# Stone Vessels and Values in the Bronze Age Mediterranean

The societies that developed in the eastern Mediterranean during the Bronze Age produced the most prolific and diverse range of stone vessel traditions known at any time or anywhere in the world. Stone vessels are therefore a key class of artefact in the early history of this region. As a form of archaeological evidence, they offer important analytical advantages over other artefact types – virtual indestructibility, a wide range of functions and values, huge variety in manufacturing traditions, as well as the subtractive character of stone and its rich potential for geological provenancing. Stone also has wide anthropological and archaeological relevance. It offers a favourable vantage from which to consider concepts of object value and how these might be approached in the archaeological record. In this book, Andrew Bevan considers individual stone vessel industries in great detail. He also offers a highly comparative and value-led perspective on production, consumption, and exchange logics throughout the eastern Mediterranean over a period of two millennia during the Bronze Age (ca. 3000–1200 BC).

Andrew Bevan is a lecturer at the Institute of Archaeology, University College London. His work has been supported by fellowships from the Leverhulme Trust, the Institute of Aegean Prehistory, and the Dr. M. Alwyn Cotton Foundation. He also received the Michael Ventris Memorial Award for Mycenaean Studies.

# Stone Vessels
# and Values in the
# Bronze Age Mediterranean

*Andrew Bevan*

UNIVERSITY COLLEGE LONDON, INSTITUTE OF ARCHAEOLOGY

CAMBRIDGE UNIVERSITY PRESS
Cambridge, New York, Melbourne, Madrid, Cape Town, Singapore, São Paulo, Delhi

Cambridge University Press
32 Avenue of the Americas, New York, NY 10013-2473, USA

www.cambridge.org
Information on this title: www.cambridge.org/9780521880800

First published 2007

Printed in the United States of America

*A catalog record for this publication is available from the British Library.*

*Library of Congress Cataloging in Publication Data*

Bevan, Andrew, 1974-
Stone vessels and values in the Bronze age Mediterranean
Andrew Bevan.
   p. cm.
Includes bibliographical references and index.
ISBN 978-0-521-88080-0 (hardback)
1. Bronze age – Mediterranean Region. 2. Stone implements – Mediterranean Region.
3. Excavations (Archaeology) – Mediterranean Region. 4. Commerce, Prehistoric – Mediterranean Region.
5. Mediterranean Region – Antiquities.   I. Title.
GN778.25.B48   2007
909'.09822–dc22       2007000175

ISBN   978-0-521-88080-0 hardback

Cover Illustrations: a chloritite box and lid with dog-shaped handle from Zakros, Crete (HM 2719,
photograph courtesy of the Heraklion Museum); a sardonyx flask from Ebla, Syria (TM.78.QIA.76, photograph
courtesy of the Ebla Expedition), and a travertine flask with original cord from Gurob, Egypt
(UC 7970, photograph courtesy of the UCL Petrie Museum).

*For my parents*

# Contents

# Acknowledgments

*This book first began as doctoral research, for which I benefited from generous financial support* from the Arts and Humanities Research Council (then AHRB). During this time, I was able to conduct fieldwork and attend conferences largely through the further support of the Institute of Archaeology, the University College London (UCL) Graduate School, and the British Institute of Archaeology at Ankara, to all of whom I am extremely grateful. A Leverhulme Trust postdoctoral fellowship, while dedicated to other research goals, allowed time for me to acquire additional skills and to develop my ideas further. Thereafter, I was able to devote a crucial year to new research and writing-up with the benefit of an Institute of Aegean Prehistory fellowship, a Cotton Foundation grant, and a Michael Ventris Memorial Fund award, all of which led to late insights into particularly thorny problems. The final stages of writing were challenged and yet also inspired by the demands of full-time teaching at UCL.

There are numerous people who helped at different stages of this study. I am especially grateful to the academic and administrative staff and students of the UCL Institute of Archaeology for providing such a friendly and inspiring research environment. Cyprian Broodbank has been, and still is, a source of endless guidance and encouragement. Todd Whitelaw has provided help with an array of research and teaching questions, some of which I hope has made an impact here. Also, many thanks to Alexander Ahrens, Daniel Antoine, Carol Bell, Lisa Bendall, John Bennet, Elizabeth Bloxham, Stuart Brookes, Tristan Carter, Steffie Chlouveraki, James Conolly, Jago Cooper, Lindy Crewe, Joanne Cutler, Helène David, Don Evely, Lesley Fitton, James Harrell, Eleni Hatzaki, Christophe Helmke, David Jeffreys, Peter Jordan, Evangelia Kiriatzi, Carl Knappett, Olga Krzyszkowska, Lorenzo Lazzarini, Mark Lake, Borja Legarra, Christine Lilyquist, Kris Lockyear, Christina Luke, Marcos Martinón-Torres, Roger Matthews, Nicoletta Momigliano, Orazio Palio, Ian Patterson, Edgar Peltenburg, Jacke Phillips, Claude Poursat, Laura Preston, Stephen Quirke, Lucinda Reeves, Thilo Rehren, Brian Robertson, Christopher Roosevelt, Joanne Rowland, Jerry Rutter, Robert Schaub, Vincent Serneels, Susan Sherratt, Ruth Siddall, Karin Sowada, Rachael Sparks, Denys Stocks, Geoffrey Tassie, Peter Ucko, Peter Warren, Vance Watrous, David Wengrow, and the two anonymous Cambridge reviewers for discussing different aspects of the subject with me, providing digital data, reading chapter drafts, or otherwise contributing to this effort. No doubt there are others who I have omitted for which I offer my sincere apologies. Any remaining errors are my own responsibility.

Permissions to reproduce photographs and/or include illustrations were kindly supplied by the following people and institutions (in alphabetical order): the Ashmolean Museum, Barbara Aston, the British Museum, the British School at Athens, the Cairo Museum,

Pierre de Miroschedji, Christos Doumas, Ebla Expedition, Don Evely, Pat Getz-Gentle, James Harrell, the Herakleion Museum, the Italian School of Archaeology at Athens, Vassos Karageorghis, Gernot Katzer, Kay Kohlmeyer, Karla Kroeper, Olga Krzyszkowska, the Louver Museum, Paolo Matthiae, the Metropolitan Museum of Art, the National Museum of Greece, the Oriental Institute at the University of Chicago, Nimet Özgüç, Philip von Zabern Press, Ingo Pini, Frances Pinnock, Sue Sherratt, Jeffrey Soles, Denys Stocks, the ST Ephorate of Prehistoric and Classical Antiquities (Patras), Turan Takaoğlu, Francesco Tiradritti, Jonathan Tubb, the Turin Museum, University College London, the UCL Petrie Museum, the University of Wisconsin Press, Gert van Wijngaarden, Shelley Wachsmann, and Peter Warren. In addition, the opportunity to study unpublished material was of huge benefit in the early stages of this research, for which I thank Phillip Betancourt, Gerald Cadogan, Sinclair Hood, Mervyn Popham, Jeffrey Soles, and Peter Warren. I am also grateful to Lesley Fitton, Louise Schofield, and Jonathan Tubb at the British Museum; Sue Sherratt and Roger Moorey at the Ashmolean Museum; Penny Wilson and Eleni Vassilika at the Fitzwilliam Museum; Sally MacDonald and Stephen Quirke at the Petrie Museum; Despo Pilides at the Cypriot Museum; Sophie Cluzan and Norbeil Aouici at the Louvre; Tom Brogan at the INSTAP-EC Study Centre; and Eleni Hatzaki and Don Evely at the Knossos Stratigraphical Museum for facilitating my various visits to these institutions.

A final heartfelt thanks go to Brenna, my parents, and my sister.

# 1
## Introduction

This book examines the role of stone vessels throughout the eastern Mediterranean and over a period of two millennia during the Bronze Age (ca. 3000-1200 BC). This period and region saw perhaps the most prolific and diverse tradition of such objects in human history and their treatment as a group represents an unusual interpretative opportunity. Stone vessels offer important analytical advantages over other classes of material, making them a favourable vantage from which to consider concepts of object value and how they might be approached in the archaeological record. Although comparative longitudinal studies like this one are increasingly rare, they provide a clarity which a narrower focus does not and are the type of contribution to the social sciences that archaeology is particularly well placed to provide. The following discussion addresses why a seemingly straightforward object-based analysis might offer wider archaeological insight, especially with regard to object value. It then goes on to justify the scope and coverage of the book before setting some relevant terms for comparative analysis. Finally, it outlines the main focus of each the succeeding chapters.

Stone vessels offer interpretative advantages over most other classes of material culture for at least five reasons: (1) their virtual indestructibility, (2) the subtractive properties of stone, (3) the potential for macroscopic, petrographic, or geochemical provenancing, (4) their numbers and regional diversity within the Bronze Age eastern Mediterranean, and (5) their flexible range of values and functions. Firstly, stone is one of the most consistently preserved types of material in the archaeological record, matched perhaps only by pottery and with a considerably longer history. Occasionally, the physical robustness of stone vessels can make for a rather bewildering archaeological picture, because it encourages these objects to have long use lives and potentially confusing reincarnations as heirlooms, antiquities, or stratigraphic kick-ups. However, for the most part, their frequent survival in the archaeological record means that we can hope to recover a much more representative sample than metals (that get recycled) or organics (that biodegrade) and, under the right conditions, even use them as tracers to understand the more elusive social lives of other material classes (e.g. through skeuomorphs). Secondly, stone is a subtractive medium which often retains marks from human alteration. Refits of knapped stone debitage are the most well-known and evocative example of this, but ground and carved stone artefacts also preserve informative traces of manufacture, use, modification, and repair. Thirdly, stone can often be provenanced to specific source areas on the basis of visual identification, study under a microscope, or analysis of trace elements. The first of these, macroscopic recognition, is a particularly important property, lending certain stones a prominence both in the past (as fundamentally branded objects) and in the present (as equally branded finds that consistently catch the archaeologist's attention).

Fourthly, stone vessels are not only found in comparatively large numbers in the Bronze Age eastern Mediterranean but also made in a variety of distinctive crafting traditions revealing spatial and chronological variation which is of considerable interest. As suggested earlier, the prehistoric Mediterranean sees arguably the most intensive and diverse outpourings of this type of material culture in human history, linked unequivocally to important large-scale changes such as the move to more sedentary foraging, the spread of farming, the emergence of early state societies, and the Bronze Age intensification of interregional exchange. Finally, stone vessels can have a wide variety of perceived values and functions, not least because different stones have very different working and aesthetic properties and vary tremendously in the location and frequency of their source outcrops. Stone vessels occupy a very wide range of roles, from those used for grinding crops or pigments to cooking pots to lamps and possible fumigatory devices to containers for well-known organic commodities to highly charged and heavily decorated ritual objects. By comparison, and in contrast, metals are often more precious (relatively rare and complicated to process), more heavily commodified (in part due to their convertible bullion value), and susceptible to very different recycling patterns, while pottery is usually more commonplace and almost always of lower value.

More broadly, few other areas of the world offer such a rich setting in which to explore the relationship between material culture and society as does the eastern Mediterranean, and it is no surprise that most of the key anthropological approaches to issues such as trade or early state formation were developed with this area partly in mind or were applied to it at a very early stage. In this regard, the combination of textual sources, a wide range of representational art, and a richly explored archaeological record are both a boon and a curse, challenging us to reconcile three very different types of evidence. For example, both chronologically and geographically, the eastern Mediterranean straddles the divide between areas with written sources and those without. On the one hand, this throws up textual deserts where studying concepts such as value present a greater challenge. On the other, it provides sufficient texts in certain regions to allow written evidence and archaeological interpretation to complement and, if necessary, to correct one another. Many of the subtleties of how materials and shapes were perceived by particular societies may well be best understood with the help of written texts or images, but it would be a mistake to assume that either of the latter sources is wholly unproblematic. Both are partial samples biased by the archaeological robustness of the material on which they were produced and the priorities of the people or institutions by or for whom they were created.

The archaeological material that can be harnessed in an analysis of stone vessels is impressive. In the Aegean, a substantial amount of research has already been carried out and more than 5,000 stone vessels are known from Bronze Age contexts. Elsewhere, there are perhaps fewer than 100 published Bronze Age Anatolian vessels, a slightly greater number of Cypriot examples, nearly 2,000 vessels published from Levantine contexts, and literally hundreds of thousands from Egypt. This skewed distribution reflects some recovery bias (e.g. with less attention having been paid to Anatolia), but nevertheless it offers a broad indication of the relative importance of this class of material culture in different regions. These varying numbers also demand very different analytical strategies, especially for Dynasties 1–4 in Egypt, where a selective approach to the primary evidence is inevitable. Moreover, the ease with which museum collections of stone vessels can be accessed, the extent of published records, and the depth of existing synthetic or interpretative discussion are highly varied and often biased by the traditional archaeological preoccupations with monuments, palaces, and cities. The approach adopted throughout this book is to be comprehensive and quantifying where possible,[1] to build on existing studies where available, and to balance a broad general analysis with the detailed investigation of a few particularly rewarding contexts.

## Comparative Terminology

One awkward result of the emphasis on specialist study in the region is the lack of coherent terminology. The analysis in succeeding chapters crosses several regional disciplinary specialties and draws heavily on more focused typological works. However, for such a broader comparative perspective to be effective, especially in the context of early complex societies (e.g. Trigger 2003), it needs to declare a particular set of terms that are sufficiently broad for general application but do not lose all analytical strength. This section outlines the chronological framework, vessel shapes, stone identifications, and social categories used throughout the rest of the book.

Stone vessels rarely allow the kind of chronological resolution that can be found in pottery. This is partly a result of less intense modern study of their forms and materials but also because of lower levels of surface decoration, the smaller numbers of artefacts produced, and the increased possibility that any given vessel might be deliberately curated for quite long periods before deposition in the ground. So while chronology provides an important analytical framework, it will rarely be appropriate to attempt extremely fine temporal distinctions. A rough correlation of established regional period divisions is presented in Figure 1.1, along with the period and regional abbreviations used throughout the rest of the book. This study follows the Egyptian chronological sequence outlined by Hendrickx (1996, 1999) for earlier periods and by Kitchen (1987, 2000) for later ones. For the Levant, it uses the period divisions suggested by Albright and others (Albright 1949: 84; Mazar 1990: 175, 238, 295). In the Aegean, it follows the Early Bronze Age (EBA) radiocarbon chronology outlined by Manning (1995) but assumes a traditional short chronology for later periods (Warren and Hankey 1989), addressing specific problems of interregional synchronisation (e.g. those raised by the debate over the dating of the Theran eruption: Wiener 2003, 2006; Manning et al. 2006) when necessary. All dates are BC unless stated otherwise.

The individual terms used for vessel shapes have been standardised where possible to conform to more explicit modern definitions (in particular Aston 1994: appendix C), but existing terms have been retained where they refer to particularly well-known artefact types (e.g. alabastra). Summary regional vessel typologies are offered in the appendix, adopting existing schemes where these are broadly reliable and developing new ones where necessary. As with the shape terms themselves, this complementary (some old, some new) strategy has its problems, not least because levels of classificatory detail vary as a result, but it seems more important to conform to an existing consensus where one exists rather than offer yet another alternative. Shapes are frequently referred to in Chapters 5–7, along with their type identifier in brackets (a regional prefix followed by a shape number) to allow easy cross-referencing with the type drawings, short descriptions, and relevant references in the appendix. There remain particularly ill-defined analytical boundaries between straightforward stone vessels and various forms of permanent stone installations, rough mortars, or grinding slabs. None

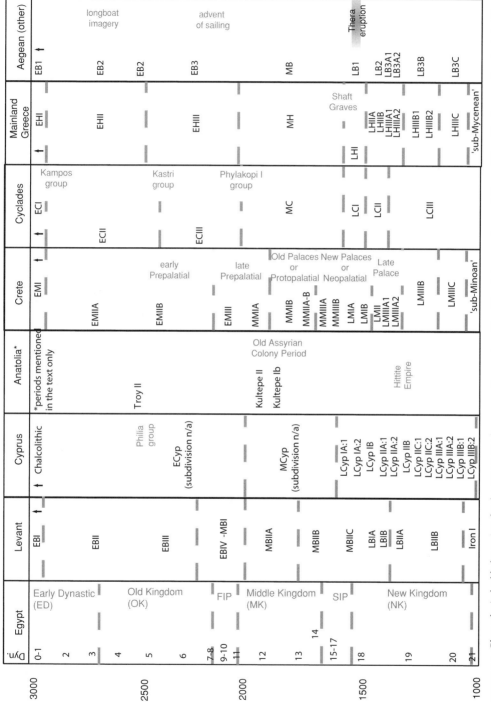

FIGURE 1.1. Chronological table by region for the eastern Mediterranean Bronze Age. The abbreviations used are as follows: FIP = First Intermediate Period; SIP = Second Intermediate Period; E, M, L = Early, Middle and Late, respectively; and are found with B = Bronze, Cyp = Cypriot (elsewhere this is usually abbreviated as 'C' but extended here to avoid confusion), M = Minoan, C = Cycladic, H = Helladic.

4

of the latter are treated in as much detail here although the long-term links between them and more clearly defined stone vessels are an extremely interesting issue and are returned to in Chapter 8.

The study of stone vessels is bedeviled by a lack of clarity when it comes to stone identification. This is nowhere more obvious than in published descriptions of gypsum (hydrated calcium sulphate and, for vessels, mainly the alabastrine variety) and travertine (calcium carbonate, 'Egyptian alabaster'), both of which have misleadingly been grouped under the label *alabaster* in much of the archaeological literature. Likewise, *steatite* is the most commonly published term for a range of dark-coloured softstones (that all come from the same broad green schist facies), even though in most cases where vessels have been studied by a geologist, the actual material turns out to be either a chlorite-rich rock (hereafter occasionally shortened to the overly specific term *chloritite* for convenience) or a slightly harder serpentinite.[2] Where it has not been possible to correct traditional terms or problematic identifications, these have been deliberately broadened into a wider classification (e.g. steatite/chloritite) and, for Egyptian stones, Aston's terminology (1994) has been adopted whenever possible. We can also draw upon relatively well-studied evidence for ethnotaxonomies of stone, in both Egyptian (Harris 1961; Aufrère 1991) and Sumerian/Akkadian (Postgate 1997). In fact, these typologies prove to be both subtle and relatively precise, given that they were based on provenance, colour, and working properties rather than any microscopic or geochemical profiling. Even so, one-to-one correlations with our own geological categories are often elusive, arguably less because of gross mismatch (though this does occasionally exist) and more because of the imprecise nature of our evidence.

The discussion in succeeding chapters refers repeatedly to the relationship between stone vessel use and the expression of social identity and status. Some key vectors for variation in object use and value are likely to be age, gender, lineage, social class, and political faction, but many of these will be difficult to identify in the archaeological record (e.g. gender distinctions in the absence of clear iconography or carefully sexed burials). Social class is probably the one most open to analysis. For smaller-scale societies that were still present in many areas at the beginning of the Bronze Age, particularly in the Aegean, neutral descriptions are initially preferred for discussing apparently powerful or influential people over those that might assume too specific an organising principle (e.g. 'chief'). For the larger, more complex, and palace-based societies whose interactions with each other were often important, we require some generally applicable comparative terminology for discussing social categories, despite the fact that any scheme of this coarseness will inevitably fail to capture many important regional variations. Nonetheless, during the Bronze Age, much of the region was broken up into kingdoms of various sizes and types of territorial organisation. Most of these polities were ruled by kings who often referred to their dominions as a royal household and estate and, beyond this, carefully ranked their relations with other kingdoms, treating some as potential equals and others as vassals. Across society as a whole, we can usually suggest a three-way division amongst a small upper elite group, a larger lower elite, and the wider population which offers us a comparative framework for thinking about the way stone vessels, object value, and status relate to social structure.

While these crude distinctions are useful in a general analytical sense, there is important cultural variation in the sharpness of social hierarchy, the relative size of different social groupings, and their particular ideological preoccupations.[3] Even so, the upper elite was an often volatile and incestuous inner community, usually surrounding a royal family (where we know one exists) and including extended family members, concubines, and the most powerful state and religious administrators. These people sometimes owned impressive rural houses but frequently dwelt in cities, and we see them in close contact with the politics and fashions of the court. There is often a degree of overlap in official roles with courtiers also being administrators, priests, traders, and/or important patrons. Likewise, at this level there were relatively common instances of direct contact between courtly circles, sometimes over long distances, with the exchange of messengers, wives, and palace personnel that encouraged the convergence of elite taste (or, conversely, the conscious expression of difference) over quite a wide area of the eastern Mediterranean. By contrast, the lower elite often held lesser bureaucratic posts and/or appear as powerful figures in certain local or provincial contexts but were generally much less well connected. The rest of the population is by far the largest group, including both urban and rural populations, but their archaeological visibility varies tremendously, depending on recovery bias (e.g. whether survey and excavation beyond the monumental urban structures have considered them directly), textual samples, archival reach, and their varying mobility and material impact within the wider landscape.

## Chapter Summary

The structure of this book reflects a compromise between the need to proceed in a sensible chronological and geographical order and a desire to address certain issues more holistically. Chapter 2 looks at theoretical approaches to value, drawing in particular on recent studies of cultural transmission and the logic of social relationships to suggest ways in which a potentially ephemeral property such as value might reveal itself in archaeological recoverable ways. The next two chapters define some practical and analytical parameters: Chapter 3 begins with an analysis of the Mediterranean environment and how Bronze Age people and objects might have moved around it. Thereafter, it addresses the theoretical models through which we have traditionally considered Bronze Age trade, devoting particularly critical attention to the conceptual divisions that have often been drawn between what we construe as modern and premodern behaviours. Finally, it offers a brief summary of the overall evidence for interregional interaction in the third and second millennia BC. Chapter 4 then looks closely at how stone vessels are made, offering a summary of the range of possible manufacturing strategies, the working properties of different stones, common manufacturing sequences, and what departure from these norms might imply in terms of local production priorities. Chapters 5–7 deal with the regional stone vessel traditions found in the Bronze Age eastern Mediterranean. The chapter breaks were chosen because they provide a convenient and necessary subdivision of the bulk of the analysis, but they also reflect important points of large-scale, sociopolitical change. The third millennium is treated in a single block in Chapter 5, though reference is occasionally made to earlier periods where this seems particularly relevant (e.g. the later fourth millennium). Chapter 6 considers the earlier second millennium, a period that sees the emergence of new political, social, and economic structures throughout much of the region, including the Middle Kingdom Egyptian state, increased urbanism in the Levant; Assyrian colonies in Anatolia, and the appearance of palatial society on Crete. Chapter 7 addresses the highly connected world of the later second millennium and begins at another relatively convenient break in discussion, ca. 1500–1450 BC, with the reign of Thutmosis III and his expansion of Egyptian power into the Levant. This conquest has clear implications for patterns of production, consumption, and exchange and is also roughly contemporary with the apparent collapse of Neopalatial Cretan society. For each of these three chapters, analysis begins with Egypt and continues in an anticlockwise path via the Levant, Cyprus, Anatolia, and the Aegean, which has the interpretative advantage of following both the prevailing movement of Bronze Age maritime traffic (see Chapter 4) and the flow of stone vessel exports from Egypt, the industry with the largest and most extensive foreign impact. Following these detailed regional discussions, the last two chapters adopt a broader perspective once again. Chapter 8 takes a comparative approach to its logical conclusion by briefly considering the roles played by stone vessel industries across the world and throughout human history. It aims to distinguish both smoother cross-cultural regularities (of which several important examples are considered) and those rougher idiosyncrasies specific to the cultural development of the Bronze Age eastern Mediterranean. Chapter 9 ends the book by returning to the theoretical challenges raised in Chapter 2, identifying where the preceding analysis has important insights to offer on the concept of object value and where further research might lead. Value is too resonant a social concept to avoid but too analytically fraught to treat lightly, and it is to the discussion of useful theoretical perspectives that we turn first.

# 2
## Agreeing on Things

⌘⌘⌘⌘⌘⌘

*Value is a term that cries out for careful definition. It has a curiously ambivalent semantic* power, referring to both tangible and intangible culture, to objects that we think of as commodities and those that we do not, and to meanings that we think of as personal and those that we treat as collective social givens. Indeed, object value arguably inhabits exactly this social space, an interface between what we assume to be objective and what we recognise as subjective (Simmel 1900). This is reflected nicely by the fact that the terms people often use to describe this domain—for example, in English, *value(s)*, *taste*, *worth*—evoke wider social mores, natural sensory skills, or even innate moral rules but thereby often conceal definitions that are potentially vulnerable and up for negotiation (Bourdieu 1994: 99). This chapter considers these rather ambiguous meanings, the way object value may reflect the wider ordering of human relations, and how, if at all, it might manifest itself archaeologically. Some of the issues raised are declared merely to make the analytical preoccupations of Chapters 4–8 more transparent, while others are revisited directly in later analyses, particularly in Chapters 8 and 9.

Value is not something inherent in things but is a culturally constructed property. The following discussion is interested primarily in object value; intangible things can have value (e.g. a piece of music, an idea, a brand) in a way which floats free of any particular physical object, but it is curious that such value is often most obvious when manifested concretely and objectified in some way (e.g. a recording, a performer, a patent, or a branded commodity). Shared logics about ways of making, exchanging, using, and destroying objects are cultural norms and as such structure people's individual social strategies. These norms can be argued over and modified, but they are also learnt and passed on, both horizontally between people and vertically between generations. They therefore form part of inherited cultural traditions that have a wider evolutionary context and reveal a degree of cross-cultural consistency about which it might be possible to generalise. Because value logics are often grounded in material things, they are partially structured by this physicality. Indeed, if value is to be more than merely an evocative term for archaeologists, its study needs to focus on material variation whose physical or contextual signature we can reasonably hope to distinguish in the ordinary archaeological record.

With this inferential leap in mind, five possible approaches are combined in the following chapters: (1) highly comparative analysis across time and space; (2) contemporaneous comparisons between different types of objects; (3) highly contextual analysis of archaeological deposits where possible; (4) attention to the wider implications of typological variation; and (5) careful combination of archaeological, documentary, and representational evidence. The first of these allows us sufficient investigative scope to address the broadest temporal and spatial scales at which object value is likely to be influenced, for example, in the form of long-lived cultural traditions or supraregional economic systems. It also encourages us to distinguish the socially and historically contingent features of stone vessel value from those that are repetitive and cross-cultural in their impact. The second approach involves a similarly wide-ranging strategy but seeks to break down the traditional barriers separating the study of specific material categories, wherever such synthesis can be achieved efficiently. The third approach refers to the need to pay particularly acute attention to archaeological contexts where our preservation, recovery, publication, and/or sample size is unusually good. This needs little justification in terms of archaeological practice but can sometimes be sidelined in the search for broad-scale comparisons. The fourth approach is, of course, reflected in the construction of object typologies, a fundamental aspect of archaeological method but given greater significance where such phylogenies are suggestive of the selective pressures and processes of cultural transmission. The fifth and final approach allows us to explore the consistent or contradictory expressions of value present in textual, iconographic, and material records.

Value evokes a whole host of overlapping but potentially conflicting meanings: labour cost, use value, exchange value, added value, social value, moral value, sentimental value, and shock value, to name but a few. At one extreme are traditional economic perspectives such as Marx's emphasis on value as embodied labour-time (i.e. the cost of making or doing something; 1969: 45) or the tyrannical, if often unfairly stereotyped, utility functions associated with classical economics (e.g. Nash 1950). These perspectives tend to assume, either as a theoretical proposition or for analytical convenience, that value can be treated as a rational variable, inherently measurable and universally understood. At the other extreme are valuations construed as inherently personal and sentimental, which only really have meaning for the individual concerned. Ironically, both ends of this spectrum provide models that are almost wholly asocial, whereas in fact value is usually part of wider social norms and crucial to the way people forge and structure their relationships with one another (see below).

Assumptions about object value exist in most artefact-based studies, but the degree to which they are recognised and accounted for varies wildly. For example, arbitrary measures of prehistoric wealth (e.g. the 'scoring' approach used on some cemetery assemblages), art historical speculation about the creative intentions of prehistoric craftspeople, or unmoderated emphasis on the past importance of an archaeologically prevalent indicator such as pottery are all examples where value is undertheorised. However, following a wider reorientation of social science research on such problems, the more theoretically explicit of existing archaeological discussions (e.g. Voutsaki 1997) emphasise the need to move away from seeing value as related to a unique process such as production (prioritised by Marx), exchange (emphasised by Simmel and others), or consumption (often emphasised by anthropologists: e.g. Miller 1995) to one in which this property can potentially be transformed at any of these stages. Revaluation is in fact a very important part of an object's biography (Kopytoff 1986), sometimes seen as a subversive act and subject to strong social sanction but also recognised as a recipe for success. A range of examples are discussed herein, but archaeologists most commonly encounter the ambiguities of revaluation in the spectre of the modern antiquities market and the destructive effect that Western value determinations and connoisseurship can have on the surviving archaeological record (e.g. Broodbank 2000: 58–65).

## Classification and Transmission

A useful first analytical step in understanding this topic is to ask what encourages things to be ascribed high value regularly and in a manner which is sometimes *perceived* as intrinsic by the people who esteem them (Colin Renfrew's 'prime' value, 1986: 159ff). For example, the ability of certain things to be recycled (e.g. metals) or reproduced (e.g. certain livestock) encourages their recurrent use as wealth indices and/or exchange media. The durability of objects is another important factor, especially their ability to resist decay, heat, breakage, or wear. The direct effects that objects have on the human senses (e.g. shiny, hard, colourful, textured, melodic, sweet) is another, though there is a balance here between those sensory responses that are evolved propensities and those that are culturally learnt. Finally, the natural rarity of a material or the symbolic potential offered by its provenance (e.g. gemstones from a particular mountain) can be very significant, especially if it can be tied to the preferred cosmology of the consumer in convenient ways (Helms 1993). Similarly, we might expect groups of materials and products from the same natural landscapes to engender shared values and consistent associations, based on the fact that they will often be acquired, manufactured, and distributed along very similar paths (see Chapter 8). All of these properties encourage certain objects to be valued highly and/or more consistently than others, but the particular meanings assigned to them will nonetheless be formulated in culturally specific ways. For example, objects will be associated with particular epithets and/or adjectives, a periodicity of use (e.g. occasional or everyday), and appropriate human actors, props, or gestures. Their value may be further enhanced by conspicuous acts of added investment (e.g. labour-intensive decoration) or reflected in repeated references by other material culture (e.g. skeuomorphs).

Value is also a comparative concept, one defined between perceived social and physical classifications (Thompson 1979: 7–8). While a fundamental part of this classificatory process is the reification achieved through language (Tilley 1991), objects can also carry meanings in ways that are not analogous to language (Chippindale 1989; also Miller 1985), such as those often evoked by their choreography with the human body. Some objects resist convenient classification, but for many, a combination of style, material, and/or habitual function makes them highly recognisable members of a particular category of thing, at least for those with the relevant cultural background. The drive to categorise, and thereby to recognise, is arguably a fundamental aspect of human cognition, but in all such orderings, there is a necessary balance between too much lumping (offering insufficient capacity to distinguish) and too much splitting (leading to a scheme which is confusing and cumbersome to use).

Given that such classifications structure the way individual human actors think and act, it certainly makes sense to try to reconstruct their meaning and understand them as a kind of information system (albeit an imperfect and polysemic one). However, while undoubtedly necessary, such an approach, at best, offers interestingly thick description and, at worst, risks becoming no more than a frustrated ethnography (Shennan 2002: 9). An important complementary perspective which the archaeological record is far better placed to offer is to explore object value over larger spatial and temporal scales, including ones that individuals may not have necessarily been conscious of in the past. For the transmission of such ideas through time, we can turn to insights offered by evolutionary perspectives on cultural variation which have emphasised the fact that humans receive both a genetic and a cultural inheritance from their predecessors, each of which is subject to descent with modification through time (though potentially by very different mechanisms; Shennan 2002; Richerson and Boyd 2005). However, unlike biological selection, which can operate at the level of the group or individual but for which genes represent a crucial unit of replication, there are no clear and permanent units of cultural inheritance, only more or less discrete packages of decorative motifs, shapes, materials, and wider panoplies of goods and behaviours that can coalesce for comparatively long periods of time or sometimes only briefly.

There are certainly plenty of historical instances of purposeful innovation (i.e. the deliberate creation of new designs or roles for things) or the careful selection between existing alternatives, but a significant proportion of cultural traits seem to be passed on indirectly, through random drift (e.g. the accumulation of minor, random variation in crafting habits or object microstyle), frequency-dependent and/or deliberately conformist copying, or the indiscriminate and blanket imitation of elite individuals (without regard to what specifically makes them successful; Boyd and Richerson 1985). Indeed, were it not for these mechanisms, reinforced occasionally by moral sanction, the rapid turnover associated with cultural variation might theoretically lead to extreme relativism and a complete absence of the sorts of recognisable cultural groupings that are indeed present in the archaeological record (Richerson and Boyd 2005: 203–36). Such regularities may come about by either branching processes of cultural descent or blending processes due to regional interaction or similar environment, and it appears as if both have been important in human history. Likewise, the social conventions associated with object value can be passed on in a variety of ways, which have different implications and follow different tempos. For example, we should distinguish the routinizing impact of everyday activities, from the effects of occasional, more socially charged events, especially given that there is often an inverse correlation between the perceived value of objects and the frequency of their use (Douglas and Isherwood 1979: 83ff). Indeed, for the characterisation of high-value goods, occasional ceremonies are particularly important (Arjun Appadurai's 'tournaments of value', 1986: 20–3), with objects playing a fundamental role in establishing aspects of performance space (off-stage/on-stage, nearby/far away), time (event-related/symbolic), narrative, omission (with objects acting as mnemonics for more complex real-world concepts), and choreography (particularly in relation to the human body; Pearson 1998).

Moreover, both practical skills and broader social logics can be learnt from parents (one-to-one, vertical), acquired from a peer group (one-to-one, many-to-one horizontal), the subject of public polemic (one-to-many, horizontal), or reinforced by the received wisdom of elders (many-to-one, vertical; following Shennan 2002: 42–64, fig. 4). There is often an inertia to social learning, especially by vertical transmission, which can lock people into potentially maladaptive (e.g. in biological terms) or runaway behaviours. The latter are sometimes visible in patterns of escalating and increasingly fine-grained quality distinction or boom-and-bust trajectories of certain types of prestige behaviour (e.g. feasting), with these spirals sometimes identified as harbingers or contributors to wider social collapse (e.g. Miller 1993). Existing elite groups have a lot invested in established status markers and an obvious interest in maintaining the status quo. Investments of this kind encourage those in power to be conservative in altering their socioeconomic strategies and to portray existing social relationships and value logics as natural or inevitable ('sunk-cost' effects: Janssen et al. 2003). In such situations, change usually occurs only from the outside, on the whim of a particularly eccentric individual at the top of the hierarchy, or after abrupt social or economic collapse when conditions are ripe for human and material *parvenus*.

## Social Relationships

Occasionally, we can identify instances where the value of things is relevant only to one individual (e.g. objects with purely sentimental value or an immediate and transitory use value), but usually the term makes better sense as an emergent property, expressed and confirmed through a wider set of social relationships. In this sense, it is at the heart of a more general and long-running debate in the social sciences about the relationship between individuals and social institutions, especially with respect to the structuring mechanisms by which the one constitutes the other (e.g. Giddens 1984).

Game theory provides a useful for framework for understanding why individual decision-making is so dependent on social norms. In particular, this branch of research has emphasised how closely tied people's behavioural strategies are to their understanding of what might be called the game conditions. Even so, the rather simple rules used in many game theory models of human behaviour rarely reflect the complex asymmetrical payoffs involved in real-life decision-making. In the latter, rewards and punishments can vary for different individuals (e.g. as a result of their social position), for different types of interaction (e.g. according to the time or place), where the expected number of social interactions is unpredictable (e.g. how often people meet), or where information costs vary (e.g. the knowledgeability of the people involved), all prompting different behavioural equilibria (Boyd 1992). Such features also depend on the structure of social networks, with value logics clearly more malleable for some people than for others (Molm et al. 2001), particularly because their prestige, wealth, and/or social connections make them better known and more likely to be imitated (Appadurai's notion of the 'turnstyle' function of upper elite individuals; 1986: 31). Indeed, many social networks exhibit 'small-world' properties, in which most social relationships are small scale and local, but a few key individuals have wider connections that help to create the sense of a much larger-scale community (e.g. Milgram 1967; Watts and Strogatz 1998). Because social systems represent the aggregate behaviour of interacting human agents, they can often involve strange feedback effects, in which there are regimes of misleading social stability punctuated by occasional, sharp discontinuities (Renfrew 1978; Thompson 1979: 152ff; Kirman 1993; Ormerod 1998). In particular, the disappearance of well-connected people—and we might think at a coarser scale about well-connected communities—can collapse an existing social or economic structure quite abruptly.

What is clear from the more recent of this work on social networks is that people making decisions in such an environment have imperfect knowledge and limited time to inform themselves. Such conditions encourage rule-of-thumb reasoning and we should see many of the social strategies people adopt as falling into this imperfect, heuristic world. Fortunately, there is an increasingly well-founded and interdisciplinary body of theory addressing how people understand, organise, and signal their relationships with each other that moves beyond the mere construction of sociological types and provides a concrete basis for thinking about the role of objects and the likely selective pressures that might apply to them. In particular, Alan Fiske's description of four structural logics behind social life offers an extremely useful way forward (1991, 2004b). He suggests that individuals implicitly use one or more of four generative grammars for thinking about their relationships with others, emphasising (1) communal sharing, (2) authority ranking, (3) equality matching, and/or (4) market pricing. When people think in terms of the first of these relational models, communal sharing, they usually emphasise membership of a carefully defined in-group (e.g. the family being both an example and common metaphor for the way these relations are framed). Here the key is the creation of a very simple set of us-and-them categories: within the community, there is usually a readiness to perform altruistic acts and a strong sense of common identity. Issues of group purity and intimacy are important, possessions may often be shared at need without any perceived accounting, specific taboo behaviours are sometimes present that reinforce group cohesion, and ostracism is a common mechanism for dealing with conflict situations. In contrast, people use the second logic, authority ranking, when they emphasise ordered differences between each other, in particular, their relative position within vertical social hierarchies, be these based on age, caste, gender, office, or some other index. Rank can also assert itself at different scales within a group (e.g. among kings) or between groups within a society (e.g. nobles and commoners). Notions of obedience to your betters (whether gods, ancestors, or human superiors) are a common feature. The third logic, equality matching, usually implies peer-to-peer or collegial relationships in which the maintenance of balanced contributions is extremely important. Tit-for-tat reciprocity is one dominant feature, with respect both to the way positive social relations are structured and to the types of punishment seen as appropriate for violation of these norms (e.g. an eye for an eye). Turn-taking (e.g. over invitations to feasts) and equal representation (e.g. one person one vote elections) are also common. Repeated interactions between strangers are often best organised by such logics because they can lead to cooperation but are fairly resistant to exploitation (Axelrod 1990; Sigmund 1993). The fourth and final relational model, market pricing, structures relationships in terms of proportions or ratios and can involve a range of calculations associated with cost and benefit or supply and demand. The influence of this latter way of thinking (even on emotionally charged topics such as childcare or love) is particularly obvious in modern capitalist societies, but rather than contrast it too simplistically with a model of premodern, marketless sharing or reciprocity, it is better to see capitalist behaviour as just one very specific expression of a more generic propensity for market-style calculation that is present in most if not all societies (see below and Chapter 3).

At a more abstract and formal level, Fiske's logics imply four increasingly complex scales of measurement, from nominal (in- and out-groups) to ordinal (ranked) to interval (metrically equivalent and hence able to support additive or subtractive concepts) to ratio (metrically flexible and amenable to division, multiplication, etc.). What makes this way of looking at things considerably more insightful than the usual sociological typologies are Fiske's further contentions that, apart from a few null cases where people's social relations with each other are extremely limited or transitory, these are the only four relational models that people use and that such logics are distinct from each other, fundamental in the sense that people use them as building blocks for more complex and culturally specific social relationships and scale-free in the sense that they can apply to the way people think about their one-to-one relationships, small group identities, and roles within wider society. There is also theoretical and experimental evidence to suggest that they reflect evolved cognitive features, innate to all modern humans but implemented during childhood in a wide range of culturally specific ways (Fiske 2000). Such a complementary scheme, of evolved proclivities and culturally learnt implementations, has much in common with modern theories about language development, as well as about the modularity of the human mind, and strikes an attractive balance between behavioural determinism and cultural relativism (e.g. Fiske and Haslam 2000). The scheme also enjoys an impressive degree of ethnographic and psychological support (Haslam 2004), as well as congruence with a wide range of existing sociological theory, including the similar, if arguably less complete and more firmly typological, distinctions raised by Weber, Piaget, Ricoeur, Mauss, Sahlins, and Douglas to name but a few (also see Whitehead 1993: 11–12). It encompasses both competitive and cooperative behaviours but assumes neither that each logic operates in isolation nor that simpler relational models are eventually replaced by more complex ones. Rather, all four ways of thinking are generically available to any individual but learnt differently in different cultures and applied differently in different social contexts.

Such a perspective has clear relevance to the study of objects: some things, for example, can be bought and sold between two individuals according to a clear sense of market price, be thereafter distributed amongst others according to precedent and rank, then offered out more narrowly within a peer group on a reciprocal basis, and eventually shared without regard to such distinctions within a carefully defined in-group such as a family. Moreover, following a line of reasoning suggested by Annette Weiner (1992), an object can also be deliberately kept out of horizontal circulation during the lifetime of an owner according to any one of these ways of thinking. It can be preserved as an inalienable emblem (e.g. a family heirloom), sometimes with an explicit associated cosmology that ensures that it is seen as somehow equivalent with the people and ancestors in the group (e.g. a Maori feather cloak). In addition or in contrast, it could be kept as a clear sign of rank and the stability of the social order, whose exchange, when utterly necessary, is itself a symbol of the tension present during transitions of power (e.g. the death of a ruler). It can also be curated as an expression of peer-group responsibility, invoking reciprocal social relationships without actually being exchanged as part of them. Finally it can be given a valuation according to a market-pricing model but never actually be commodified in this sense (e.g. in the modern context of insurance) or can be hoarded out of a concern to avoid inflationary spirals.

All of these behaviours make no sense except as inherently social strategies, with implicit reference to other people or groups, even if they often involve acts of keeping that deliberately refrain from engaging in interpersonal exchange. Thus the same person is capable of thinking in very different terms about their relationships with other people depending on context, and the social life of an object can involve numerous diversions from one logic to another and back again (Appadurai 1986: 16ff). An apparently simple but anthropologically famous strategy such as gift-giving can in fact invoke any one of these four logics, from gifts that reflect altruistic sharing within communities to those that express clear ranked social differences to those traditionally associated with Maussian delayed reciprocal exchanges to those such as bribes that reflect market-style calculations (Komter 2001, 2004; also see Chapter 3 on the Amarna correspondence). In individual contexts, some objects are protected from such diversion by social convention and a certain degree of moral outrage will surround their use according to what is otherwise deemed as an unacceptable logic (Appadurai 1986: 14–15; McGraw et al. 2003). Such enclaving is not restricted to premonetary societies and even something as seemingly promiscuous as the flow of cash can sometimes be confined to specific social spheres, for example, in the context of multiple currencies and 'black markets' (Dominguez 1990). Agreed ways of valuing things offer socially sanctioned avenues of competition and cooperation, but because there is room for the relational models that people use to conflict with one another (even inside one person's head), success can also take the form of semilegitimate acts of diversion from one value logic to another. Excellent examples are the buying or selling of things not otherwise thought to be appropriate commodities (e.g. some but not all examples of trafficking in sacred relics or people, Kopytoff 1986) or the recasting of reciprocal exchanges as ones expressing rank differences (e.g. passing gifts off as tribute). Beyond this realm of semiacceptable negotiation – itself a process that can be quarantined to specific offices of individuals such as traders, prostitutes, and pawn brokers – are acts of more obvious cheating or defection for which a variety of social sanctions might apply.

A further feature of interest associated with these four relational models is Fiske's suggestion (2004a) that there are distinct and commonly occurring ways in which they are constituted as norms. In this respect, the recognition of these patterns by children, outsiders, or anthropologists is made easier by the presence of extremely common (though certainly not exclusive) ways in which such relationships are expressed. Hence communal sharing relationships are often reinforced by acts of food-sharing, emblematic body modification, physical intimacy, initiation rites, and purity taboos, all of which forge and maintain a strong sense of group communion. The ordered differences of authority ranking are commonly forged and maintained through a sort of social physics that emphasises people's relative position in hierarchies of space (above/below, in front/behind), time (before/after), size (bigger/smaller), and force (stronger/weaker), with these distinctions revealing an impressive degree of cross-cultural consistency. Equivalence matching logics are usually forged and reinforced by transparent, concrete matching procedures such as turn-taking, random lotteries, overt matching of object sizes or quantities, and/or the use of physical place-holders as reminders of delayed reciprocal obligations. Market-pricing logics tend to be expressed in various types of propositional language (if you do or give this, I will do or give this) and supported by an abstract set of symbols such as contracts, coupons, dockets, weight systems, and, perhaps the most powerful of all, various forms of money. It is perhaps fair to say that for societies where ratio-scale, market-style social logics are very important (e.g. recent capitalist democracies), such representational symbols become increasingly prevalent and abstract. For example, we could distinguish barter-based calculations where the items are physically present for the exchange from those in which independently valuable exchange units are used as a point of reference but are not physically present in all transfers (e.g. pigs or bullion), from increasingly symbolic, but still materially concrete, monetary units (e.g. banknotes or so-called flat money), from purely theoretical ones (e.g. the numbers on a modern stock trader's screen; Fiske 2004a: 113–14; see also Appadurai 2005). These differences imply an increasingly efficient approach to market-pricing relationships in the modern world but certainly do not argue for an explicit modern/premodern split in terms of behaviour.

A key issue from an archaeological perspective is whether the varying emphasis placed on these different ways of thinking about social relations and the objects associated with them regularly leaves identifiable material traces that we might hope to identify in the archaeological record. More precisely, we deal with static, chronologically blurred patterns and need to build up more holistic and dynamic understandings from the detail of the objects themselves, including their archaeological context or population-scale indicators such as relative wealth or typological diversity. Although we cannot expect exact correspondence, we might hope that where objects are used *primarily* according to a consistent relational logic, their physical attributes (e.g. size, shape, material, and decoration) may be subject to selective pressure over time. For example, when objects are commonly shared within a notionally egalitarian in-group, we might expect that major differences in shape, material, size, elaboration, and quantity will be selected against, because such variability would reduce the potential emblematic qualities of the artefact and would leave room for unwelcome expressions of difference (i.e. people would tend to adopt highly conformist strategies in such contexts; Richerson and Boyd 2005: 162–3). However, exact consistency will be rare because it would imply unnecessarily precise levels of comparison. We might also expect a few distinct, highly recognisable categories of goods, including particularly charged examples such as heirlooms and relics, which emphasise the timeless and 'consubstantial' quality of the group (Fiske 2004a: 69–94), as well as those that physically encourage shared group acts (e.g. the proverbial round table and a wide range of other commensal paraphernalia).

For objects that are frequently used as part of ranked social relationships, we might expect both guided and indirect selective pressures encouraging them to mirror the hierarchical divisions present in society overall (Mauss and Durkheim 1963: 83–4). Variations in shape, material, size, elaboration, and quantity will be important factors but carefully organised into explicit vertical grades and occasionally enclaved from widespread use by sumptuary law (e.g. royal monopolies). The vertical flows of such items, as rewards from superiors or tribute from subordinates, often serve to cement the existing social hierarchy. Whole groups of values are likely to be transmitted together as people copy the behaviour of successful individuals indiscriminately and this can lead to both increased competition and to 'runaway' patterns of increasing elaboration (Richerson and Boyd 2005: 163–4). For objects that are used in reciprocal and/or equivalent social relationships, variations in shape, material, size, elaboration and quantity of particular classes of object are likely to be avoided or evenly matched. In this respect, there may be selective pressure favouring objects that encourage balanced contributions (e.g. miniature votives), easy matching (e.g. the equipment required of a hoplite), or turn-taking (e.g. a loving cup). For objects primarily involved in social relationships associated with pricing mechanisms and carefully measured ratios, variation in most of these object properties will be actively encouraged, but object types that encourage convertibility and mensurability (e.g. exchange rates, bullion weight, purity) will be preferred. Propositional offerings (e.g. samples), brand mnemonics, and accounting symbols (e.g. logos, labels, seals, and weights) are also likely to be important.

## Wealth Measurement

A related approach that may illuminate concepts of value is to consider the logics by which wealth and status are expressed in society, particularly with respect to the priority given to various forms of accumulation and vertical or horizontal classification. The overall amount of wealth, its material expression and distribution across a population, varies cross-culturally, but in most complex societies it is a heavily skewed property such that the vast majority of wealth and power is monopolised by a small minority. The multiplicative nature of the way wealth flows through social and economic networks also tends to lead to rich–get–richer effects and the persistence of well-defined elite groups (e.g. Pareto 1982: esp. section 964; Bouchard and Mézard 2000; Bentley et al. 2005). It is therefore important to explore how any given object class distributes itself through the social hierarchy (and, in spatial terms, through the settlement hierarchy), noting when there appear to be sharp thresholds between those who deploy such items and those who do not. In other words, it is useful to consider object value at the population scale wherever this is feasible. Following on from the points made above about the potential correlation between object variation and relational models, we also might look at the varying emphasis placed on three different structuring logics that might be used to measure wealth: quantity, quality, and diversity. Mortuary custom is a good example of an archaeologically recoverable pattern which is amenable to exploring these issues, and several commentators have already highlighted one or more of these three logics as a better way of exploring burial wealth than, for example, arbitrary scoring methods (e.g. Voutsaki 1993; Quesada 1998). However, the study of such patterns in burial urges particular caution, because it is classic example of a context-specific performance that can have its own specialised paraphernalia and norms, serving to remodel the social arena of the living rather than mirror it in any straightforward manner.

Varying emphasis on quality, quantity, and diversity are part of social logics governing the appropriate classification of objects and the way they are accumulated. Two already well-known variables are the degree to which a society allows or encourages the collection of private property and whether it is acceptable to pass this wealth on from one generation to another. Beyond these, there can be many different types of wealth indexes or prestige markers or just one or two key items (a question of diversity). Each type of item can then be arranged more or less tyrannically into vertical grades of better and worse examples (quality). Finally, there are often very specific rules governing how much or how many of any given item it is appropriate to accumulate or display (quantity). For example, in modern capitalist societies, wealth is often expressed by the possession of a relatively diverse array of personal accessories and modern conveniences (e.g. watches, clothes, cars, stereos, and computers) and for any one of these status objects, there are well-defined quality grades. However, while it is acceptable to collect and store certain types of wealth (e.g. money or clothes), a degree of disapproval, social sanction, or legal intervention can accompany the accumulation of others (Douglas and Isherwood 1979: 90–1), particularly where this is deemed overly ostentatious or maladaptive for the group (e.g. owning 50 cars).

Measuring vertical quality and horizontal diversity distinctions is not without method-ological pitfalls, particularly with respect to variable sample size (Grayson 1988). Moreover, quality and diversity can vary both within and between perceived object classes, making the definition of baselines ('typical' or average examples) and class boundaries (what is or is not deemed part of an object category) very important. Usually, however, amidst a potentially bewildering array of cultural products, there is a classificatory threshold be-yond which people no longer feel they are comparing like with like. Quantity usually involves distinctions made on the basis of size, weight, and number that allow relatively complex ratio-scale comparisons. Diversity, on the one hand, is often equality matched to the extent that having one (or a limited number) of each prestige indicator is often the most appropriate form of behaviour because it encourages formal equivalence amongst peers (see above). On the other hand, sometimes class diversity can be so low that only one dominant wealth index exists, such as cattle or pigs (Evans-Pritchard 1940; Lemonnier 1993). This does not imply that other objects are somehow left completely outside local value regimes, only that they are used less clearly to carry this sort of status-related information.

In contrast, quality refers to linearly ordered, ranked variations. Highly articulated hierarchies of object value, including both real and spurious distinctions, often emerge within the context of elite competition. The types of distinction that are commonly important include colour, texture, taste, hardness, elaboration, provenance, maker, and vintage. Imitation and skeuomorphism are particularly curious features of objects caught up in such quality hierarchies. Imitation can refer to a vast range of phenomena from deliberate fakes to symbolic substitutions to partial and isolated copies of material, style, or technique from one medium to another. The latter allusions are indicators of value and esteem that usually confirm rather than undermine existing valuations. Fakes, however, threaten to short-circuit existing value hierarchies by successfully being accepted as the real thing. In this respect, consumer brands, heirlooms, and sacred relics are often faked because they all act as passports into a specific ranked group, such as a political and social elite or a community of the divinely blessed. Particularly heated debates about authenticity and forgery tend to occur in such an elite climate, where the negotiation of taste is highly nuanced, fakes are common, and social competition is fierce. Indeed, the possession of obscure, sometimes wholly fictitious, skills of quality distinction or discernment is a powerful way of controlling social mobility and vetting *parvenus*. In between these two categories of imitation is the use of models or other symbolic place-holders for real valued objects. These are acts of omission most easily made during transformative rituals such as burial (Pearson 1998), but the wider acceptance of such substitutions (e.g. the degree to which they are believed to involve actual transubstantiation) varies greatly.

This chapter has suggested a practical course through the rather ambiguous meanings of the term value. It has emphasised the fact that object value is often embedded in wider social strategies that are deliberately naturalised by their practitioners, making them seem effortless, timeless, and/or inevitable. It can also be defined and redefined at various stages in an object's social life and is in fact best understood as a social phenomenon, part of the logics through which people think about their relationships with each other. Wealth measurement is a particularly crucial domain where object value is harnessed and we should approach the issue of how it manifests itself archaeologically both by unpacking the contemporary and context-specific norms that affect human decision-making and by considering its wider comparative and longitudinal implications. The following chapters turn to consider the material culture of the Bronze Age eastern Mediterranean: the relevance of the ideas proposed here will hopefully be obvious amongst the detail of substantive discussion and are also returned to more explicitly in Chapter 9.

# 3
# Moving People, Objects, and Ideas

🖿🖿🖿🖿🖿🖿

*This chapter shifts away from theories of value to concentrate on understanding the movement* of material culture around the Bronze Age eastern Mediterranean. It places the study of stone vessels in a wider exchange and consumption context and in so doing declares a particular theoretical and empirical perspective on how we should go about reconstructing the importance of interregional contact in a pre- and protohistoric context. The discussion begins by exploring the Mediterranean environment and how Bronze Age people and objects might travel around it, before then considering the conceptual models with which modern commentators have approached Bronze Age trade, through which the most frequent and important fault line is the extent to which premodern economies can and should be distinguished from modern, capitalist ones. In this respect, we find it hard to assign priority to a range of types and scales of explanation for the movement of objects, just as we sometimes struggle to know how the picture presented by the archaeological record must be calibrated up or down to capture the real quantity, variety, and significance of material moving about. The final three sections address the third, earlier and later second millennia BC more directly and explore how specific flows of material integrated or distinguished different areas at different times.

## Moving Around the Eastern Mediterranean

At first glance, the Mediterranean might seem a curious choice of region within which to study human society—an expanse of sea surrounded by fringes of land and groups of islands, occasionally opening out into deeper hinterlands. However, this body of water not only delimits an area of broadly similar climate, it also provides the critical means by which otherwise disparate communities can be connected into a much larger maritime network. The social and cultural interaction occurring over this network has been particularly intense in the eastern half of the Mediterranean, from the Bronze Age onwards, forging a range of shared cultural forms that often cross-cut perceived political boundaries. Certainly, there are also important contacts with the Pontic and Balkan regions to the north, Mesopotamia to the east, Nubia and Sahel Africa to the south, and the central Mediterranean to the west, but these are often on a more restricted scale, and the eastern Mediterranean remains an extremely useful analytical unit.

Within this area, a combination of topography, winds, and currents encourage travellers and their possessions to follow specific directional patterns, on both land and sea, and many major settlements owe their prosperity to nodal locations along preferred overland routes, river junctions, or maritime corridors. On land, domesticated equids were commonly used as pack animals in the Bronze Age but were comparatively slow and the caravan trade involved significant logistical problems if large loads or great distances were involved (e.g. Cooper 1992). In a few favoured areas, major perennial rivers (e.g. the Nile and the Euphrates) provided faster and more cargo-friendly links and these were clearly a factor in the precocious socioeconomic development of the Egyptian and (east of our area) Mesopotamian states. However, it is the eastern Mediterranean sea which plays the most crucial connective role in the region and there are a series of important environmental and historical patterns that affect the distribution and value of material culture traded across this body of water. Firstly, the technology of seagoing ships developed in significant ways over the course of the Bronze Age. Canoe-borne movement is common from a very early stage (Marcus 2002a: 404–5) and encouraged relatively flexible, but short range and low-bulk, voyages.[1] These travelling parameters remain fairly constant until the third millennium despite a wide variety of materials with which such canoes could be made. Occasional larger multipaddle canoes might voyage slightly longer distances but were substantial, risky investments in terms of human resources and therefore only viable for communities of a certain size and outlook (Broodbank 2000: 96–102).

A key development during the third millennium, however, is the spread of sailboats and sailing know-how. The first experimentation with sails on the Nile seems to occur in the later fourth millennium, though there may have been a roughly contemporary invention in Mesopotamia as well (Bowen 1960: 117, fig. 1; Casson 1995: fig. 6). By the third millennium, literary references to 'Byblos ships' and pictures of seagoing vessels (Wachsmann 1998: 12–18; Marcus 2002a; Fabre 2005: 89–129) all attest to the increased importance of sailboats and to Egyptian maritime links with the Levantine coast. Thereafter, sailing activity in the eastern Mediterranean appears to increase in scale, intensity, and reach but with a more immediate impact on some regions than on others. In the Aegean, evidence for sailing ships appears quite late, towards the end of the third millennium (Broodbank 2000: 96–102). More generally, the apparent design of these early ships suggests performance parameters for maritime travel that remained relatively unchanged until at least the later second millennium. All of the well-identified depictions show sailboats with symmetrical round hulls and double-boomed square sails (probably also without keels in many instances; Vinson 1993; Wachsmann 1998). The precise degree of navigational flexibility offered by this general design remains a little unclear, but it nonetheless suggests a more finite range of travelling directions with respect to the wind than either Classical or later Medieval shipping (that were rigged in more complex ways and had lateen sails, respectively; Roberts 1991; Casson 1995: 21, 273; Roberts 1995). At times, some ships may have been able to use oar power to improve their routing options, but this strategy was mainly available to galleys (that really only become visible late in the period) and not to merchant ships with larger holds, higher freeboards, and fewer oars (Georgiou 1991: 62).

So for most of the Bronze Age, analogies with the performance of better-documented, later Mediterranean sailing craft and with later sailing routes may well be misleading. The eastern Mediterranean's winds and currents encourage anticlockwise shipping (Pryor 1988; Mantzourani and Theodorou 1989; Lambrou-Phillipson 1991; Georgiou 1995; Agouridis 1997; Georgiou 1997; Wachsmann 1998: 295–301), and these parameters are likely to have been slightly more tyrannical for Bronze Age craft than for many later sailing vessels. This prevailing pattern strongly influenced the configuration of maritime networks but also varied depending on the departure points and destinations involved, the local knowledge of travellers, the risks they were prepared to take, and the capabilities of their watercraft. Open-sea voyaging is perhaps the most direct but also the most inherently risky maritime voyaging strategy due to the likelihood of storms, windless periods, and loss of orientation. Coast-hugging is an alternative tactic which might circumvent larger-scale winds or currents and take advantage of local conditions to chart a wider variety of courses, but it required specialist local knowledge and dramatically increased risk of running aground in bad weather (Marcus 2002b: 249). Harbour navigation is often tricky, and while canoes, row-boats, and smaller keel-less sailing ships could be beached and dragged ashore, larger vessels required more elaborate facilities or had to wait at anchor and disembark their people and cargoes off-shore.

So the Mediterranean environment encourages the flow of people and objects in specific directions. As we shall see repeatedly, this has important effects on the structure of inter-regional contact and on the values assigned to specific trade goods. The adoption of new transport technologies such as equids or sailing ships adds a dynamic quality to these flows over the course of the Bronze Age, and throughout, we should bear in mind that individual itineraries and commercial agendas might diverge from these central tendencies, especially for shorter trips (Horden and Purcell's 'Brownian motion of caboteurs', 2000: 143). With these possibilities in mind, the following sections consider first the theoretical positions that commentators have adopted when addressing Bronze Age exchange and then the nature of the material patterns themselves.

## Bronze Age Economies and Exchanges

Exchange is a heavily theorised topic and the protohistoric eastern Mediterranean has been a battleground for rival academic narratives, emphasising either the otherness of Bronze Age exchange mechanisms or their similarity to modern examples. The previous chapter touched briefly on the analytical distinctions often made between modern and premodern values and indeed similar types of opposition are paradigmatic for many long-term perspectives in the social sciences and humanities. However, while we need to think carefully about what attitudes are behind prehistoric exchange economies, this modern vs. premodern split is a potentially misleading one, from and around which a number of other us-and-them models have coalesced (Bloch and Parry 1989: 7–8). In the Bronze Age eastern Mediterranean, such a dichotomy is particularly persistent, not least because the survival of textual sources (limited in subject matter, distribution, and/or quantity) coupled with a wide range of representational art and a richly explored archaeological record has meant, ironically, that rival narratives have concentrated at the awkward interface of these data sets, often making the three types of evidence difficult to reconcile with each other. With these concerns in mind, the following discussion begins rather simply by considering the different ways in which objects move from one place to another and the varying degree to which we might recognise these processes archaeologically. Subsequent sections then go on to address the thorny issue of the scale and nature of mercantile activity during the Bronze Age.

There are two basic distinctions that characterise the movement of objects (Figure 3.1): (1) whether they travel along with their owners or between different people and (2) whether

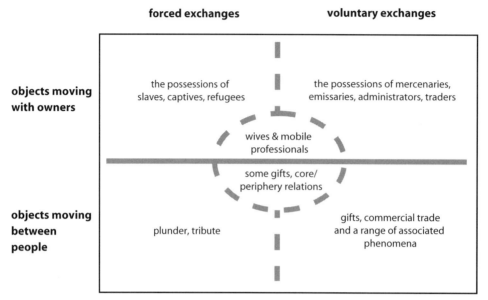

FIGURE 3.1. A schematic model of the movement of objects.

the objects' movement is compelled upon their human owners in some way or voluntarily undertaken by all parties. The first distinction, between objects moving with owners and those exchanged between them, is important because it implies quite different levels of information transfer (Renfrew 1993). Objects moving between people leap over a cognitive divide across which there is only a partial transfer of information about the purpose of the thing being traded (e.g. about its value or history) and in extreme cases, objects exchanged down-the-line become completely deracinated of their original meaning. In contrast, objects moving with their owners potentially retain much more of their own cultural baggage, but a new consumption environment may nonetheless make them more or less desirable or appropriate than before.

The second distinction is useful because it identifies the fact that power relationships between people often feed back into the value of the objects involved. Objects can move as part of arrangements that are either forced or voluntary for the human parties involved. There is some degree of categorical overlap here, however, as apparently voluntary exchanges can sometimes be compelled by a perceived network of reciprocal obligations (see below with respect to traditional gift exchange models). Likewise, real power relations can sometimes be disguised to fuel local sociopolitical agendas: gifts can be passed off as tribute and stolen goods as traded ones. Moreover, some exchanges can be voluntary but unbalanced, to the extent, for example, of being perceived as morally better and worse goods flowing in opposite directions (Shennan 1999).

Without losing sight of this intriguing overlap, the two main distinctions and their impli-cations can be usefully described as a matrix. Each of the four quadrants shown in Figure 3.1 has a different level of archaeological visibility and different implications for the transfer of object value and meaning. The top left quadrant refers to those situations where objects travel with their owners and where this movement is compelled in some way. This includes the possessions of slaves, captives, and refugees, who have huge social impacts but are difficult to identify archaeologically. Such people often carried few if any objects that might mark them out in new contexts and/or might be unable to exercise the same freedom in expressing social identities through material culture, burial, or depositional practice in their new surroundings (Parkin 1999).

The top right quadrant refers to more voluntary ways in which humans and their artefacts travel together and includes the impact of mobile professionals such as mercenaries, traders, artisans, pilgrims, and emissaries. With some of these groups, a degree of external control might also be involved, for example, in the exchange of wives or palace personnel between different courts attested in Near Eastern texts (Zaccagnini 1983; Moorey 2001). Not only is it often hard to prescribe a set of material traces that might characterise such people, it is also worth considering that the material identities projected by expatriates might well be different (e.g. more extreme or more subdued) from the ones the same individuals would have adopted in their home countries. Furthermore, travelling craftspeople inevitably blur the distinctions between local products and imports, and this type of artisanal fluidity is probably behind the genesis of transregional or international decorative styles, especially during the Late Bronze Age (see below). Nevertheless, mobile professionals represent a powerful means by which information about objects and the way they might be used could be transferred directly to local groups.

The bottom left quadrant of Figure 3.1 refers to forced exchanges between people. Plunder and tribute are two phenomena that fall into this category and are both ways in which large amounts of material might move around. For example, the annals of Thutmosis III provide a good picture of how such forces operated and the scale of transfers they might entail (Breasted 1907: passage 406). However, the inflow of wealth resulting from plunder or tribute is not always advantageous and can be both economically and socially destabilising. Plunder can lead goods that previously circulated in quite restricted spheres of exchange to become available more widely. Tribute is also a two-edged sword, prompting structural changes in the economies of both vassal and overlord that can have far-reaching effects. Both war booty and tribute expose communities to novel ways of expressing wealth and prestige, introducing new values and transforming old ones. Evidence for plunder might be found in burial deposits displaying foreign objects alongside clear warrior identities or, more rarely still, might be spelt out by artefact inscriptions (e.g. Lilyquist 1988; Potts 1989), but the archaeological visibility of such processes is often very low.

## Behind Bronze Age Gifts

Perhaps the thorniest problems of description arise when it comes to the bottom right quadrant of Figure 3.1, voluntary exchanges between people. This fourth domain is arguably given a disproportionate amount of emphasis by archaeologists compared to the other three, and again two rival models have often been used to understand it: gift-giving and trade-for-profit. Gift-giving was a fundamental part of the socioeconomic life of the Bronze Age eastern Mediterranean and our best-known examples usually reflect upper elite behaviour, for which specific types of object, such as drinking cups, rhyta, chariots, horses, anointing oils, and luxury garments were seen as particularly appropriate (Zaccagnini 1987: 58). Similar gift-giving regimes no doubt existed for the rest of society, but (1) are inevitably less visible in surviving written correspondence, (2) are not such highly recogniseable and curateable products, and (3) often occurred at the smaller spatial scale of the household or community where they would be harder to discern archaeologically. The notion of the gift has often been set up in opposition to the concept of commercial trade, and the balance between these two apparent structuring principles has been at the heart of academic debate about premodern economies for a long time (e.g. Revere 1957; Dumont 1980; also Gregory 1982; Godelier 1996). With respect to the early eastern Mediterranean, it has also fed into a number of other disciplinary oppositions with respect to the scale of ancient economies, the degree of institutional control by palaces or temples, as well as the relative importance of trade vs. agriculture and external influence vs. indigenous development (Sherratt and Sherratt 1998: 330–3, with references). However, these divisions also took on a new lease of life with the studies of Karl Polanyi and others who again emphasised the embeddedness of premodern exchange systems in wider social practices (e.g. Polanyi et al. 1957; Sahlins 1972; Polanyi 1977) and cautioned that the extreme monetisation, commodification, and ubiquitous markets of modern capitalist societies are unique in human history, making it inappropriate for us to apply our own commercial perspectives to ostensibly economic patterns in the past. Rather, for Polanyi et al., gift exchange is a dominant feature of less stratified societies, while redistributionary mechanisms are responsible for the main flows of goods between people belonging to more complex ones.

Such a 'substantivist' perspective still remains prominent, if often implicit, in many recent analyses of eastern Mediterranean society and economy (including the continued emphasis on redistribution models; see Halstead 2004: 192–3 for discussion). A similarly polarised debate has occurred over the relative importance assigned to trade or agriculture in early Mediterranean societies, initially driven by classical historians (Jones 1964; Finley 1973) who emphasised the complete dominance of agricultural concerns and suggested that trade was fairly limited both in scale and impact. Renfrew's model (1972) of indigenous change behind the emergence of complex societies in the Aegean was also in rough agreement with these principles, describing a Bronze Age world full of socioeconomic continuities, dependent for its gradual changes more on local economic and demographic processes than on diffusion of ideas and objects from the outside. From a structural point of view, models that minimise the impact of Bronze Age trade tend to point to a combination of redistributionary mechanisms operating within state-level societies and to gift exchange arrangements, accounting for a limited transfer of luxury goods between and beyond them (Janssen 1975b: 139, 183; Snodgrass 1991). Trade is often seen as a monopoly of palaces or major temples that organised it to supply necessary raw materials or luxury materials for their attached workshops.

However, while the emphasis on gifts and the redistribution of agricultural surpluses has been beneficial, the creation of a premodern, anthropological 'other' has also produced some rather abstract and misleading models. For example, a major sources of substantivist exchange theory is the complex reciprocal gift systems documented in late-nineteenth- to early-twentieth-century Melanesia (e.g. Malinowski 1950; Mauss 1990) and many prestate societies in the eastern Mediterranean have been approached with this perspective in mind. Unfortunately, these traditional Melanesian ethnographies described a world which was already profoundly affected by European contact and therefore unlikely to provide the unmediated impression of 'primitive exchange' that is so often assumed (see Leach and Leach 1983). Moreover, recent work has questioned if this paradigmatic Melanesian gift society *ever* existed, emphasising that multiple valuations of goods and services appear to have been present in the Melanesian heartland long before colonial times (Aswani and Sheppard 2003; also Weiner 1992: 44–65). In other words, we should be extremely cautious of deploying such models as an explanatory framework within the Mediterranean, without arguing, as Cyprian Broodbank has done successfully (2000), both a far less essentialist position and a more detailed comparative case (see also Wolpert 2004: 132–5).

Rather than placing this priority on reciprocity, it is more useful to see gifts as embracing a range of human relationships, which also include thinking about them as acts of altruism within a community, as expressions of hierarchical power, or indeed as inextricable elements of commercial manoeuvering (see previous chapter). For instance, in the Bronze Age eastern Mediterranean, the ideology of gifts, community, and commerce are particularly intertwined. The logic of the Amarna period correspondence is perhaps our best example and many commentators have viewed the relationships expressed there, amongst rulers who matched greeting gifts, emphasised reciprocal fair-dealing, and called each other 'brother', as only the most ostentatious feature of a classic premodern, Maussian economy. However, there is much going on beneath the surface of this phraseology (see also Feldman 2006), such as a preoccupation with the exchange value of goods (Moran 1987: EA 13, 14, 22, 25)[2] or the fact that, to an internal domestic audience, the same gifts might be used to refer to the subordinate status of the giver rather than to their equality (e.g. Wachsmann 1987; Liverani 1990: 240–70; Bleiberg 1996: 90–114). Likewise, there is huge ambivalence between the labels used for merchants (*tamkāru*) and messengers or ambassadors (*mar šipri*; Rainey 1964: 315; Kestemont 1977: 191–3; Zaccagnini 1987: 58ff) which is part of a wider array of ambiguous vocabulary (brotherhood, family adoption, friendly conduct, and gift-giving) present in the royal letters between Great Kings but also used in private correspondence between Near Eastern merchants (Zaccagnini 1984: 150ff; Silver 1985: 32–9; Ben-Barak 1988). What we can be sure of therefore is that, for different areas of the Bronze Age eastern Mediterranean, there existed a superficially noncommercial protocol that styled itself on codes of honorable conduct pertaining within families or small village communities (Liverani 2000) but which choreographed a much wider range of diplomatic, social, and economic activities.

So at least some of the high-level gift exchange scenarios that we might wish to treat as straightforward either disguise or facilitate commercial arrangements. Rulers were clearly aware of how ideologies could conflict and how distorted they could become. The king of Babylon alludes to this in his Egyptian correspondence when he expresses annoyance that his gift of chariots was misleadingly being displayed along with the tribute of vassals during an Egyptian parade (Moran 1987: EA 1). Likewise, he refers disparagingly to his rival, the king of Assyria's, attempts to initiate diplomatic relations with Egypt and requests that they not be allowed to carry out any business in Egypt. Such a request was almost certainly aimed at restricting commercial trade, and thus the term business (*šimati*) was used deliberately as an ugly contrast with the greeting gifts (šulmanu), which was superficially more befitting relations between kings (Zaccagnini 1987: 63–5).

## Scale in the Archaeological Record

These examples of Bronze Age gifts therefore offer a useful cautionary tale, suggesting that even the most apparently clear-cut instances of noncommercial Bronze Age exchange are rarely straightforward. Another contribution that the Amarna correspondence and a few other privileged contexts make is to highlight the often severe discrepancy between real levels of Bronze Age exchange and those superficially implied by most of the surviving archaeological record. This problem of archaeological scale is a common but extremely difficult one, and we are forced to take a critical position not only on the quantities of trade goods involved but also on their corresponding social and economic impact, particularly in cases where foreign objects might be used as exotic status markers (e.g. Helms 1988; Sherratt and Sherratt 1991). We are lucky in the eastern Mediterranean to be able to examine a rich combination of archaeology, text, and iconography, but none of these types of evidence are unproblematic on their own. A few rare archaeological snapshots (e.g. shipwrecks or unplundered single interments) often point to the gaps present in most of the record due to poor preservation or recovery bias. Our surviving textual record leaves many subjects patchily represented, reflecting as it does the context-specific uses of Bronze Age writing, the administrative reach of particular people or institutions, and the records kept on nonbiodegradeable or otherwise freakishly preserved materials (e.g. Bennet 1988: 509–10; Postgate 2001). Likewise, representational art often provides a highly biased impression of reality, filtered through the ideologies of the maker and/or their patrons. Scale problems are usefully highlighted by considering three broad categories of material: organics, metals, and pottery. To take the case of organic materials first, we have almost no quantifiable archaeological data about the trade in such products. From the texts and images that survive, it is clear that vast quantities of textiles, resins, oils, wines, dyes, spices, and woods were being made, sometimes traded, over considerable distances and then repackaged, reworked, and consumed in a variety of ways, beginning in earnest in the third millennium and apparently increasing in tempo throughout the second (Knapp 1991; Haldane 1993; Serpico 2004). Very little of this material is recoverable under normal archaeological conditions, and it is only exaggerating slightly to suggest that whole Bronze Age industries can appear and disappear from our analysis based on a limited number of philological or chemical identifications (e.g. opiates; Merrillees 1962; Bisset et al. 1996).

Precious metals were an important objective of interregional trade but also offer a highly problematic material record, because they were extensively re-cycled (e.g. Sherratt and Sherratt 2001; Budd and Taylor 1995). For example, the Karnak dedications of Thutmosis III, the Ulu Burun shipwreck, and the Kültepe tablets represent contrasting types of evidence, separate chronological periods, and very different methods of transport, but all indicate very large amounts of metal moving in single transfers and contrast dramatically with the relatively small amounts found in ordinary archaeological deposits.[3] Moroever, while there is clearly a concentration of luxury finds in high-status contexts, the written records suggest a substantial amount of metal, including silver and gold, circulating in private hands, though the circumstances and scale of such activity clearly varies over time and from region to region (Heltzer 1984; Zaccagnini 1984). In contrast, to metal or organics, the trade in pottery is something over which we usually feel we have relatively good control, and yet we frequently misrepresent its scale and importance as well. The number of imported pots in any given context is often vanishingly small, both as a sampling fraction of the original population (about which we might hope to generalise) and as an overall proportion of the local ceramic assemblage. As Susan Sherratt has pointed out, pottery "has both less importance and more importance than has often been accorded it" (1999: 195)—less in the sense that written accounts clearly show how unimportant it was to the high-level exchanges with which these records are usually concerned and yet more, because pottery therefore represents absolutely undeniable evidence for a very substantial degree of production and trade below and beyond that which these sources discuss (also Whitelaw 2001).

This issue of scale relates directly to how elaborate an explanation we adopt for describing macroregional patterns, and it is worth considering two common models used to clean up an otherwise troublesome and messy picture: trading monopolies and 'world systems'. The first of these simplifies the explanation of regional trade into a series of national actors, suggesting that trading practices, like political manoeuvering, were monopolised by either particular institutions or ethnic groups. Limited support for this is offered by textual references to fleets or ship designs associated with specific states or regions (Breasted 1907: passages 492, 537; Moran 1987: EA 36, 40; Lambrou-Phillipson 1993; Fabre 2005: 89–152), but the sheer diversity of examples mostly argues against such a simplification. Moreover, the question of who crewed and managed these boats is more complicated than it might first appear: in the case of shipwrecks, for example, far too many analyses assume that the ethnicity and/or political allegiance of crews can be read off from the archaeological provenance of the cargo. In fact, the possible role of multinational traders in the LBA has been emphasised by a number of authors (Renfrew 1972: 468–70; Wachsmann 1998: 163–212; Knapp 1999; Gillis 1995: 62–5; Fabre 2005: 143–89), suggesting the tip of an iceberg in which boats, sailors, merchants, and cargoes might all have varying nationalities and agendas. Certainly, this is all the more plausible given our clear evidence for mercenaries, mobile artisans, and refugees abroad during this period (Parkinson and Schofield 1995; Artzy 1997: 4–5; Moorey 2001). In another sense, the priority assigned to institutional or state control of trade requires some sober revision, reflecting as it does particular theoretical agendas about the redistributive economies of early states or modern nationalist perspectives. For example, many commentators have questioned both the detail and the overarching assumptions behind Polanyi's palace and temple-based, marketless economies (Foster 1987; North 1977; Powell 1977; Silver 1985; Larsen 1987: 49; Postgate 1991: 79, 191–221). Such institutions clearly did have a crucial role to play as heavyweight producers, consumers, arbitrators, and/or patrons, inevitably controlling trade to some extent, by the impact of their invested wealth, their control of taxation and their support for key port or caravan facilities (e.g. Kestemont 1977: 194–6; Kemp 1989: 323–60), but both these institutions and private individuals often appear relatively flexible to market conditions that were not wholly of their own making.

Another approach to the large-scale description of long-distance contact has been an emphasis on 'world-systems', following the model of interregional trade that Immanuel Wallerstein developed for the colonial and postcolonial, capitalist world (1974). Such a model emphasises the importance of long-distance commodity flows, often across perceived political and cultural boundaries, produced by a division of labour and organisation between core regions and peripheral ones. Wallerstein identified a powerful dynamic property to these activities—often a picture of social and economic complexity cascading outwards from the centre—which produced far-reaching socioeconomic changes, particularly in the peripheral areas, and could eventually transform them into secondary cores themselves. Archaeologists and historians have understandably found this dynamic, macro-scale approach useful in other periods as well. At their most persuasive, world-systems perspectives emphasise that social and economic analysis should not be predefined as operating at the same scale as perceived political or cultural boundaries, but rather we should seek to explore empirically what unit of analysis is most relevant by looking at economic interdependence (Chase-Dunn and Hall 1997; Stein 1998; Peregrine 2001). However, most approaches simply identify some form of interregional trade and reify it as a deliberate, directed system. In fact, it is increasingly clear that while large-scale social and economic structures can certainly exhibit a degree of system-level order they are often better explained by identifying the more simple decision-making mechanisms operating behind them, that is, at the scale of the individual or small group (see Chapter 2). In other words, while we are describing systemic patterning we are not always explaining underlying process or imbuing it with any satisfactory human context.

Moreover, wherever archaeologists have adopted the theoretical lens of world systems, they have usually had to alter it, sometimes quite radically (e.g. Schneider 1977; Rowlands et al. 1987; Algaze 1993; Ratnagar 2001). Unfortunately, with this renegotiation, the descriptions often lose much of their explanatory power: we offer nothing particularly insightful by labelling the material interaction of neighbouring societies a world system, unless we can retain the dynamic structural properties (technological gaps, division of labour, political power, and bulk commodity transfers) of core and periphery that Wallerstein described. Stripped of these, there is a danger that what remains is merely a broadly diffusionist meta-narrative (in broad agreement with Renfrew 1993: 7). As we shall see, in the Bronze Age eastern Mediterranean, the flows of both prestige items and bulk commodities are indeed sometimes directional and assymmetric, and Andrew Sherratt's treatment of the long-distance trade in metal ores from a number of well-defined source areas makes it clear that a world-systems approach can be extremely effective (1993). However, many regional patterns are clearly not so imbalanced, and even metals often flowed in multiple directions and through multiple exchange links. Many of the source areas (e.g. highland Iran especially but to some extent also Anatolia and the Aegean) were themselves highly developed societies during the Bronze Age and produced a range of manufactured items that piggy-backed on the trade in metal.

What the rest of the chapter and those that follow therefore try to suggest is that any comparative, pan-regional approach demands deliberate shifts in the spatial scale of its explanations, from the general to the particular and back again where the evidence will sustain it. We must adopt a spatial equivalent to Braudel's temporal scales (*structure*, *conjoncture*, and *événement*: e.g. 1966: 13–14) that, unquestionably, is concerned with the overall, emergent properties of long-distance interactions, but also foregrounds characteristic regional responses and, at an even lower level, glimpses smaller communities and the actions of individuals wherever possible.

## Merchants and Their Roles

In this regard, one important category of person in the modern vs. premodern debate who requires our attention is the merchant. In the third millennium eastern Mediterranean, the paucity of written texts makes it difficult to pin down the specific role of trading groups in relation to existing or emergent polities. For example, Egypt has traditionally been characterised as a highly hierarchical state with little room for private overseas trade or merchants (Janssen 1982; Helck 1987; Bleiberg 1996). Its restricted number of viable points of access from the outside world probably did prioritise the role of the central authority in organising long-range expeditions, particularly at an early stage, and while small market places may be depicted in a few Old Kingdom tombs (e.g. Altenmüller and Moussa 1977), we see no clearly expressed trading personae during most of the Bronze Age. In the 19th Dynasty, we suddenly have written records referring to merchants being 'as busy as copper' on the Nile (Blackman and Peet 1925: 288; Gardiner 1935) and it unclear whether this reflects an increasing textual sample (surviving papyri) or a real socioeconomic change (Fabre 2005: 155–89). In the Near Eastern texts from the third millennium onwards, there are a range of terms apparently referring to merchants, of which by far the most well known is the Akkadian *tamkāru* (Sumerian *dam-gàr*; e.g. Rainey 1964; Astour 1972; Garelli 1977; Zaccagnini 1977; Hallo 1992). This term probably meant slightly different things at different times and places, but *tamkāru* consistently seem to have been agents involved in the actual execution of exchanges and the journeys they involved rather than immobile speculators. The activities of merchants were officially regulated and protected both within and between states and rulers themselves could get involved in the settlement of disputes and contracts (Knapp 1983; Heltzer 1984: 164–5; 1988: 9–14). In the northern Levant and Anatolia during the second millennium, merchants were mostly men, found at a range of levels in the social hierarchy and often organised into more or less formal cooperative partnerships. They were also often included amongst the professional groups listed as dependents or associates of the king (Rainey 1964: Astour 1972; Heltzer 1978: 126–8; Vargyas 1988: 119) Such relationships are hard to decode entirely, but probably involved the allocation of royal rations, lands, and political protection in return for a degree of royal service. This palace or temple regulation clearly varied over time and from region to region, but while the prestige, surplus capital, and political or juridical weight of such institutions might strongly influence mercantile arrangements, this does not automatically mean that merchants conducted all of their trade with palace-owned goods, that their routes were predetermined or that they could not form exclusively private enterprises. Where we have written records, there is good evidence for large amounts of private property or capital (e.g. Heltzer 1984; Zaccagnini 1984) and for a high degree of personal freedom in the way such people operated (Liverani 2003).

So merchants are good individuals with whom to conclude this discussion, embodying as they do a range of disciplinary standoffs over the extent and nature of Bronze Age trade. The following three sections (for the sites mentioned, see Figure 3.2) therefore provide some necessary contextual background to the discussion of stone vessels by discussing the types of objects in circulation within the Bronze Age eastern Mediterranean and how these patterns varied over time and space.

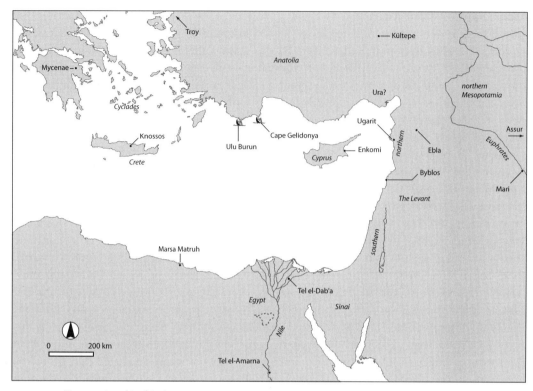

FIGURE 3.2. Sites mentioned in this chapter.

## Third Millennium Trade

The third millennium is a period of emerging interregional communication, in many ways the genesis of a coherent trading system. The impact of linkups can be seen across a vast area. In many instances, this was set against the backdrop of the importance of metals as status markers whose acquisition and processing could be controlled in a variety of ways. In the north and east, cities such as Ebla and Assur begin to establish a wide array of trading connections towards the end of the third millennium, driven for the most part by long-distance donkey caravans. Further south, Egypt's contacts with the Levant were mediated initially by overland caravans and perhaps short-range canoe hops along the coast but are later transformed by the appearance of sailing ships. The latter have the single most important impact on trading dynamics in this period, but were a new strategy that was adopted unevenly across the region. In the Aegean, for example, canoe-based regimes persist until near the end of the millennium, suggesting there must have been an important and shifting cultural interface between these two voyaging zones west of Cyprus and along the southwestern Anatolian coast.

By the late fourth millennium, Egypt had developed a relatively coherent material and political identity and an increasingly stratified society involved in trade with neighbouring areas such as the Levant and Nubia (Wengrow 2006: 13–40, 135–50). During Nagada IB-II, there is substantial contact with the Chalcolithic Levant, probably driven by the metallurgical output of the Wadi Feinan area, but supplemented by trade in other commodities such as Levantine wines and oils. The Late Uruk expansion may also have had an impact on the dietary, administrative, and iconographic forms that emerged during the period of Egyptian state formation, but if these links existed, they were extremely attenuated and filtered through intervening Levantine communities (Wengrow 2006: 38–40). Small amounts of lapis lazuli were probably also obtained via such extended exchange networks (Aston et al. 2000: 39). By the 1st Dynasty, a much stronger Egyptian presence in the southern Levant is visible, but this influence makes itself felt to very different degrees from site to site, with both evidence for Egyptian resident populations and in other cases, communities almost entirely devoid of Egyptian-style material (van den Brink and Braun 2003). Despite some evidence for contemporary canoe use, the key corridor along which this early contact took place was a terrestrial one, via the desert caravan route from the eastern Delta across the northern Sinai (Oren 1973, 1997; Marcus 2002a). However, in the 2nd to 3rd Dynasties, the Egyptian presence in the southern Levant and northern Sinai declines dramatically and by the Old Kingdom, if not some time before, the focus of Egyptian trade had moved northwards, particularly to the site of Byblos (Ward 1963; Saghieh 1983: 104–6; Marfoe 1987: 26–7). This also involved a shift from a primarily land-based trade route to a maritime, sail-driven one, and in return presumably for high-value raw materials such as gold and manufactured items, Egyptians sought coniferous woods for shipbuilding, coffins, and other objects, as well as Levantine arboreal oils, orchard fruits, bitumen and perhaps silver, tin, and lapis lazuli. Northern Levantine pottery containers now also begin to be imported into Egypt (Esse 1991: 103–16; Greenberg and Porat 1996), and the increasing size and standardisation of these vessels probably indicates their growing role as maritime transport containers (Marcus 2002a: 409–12). This relationship seems to continue through the FIP and an equally disrupted period in the Levant, but at a much reduced scale, picking up again only in the 11th Dynasty (Ward 1971: 49–64).

Further north, there is evidence that the connection between Assur and central Anatolia may have begun as early as the later third millennium (Leemans 1977: 6), and this seems to be the period when the Near East begins to use silver as a consistent exchange standard (Powell 1999), perhaps related to increased access to Anatolian silver sources (Foster 1977: 35). The effects of this established standard may well be echoed even as far away as northwestern Anatolia where silver ingots are found in Troy II and perhaps the Aegean where silver was probably being cupellated from lead on Siphnos (Wagner et al. 1985). A major window on northern Levantine trading systems is also provided by the Ebla archives, which reveal a thriving trade in metals, oils, and textiles (Pettinato 1986: 229–30).

The third millennium also sees an intensification of interregional contact within the Aegean, encouraged in particular by the longboat-voyaging communities of the ECII Cyclades (Renfrew 1972: 225ff). Metal objects become more obvious, influential status goods and we also have good evidence for a substantial trade in obsidian, marble objects, andesite millstones, and pottery (Runnels 1985; Nakou 1997; Carter 1998; Broodbank 2000: 211–75). The possible emergence of vine and olive cultivation and increasing use of secondary animal products (Renfrew 1972; Sherratt 1981; Runnels and Hansen 1986; Runnels and van Andel 1988) suggests, along with the increased visibility of drinking, pouring, and container vessels, that a small-scale trade in organic products (oil, wine, textiles) was developing. Despite these Aegean-wide trends, the first indications of contact with the Near East are generally restricted to Cretan contexts in the form of tiny and often disputed items made of faience, carnelian, and hippopotamus ivory (also see Chapter 5). As with the rather ephemeral traces of Mesopotamian influence in Predynastic Egypt, these exotic objects in the Aegean are hard to place in a wider context but suggest extremely attenuated and infrequent long-distance links that may have had more ideological impact than the quantities at first suggest (Sherratt and Sherratt 1991).

In late EB2, a different pattern begins to emerge, visible in new, shared forms of material culture, in technological borrowing, and in a particular demand for raw materials. The local adoption of these elements was often rather parochial and piecemeal, but the overall impression is of a breaking down of distinct regional patterns (Nakou 1997). The importance of metal ores (from Pontic/Balkan and Attic/western Cycladic source areas) and a few other resources, seems to have encouraged more directional trade, featuring sites at geographically advantaged points along the lines of pan-Aegean and extra-Aegean communication. Along with this set of contacts and preoccupations also came a series of new metalworking technologies such as tin alloying, spear, and dagger hafting and various casting/smithing processes.

Towards the end of the third millennium, we can identify a crucial change, marked archaeologically by when the first sail-driven vessels appear in Aegean iconography (Broodbank 2000: 341ff; Bevan 2004: 109), though it is unclear whether sailing remained a largely foreign strategy (Anatolian, Levantine, or Egyptian) for some time or was taken up rapidly by indigenous populations. The routes taken by sailing ships, the amounts they could carry, the distances they could travel, and the organisation they required imply major changes for those communities that actively embraced them as much as for those that did not. It is no accident that by the late third or early second millennium BC we see more substantial evidence for links between Crete and the Near East, particularly with Egypt, including goldwork, faience, ivory, seals, and stone vessels (e.g. Whitelaw 2004). Major elements of the Cretan palatial lifestyle such as ashlar orthostat architecture, the use of writing and wheel-assisted fine ceramics appear or develop at this time, perhaps partly as the result of peripheral exposure to models from further east (Watrous 1987). A direct maritime journey linking the southern coast of Crete to Egypt remains a possibility given the scarabs found at small communities on the south-central Cretan coast, but the return voyage would have been extremely difficult for Bronze Age craft, and it seems likely that much of this contact was filtered through intermediate Levantine sites such as Byblos.[4]

## Earlier Second Millennium Trade

The Middle Kingdom in Egypt saw a new flurry of trading activity with the southern Levant, evoked, for example, by the Beni Hassan tomb paintings (Newberry 1893). The traditional land routes connecting these two areas may have been given added significance by renewed mining expeditions to the Sinai for turquoise and possibly copper (Bietak 1996: 14–19, figs. 13–15; Gardiner et al. 1955: 11, 18–19, 103–4). Further north, Middle Kingdom finds from Byblos imply that this important exchange link survived the social and political upheaval of the the FIP/EBIV period or was reestablished thereafter. Alongside this, tin and textile trade between northern Mesopotamia and both northern Levantine and central Anatolian cities provided an avenue by which Mesopotamian influence and material culture might move into the eastern Mediterranean region (see below). We can also see the re-emergence of an agricultural commodity trade in which Levantine oil juglets and storage jars played a prominent role. Amenemhet II's court annals record two maritime expeditions to the Levant, and while the rhetorical nature of the source does not allow us to know whether the objects acquired during these were trade items or plunder, they record the large-scale transfer of people, weapons, gold, silver, copper, lapis lazuli, gems, wine, wood, and oil (Redford 1992: 78–80).

Levantine pottery in particular is found in many later Middle Kingdom contexts in Egypt (Petrie 1891: 16–22; Arnold 1982; Kemp and Merrillees 1982: 34–6, 39, figs. 15–16; McGovern et al. 1994; Arnold et al. 1995), while smaller quantities of Cretan, Cypriot, and Anatolian pottery are found in the Levant and Egypt around the same time (MacGuire 1995) and intercultural combinations of styles also become more common. A major conduit for this inflow of Levantine and other foreign pottery into Egypt was the site of Tel el-Dab'a in the eastern Delta. As the 'mouth of the two ways', it lay at the intersection of both maritime and land routes to the Levant and beyond. A wide variety of evidence all indicates its close economic and social connections with the southern Levant (van den Brink 1982; Porada 1984; Bietak 1989, 1991; Phillip 1995; McGovern and Harbottle 1997: 150–5; Redford 1997: 20–1; Wapnish 1997). Immigration of Levantine groups into Egypt from as early as the 12th Dynasty seems probable and this process arguably crystallises in the political form of later Hyksos rule in the eastern Delta, as well as in the increasingly impressive, urban character of southern Levantine coastal communities (Marcus 2002b).

In Anatolia and the northern Levant, a phenomenon of increased importance was the trade in tin. Cities such as Assur, Ebla, Kültepe, Mari, and Ugarit owed some of their prosperity to the tin trade, which arguably created opportunities for an accompanying exchange of fine textiles and/or lapis lazuli (Dalley 1977; Rouault 1977). The actual routing of the tin trade appears to have been very much at the mercy of interregional politics. Written evidence from two major beneficiaries of this trade, Kültepe and Mari, show how important and peripatetic it was. In the first case, a vast array of written correspondence from the site of Kültepe on the central Anatolian plateau reveals the impressive scale of long-distance commercial exchanges between this region and the Mesopotamian city of Assur during the early centuries of the second millennium (Larsen 1967; Veenhof 1972; Garelli 1977; Larsen 1987; Veenhof 2003). The main commodities at the Anatolian end of the network were wool, textiles, copper, silver, and gold, and of these, the last two were the ones most frequently exported back to Assur, while the others mainly formed part of smaller Anatolian trade circuits in which the Assyrian traders were also involved. At the other end of the network, Assur's advantageous geographical location and commercial infrastructure (donkey caravans, merchants, reputation, etc.) made it a key market for the exchange of fine Mesopotamian textiles, copper, tin, lapis lazuli, and occasionally even meteoric iron. With the exception of the copper, all of these materials were sometimes sent on to Anatolia, though tin and textiles were by far the most important. The amounts being traded were enormous given the attenuated donkey-caravan routes by which they moved. Family trading firms managed much of this trade, often with different relatives acting as representatives at particular ends of, or stops along, the route. Although merchants frequently had to deal with local rulers, occasionally used temple funds and were nominally supervised by representatives of the city of Assur, they were essentially involved in private ventures that relied quite explicitly on an ability to exploit market forces.

The demise of these Assyrian colonies, towards the end of the first quarter of the second millennium, coincides with two important political developments in the northern Levantine and Mesopotamian sphere: the rise of the Hittite state in Anatolia and the temporary decline of the kingdoms of Assur and Eshnunna (Charpin and Durand 1991). The latter allowed the Elamite kingdom to wrest some control of the tin trade from Assur, and Mari's cordial relations with the former temporarily, and unusually, allowed it to become an important transhipment point for this metal, as it came up the Euphrates (Joannes 1991). The Mari archives provide our second important textual vantage on the metals trade, particularly its impact on the northern Levant (also see Dalley 2002). To the southeast, the king of Mari proves to be in intense diplomatic contact with the Elamite ruler at Susa, in which letters tin and lapis lazuli are prominent issues and, in one trip to the northwest, gives away almost half a ton of tin in largesse to neighbouring Levantine kings. Other major cities were clearly jostling for preferred rights in a commerce with Mari which again included gold, silver, tin, lapis lazuli, and fine textiles (Albright 1940: 27; Limet 1985: 16–17; Heltzer 1989; Bonechi 1992: 11–13). However, Mari's favoured trading status was to last only two and a half years, indicating that while there was a degree of stability in the flow of long-distance trade as a result of the limited source areas of certain raw materials, the privileged positions of individual traders, cities, or rulers were very much up for grabs, in a competitive political and economic arena that often descended into out-and-out warfare. The role of Cyprus at this time is difficult to assess, but the Mari texts contain several references to Alasiyan copper and bronze (Heltzer 1989: 8; Muhly 1996: 49), suggesting the contemporary expansion of the Cypriot metal industry. If the references are correctly interpreted, then Cypriot ore would have flowed via the Levantine coast and explains an accompanying trade in Cypro-Levantine pottery which may possibly have begun as early as MBIIA (Aström 1972: 206–33; Dever 1976: no. 104; Gittlen 1981: 50; Merrillees and Tubb 1979).

A palace-based society developed in Crete at the end of the third and beginning of the second millennium. Within the Aegean, the influence of the earlier Cretan palaces is patchy but increasingly apparent during the Neopalatial period (Broodbank 2004). At the same time, more complex political structures and exotic lifestyles are suggested by the Shaft Grave assemblages at Mycenae and other centres on the mainland. However, Crete remains the most obvious point of Aegean articulation with the rest of the eastern Mediterranean until relatively late (perhaps the fourteenth century BC: Phillips 2005). While the later EBA Aegean may have been a very peripheral source of raw materials or rare exotica for Near Eastern elites earlier on, it is during the Protopalatial period that we first see Crete exporting high-status goods in its own right. Cretan decorated fineware Kamares pottery has been found at a number of sites in Cyprus, the Levant, and Egypt (Kemp and Merrillees 1982; Warren and Hankey 1989: 115; Walberg 1997; Betancourt 1998: 6; Fitton et al. 1998). These finds are particularly visible in Middle Egypt, along with the first possible evidence for organic trade items such as fine textiles and medicinal herbs (Manniche 1989; Barber 1991: 338–51). More broadly, the striking feature about Kamares fragments found abroad is that they mostly come from cups or bridge-spouted jars, in contrast to the predominance of container shapes among Levantine imports. In other words, the Cretan trade principally filled the need for a set of exotic, lower or subelite tableware and there is a reasonable case for suggesting that the fine polychrome designs of Kamares pottery also imitate Cretan silver vessels, for which we have both rare instances on Crete and, more contentiously, tantalising candidates from Byblos and Egypt (Warren and Hankey 1989: 131–1, pls. 5–11; Jidejian 1971: figs. 40–1; an Anatolian origin for these silver vessels is possible). The trade in high value manufactured craft goods is also evoked by texts from Mari that refer to Cretan traders or emissaries present in Ugarit in the eighteenth century BC and trading Cretan-style goods such as weapons, clothing, and possibly pottery (Heltzer 1989: 13–14). One likely objective for such trade is the acquisition of tin, especially given the extensive use of tin alloying in the contemporary Aegean (Branigan 1974: 73–6, 1982).

In Crete itself, there is an apparent peak in Near Eastern influence in MMI, with imported Egyptian stone vessels and seals, local imitations of these two object classes, the more general use of raw materials such as hippopotamus ivory, carnelian, and lapis lazuli (e.g. Krzyszkowska 1988), and the apparent transfer of practices or ideas linked with Egyptian religion (sistra, scarabs, Taweret: Warren 1995: 2–3; 2005). Even so, it remains unclear whether we should see this activity as something occurring just prior to the appearance of palatial authority in Crete and therefore an influential factor in this process or in tandem with this socio-political transformation and merely one further way in which it was expressed. Evidence for such connections becomes even more obvious in the Neopalatial period, and a relatively important relationship seems to exist with Egypt, given the large numbers of Egyptian goods—stone vessels, raw stone blocks, gold, ostrich eggs, faience vessels, ivory—that have been found in MMIII–LMI contexts (Warren 1995). In return, Crete probably exported consumables such as oils, silver, textiles, and jewelery, though the evidence for this is often circumstantial rather than direct (Barber 1991: 338-51; Knapp 1991: 37-42; Wachsmann 1987). In addition, the technical and stylistic details of Aegean-style painted wall, ceiling, and floor decorations at various important sites in Egypt and the Levant reflect, at the very least, a tightly focused, upper elite decorative agenda and probably also indicate the mobility of and an esteem for Neopalatial artisans (rather than mere emulation, e.g. Niemeier and Niemeier 2000; Brysbaert 2002).

## Later Second Millennium Trade

The earlier second millennium BC therefore sees the emergence of a much more integrated system of exchange between different regions, a good indication of which is the role of silver as a widely accepted measure of equivalence. The trading regimes that appear thereafter during the later second millennium are transformed by some major political developments. In the south, Thutmosis III's extensive campaigns brought large areas of the Levant under Egyptian control, but arguably also prompted a greater demand for foreign products in Egypt itself, perhaps on the back of an initial influx of war booty and tribute. In Anatolia, Hittite power steadily increased and this period sees a set of standoffs between these two most powerful states in the region as well as, in the early stages, with the powerful northern Levantine kingdom of Mitanni. At the same time, the increased cultural and economic influence of Cyprus coincides with the growth of larger settlements on the island, both probably the result of more intensive exploitation of its copper resources. In the Aegean, the end of Cretan Neopalatial society and the rise of the Mycenaean palaces transformed the role and importance of Aegean products within the exchange relationships of the rest of the eastern Mediterranean.

Overall, we can draw a picture of eastern Mediterranean trade that was expanding in scale during late fifteenth to thirteenth centuries BC, increasingly standardised in terms of quantities, qualities, shapes, and manufacturing methods but also diversifying in terms of producers, distributors, and consumers. A good impression of the scale of activity is given by written evidence for numbers and sizes of contemporary merchant ships. We find an Ugaritic reference to ships carrying 450–500 tons of cargo as if it was not unusual and we have mention of fleets of 100–150 ships (Sasson 1966: 133; Casson 1995: 36). The late fourteenth-century Ulu Burun shipwreck at ca. 15 m long is probably representative of an important, but not necessarily unusual, shipment, while the Cape Gelidonya ship (Bass 2006; Pulak 2006), which is slightly smaller and sunk perhaps a century later, was probably closer in frequency and status to Medieval *caboteurs* than to the larger merchantmen. The very end of the Bronze Age is a time of apparent social, economic, and political dislocation across the entire area, though the specific effects of this vary at a local level. Decentralised patterns of interregional interaction and trade, of which the Gelidonya ship may be a good example, now seem more important, eventually extending as far west as the central Mediterranean, but increasingly associated with people from Cyprus and the central Levantine coast (Sherratt 1998).

The bulk trade in metals continues to be a key aspect of this trade, alongside which a range of other goods flowed. Large quantities of copper and tin were in circulation at this time (Wachsmann and Raveh 1984; Galili and Shmueli 1986; Pulak 2006), most prominently as major upper elite transfers, though with the increasing visibility of lower-level circuits towards the end of the Bronze Age (Bass 1967; Sherratt 1999). The main reason for the growing importance of Cyprus appears to have been the increased production and marketing of its copper resources (Knapp and Cherry 1994; Knapp 1997: 156ff). A wide variety of other Cypriot products accompanied this exchange of bulk copper. Hittite texts record Cyprus sending a range of fine manufactured goods along with metal, including gold vessels, rhyta, girdles, garments, wool, and linen, along with copper and bronze (Portugali and Knapp 1985: 65), while various herbs, spices, and plant dyes may also have been Cypriot exports at this time (Merrillees 1962; Bisset et al. 1996; Karageorghis 1996: 63ff). Egypt continued to export gold and this is the commodity most sought after by the foreign correspondents in the Amarna letters. In addition, for Tushratta's marriage gift from Amenhotep III, Egypt sends copper, stone vessels, oils and aromatics, leather, hides, cloth, and dyes (Moran 1987: EA22).

More generally, organic cargoes are if anything now more prominent, both in the written texts and in the archaeological record, including various hardwoods, murex shell, wine, resins, oils, and textiles (e.g. Knapp 1991; Pulak 2006: 19–22). Pottery, however, is the most archaeologically visible of these exports and includes both container shapes for oil or wine and empty open vessels. Perhaps the four areas most deeply implicated in this trade were the Mycenaean Argolid, eastern Cyprus, the Egyptian Delta, and the northern Levant, though other places were also involved to varying degrees (e.g. Knapp and Cherry 1994; Knappett

2000; Bourriau 2004: 48-50). The fortunes of individual producers is difficult to discern archaeologically, but on a broader scale, the taste for oils from particular areas seems to fluctuate over time, with Aegean, Cypriot, Levantine, and Egyptian products in and out of favour in neighbouring regions over four or five centuries.

Mycenaean LHIIIA2-B decorated ceramics, for example, are found all over the eastern Mediterranean, but they appear to have reached their destinations in a variety of ways and to have taken on slightly different roles in different places (Day and Haskell 1993; Hirschfeld 1993; Sherratt 1999; Van Wijngaarden 2002; Bell 2005, 2006). These exports included both large coarseware stirrup jars for bulk transport of oil, smaller versions for personal use, and open shapes for the consumption of food and wine. While there were clearly many different types of arboreal oils and resins in circulation, olive oil appears to have been an increasingly important cargo, making a notable appearance in the Egyptian archaeological and written records at this time and apparently the focus of specific Mycenaean and northern Levantine industries (Manniche 1989: 17; Hankey 1995; Ahituv 1996; Serpico 2004). The latter region has perhaps the longest, substantially unbroken tradition of oil and wine production for the maritime export trade, developing initially alongside the emergent Byblos–Egypt links in the mid-third millennium, seemingly responsible for the appearance of typical Canaanite-style handled jars during the later MBA, and continuing to expand in the LBA with the possible introduction of more elaborate oil-processing methods such as the lever press (Bourriau 2004; Serpico 2004; Smith et al. 2004). Three clear developments are the increasing size of these associated pottery containers (for an extreme and late example of this trend, though possibly related to the incense trade; see Wengrow 1996), their general similarity in form despite several different regional production centres, and a diversification of producers. Increasingly by the thirteenth century BC, large-scale local imitation and import substitution was occurring, certainly for pottery (e.g. Sherratt 1999; Killebrew 2004), but perhaps for popular foreign oil and wine recipes as well.

Pottery, oil, and wine were not the only goods to show signs of more highly standardised output. Glass-making was a craft which is initially linked to the Mitanni state but becomes a more widely accepted elite commodity around the time of Thutmosis III and along with its poorer cousin faience (and several other related processes) develops into a highly organised industry, particularly in Egypt (Shortland 2001; Rehren et al. 2001). Similarly, a close look at the manufacturing logics behind the hippopotamus ivory boxes made during this period suggest a similar concern with efficient output (Gachet 1987). The hub of this trading activity was undoubtedly the triangle mapped out by the big coastal emporia of Ugarit, Ura, and Enkomi, which also included a host of other trading centres (Yon 2003; Heltzer 1977: 207–9; Archi 1984: 204, though the exact location of Ura in the Cilician delta is unknown). Import substitution and aggressive marketing appears to be particularly intense within this zone, to the extent that a suite of objects and their contents were manufactured, moved, stored, and consumed together despite the fact that they directly or indirectly express a diverse range of cultural origins. These intercultural packages, coupled with the mobility of highly skilled craftspeople, reflect a sharp convergence of upper elite tastes, one further manifestation of which are a series of synthetic, 'international-style' products in precious metal, stone, faience, glass, ivory, and pottery with an eventual distribution across much of the eastern Mediterranean (e.g. Peltenburg 1991a; Caubet and Matoïan 1995: 105–9; Smith

2003; Feldman 2006). The degree to which other regions such as the Aegean were a direct part of the process or were connected by feeder links of smaller scale and narrower impact remains unclear. As before, prestige goods seem to concentrate at a few privileged Aegean centres though it sometimes remains difficult to judge whether this is a direct result of centralised palatial control or merely the route-driven nature of interregional trade at this time (e.g. compare Voutsaki 2001; Sherratt 2001). In the central Mediterranean, Mycenaean pottery was also consumed in reasonable quantities and by LHIIIB local imitations appear (Jones and Vagnetti 1997).

A flood of late thirteenth and early twelfth century boat images attests to an important change in ship design with the introduction of the loose-footed, brailed sail (Millet 1987; Roberts 1991; Vinson 1993; Casson 1995: 37–9, 273–7, no. 19; Roberts 1995). Brails allowed much closer trimming of the sail area and could be used in stronger seas because of the different implications they had for controlling lateral movement of the boat. While the precise increase in navigational flexibility that this allowed over previous ship designs is hard to judge, it is likely to have made feasible a wider range of voyaging strategies. These developments coincide with other general advances in the maritime sphere, including new storage jar shapes, harbour facilities, and boat equipment, all of which are probably linked to ill-defined polyethnic maritime groups that become visible in the textual and pictorial records from the mid-fourteenth century and increasingly towards the end of the Bronze Age (Raban 1988; Tubb 1995; Artzy 1997; Basch 1997; Sherratt 1998; Wachsmann 1998: 163–97). Diversity of background and allegiance aptly characterises these groups and their ambivalent role as nonaligned players, with both constructive and potentially detrimental impacts on the political and economic structure of existing states (Liverani 2003: 125–6).

## Summary

This chapter has set out a methodological perspective for tackling the way stone vessels might move around the eastern Mediterranean and offered some background to the social and economic context in which this movement occurs. Commonly favoured heuristic distinctions between our own modern and various other premodern worlds are actually rather unhelpful for considering Bronze Age eastern Mediterranean trading regimes. Likewise, neither the ordinary archaeological record nor surviving written and pictorial evidence offer a comprehensive or unequivocal picture of such activity, and we must attempt to play these different data sets off against each other if we are to identify the real scale and character of past economic activity.

A combination of factors do undoubtedly suggest a marked increase in the amounts of material being traded over the course of the Bronze Age. In the EBA, we can identify region-specific scales of interaction and exchange due to varying levels of social complexity and differing local transport technologies. Even if we reject the assumptions behind a world-systems model, there is certainly a pattern of expanding cultural and economic influence, westwards out of the core urbanised zones of Egypt and Mesopotamia and thereafter the Levant and Anatolia. In many instances, metals were the driving force behind these long-distance interactions, though a range of other resources and manufactured items were also incorporated within them. Textiles, oils, and wines are three further commodities that were clearly important at an interregional level from an early stage but which are poorly preserved in the archaeological record. Together they encouraged an ever-increasing set of common elite symbols beginning in the EBA, continuing during the MBA and firmly established in the international styles and complex cultural inventories of the LBA. The following four chapters now look in detail at how stone vessels industries fitted into both local social life and this wider, increasingly integrated world.

# 4
# Making Stone Vessels

⊡⊡⊡⊡⊡⊡⊡

*The last two chapters considered some general approaches to value and then concentrated on the* subject of eastern Mediterranean trade. This chapter is yet more specific, looking closely at the details of how stone vessels are made. Production strategies are not simply a sum total of local technical knowledge but are steeped in local values. Working stone into vessels involves balancing a variety of sometimes conflicting priorities and parameters: the properties of the stone, the availability of specific tools, a preference for particular designs, the intended quality of the finished product, and acceptable levels of accidental breakage. In any given cultural context, this balance will reflect both some conscious, strategic choices on the part of the artisan and the inertia of an inherited crafting tradition (for a similar perspective on potting, see Gosselain 2000).

Both short-term decisions and longer-term traditions can be interrogated for how they reflect value-led priorities and stone objects offer particularly rich opportunities for such analysis (though chipped stone has hitherto received most of the limelight: Renfrew and Zubrow 1994). Stone-working is a subtractive process, one which begins with a raw lump and gradually reduces it to a finished artefact by removing fragments, usually in a carefully ordered sequence. Telltale traces of these production stages are often well preserved both on half-finished objects and on final products. Understanding the details of such sequences casts light on a whole range of producer and consumer-driven interests. This chapter begins by describing the common stone-working tools and techniques and then proposes a template operational sequence for making vessels, based on the fact that, cross-culturally, there is significant regularity in the order and nature of different stages. Such a template should be seen as a heuristic tool for us rather than a technological straightjacket for the original artisan. Its most important role is to expose precisely those situations that vary from the general pattern, because this divergence is an excellent guide to the idiosyncratic values of a given community.

## The Working Properties of Stones

Different stones possess different working properties, based on two main parameters (Attewell and Farmer 1976; Prentice 1990: 33–40): (1) the cohesiveness of the overall rock when put under sustained stress and (2) the hardness and durability of its constituent minerals. Rock cohesion depends greatly on the porosity of the stone in question, as well as the size and shape of its mineral grains. More cohesive rocks endure more aggressive working, take a better polish, and can be more intricately carved. In contrast, other rocks cohere relatively poorly, for instance, because they have a banded structure that makes them prone to breakage along specific fracture planes.

Some stones comprise one main mineral (e.g. chlorite or calcite), while others are composed of several minerals of varying durability. At this smaller scale, we need to consider not only a mineral's basic ability to resist abrasion or indentation but also its propensity to fracture under impact. For example, some minerals such as feldspar are very hard, but their crystalline structure is prone to splitting in certain directions (known as cleavage; Wenk and Bulakh 2003: 269–71; Solenhofen 2003). This can be beneficial as well as problematic: many Egyptian stones (e.g. granites, diorite gneisses) used for vessels are highly cohesive rocks but rich in feldspar. This means that when they are hit using pounders of equivalent or greater rock hardness, their surface can be worked because the fragile feldspar is broken down, but no larger fractures are made.

So there is a general association between rock and mineral hardness but also sufficient variation, at both the rock and mineral scales, that an expert's familiarity with the properties of particular stones becomes a valuable commodity in its own right. Nevertheless, while remaining aware of this complexity, we can usually refer to the Mohs scale as a useful shorthand for indicating the likely working properties of a particular stone (Figure 4.1). The Mohs scale is a relative index based on the ability of one mineral to scratch another and is used repeatedly in the following chapters.

Even more broadly, we can lump the stones used for vessels into 'soft', 'medium', and 'hard' categories. Stones in any one of these categories share many working parameters. For example, a major threshold exists at about Mohs 3. For 'soft' stones below this threshold, carving-based techniques (the percussive use of chisels and points) are very effective for shaping both the insides and outside of vessels. In contrast, 'medium' stones above Mohs 3, demand alternative methods: a rock-hammer or toothless saw will be needed to rough out the exterior, and some form of manual abrasion or drilling is necessary to remove the interior. Travertine is a interesting example of a stone right on the boundary of this group. It consists almost exclusively of the Mohs 3 mineral calcite, but its rock cohesion is usually very good so copper chisels struggle to make an impact and their working edges are quickly worn away (Stocks 2003: 64–9). 'Hard' stones of Mohs 6–7 often require innovative tools and techniques. For example, an Egyptian stone such as Aswan granite encourages specific working procedures: it is best quarried with stone pounders because it is feldspar rich (as above), but further shaping must then be done by sawing and drilling. Flint tools are not appropriate for this main shaping task, but can still be used to cut shallow decoration or inscriptions because the flint is harder (Mohs 7) than the granite's feldspar crystals (Mohs 6) and, on a small scale, can break them down and isolate the remaining quartz and mica grains, allowing the latter to then be removed (Stocks 2001). Finally, polishing granite is particularly time-consuming because it includes minerals (e.g. feldspar, quartz, and mica) of varying hardness.

The following sections consider specific stone-working techniques in greater detail.

## Unassisted Manual Abrasion

Abrasion is part of almost all stone vessel manufacturing procedures, whether they involve loose abrasive, a grinding stone, and/or techniques for smoothing the end product (Figure 4.2). Polishing stone vessels is a relatively simple but time-consuming process, proceeding through stone rubbers (haematite, pebbles) and/or loose abrasives of ever finer

| Mohs' Hardness | Characteristic Mineral | Knoop's Microhardness | Stones (with approx. Mohs' hardness) |
|---|---|---|---|
| 1 | talc | / | |
| 2 | gypsum | 61 | |
| 3 | calcite | 141 | |
| 4 | fluorite | 181 | |
| 5 | apatite | 483 | |
| 6 | feldspar | 621 | |
| 7 | quartz | 788 | |
| 8 | topaz | 1190 | |
| 9 | corundum | 2200 | |
| 10 | diamond | 8000 | |

Stones column (with approx. Mohs' hardness): gypsum (2); travertine (3); steatite (1–1.5); serpentinite (3–4); limestone (1–3.5); marble (3.5–5); basalt (6); gabbro (5–6); haematite (5–6); diorite (6); granite (6); quartz crystal (7); amethyst (7); obsidian (6–6.5); silicified sandstone (7); carnelian (6.5–7); sardonyx (6.5–7); flint (7); emery (8). Groupings marked 'SOFT', 'MEDIUM', 'HARD'.

FIGURE 4.1. Table showing the Mohs scale of mineral hardness. Approximate Knoop's microhardness values are included as a guide to absolute differences in hardness between each point on the scale. The stones shown on the left are those used for vessels or in stone-working toolkits.

grades (down to ca. 5–0.5 $\mu$: Stocks 1993). Simple grinding by hand represents one of the earliest methods by which stone vessels were probably made, and in industries where there are no obvious signs of edged tool or drill marks, this is likely to have been the main production technique. Grinding technologies are often associated with sedentary foraging and intensified exploitation of wild resources such as seeds but become even more prevalent with the appearance of agricultural communities (see Chapter 8). Activities such as grinding cereals provide an obvious nursery for technical experimentation and it is therefore unsurprising that in such communities, early vessel production often focuses on finer versions of rocks otherwise used for local quernstones. As local

FIGURE 4.2. An Egyptian artisan smoothing off the exterior of a vessel using a small stone. From a 5th Dynasty tomb relief at Abusir (after Borchardt 1910: 37, fig. 33).

experience of vessel-making developed, the limited rotation of a grinder by hand probably provided a platform for experimenting with more elaborate, device-aided drilling methods.

## Carving

Most prehistoric carving tools were chisels or tiny punches, made of flint or metal. In later periods, multipronged hand-picks were also sometimes used in similar ways (e.g. Kohl 1977: 121; Weir 2007), but there is as yet no clear Bronze Age evidence for the types of grouped percussion scars that such implements leave and it seems likely that they only become popular in later periods with the widespread availability of socketed iron tools (Nylander 1966). For prehistoric flint and metal chisels, some *in situ* retouching or resharpening of the working edge was necessary as work proceeded. Chisel shapes can vary but tend to leave wide, shallow marks on the side of a vessel and closely packed scars on its interior base if worked from a vertical angle (Figure 4.3). Punches are smaller and often less finely made tools. They leave smaller, denser sets of vertical or diagonal scars and are more accurate, but more time-consuming to use (e.g. Kohl 1977: 117, figs. 15–7). Both tools were hammered into the stone using a cobble or mallet. Carving vessels can therefore be risky, because this percussive stress increases the chance of breakage, especially to the vessel sides. Nevertheless, vessels made of 'soft' stones (below Mohs 3) are almost always carved (with copper tools where available), because this method is quicker than drilling, less difficult to learn, and requires very similar tools and skills to those used for other soft media such as ivory, bone, or wood. The implications of these cross-media links are taken up in detail in Chapter 8. Harder stones cannot be worked with metal tools and progress is slow with flint chisels (ca. Mohs 7, e.g. Stocks 2001) and so the vessel interior is usually drilled and/or ground down by hand.

## Pounding and Sawing

Two techniques that are intricately associated with the earlier stages of stone vessel manufacture are pounding and sawing. Pounding refers to the blunt percussion of stones or quarry faces using a rounded stone hammer (a 'stonemason's maul'). These hammers were used

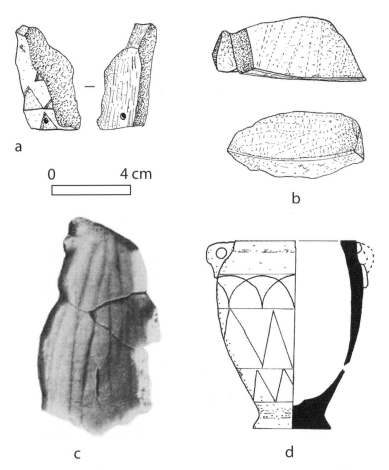

FIGURE 4.3. A selection of carved softstone vessels: (a) an EMIIA chloritite vessel from Knossos with punch or chisel marks on its interior (KSM Evans box 1893); (b) two LMII-IIIA gypsum fragments from Knossos with traces of chiselling and compass guidelines (KSM Evans boxes 551–2); (c) an MBII gypsum vessel from Jericho with chisel marks on its interior (after Ben-Dor 1945: pl. 23.8); (d) an LCypIII chloritite jar from Kourion (BM 1896.2-1.391). The last vessel is unusual because it has both punch or chisel marks on its inside and evidence for the initial use of a drill (a depression in the base). Compass-drawn decoration and guidelines are also visible.

mainly to quarry harder rocks while chisels were used for softer ones. Sawing was used to cut large blocks in the quarry and to produce squared-off vessel shapes. Bronze Age stone-working saws were toothless and made of copper, and larger examples of up to several metres long were most likely worked by gangs of two to three people. They were also probably all cast to a rigid thickness and employed a loose abrasive such as quartz sand or emery to do the actual cutting work (Stocks 2001). Notched saws were used only for working much softer media such as wood.

## Drilling

Drilling refers to rotary abrasion techniques that rely on the ability of a harder mineral to scratch and erode a softer one. Rotation provides the most efficient means of achieving this effect while, at the same time, maintaining downward pressure on the working surface. Drilling can involve a variety of scales of activity, from one person rotating a small awl by hand to a team of several people manipulating a large mechanical device (Bessac 1986: 231–52). Many different techniques are possible, but much of the variability can be expressed by considering three main areas: (1) cutting technologies (drill-bits and accompanying abrasive), (2) drill-driving methods (how the cutting tools are set in motion), and (3) drilling strategies (decisions made by the artisan about the sequence of manufacture).

## Cutting Technologies

Some forms of drill, including many modern ones, rely on the actual drill-bit to do the work of abrading the stone surface. This has led to consternation over how past societies managed to make effective inroads into very hard stones (e.g. Petrie 1917: 45, who initially presumed the use of diamond drills). In fact, the key process actually involves using a drill-bit alongside a loose abrasive powder. The abrasive embeds itself into the matrix of the drill-bit and does most of the actual cutting, while the drill-bit itself gets the material moving and gives shape to the resulting cavity. Indeed, even fairly soft materials such as reeds can be used in association with loose abrasive to cut extremely hard stones. In some cases, powdered emery (ca. Mohs 8) may have been employed as an abrasive and its residue has been identified on manufacturing debris from Crete (Warren 1969: 160).[1] However, quartz sand was probably more common, both because its grains are hard enough to cut most stones (Mohs 7 and below) and because it is naturally available in abrasive form from beaches and river beds. Abrasives can be used wet (with the addition of oil or water) or dry, depending on the type of drill and the object being made. Several experiments suggest that a wet slurry of fine abrasive is particularly effective for drilling beads, but dry quartz sand is more efficient for vessel manufacture and is easier to remove from the drilled cavity after manufacture (Stocks 1986a: 27; Gwinnett and Gorelick 1993). In fact, these two industries might well cooperate over their use of this resource, as the coarser dry abrasive used for vessels is eventually ground down into a slurry that is ideal for drilling beads or for polishing (Stocks 2003: 235–6).

There are two main types of drill-bit: solid and tubular. Solid drill-bits made of stone or metal can be used with or without loose abrasive. However, the bigger the drilling, the larger the contact area between drill-bit and stone and the more inefficient a solid drill-bit becomes. One solid drill-bit that was used without abrasive to hollow out Predynastic–Old Kingdom Egyptian vessels is the crescent-shaped flint gouge (Figure 4.4). Many of these gouges have been found at the gypsum quarries at Umm-es-Sawan (Caton-Thompson and Gardner 1934), probably indicating they were best for working softer stones. Drill-bits of this shape leave U-shaped interior cavities scored with coarse, irregular striations. Flint bits were probably retouched intermittently to maintain a sharp working edge.

Other solid drill-bits were used with loose abrasive and the Anatolian, Cretan, Egyptian, and Mesopotamian industries all preserve examples of shaped abrading stones ('grinders'), made of granite, basalt, or quartzite, that worked in very similar ways. The most common Egyptian version was made in a figure-of-eight shape [Figures 4.5(a) and (b)], which may first have been developed in Mesopotamia (see Chapter 8). The neck of the figure-of-eight was designed to be gripped by a forked stick which turned the drill-bit around the inside

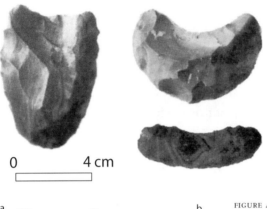

FIGURE 4.4. Three crescent-shaped flint drill-bits from the Umm-es-Sawan gypsum quarries in Egypt (Caton-Thompson and Gardner 1934: pl. lxviii.6,15, lxix.18).

0    4 cm

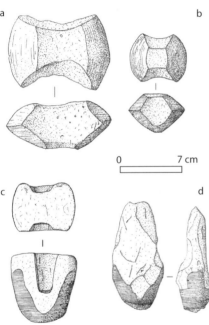

a

b

c

d

0    7 cm

FIGURE 4.5. Egyptian grinding stones (striations have been emphasised for clarity): (a) a large quartzite figure-of-eight shaped example, from an early OK workshop at Hierakonpolis (UCL 14887); (b) a smaller quartzite example, possibly from Memphis (UCL 38386); (c) a slotted quartzite grinder (UCL unnumbered); (d) an elongated basalt grinder (UCL unnumbered).

of the vessel [Figure 4.9(d)]. The coarse stones used as grinders provided an ideal matrix on which the loose quartz sand abrasive could purchase. A grinder often required an initial slot to be prepared for it in the vessel, but thereafter, it was ideal for undercutting the vessel shoulder. It could be placed diagonally into the prepared slot along with some loose abrasive and gradually twisted back and forth (not fully rotated) until it ground out a space for itself and returned to a horizontal position. The consecutive use of abraders in different sizes and shapes allowed the artisan to control the form of the resulting hole. The interior of vessels worked in this way reveal a series of wide concave grooves made by successive grinders, each finely striated by abrasive powder (Figure 4.6). In some cases, a small raised lump remains in the middle of the vessel base, because the grinder forces the abrasive round more quickly (and therefore abrades more effectively) near the edge and more slowly near the centre. Such central lumps have fine, concentric striations and can come to a sharp point in the middle

FIGURE 4.6. Two vessel interiors hollowed out using grinders and loose abrasive (striations have been emphasised for clarity): (a) a 12th Dynasty jar from Mazghuneh, Egypt (Manchester M. 5341); (b) an MM–LM bowl from Pseira, Crete (INSTAPEC PS 933).

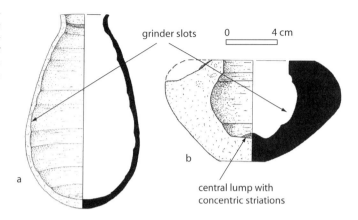

or be slightly rounded. They are often confused with the scars made by tubular drilling, but the latter leaves ring-shaped marks that are recognisably different (see below).

The second main type of drill-bit is a hollow tube. Hollow tubular bits are meant to be used with loose abrasive and can be made of organic material such as reeds but are often of copper, especially the larger diameter versions used for making vessels. There are no surviving archaeological examples of such tubes, but this in unsurprising given that they were worn down during use and no doubt reused and recast. However, the existence of copper versions is clinched by the bluish-green colour of abrasive mixed with oxidised copper fragments found in a number of drilled tubular slots (e.g. Reisner 1931: 180).

Copper is an excellent material for such a drill-bit because it can be rolled into an appropriate shape and is soft enough so that loose abrasive gets embedded into the copper matrix and thereby cuts more efficiently. Tubular drill-bits create cylindrical 'drill-cores' (Figure 4.7). The latter have straight sides or narrow slightly towards the top, depending on the technology used to drive the drill and the hardness of the stone being worked (see below). The sides of a drill-core are marked with fine, even striations made by the loose abrasive. As a general rule, the closer the relative hardness of the abrasive and the stone being drilled, the finer these striations will be. As drilling proceeds, the core is either deliberately or accidently broken off. The resulting cavity is also cylindrical or narrows slightly towards the base (the opposite of the core). Often all that is visible of such a procedure, once further shaping of the vessel has occurred, is a shallow 'drill-ring' in the base or sides. This production mark is very different to the central lump left by a grinder, because it has both a clear, even ring-shaped scar where the drill-tube was in contact with the stone and, within this ring, a fractured appearance where the stone has broken away [Figure 4.10(b)].

### Drill-Bit Driving Technologies

There are not only a variety of drill-bits, but also a variety of ways of driving them. The clearest picture of a Bronze Age drill comes from Egypt, but before looking more closely at this particular technology, it is first worth exploring five other potential drilling methods and the diagnostic physical traces, if any, that they might leave. One of the simplest types of drilling operation involves manually rotating a stick, needle, or awl. This could involve

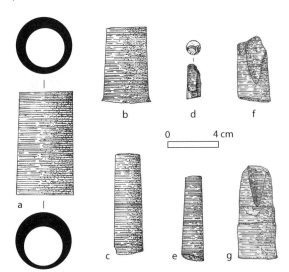

FIGURE 4.7. A selection of Egyptian and Cretan drill cores (striations have been emphasised for clarity): (a) basalt with concentric drillings from Egypt (UCL 44985); (b) black and white andesite porphyry from Egypt (UCL 44986); (c) basalt from Egypt (UCL 44988); (d) gabbro with multiple diagonal drillings from Knossos (KSM Evans 1893); (e) banded grey/white limestone from Knossos (KSM Evans 1894); (f) serpentinite with two diagonal drillings on top from Knossos (KSM MUM 72/394); (g) serpentinite with several 'stacked' drillings from Knossos and one diagonal drilling on top (KSM MUM 72/33).

either turning the drill using the wrist of one hand or spinning the drill between the palms and applying downward pressure with the chest or forehead. Wrist-rotation leaves an eccentrically shaped hole caused by the limited freedom of movement of the human wrist joint (Gwinnett and Gorelick 1983). Both processes enlarge the drill-hole more severely at the top than at the bottom, because the drill-bit is wedge shaped (e.g. a flint point) and also because it wobbles during drilling (like the final turns of a spinning top). Perforations made in this way are therefore drilled from both sides and result in characteristically hourglass-shaped holes. While vessels were often hollowed out by manually rotating a large grinding stone, making small drillings by hand was too slow for this purpose, and the latter is a strategy that was usually confined to perforating lugs or making holes to repair broken vessels.

A second drilling mechanism is the bow-driven drill (Figure 4.8). This comprises a drill-bit, a drill-shaft, a socketed capstone in which it rotates, and a bow which is usually twisted around the drill and pulled back and forth to turn it. Extra downward force can be applied by adding weights or by leaning on the end of the drill. Egyptian depictions show the bow-drill being used for perforating beads (often working up to five at once) and making furniture but never for hollowing out vessels. Experimental results also indicate that while bow-driven drilling is indeed a fast and efficient technique, its push-pull motion causes significant lateral stress and would not be a very reliable method of drilling vessels (Stocks 2003: 155). In theory, these stresses might be less important for very hard stones and might be alleviated by burying the vessel in the ground or by fixing the top end of the drill more firmly, but even so, the bow drill's advantage of increased drilling speed was offset by the increased risk of breakage that it posed.

A third possible drilling method is a horizontal lathe. Machine-driven lathes are in widespread use today and before this, bow-driven versions were employed in a variety of crafts throughout the Near East, probably beginning in the Graeco-Roman period (e.g. Magen 2002) and becoming particularly common in the Islamic world (e.g. Kohl 1977:

FIGURE 4.8. A bow-drill being used to make furniture, from the 18th Dynasty tomb of Rhekmire at Thebes (after Davies 1922: pl. liv).

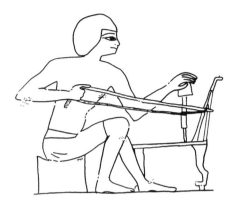

fig. 25). Such a method leaves few production marks to distinguish it from vertical-drilling techniques except perhaps where the worked object was glued or attached to the lathe (e.g. a rough lump or a small indentation on the exterior base). However, there is no real evidence that such a mechanism was used during the Bronze Age, either for stone or woodworking. Furthermore, unlike the other methods mentioned here, on a lathe, it is the vessel which is rotated not the cutting tool. Such a strategy works well for lighter materials such as wood or for small softstone vessels, but there are considerable practical problems in rotating a heavy stone vessel against a fixed point (Warren 1978: 567), and it is noticeable that even in the Islamic period, large vessels such as cooking pots were rarely lathe-made.

A fourth means of driving a drill is a bit-and-brace mechanism, such as the one used until recently to make vessels in Egypt (Hester and Heizer 1981). The design involves a fixed handle at the top of the drill against which the lower half of the drill was rotated by way of another handle, usually offset to one side. In the modern Egyptian case, the drill itself was valuable, as it consisted of a relatively complicated set of interacting components. The fifth possible type of mechanism is the pump drill (MacGuire 1894: 733; Bessac 1986: 232, figs. 53.4–5). This was operated by manipulating a cord attached to the handle of the drill, often alternately winding one end and unwinding the other. Neither of these last two mechanisms would necessarily leave any diagnostic production marks, but we have no iconographic evidence for their use in the Bronze Age.

In contrast, the clearest picture of a stone vessel drilling mechanism known from the eastern Mediterranean Bronze Age is the Egyptian weighted drill with offset handle (Figure 4.9). Such a drill is shown on many late Old Kingdom tomb reliefs and was used to signify 'artisan' in hieroglyphic (Gardiner 1988: 512).[2] The device was made up of several separate components: (1) a main upper section with an offset handle, (2) one or two weights fixed near the handle, and (3) a separate drill-shaft spliced onto the main section. The weights placed at the top of the drill added pressure against the drilling surface.[3] The number of weights shown on hieroglyphs and tomb reliefs changes over time, from two attached to the handle in the Old Kingdom to only one by the New Kingdom [Figures 4.9(a)–(d)]. Two weights would have moved about more than one fitted centrally to the shaft and this development probably reflects efforts to reduce the amount of lateral stress placed on the vessel (Goyon 1991; Stocks 2003: 147–8). The lower section of the drill was a spliced separate piece not only because it would suffer the most wear and tear during drilling but also because

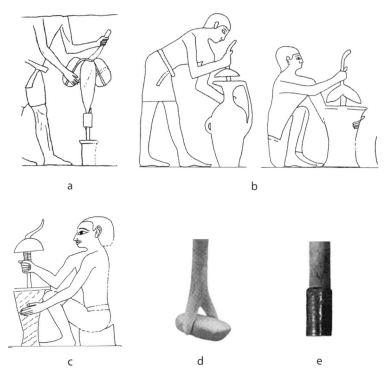

FIGURE 4.9. Depictions of Egyptian drills and two types of drill-bit: (a) 5th Dynasty (after Borchardt 1910: 37, fig. 33); (b) 12th Dynasty (after Blackman 1953: pl. xvii); (c) 18th Dynasty (after Davies 1922: pl. liv); (d) a figure-of-eight grinder held by a forked drill-shaft (after Stocks 1993: fig. 5); (e) a copper tube force-fitted onto a straight drill-shaft (after Stocks 1986b: 26).

it allowed the use of different drill-bits: a tubular copper bit could be force-fitted onto a straight drill-shaft or a grinder could be held in place by a forked drill-shaft [Figures 4.9(e) and (f)].[4]

The most critical feature of this drill is the fact that it is perhaps the only one of the six designs discussed above that could drive an abrading stone effectively. Rotating the drill probably involved a 'twist-reverse twist' action moving within a ca. 90° arc rather than in a series of complete revolutions (Stocks 2003: 148–55). This again reduced the degree of lateral stress and also made it possible to use a grinding stone for undercutting the shoulder of a vessel. The latter abrader could be placed diagonally into a prepared slot and then gradually twisted back and forth, until it returned to horizontal by grinding a larger opening that curved underneath the vessel shoulder. Bow-driven and other fully rotating drills might achieve undercutting by drilling cores at an angle into the sides of a vessel, but are unable to use a grinding stone to fulfil this task.

## Drilling Strategies

The last two sections should have made it obvious that different drills and drill-bits offer different advantages and disadvantages. For example, Stocks' experimental calculations (1993: table 1) suggest that a bow-driven drill was perhaps 5 times more efficient in removing a drill core than the Egyptian weighted drill and both types were up to 15 times slower in drilling granite than limestone. The volume of copper worn away from the drill tube was also much greater in drilling granite, suggesting that large, hardstone vessels could require a significant outlay in copper for drill-tubes. Bow-driven drilling also creates relatively severe lateral motion that would often have been unsuitable for vessel-making. So the choice of drill and drill-bits involved weighing up what kinds of lateral stress the stone could withstand, the shape of the intended product, the desired speed of production, what levels of accidental breakage were acceptable, and the abandon with which resources such as copper and loose abrasive could be used up.

However, the most complex decision-making relates to the sequence and character of the interior drilling, and ethnographic examples suggest that this process demands the attention of the most experienced artisan in a workshop, while other aspects of production can be left to apprentices (e.g. El-Khouli 1978: 790–2). For example, choices must be made about the number and shape of grinding stones to use and/or how to manage the removal of drill-cores. The artisan must choose how deep to continue the first preparatory slot, especially if he or she wants to insert an abrading stone to undercut the vessel shoulder.

Furthermore, if tubular drilling is the main technique being used, then the artisan must decide whether to make a single, large-diameter drilling or a series of smaller, adjacent ones. Either method will create drill-cores and depending on the stone involved and the size of the drilling, these cores can break off accidentally or they may need to be removed deliberately. There are three different methods by which the latter might be achieved. The first option is to use wedges or chisels to split off the core, but this would also risk fracturing the sides of the vessel (Stocks 2003: 134–5). A second option is to remove a primary core by one or more secondary drillings within it, arranged either concentrically or adjacent to each other in a honeycomb pattern [Figure 4.10(a)]. Removal of these secondary cores can then proceed more quickly because the sides of the vessel are protected by the walls of the primary core and the risks of vessel breakage are lower. A final alternative is to abandon drilling a primary core altogether and use a large number of small adjacent drillings [Figure 4.10(b)].

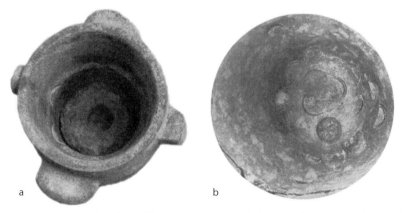

a                    b

FIGURE 4.10. Examples of two different core-removal techniques: (a) 'honeycombing' on the inside of an unfinished LMIA bucket jar from Akrotiri (Warren 1978: pl. 3) and (b) scars from adjacent and diagonal tubular drilling on the inside of an LHIIIB1 jar from Mycenae (Wace 1955: fig. 23b).

| Stage of Manufacture | Practical Options | Equipment | Archaeological Residues |
|---|---|---|---|
| **1** Collect the raw material | formal quarrying<br>surface collection of cobbles<br>traded raw stone | saw<br>adze<br>chisel<br>wooden wedges etc. | sawn blocks<br>boulder-sized pieces<br>large chips (at quarry)<br>firesetting residues |
| **2** Rough out the vessel shape | at quarry or in workshop<br>include attachments (e.g. handles, spouts) within blank or not | punch<br>chisel<br>adze<br>saw | tools (as left)<br>vessel 'blanks'<br>large chips<br>(some may have saw marks) |
| **3** Prepare the vessel before removing the interior | protect vessel against breakage and set in place (cloth wrapping, glue covering, burial in the ground, dedicated vessel fixture)<br>soak stone to improve workability<br>peck a rough depression to start drill<br>add working guidelines | cloth<br>glue<br>punch/chisel<br>vessel fixture<br>compass<br>ruler | tools (as left)<br>pits<br>some fine stone debris |
| **4** Remove the interior *(subtractive)* | carving<br>solid drilling<br>removal of drill core(s)<br>use of shaped abrading stones<br>use of emery with loose abrasive(?) | punch<br>chisel<br>hammer(stone)<br>drilling mechanism<br>tubular drill bits<br>shaped stone abraders<br>quartz sand/emery | tools (as left)<br>medium-sized stone chips<br>drill cores<br>fine abrasive slurry |
| **5** Refine the external form *(subtractive)* | further abrasion<br>incised decoration<br>shallow relief carving<br>finishing of handles, spouts etc.<br>inscription | chisel/punch<br>bow-drill<br>burin<br>compass | tools (as left)<br>fine stone chips<br>tiny bores cores |
| **6** Finish the surface | polishing<br>waxing<br>heat treatment for colour | oil<br>leather cloth<br>burnishing stone<br>fine abrasive slurry<br>oven | tools (as left) |
| **7** Assemble any vessel parts *(additive)* | gluing<br>pinning<br>inlay | hammer(stone)<br>glue | tools (as left)<br>nails/pins<br>inlay pieces<br>various attachments<br>(handles, spouts, etc..) |
| **8** Add the final decoration *(additive)* | gilding,<br>painting<br>accessories (ribbons etc.) | glue<br>gold-leaf hammer<br>gold-leaf<br>paints and brushes | tools (as left)<br>gold leaf<br>paints/pigments |

FIGURE 4.11. A template operational sequence for making stone vessels. The chart suggests a generalised order of manufacture, the practical options possible at each stage, the tools involved, and the material residues we might expect to find in the archaeological record.

## A Template Production Sequence

Figure 4.11 suggests a general sequence for making stone vessels. Cross-culturally it is clear that the manufacturing stages follow a fairly standard order but that within this general pattern the strategies adopted by specific industries reflect a combination of local technical know-how and conscious choices about where to invest more or less time and effort.

Moving through each of the eight outlined stages, we can propose what production values some of these strategies might imply. For example, in the first stage, random collection of stones for making vessels is apparently rare. Rather, the acquisition of raw material relied on quarrying, formal boulder collection sites, markets trading in raw stone, or gifts between powerful individuals. Depending on which of these methods of acquisition is used and how involved it is, the quest for raw materials can be relatively straightforward or laden with significance and a prime subject for propaganda. Circumscribed access to a particular stone, whether real or deliberately restricted, affects the value not only of finished products but also of the specialist artisans who had experience in working it, particularly for materials with idiosyncratic properties. For example, Egyptian anorthosite gneiss comes from a single source in the western desert that seems to have been accessed almost exclusively by royal expeditions (Shaw 1999). It is not only a very hard stone but also difficult to work because it is feldspar rich and susceptible to certain types of fracturing on impact (see above). Having an artisan familiar with the techniques to work such materials was necessary and probably prestigious in its own right.

Roughing out (stage 2) could be done at the quarry or in the workshop, and such a choice has obvious implications for the degree to which both the size and shape of finished products is standardised. Moreover, the moment of defining the shape of a vessel can be relatively mundane or highly valued, for instance, with claims that the shapes of the vessels have been decided upon by the ruler or a celebrity artisan.

Hollowing out a vessel (stages 3–4) can also be more or less complicated. Carving traditions tend to simplify this process and require a limited range of skills and tools. By contrast, drilling the interior of harder stone vessels involves a whole series of complicated procedures and choices, demanding the attention of the most experienced worker. Choices made while removing the interior have implications not just for speed of production and risk of breakage, but also for what could be done with the resulting debris. For example, drill-cores can and were made into smaller stone vessels, pestles, seal blanks, and jewelery. Stocks' experimental results suggest that the abrasive residue from drilling vessels could also be reused in bead drilling (as mentioned above) or as raw material for making faience (Stocks 2003: 235–7). Further experiments provide important insight into the labour-time necessary to shape and hollow out a stone vessel (stages 2–4; Stocks 2003: 155–66). For an 11-cm-tall limestone jar, it took 6.5 hours to prepare the external shape, 5 hours to drill an initial tubular core, and 11 hours to undercut using a grinding stone. Experienced workers no doubt achieved faster rates, but this is a useful indication that a medium-sized vessel in a ca. Mohs 3 stone (e.g. limestone, travertine, or serpentinite) might take two to three person-days to make, but not polish. A similar vessel in a harder stone such as granite might take four to five times longer.

The final stages of production (5–8) can also be more or less elaborate. Surface decorations or inscriptions are a classic example of added value elements that could be either completely avoided or invested in heavily. For softstone vessels, this is often the area where a carver might choose to display his or her skill and expend most effort, perhaps with intricate added decoration. Polishing is also extremely time-consuming but could often be delegated to far less experienced workshop personnel. Multiple assembly of vessel parts (separate handles, spouts, feet, lids) is sometimes an involved process requiring careful pinning and gluing but is usually done to save effort during the earlier stages of roughing out and drilling or to conserve stone. Final decoration such as gilding can also either be ignored or be charged with meaning; in Egypt, gold leaf was associated with the flesh of the god Re (Aufrère 1991: 725–8).

So different stages in the crafting sequence can be given more or less emphasis for a variety of reasons. The location of these activities can also vary, but the dotted horizontal lines in Figure 4.11 suggest three major thresholds. The first two stages of manufacture often occur at or near the stone source, not least because of the advantages gained by both detecting flaws in the stone early and reducing the amount that was subsequently transported away. The next three stages often occur in more formal workshop spaces. These workshops can be inside and might occasionally include elaborate installations for fixing vessels in place (e.g. Quibell and Green 1902: 17, pls. lxii, lxviii) or for larger drill rigs. However, vessel-making is also a craft that benefits from being done outside, in courtyards, or on rooftops, where there is good light and a breeze to help disperse the fine silicate dust that can cause lung damage (Curry et al. 1986). Outdoor production is suggested by the large amount of evidence for on-site vessel manufacture during the construction of Netjerikhet's pyramid complex and by the Middle Kingdom model of a private estate where vessel-makers are working in the courtyard (El-Khouli 1978: pl. 147). The numbers and integration of the people working in these places clearly varied, from an isolated individual or family concern to the hot-house environment of attached specialists working in multimedia elite workshops. Finally, the last three stages of production often occur in the same place as actual vessel-making but can also occasionally be spatially distinct activities. Vessels can, for example, be made in one place and then kept in store or sent to a clearing-house where they are assembled and given final decoration before use.

## Bronze Age Production Traditions

The evidence for production techniques in the Bronze Age eastern Mediterranean is unevenly preserved, with a notable bias towards the Egyptian material. Nevertheless, there are clear chronological and regional differences and the following sections address these variations in greater detail.

### Egypt

The rather simple shapes and lack of complex undercutting of the earliest Egyptian stone vessels suggest that they were crafted using a simple shaped grinding stone, operated by hand or with a very simple drilling device. By the later Predynastic, however, more complex shapes were being produced and crescent-shaped flint drill-bits (Figure 4.4) and various shaped grinding stones (Figure 4.5) begin to be found, almost certainly driven by the type of drills shown on later Old Kingdom tomb reliefs (Figure 4.9). Flint gouges produced rounded interior cavities and coarse, irregular striations, while shaped grinders produced more uniform curved slots, marked with finer striations. The exteriors of Predynastic vessels were smoothed off by hand (leaving diagonal abrasion facets: Petrie 1937: 2) and handles were perforated from both sides using a chipped flint drill-bit.

By the end of the Predynastic, there are significant changes and third millennium Egypt offers perhaps the clearest picture of stone vessel production in the entire Bronze Age eastern Mediterranean. We can draw on wide-ranging studies of quarrying tools and techniques, funerary depictions and archaeological traces of workshop activity, clear production marks on both finished and unfinished vessels, and modern experimental reconstructions. Much of this information was introduced earlier in the chapter and a shorter summary is offered here.

Unsurprisingly, this peak in our evidence correlates with a period of particularly intense Egyptian stone-working activity, with extremely high levels of stone vessel, sarcophagus, and statue manufacture, as well as massive pyramid-building operations (see Chapter 5).

Softer stones were quarried with flint or copper picks and chisels (Arnold 1991: 257–68; Aston et al. 2000). The copper versions were of round bar and flat mortise type and their edges would have needed periodic resharpening, just as the chipped stone versions required occasional reknapping. Harder stones were extracted by fire-setting along fracture planes in the existing rock outcrops (Heldal et al. 2003) but also using stone pounders, adzes, saws, and wedges. At a variety of quarries we find a toolkit of dolerite, basalt, or anorthosite pounders that seem to have been carried by the OK hardstone quarry workers (Bloxam 2003: 318–21). Early Dynastic and Old Kingdom vessels were hollowed out using a combination of flint gouges, shaped grinders, and/or tubular drill-bits, all three driven by the types of weighted drill shown on Old Kingdom tomb reliefs (Figure 4.9). Crescent-shaped flint gouges continue to be used to work softer stones, though the cut-off point at which these ceased to be an effective strategy for harder stones is unclear. Shaped grinders in quartzite, basalt, and granite also continue to be deployed, with quartz sand abrasive to grind out harder stones and undercut vessel shoulders. By Dynasty 1, tubular drilling becomes a prominent technique too. Copper tubes and quartz sand abrasive were used in tandem to work everything from small beads to large sarcophagi.[5] Rotary abrasion marks on both the insides and outsides of some Old Kingdom vessels also indicate that they were being rotated to speed up the smoothing and polishing process (e.g. UCL 16042, 42075). A horizontal lathe might conceivably have been used for this purpose, but there are no clear attachment marks on vessels bases to suggest this, and vertical rotation on a potter's wheel would have been more practical, especially for heavier vessels.

From the Middle Kingdom onwards our evidence of changing production techniques is hampered by a lack of tools, unfinished vessels, and obvious workshop contexts. Depictions of stone-drilling equipment on tomb walls are rarer, but there is no obvious change in the technical skill of vessel-makers. Copper tubes and grinding stones are both still in evidence, but we have far fewer preserved drill-cores, either because tubular drilling was now a less popular strategy or because drill-cores were more commonly reused to manufacture other objects.

## The Levant

The exact method used for making the pre-EBA and EBI stone vessels found in the Levant is unclear though the use of manual abrasion and, where necessary, a stone grinder and simple drill seems most likely. By the MBA, there are a range of Levantine industries that worked softstones into vessels using carving-based techniques. These include chlorite and soft limestone vessels from the EBII-III northern Levant (with an emphasis on inlay, in-the-round sculpted elements and incised decoration; e.g. Money-Coutts 1936), chlorite vessels at MB Ugarit (Caubet 1991: pl. viii. 3; Eliot 1991), and gypsum vessels from the MBII-Iron I southern Levant (Sparks 2007: 7.4.3). In the past, such Levantine carving industries have been contrasted with Egyptian drilling methods and identified as regionally distinct production traditions. However, their apparent differences merely reflect the commonly preferred ways of working travertine (abrasion and drilling) on the one hand and softer stones such as chloritite or gypsum (carving) on the other. In fact, it is possible that some of the Egyptian-style travertine vessels found in the Levant were made locally (see Chapters 6 and 7) and drills were certainly used in the southern Levant because we find traces of them on other objects (e.g. Ben-Dor 1945: 97 no. 4).

In the northern Levant, in a MBIIB-C workshop at Alalakh, we also find drills used to make obsidian vessels (Woolley 1955a: 109, 293, pl. lxxxiii.a–d). Here, unfinished vessels appear to have been worked with an innovative combination of both small, solid and larger, tubular drill-bits, while their exteriors are far more fully finished than might normally be expected before work on the interior was begun. Such unusual methods are typical of the virtuoso crafting skill necessary to work hard stones such as obsidian. In addition to these methods, two serpentinite vessels of apparent local manufacture were hollowed out using a shaped grinding stone (BM 1939.6-13.111, 1951.1-3.42) and, in combination, these diverse techniques are impressive given the limited overall number of stone vessels known from this site. Such upper elite crafting has parallels in neighbouring Anatolia and is probably a good reflection of a world in which skilled artisans, including stone masons, were highly prized and exchanged between royal courts (Zaccagnini 1983; Lackenbacher 1995).

## Cyprus

In LBA and EIA Cyprus, chloritite and gypsum vessels were produced by an unusual combination of carving and drilling. For example, one chloritite vessel reveals a mixed technique in which the interior was first drilled to make a preliminary cavity and then chiseled (Figure 4.3). The same vessel also displays very careful use of a compass both for outlining the shape and applying decoration. More unusual still, a series of three-lugged gypsum alabastra (Cyp2) were all undercut using a single abrading stone and loose abrasive that left clear striations on their interiors. This method of manufacture is interesting because gypsum is usually carved, and it suggests that making sure the interior of this shape was undercut properly (a task that a chisel could not achieve given the size of the vessel mouth) was important, unlike in the contemporary southern Levant, where similar shapes (e.g. L19–20) were increasingly simplified (with less undercutting) to make them easier to carve.

## Anatolia

Neolithic and EBA Anatolian stone vessels appear to have been fashioned by a combination of manual abrasion and in some instances, some form of device-aided drilling. By far the best perspective on these methods is offered by workshop debris found during surface survey of the size of Kulaksızlar in western Anatolia, where marble bowls, beakers, and figurines were made (Figure 4.12; Takaoğlu 2005). The striking thing about this site is the clear evidence for a relatively specialised production environment, on the margins of the fertile agricultural landscape and apparently producing for a geographically extended market. Marble cobbles appear to have been collected from nearby stream beds (though this is unlikely to have been a haphazard activity); vessels were roughed out on-site using pounders and picks, then drilled using a series of shaped sandstone drill-bits, and finally polished.[6] The Kulaksızlar debris offers us a vivid impression of village-based specialisation during the earlier fifth millennium

FIGURE 4.12. Unfinished vessel and stone grinder from Kulaksızlar, western Anatolia: (a) concentric striations on the inside of a marble bowl; (b) a sandstone abrader, with neck possibly shaped to fit a forked stick (Takaoğlu 2005: pls. 12.72, 23.148, 40.148).

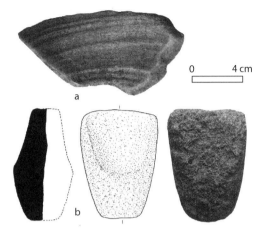

BC and provides a plausible model for the types of manufacturing know-how behind many other early industries in the eastern Mediterranean.

More complex techniques are visible by the MBA, including the use of both large and small tubular metal drill-bits. For example, one long obsidian rod from Kültepe is probably a drill-core and, if so, a real virtuoso effort of production involving very careful control of lateral drill movement to avoid the core breaking off at an earlier stage (Özgüç 1986: pl. 97). In addition, several chloritite or steatite vessels show the typical signs of being carved (e.g. Özgüç 1986: pl. 133.4). During the LBA, various tools, drill-cores, and drill-holes attest to the common use of tubular drill bits, but these seem to be primarily for architectural features and smaller items such as stone hammers and axes rather than for vessels (Seeher 2005).

## The Aegean

The earliest Aegean stone vessels were generally of marble or limestone and were probably produced using methods similar to those deployed in Neolithic to early EBA communities throughout Anatolia, Cyprus, and the Levant. Flint or obsidian chisels do not seem to have been used, as there are no surviving marks that conform to these techniques, but both blunt and pointed stone pounders were probably deployed to rough out vessel shapes, while knapped flint or obsidian drill-bits were used to perforate handles and to make repair holes. The latter perforations are hourglass in shape and may have been made either by manually rotating the micro-drill between the palm of the hands or by a bow-drill. The vessel exterior was probably further smoothed off by hand, perhaps using emery blocks which are available from several Aegean sources (Feenstra et al. 2002: 790–1, fig. 1). Coarse, concentric striations on the interior of a number of Aegean vessels (e.g. Mylonas 1959: no. 104, fig. 165) suggest that a shaped abrading stone was used to remove the vessel interior. This may have been rotated by hand or, more likely, given the evidence from Chalcolithic Kulaksızlar, by the use of a simple vertical drill. Cycladic vessels also occasionally preserve a central lump on the interior base that suggests the use of a grinding stone is far more likely than a tubular or solid drill-bit.[7]

Chloritite vessels begin to be made for the first time in early EB2 Crete and the Cyclades. These vessels are carved both on the exterior and the interior (Figure 4.3) and the increased availability of copper-based tools (e.g. saws, chisels, and punches; Renfrew 1972: 315, 326–32, fig. 17.2) may have contributed to this development. The irregularity of the circular shapes and spiral designs suggests that neither a potter's wheel nor a compass were being used.

Thereafter, in EMIIB Crete, a combination of the denser sets of striations now visible on vessel sides, raised lumps on the base of vessel interiors, and more uniform vessel cavities all suggest more complicated and standardised drilling mechanisms. Occasional drill-ring marks also make it clear that a tubular drill-bit was now being used (Warren 1969: 161, D199, D264, D279), though it is difficult to say when within the late Prepalatial period (EMIIB-MMIA) the latter becomes a dominant technique. Sometimes the outside of vessels show signs of diagonal abrasion, but wheel-assisted smoothing of the exterior is also increasingly visible by MMI, contemporary with early experimentation in wheel-formed pottery (Knappett 1999b).

The Protopalatial period saw a series of changes in priority for the Cretan stone vessel industry (see Chapter 6), that are also reflected in the technologies chosen. The chisel continued to be used for a few vessels when the stone was soft enough (Evely 1993: 177), but drilling predominated. The consistent use of one main stone (serpentinite) and of several common shapes appears to have fostered a more uniform approach to manufacturing processes, but a few workshops associated with the palaces experimented with new methods, including compound vessels and surface treatments such as gilding and inlay (Warren 1969: 48, P279).

By MMII, we have the first instances in the groundstone record of hard spherical cobbles with a tubular slot drilled out of their side (Détournay 1981: 68, fig. 87; Poursat 1996: 120, pls. 57c–d). These cobbles become common in the Neopalatial period, and when tested, their material usually proves to be amphibolite (Mohs 6, Carter 2006), indicating that the slot would have been both time- and copper-consuming to drill. Such objects have been plausibly identified as drill-guides that helped secure the position of a tubular drill-bit when it was being used to hollow out a vessel (Warren 1969: 159, fig. 5). Some of these MMII-LMI tools have faceted faces or impact scars from their use as abraders or pounders as well, suggesting they were deployed in a variety of ways during their use-life. It remains just possible that they were actually used as vessel grinders themselves, but none show the regular use-wear striations or the uniform grinding surfaces visible on Egyptian abraders, so this seems unlikely.

By the Neopalatial period, many secondary sites show unequivocal evidence of stone vessel manufacture, and amphibolite cobbles with drilled slots are relatively common finds at various levels of the settlement hierarchy.[8] In fact, a whole range of crafting methods were being used. Some vessels were carved, including a few in stones as hard as serpentinite (Warren 1969: 161, P628). Many were being drilled with tubular drill-bits and/or basic stone grinders. Others were being undercut using more carefully shaped grinding stones. Strangely, despite relatively careful attention to Cretan groundstone assemblages in recent years, we have only one definite tool in the latter category (Figure 4.13). It is made of the same material and preserves the same use-wear marks as many Egyptian grinders, with concentric striations on

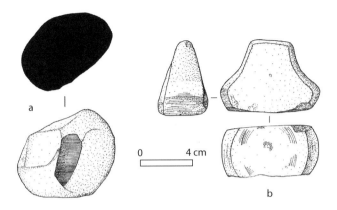

FIGURE 4.13. Two groundstone objects associated with Cretan stone vessel-making (striations have been emphasised for clarity): (a) an amphibolite cobble with drilled slot from Pseira (INSTAPEC PS168) and (b) a quartzite trapezoidal grinder from Knossos (KSM RR/72/306).

0    4 cm

its base and parallel grooves on its short ends. Its curved subrectangular shape in plan is also familiar, but it has a pyramidal projection on the top side where the Egyptian versions have a notched neck (akin to the much earlier Kulaksızlar examples). The latter is an alternative way of providing something on which the fork of a drill mechanism could purchase. In other respects the two types of grinder would seem to have operated almost identically. The Cretan example would have undercut a vessel shoulder by ca. 2 cm, constrained by the length that the grinder's shoulder projects beyond the area to which the fork was attached.

In contrast to grinder-based methods, there is a great deal of information about tubular drilling in the Neopalatial period. The large series of cores from Knossos display roughly the same proportions of different material types as the vessels themselves (Warren 1969: 159–60), suggesting that tubular drilling was not exclusively associated with any particular sort of material. The sheer quantity of these cores, when compared with other sites, is also testament to the special scale of operation at Knossos. The overall impression is of the frequent use of ca. 1.5- to 2-cm-diameter drill-tubes but without any obvious effort at standardisation (Figure 4.14). Larger drillings were probably more common than the surviving core sizes suggests but underrepresented due to their likely reuse for smaller vessels, pounders, pestles, and lentoid seals. One drilled cavity in an unfinished vessel from Akrotiri indicates a single drilling of ca. 30 cm in diameter (Warren 1978: 557–61).

There are at least three different techniques for removing a drill-core that were in use at this time (Figures 4.7 and 4.10). First, at least a quarter of the Knossian cores show signs of where diagonal secondary drillings have been made at ca. 20°–45° from vertical, with the purpose of undercutting the vessel shoulder. A second core removal procedure is visible on an unfinished bucket jar from LMIA Akrotiri where vertical secondary drillings were made in a honeycomb pattern within a larger primary core. A third technique, apparently not so common but visible at Knossos (Evely 1993: 192, pl. 47.2), indicates core removal by concentric drilling, in which repeatedly smaller and smaller vertical secondary cores are extracted from within the primary one. These were all attempts to remove the interior efficiently, but without placing too much stress on the sides of the vessel.

In Crete, emery was being used as a loose abrasive from LMIA if not earlier (Warren 1969: 160). The nearest source of this material is central Naxos (Feenstra and Wunder 2003: figs.

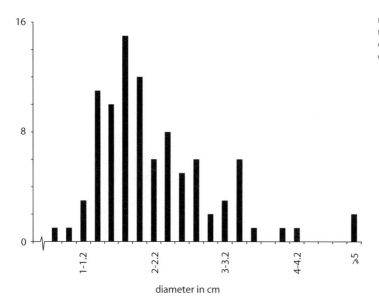

FIGURE 4.14. A frequency distribution showing the diameters of drill cores found at Knossos (n = 95, median = 2.0 cm).

2–3), and its use reflects a wider willingness, especially in the Neopalatial period, to expend time, effort and resources on producing elaborate products in unusual or technically difficult stones, such as obsidian and quartz crystal. Both of the latter materials were also used as tools in workshop contexts (obsidian flakes and quartz crystal burins, e.g. Floyd 1998: figs. 27, 33) to add fine details to seals and vessels in harder stones.

In LMII-IIIA, overall stone vessel numbers seem to decrease, but traditional production methods continue. In addition, a new class of gypsum vessels was made by carving. Worked fragments from a probable workshop at Knossos (Warren 1967; Evely 1980) suggest the high levels of accidental breakage expected from working a banded stone by indirect percussion [Figure 4.3(b)]. A compass was used to lay out guidelines and decorative schemes such as spirals and flutes.[9]

The stone vessels from LHIIIB1 Mycenae reveal a much more restricted production rationale (Tournavitou 1995). In particular, two techniques that were previously part of a wider range of Neopalatial production logics are now dominant. Firstly, the assembly of separate parts—handles, neck-pieces, spouts, and quartz crystal inlay—became the standard way to make complex vessel shapes. Even lids are made with a separate knob handle. Secondly, the interior of the vessel is now hollowed out exclusively by small, adjacent drillings, made both vertically and diagonally to undercut the vessel shoulder (Figure 4.10, this had been just one of several Neopalatial techniques). Little effort is now made to smooth away the resulting drill-rings on the interior suggesting, along with the multiple assembly of vessel parts, that rapid and efficient production was important.

## Conclusion

Many of the individual points raised here will be returned to in later chapters. When we try to understand the role of production as part of the process of creating and modifying object value, we must be very aware of production parameters: what aspects of the process are important, when, where, and why. We should expect considerable diversity, with artisans and specific technologies given a high profile in some instances and not in others. The parameters that govern stone-working and stone-drilling can be used to structure our attempts to understand this diversity, while regional evidence as to aspects of local technique, production contexts, and tool-kits can fill in specific details and point to why they are important. The next three chapters consider this regional and interregional history.

# 5
## The Third Millennium

⌐⌐⌐⌐⌐⌐⌐

*The following three chapters look more closely at the stone vessel traditions of the Bronze* Age eastern Mediterranean. Each one is organised by region proceeding from Egypt to the Aegean in a roughly anticlockwise direction. This chapter looks at stone vessels in the third millennium, the period during which many of the areas concerned begin to come into more intense contact with each other. The date ranges are chosen for convenience only and, though some sociopolitical patterns do correlate with these divisions, many stone vessel traditions discussed here begin earlier or persist until later on. As a result, some prefacing of the discussion with earlier developments or reiteration of details in later chapters is inevitable but has been limited to topics where arbitrary division might otherwise obscure the argument.

## Egypt

### The Pre-Third Millennium Background
An obvious place to begin a survey of this kind is with the earliest evidence for Egyptian stone vessels, the most prolific and long-lived industry in the eastern Mediterranean. The first Egyptian vessels attested in Lower Egypt are made of limestone, basalt, and metasiltstone and are found in the southern Delta in late fifth- to early fourth-millennium BC farming settlements such as el Omari and Merimda (Debono and Mortensen 1990: pl. 14.5, 29.3-6; Eiwanger 1988: pls. 57.1173-4). These are just one of a number of artefact types, including figurines, maceheads, and palettes that suggest limited craft specialisation and the emergence of a wider set of social roles. In contrast, stone vessels are not yet visible in contemporary Upper Egyptian contexts, the only exception being at Gebel Ramlah in the southwestern desert, where a cup made of the extremely hard stone anorthosite gneiss (see below for later use of this stone) was found buried in a Neolithic female grave (probably fifth millennium; Schild and Wendorf 2001: 17). The latter find is intriguing and probably reflects the relatively prosperous communities and favourable subsistence conditions present in the Nabta Playa area at this time, as well as the site's relative proximity to the anorthosite gneiss source area, some 50 km away.

Lower Egyptian stone vessel use becomes more prominent in the earlier fourth millennium, particularly at the site of Maadi (Mallory-Greenough 2002). These objects come primarily from the Maadi settlement deposits and local burials show only a very limited degree of mortuary elaboration. Most examples seem to be made of basalt from a nearby source at el-Haddadin (Mallory-Greenough et al. 1999) and the commonest shapes are baggy cylinders and lugged ovoid jars (Rizkana and Seeher 1988: fig. 12). Similar basalt vessels have been found at other northern sites and have contemporary parallels in pottery and ivory

(Brunton and Caton-Thompson 1928: 28; Reisner 1931: 131), indicating a shared Lower Egyptian material culture.

In Upper Egypt, a far more elaborate mortuary tradition had been developing (Midant-Reynes 2003: 87–95) and by the earlier fourth millennium, Nagada IB-IIC graves include both a few Lower Egyptian basalt vessels and similar shapes in Upper Egyptian materials such as red-and-white brecciated limestone (Plate 1). Esteem for the basalt imports was such that they were also copied in local black burnished pottery (Mallory-Greenough 2002: 90), but our appreciation of these early processes of imitation and elaboration in Upper Egypt is hampered by the poor provenance of most stylistically early examples. Only a very small percentage of Nagada IB-IIC graves were equipped with such items (e.g. Reisner 1931: 59–63, 130), but it is clear that during the broad Nagada II period, harder stones were increasingly sought from the eastern Desert and Red Sea district and a possible early workshop has been identified at Hierakonpolis (Hoffman 1982: 130). One of the most useful, published examples of the importance of stone vessels within burial performance by Nagada IIC is grave A118 from el-Amra (Randall-MacIver and Mace 1902: 17–18, pl. 5.2; Wengrow 2006: 116–8, fig. 5.8 top). Here, an individual[1] was buried in a flexed position, with a small, heart-shaped jar of limestone placed between the hands and held up to the face. Also placed around the head were two fish-shaped metasiltstone palettes, and behind the pelvis was a large D-ware pottery skeuomorph of a hardstone heart-shaped bowl. The close proximity of these vessels to the body itself probably emphasise their importance relative to the other pottery jars in the tomb that were placed on a ledge further away and may also reflect a close association between stone or stone imitations and the corpse's treatment and choreography during the mortuary ritual.

A significant change occurs in the material culture used by Lower Egyptian communities in the late fourth millennium (Nagada IIC-IIIA; Hendrickx 1996), when Upper Egyptian pottery appears in large quantities and traditional Lower Egyptian material declines rapidly (including basalt vessels). A similar pattern of expanding Upper Egyptian cultural influence can arguably be seen in the south as well, with the appearance of Nagada III stone vessels and what appears to be Upper Egyptian political imagery at the impressive cemetery L at Qustul (near Abu Simbel), alongside an interesting group of locally made stone vessels that may have been used as incense burners (Williams 1986: 108–47, figs. 49–53, pls. 26–38). In any case, during this crucial period of cultural and political convergence, new zoomorphic stone vessels and palettes (e.g. frogs, ducks), multiple-tube block vessels, and wavy-handled jars all appear. The more established Upper Egyptian stone shapes such as heart-shaped jars (E78-81, 108, also with shape parallels in D-ware pottery) are given more sharply defined rims and lugs reflecting the fact that these areas were now sometimes being covered in silver and gold (Payne 1993: nos. 1155, 1180; Wengrow 2006: 38). However, most developments are hard to distinguish chronologically from early 1st Dynasty ones and are therefore incorporated into the discussion below.

### Early Dynastic and Earlier Old Kingdom

Behind the widespread acceptance of Upper Egyptian objects undoubtedly lay new political power structures and altered rationales for elite competition. The use of palettes is perhaps the most evocative example: these appear as an item of Egyptian material culture in the

Neolithic, probably as part of body-marking practices, become extremely elaborate during late Nagada II–III and then disappear at the beginning of Dynasty 1. They are also one of a handful of small, portable, and traditionally functional Predynastic objects, including knife handles and maceheads that were invested with elaborate politically charged relief imagery (the most famous of which is the so-called Narmer palette). The particular ideological attention this implies probably reflects their assocations with deep tradition and deliberate attempts to reconcile newly entrenched political hierarchies with the social norms and customs of the past (Wengrow 2006: 176–87; see Chapter 8).

Perhaps the most obvious expression of the assertiveness with which the upper elite were now competing for power and prestige was an increasing emphasis on ostentation and accumulation in mortuary display. Stone vessels become dramatically more visible in Dynasty 0–1 graves (ca. 3300–2900 BC), as measured both by the growing proportion of burials that possess these items, their presence even at relatively provincial sites (e.g. Krzyzaniak 1989) and increased quantities and quality in the wealthiest tombs. Abydos tomb U-j is an early example of this funerary extravagance (Dreyer 1992) and, though heavily robbed, its 12 chambers still boasted a cedar box, cylinder seals, early hieroglyphic writing, pottery containers for oil, beer and resinated wine, ivory, and stone vessels, including examples made of obsidian (the nearest source for which was the region of modern-day Ethiopia; Merrick and Brown 1984; Zarins 1989). Hereafter, stone vessels become even more firmly established as a primary mechanism for such prestige display. Despite massive looting, the subsequent Dynasty 1 cemetery at Abydos produced a staggering 10,000–20,000 vessel fragments in hard stones and 50,000–100,000 in metasiltstone and travertine (Petrie 1900: 18; Amélineau 1905: 376–7 no. 1).

This Dynasty 0–1 period represents the peak in stone vessel production throughout Egyptian history, with the manufacture of large quantities in a wide range of shapes and materials (Figure 5.1).[2] It was also the crucial formative period in Egyptian pharaonic society, leaving an ideological legacy that underpinned Egyptian elite display through the Old Kingdom and beyond (Baines and Yoffee 1998). Stone vessels were a key durable artefact by which this ideology was constructed and expressed and it is therefore worth exploring in greater detail the materials, forms, manufacturing techniques, and consumption routines around which this prestige logic took shape.

Egypt is blessed with a vast quantity and variety of mineral resources (Plate 1). The earliest vessels were made of stones found close to the Nile or one of the major wadi systems draining into it (e.g. basalt, travertine, limestone). By Nagada II–III, harder metamorphic stones were being extracted from the eastern Desert. Such quarrying activities were probably by periodic expedition rather than continuous, and as a result, the use of specific hardstones varies considerably over the ED period: for example, black andesite porphyry with white phenocrysts is popular only in Dynasty 0-1 tombs and otherwise very rare [Plate 1(e); Aston 1994: 23]. Similarly, obsidian and quartz crystal are highly visible in certain Dynasty 0-1 royal tombs, but otherwise rare. Again, irregular acquisition may be the reason, as stocks of obsidian large enough for making vessels were probably obtained only by occasional trading or raiding expeditions to the south rather than in a steady flow.[3]

Large numbers of vessels in more colourful or intractable stones appear in royal and upper elite graves and in ones and twos from richer provincial burials. In comparison, travertine

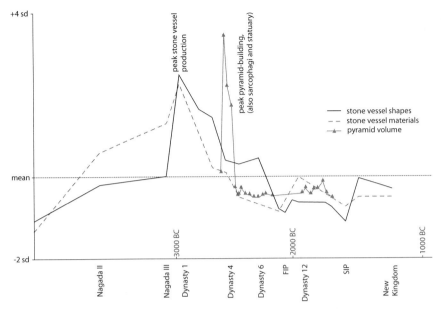

FIGURE 5.1. Chart showing varying investment in major stone-based status markers.

and metasiltstone vessels were softer, more common and less valuable. Travertine in particular becomes the dominant second-order stone and retains this role throughout most of pharaonic history for three main reasons. First, while its constituent mineral, calcite, is fairly soft, the overall rock is cohesive, which allows it to be drilled relatively easily and to take an attractive polish. Second, it can be found from as far north as modern Cairo to at least as far south as Luxor [Plate 1(a); Klemm and Klemm 1993: 199–223], but the outcrops are not particularly frequent. It therefore was a commonly recognised, but not commonplace, status marker throughout Egypt, with only small variation in the difficulty of acquiring the raw material. Third, it is a stone that lends itself well to perceived differences in quality, with a variety of colours, bandings, and textures [Plate 1(b) and (c)]. Some of these distinctions reflect practical differences in the effort necessary to acquire certain types, especially as finer varieties were often found either further from the Nile or deep below the rock exposure. The celebrated travertines from Hatnub are the best example of the upper end of this value qualification (Aston et al. 2000: 6). Travertine was used predominantly for tall cylindrical oil jars and open bowls which were also common in the pottery repertoire, while harder stones were usually made into more distinctive shapes.[4]

A range of new manufacturing techniques appear during this period that indicate both widespread experimentation with different vessel-making strategies and the hot-house crafting environment of royal workshops. Drill-made striations on vessel interiors now become significantly less coarse, suggesting that shaped grinding stones were being increasingly used rather than flint gouges as drill-bits (see Chapter 4). Quartz crystal and obsidian vessels imply improved technical ability, significant amounts of labour-time, and a desire to show off by using the hardest stones available. From the 1st Dynasty onwards, several bowl forms are

a    b    c

FIGURE 5.2. Three examples of new vessel-making techniques in the 1st to 2nd Dynasties: (a) a bowl with decorative drill impression in the interior base (Aston 1994: pl. 5c; Lowie Museum of Anthropology), (b) a metasiltstone vessel carved with reed decoration (Tiradritti 1998: 44), (c) a composite jar made with upper half of metasiltstone and lower half of travertine (Kroeper and Wildung 1985: pl. 276).

given a shallow cylindrical depression in the interior base using a large-diameter, tubular drill [Figure 5.2(a)]. Such a device was not really necessary for making simple shapes and the depression is as much a display feature as a practical one, to the extent that poorer versions imitate it with an incised circle instead. Rather, the depression highlighted the producer's ability to wield a weighted drill close to the base of the vessel and to expend copper on a larger diameter drill tube, but, perhaps more importantly, it also referenced the shape of contemporary copper vessels (e.g. Wengrow 2006: fig. 7.7 top), where such a basal feature is perhaps related to the way the bowl was originally hammered over a shaped block.

So a number of Dynasty 0–1 developments emphasise that quality and quantity logics were increasingly influential aspects of stone vessel value. At the upper end of the scale, access to hard stones from quarry expeditions in the eastern Desert supported the production of royal and elite workshops. At the lower end, travertine provided a common denominator which ambitious individuals could improve upon, by acquiring more exotic hard stone vessels, or aspire to, through lesser versions in limestone, gypsum, and skeuomorphic pottery. The acceptance of these objects as an agreed prestige index meant that there was a constant give and take between innovation and elaboration on the one hand and imitation, substitution, and mass production on the other. Two very different examples of these pressures, and how they were solved in satisfactory ways, can be seen in carved softstone vessels and composite vessels. The first are a relatively small group that were carved from metasiltstone into elaborated shapes such as footed goblets, ankh-signs, lotus leaves, reed boats, and baskets (E67, 92, 94–5). Gold leaf adhering to some examples suggests that they were originally gilded (Buckingham 1985: 9) and similarly, Figure 5.2(b) shows an example with the hieroglyph for gold (*nbw*) cut into one side (not visible in the figure). This practice of adding intensive relief-carved decoration and gilding to a few softstone vessels is also found much later in the stone vessel assemblages of Neopalatial Crete (see Chapter 6). In both cases, these objects may have been attempts to counterfeit solid gold vessels that either were cheaper to make this way or required a solid core to retain their shape.

A second group which sheds light on the priorities of lower elite consumers at this time are vessels made in a series of joining pieces (E86, 90). Constructing vessels in this manner was a way to (1) to use smaller lumps of stone, (2) reduce the risk of accidental breakage during manufacture, and, most importantly, (3) avoid the laborious process of undercutting the vessel shoulder. This short-cut technique becomes relatively common in the 1st Dynasty, just as both the overall numbers of vessels in tombs reaches its peak and when new virtuoso displays of hard stone drilling, shoulder-undercutting, and decorative carving also appear. Local versions of this composite tactic could vary: at Minshat Abu Omar, craftspeople chose to emphasise rather than hide it by creating vessels with one half each made of local travertine and metasiltstone [Figure 5.2(c); Kroeper 1985].

This last example hints at the role of stone vessels beyond the burials of the royal family and courtly elite. Unfortunately, contemporary settlement and temple contexts remain poorly investigated, but three particularly informative nonroyal cemeteries are Minshat Abu Omar and Kafr Hassan Dawood in the Delta (Kroeper and Wildung 1985; Hassan et al. 2003), and Abydos cemetery M in Upper Egypt (Petrie 1902). Cylindrical jars and shallow bowls are the dominant shapes at all three sites and travertine is by far the most common material. At the first two, these objects mark out a privileged subsection of 10–15% of the burying community (Kroeper 1985: 51). The third cemetery, Abydos M, is slightly different because it is only a small group of 12 tombs situated close to the royal funerary complexes. Unsurprisingly, given their location near the royal burial area, the tombs are more uniformly wealthy and all possess some stone vessels. However, in each of the three cemeteries, we can point to a handful of bigger, architecturally embellished tombs within the privileged group that monopolised a disproportionate number of stone vessels and other valuables. At Minshat Abu Omar, their occupants included adults and children of both sexes who were probably members of the most powerful families of the local community (Kroeper 1992).

After the explosion of diversity and innovation in Dynasty 0-1, we continue to see the production and consumption of large numbers of stone vessels in Dynasty 2, but there are also signs of the increased use of dummy model vessels (e.g. van Walsem 2003: fig. 4) and the reigns of Khasekhemui and his probable 3rd Dynasty successor, Netjerikhet (Djoser), mark consecutive stages of a critical transformation. In both cases, between the lines of two extremely impressive acts of royal stone vessel consumption, we can read a degree of uncertainty about the continued preeminence of these objects as prestige markers. Khasekhemui seems to have both paid deliberate attention to tradition in some areas, at the same time as being something of an innovator in others (Wengrow 2006: 248–51). Ideologically, he appears to have achieved a reconciliation of the Seth and Horus cults and built an impressive enclosure at Hierakonpolis (known as 'The Fort') and both a tomb and enclosure (the 'Shunet el-Zebib') at Abydos. The tomb was a monumental mudbrick construction in a traditional royal burial ground, but its stone-dressed interior also reflected the increasing role of the latter material in royal funerary architecture (Wengrow 2006: 250–1). Both the overall character of the stone vessel assemblage from this context and the large number of examples inscribed with his name make it clear that small but noticeable changes had been made to a wide range of stone vessel shapes (Petrie 1901b: 27; Amélineau 1902; Reisner 1931: types IIIc, IVe, Va, Xa3, Xd, XIa4, XIb2, XIc2, XIIb) and that a new range of materials was being exploited. The latter include the first carnelian vessels, a major use of recrystalised limestone and the first significant exploitation of anorthosite gneiss (Petrie 1901b: 27, pl. 9.2; Aston 1994: 39), all three of which were probably quarried near Gebel el-Asr in the western Desert (Plate 1).

Anorthosite gneiss in particular becomes the dominant higher-value material above travertine in royal and private tombs in the 3rd–6th Dynasties (Reisner 1931: 140, 180; Aston 1994:
63–4).[5] It was visually attractive and recognisable, hard and difficult to work, and from a single remote source that required logistically complex quarrying operations to exploit it (Shaw
1999). Indeed, the presence of preformed quarry blanks implies a degree of premeditation
about intended vessel shapes (Storemyr et al. 2002: pl. 3).

It is worth speculating about what prompted this change in shapes and materials during
Khasekhemui's reign. One possible factor is the increasing prominence of metal vessels and
improved metallurgical techniques. Beaten copper bowls are found in 1st Dynasty contexts
at Saqqara, Abydos, and in the richest provincial tombs (Ogden 2000: 157), but while metal
might rival the prestige value of stone as a material, these vessels were relatively simple
products and stone-workers could still produce much larger and more elaborate shapes.
In this respect, the rival prestige of the early metal vessels, mentioned briefly above, may
have been one of the factors promoting the increased technical virtuosity evident in the
manufacture of Dynasty 1 stone vessels, but such simple products could not yet wholly usurp
the position of stone vessels as a preeminent prestige marker. However, by Khasekhemui's
reign, we see a possible further development in metallurgical technology with the first
evidence for tin-bronze and lost wax casting methods (Petrie 1937: 25; Ogden 2000: 153,
158; Wilkinson 1999: 91–4). The potential to produce more elaborate metal vessels certainly
becomes obvious from the 4th Dynasty onwards when skeuomorphism of metal in pottery
and stone becomes common. As we shall see, other rival forms of stone-based, royal display
were also about to appear.

Netjerikhet returned to the Saqqara cemetery and seems to have taken the idea of a
monumental stone mortuary complex even further. The Step Pyramid was to provide a
chief prototype for the pyramid-building projects undertaken by the OK rulers and it
involved a colossal diversion of material, human resources, and stone-working expertise into
one dominant form of royal display. For example, inscriptions from the *phyle* work-gangs
that hitherto are found almost exclusively on stone vessels are hereafter mainly found at
quarries or on these stone monuments (Roth 1991). Both quarrying and other later stages
of stoneworking involved a highly skilled but relatively small group of people (perhaps
contrary to the popular expectation of large gangs; see Bloxam 2003) and the change in
these inscriptions is a key indication that the efforts of these individuals were being partially
redirected in the service of a new royal agenda. Even so, from only a cursory glance at the
truly staggering quantities of stone vessels buried in the complex it would not necessarily
be clear that there had been any corresponding reduction in the priority given to these
status objects (Figure 5.3). In two unrobbed subterranean galleries, for instance, there were
30,000–40,000 or ca. 90 tons of travertine vessels stacked floor-to-ceiling [Figures 5.3(b)
and (c); Firth and Quibell 1935: 107, 130; Lauer 1939]. Many other galleries appear to
have been similarly equipped but have since been plundered. The scale of human labour
implied by these quantities can be better understood, if we remember that a medium-sized
travertine vessel would probably have taken one to two days to make and polish and a
similar hardstone vessel perhaps a week (see Chapter 4). It is therefore unsurprising that
large numbers of vessels were being made on-site while the monument itself was under
construction: evidence includes unfinished vessels, over 300 flint drill-bits, many shaped

FIGURE 5.3. Stone vessels from the Step Pyramid: (a) porphyritic bowls from a pit south of the entrance colonnade (Firth and Quibell 1935: pl. 96), (b) stacked travertine vessels from Gallery VI (Lauer 1939: pl. v.1), and (c) a selection of more complete vessels from Gallery VII (Lauer 1939: pl. xiii.2).

grinders, a drill-core and more than 50 limestone blocks marked with test drillings (Firth and Quibell 1935: iv, 44, 71, 126, pls. 93–4; Lauer 1939: pl. xix.10).

The burial of these objects around and under the Step Pyramid reveals some interesting spatial patterns, despite significant looting. For example, over 400 thick-walled, heart-shaped bowls were found in a small pit near the entrance colonnade [Figure 5.3(b)] and there are signs of similar if less well-preserved caches elsewhere in the complex (Firth and Quibell 1935: iv, 44). These bowls made of porphyritic stones were very traditional forms, first popular as early as Nagada II (Aston 1994: shapes 1 and 2). While their continued importance is clear from their numbers here, the finishing of the Netjerikhet examples is extremely poor (unpolished, lopsided, handles unperforated), and the caches are isolated some way from the primary burial areas and other stone vessels. These features are hard to understand entirely but might suggest that this shape tradition was becoming increasingly detached from contemporary mortuary preparations, foreshadowing its disappearance soon after this reign.

In contrast, the majority of vessels from the Netjerikhet complex are bowls and oil or wine jars. Travertine is the most common material and seems to have served instead of pottery throughout the complex, but anorthosite gneiss and other hardstone bowls also occur in great quantities as higher value versions.[6] The latter are particularly frequent in the funerary chambers closer to the tomb of the king, whose owners probably used them to distinguish themselves from burials of less important family members (Firth and Quibell 1935: 132).

There is no doubt that Netjerikhet's vessels represent a colossal display of conspicuous consumption. However, a closer glance also reveals that the scale of contemporary royal *production* they imply is heavily exaggerated. For example, among over 1,000 inscribed vessels from the site, many earlier kings are mentioned, but Netjerikhet's name never appears. Some inscriptions also refer to gifts from important private individuals rather than to palace products (Firth and Quibell 1935: ii, v, 5, 18, 132). Furthermore, many of the materials and shapes have their best parallels in earlier 1st–2nd Dynasty tombs and several commentators have arrived at the conclusion that a large proportion of the assemblage was either drawn from stores made in earlier reigns or plundered from earlier tombs (e.g. Firth and Quibell 1935: ii, 41; Aston 1994: nos. 571–3). This type of curation and reuse is a common feature throughout Egyptian pharaonic history, but the scale at which it occurs here is impressive.

Overall therefore, the sheer quantity of vessels found in the Step Pyramid complex is misleading as an index of contemporary royal manufacture, because it is heavily supplemented by heirlooms, antiquities, private donations, and semifinished examples. Combined with the evidence of the *phyle* inscriptions, this suggests strongly that the traditional dominance of stone vessels as royal status markers was indeed faltering alongside the demands of pyramid-building. In a broader sense, OK pyramids become the new focus of mortuary ostentation and royal patronage after Netjerikhet, not least because such projects involved strong collusion between the pharaoh and powerful elite groups whose own burials gained prestige by being located next to the royal monument. In fact, this was just one of several ways in which OK rulers made use of their name, monuments, and physical presence as a form of patronage. For example, vessels inscribed with the royal name hereafter become a clear signature for royal workshops and a tool for royal propaganda (e.g. Arkell 1956; Reisner 1931: 174). A telling change is the switch in emphasis made on vessel inscriptions for the royal jubilee (see below): in the ED these are inscribed *by* private individuals *for* the king, but in the later OK are inscribed *by* him and sent out as gifts.

The funerary complexes of two of Netjerikhet's later successors, Menkaure and Sahure, confirm a major downturn in the quantity, quality, and diversity of stone vessels, with smaller overall numbers, poor vessel finishing and continued reuse of ED products (Borchardt 1910: 115–8; Reisner 1931: 178, 180). Specific combinations of shapes and materials are common, probably indicating that a few main shapes were being blanked out at the quarries.[7] Another significant 4th Dynasty pattern is the appearance of sarcophagi and statues in harder stones. Anorthosite gneiss was an established prestige material and continued to be used for a diverse array of objects, but its darkest, finest pieces (gabbro gneiss) were now reserved for royal statuary (e.g. Shaw et al. 2001: fig. 1). Moreover, Aswan granite and Fayum basalt are now more intensively exploited for fine building stone, statues, and sarcophagi but rarely for vessels. Again this implies the diversion of skilled labour from traditional vessel-making priorities: Khufu's huge granite sarcophagus, for example, would probably have taken a small group of full-time stoneworkers one or two years to make (Stocks 2003: 176).

The cache of funerary equipment associated with the burial of Hetepheres, probable wife of Snefru and mother of Khufu,[8] reveals how these changing prestige logics worked themselves out in stylistic details and specific vessel combinations. The majority of the stone vessels in this deposit are traditional bowls and oil jars, but most of these were left slightly rough. Almost the only ones that are finely polished are those skeuomorphing the thin walls, sharp carinations, or pedestal feet and spouts of metal vessels (Reisner and Smith 1955: Figs. 142–4). The latter had become highly influential prestige items by this time (Scheel 1989: figs. 34, 36, 43; Ogden 2000: 157) and in this more metal-driven environment, we see stone vessels either referencing this other material or given carefully articulated new niches.

A chief way in which the latter niches developed was through the creation of formal stone vessel sets with prominent roles in Egyptian ritual. Hetepheres' funerary deposit offers an excellent early example in a group of small stone oil containers that were kept together as a prescribed set of sacred oils [Figure 5.4(a)]. Seven of the jars were labeled with oil names and an eighth jar held green eye paint. Images of the 'seven sacred oils' appear on many tomb reliefs at this time (Pischikova 1994: 65) and indicate that a number of local and foreign products were now grouped together into one rejuvenative recipe. Specialty oils of this kind demanded extremely elaborate production and consumption routines (Shimy 1997): they comprised a complicated mixture of ingredients whose proper preparation took many days and was only really known to a few expert perfumers among the priestly class. The order of use for each oil became well-prescribed and was associated with cleanliness, renewal of the physical body, union with the gods Ra, Horus, and Osiris,

a                                        c                                        b

FIGURE 5.4. Stone vessels from three related OK rituals: (a) a sacred oil set from the funerary deposit of Hetepheres (the box is reconstructed, Reisner and Smith 1955: fig. 34a), (b) a set of black and white model vessels and tools for the opening-of-the-mouth ceremony (Naville 1914: fig. iv6), and (c) a monkey-shaped travertine vessel, inscribed for Pepi I on the 'first occasion of the jubilee [*heb sed*]' and referring to a female tenant landholder of '[the pyramid endowment] *Mn-nfr-Mryr*' (courtesy of the Metropolitan Museum of Art, 1992.338).

and the step-by-step process of passing through each of the seven gates of the underworld (Gee 1998: table 7.5).

## Later Old Kingdom and the First Intermediate Period

These changes during the 4th Dynasty are consolidated and extended in the 5th and 6th Dynasties and establish many of the ways Egyptian stone vessels would be valued and used throughout the rest of pharaonic history. One intriguing hint at how decisive this shift may have been is the series of foundation deposits, including stone vessels, which may have been part of a deliberate dumping and decommissioning of ED elite culture under later OK temples (Wengrow 2006: 182–4). The discussion below begins by exploring the continued prominence of stone vessel sets, before looking at the use of other types of stone vessel at various levels of the late OK social hierarchy. Sacred oils sets such as the one found in the Hetepheres deposit become more common in the succeeding two dynasties and are represented in less wealthy tombs by limestone palettes with seven small depressions (Roth 1992: fig. 3). Two further groups of stone vessels, opening-of-the-mouth sets and the *sed* festival oil jars, are deployed within a similar ritual context and are worth considering in greater detail.

The opening-of-the-mouth ceremony directly preceded the use of the seven sacred oils in late OK mortuary liturgy (Roth 1993). Both of these rituals represented traditional recipes for negotiating the process of rebirth into the afterlife, and they both started to use more formal vessel packages at this time. Opening-of-the-mouth sets comprised miniature white and black flasks and bowls (E137, 138) which were stored with *psš-kf* knives and other prescribed equipment in custom-made limestone palettes [Figure 5.4(c)]. Proper performance of the ritual using this equipment enabled the deceased to take food in the afterlife and was a reenactment of cutting a newborn's umbilical cord and clearing away mucus from its mouth. The Pyramid Texts preserve a rare glimpse of the rich cosmological associations of the opening-of-the-mouth-vessels (Mercer 1952: utterances 47–55). These objects occupied a specific scene in the ceremony, after the deceased had been symbolically weaned and teethed. The corpse (or a mortuary statue representing the dead indiviudal) was given a token amount of wine, first from the white stone flask which symbolised the right eye of Horus and the sun and then from the black flask (the left eye of Horus and the moon). More solid food (beer) followed from the black and white bowls. Such binary oppositions are an extremely common way in which elite groups in early complex societies construct their view of the world and these black and white stones map out a preferred Egyptian cosmology. The most impressive opening-of-the-mouth sets used quartz crystal and obsidian vessels to create such contrasts and the Egyptian names for these two stones (*mnw hd* and *mnw km*, respectively, or *ka hd* and *ka km*, Aston 1994: 24) indicate that they were essentially seen as light and dark hues of the same rock.

Sacred oils and opening of the mouth sets were both mainly used in mortuary performance but also appear to have been deployed in the symbolic rebirth of the king on the occasion of his jubilee or *heb sed*. In theory, the *sed* festival was held every 30 years to test the pharaoh's continued ability to rule. In practice, it became a highly choreographed rejuvenation of royal power whose timing appears to have reflected the demands of royal propaganda. The stone vessels inscribed with references to the *heb sed* fall into two chronological groups: (1)

a smaller, ED group from royal tombs at Saqqara and Abydos consisting of vessels produced by important individuals for the king and (2) a larger, more standardised late OK group inscribed by the pharaoh and occasionally dedicated to private individuals (Murnane 1981; Minault-Gout 1993: 307–8). More specifically, these later examples were products of royal workshops that were sent out to individuals or temples in logistically or commercially important locations as markers of central authority. Most of the inscriptions are from the reigns of the two Pepis suggesting that this sort of overt statement was an unevenly exploited political strategy, but one that might well become important at a time when provincial elite groups were becoming increasingly powerful.

The later *heb sed* inscriptions occur most frequently on cylindrical jars (E-34-5), but one on a monkey-shaped example was given to a woman endowed with land from the royal pyramid estate of Pepi I and offers a rare glimpse of the types of asymmetric gift relationship that might have been involved [Figure 5.4(b), Fischer 1993]. Indeed, though many *heb sed* vessels lack a secure provenance, the rest have a very wide distribution: Pepi I's vessels, for example, encompass not only the royal cemeteries at Saqqara but also the private tombs of governors at Balat, a temple context at Elephantine and both temple and residential contexts at Byblos in the Levant (e.g. Jéquier 1934: 306, figs. 1–2, 15; Dreyer 1986: 152, no. 455, pl. 58). These outlying sites were all important trading nodes: Elephantine as a major point on the riverine route south to Nubia, Balat at one of the principal oases along the Western Desert caravan route (Pantalacci 1997), and Byblos as the chief destination for emerging maritime trade with the Levant (see below). In other words, Pepi seems to have used the occasion of his jubilee to cement a series of long-distance trading contacts by making gifts to loyal officials, temples, and perhaps even to foreign rulers.[9] In effect, this parallels the spatial choreography of the *heb sed* ritual itself, which involved a symbolic mapping of the ruler's control over the known world.

Ritual sets and jubilee vessels were a feature only of the upper levels of Egyptian society, but it is worth considering the wider ways in which stone vessel value was changing during the late OK. At the top of the social hierarchy, royal burials continue to be provided with a range of stone vessels. For example, the tombs of Pepi II and queen Neit include many large jars, carinated bowls, and lamps of travertine and anorthosite gneiss (Jéquier 1934, 1935). The window on stone vessel use among the late OK royal family that these two assemblages provide is particularly relevant, as we shall see in discussion of similar vessels at contemporary Byblos, Ebla, and perhaps even as far away as Crete. Outside of the royal family, the overall numbers of vessels buried in elite tombs were declining (Bernard 1966–1967). Even the most powerful individuals were no longer willing to overinvest in this type of prestige display and substituted large numbers of real stone vessels for notional funerary equipment. This fits into a broader pattern in which the traditional material culture and writing styles of mortuary display were becoming increasingly economical and/or formulaic (e.g. Baer 1960; Lichtheim 1975: 1-2; Bárta 1995). Opening-of-the-mouth and sacred oil sets represent two examples of this trend, but others are also visible. For example, the vizier Mereruka constructed the largest known private OK tomb at Saqqara but included only a few larger stone vessels with him (Firth and Gunn 1926: 26, fig. 20-1), opting instead to be accompanied by a considerable number of miniature, model vessels. This contrasts with the ED period when the use of models is found only in much less important burials, and now it becomes just one of several forms of funerary substitution used by all levels of the elite. In many cases, the walls of late OK-FIP tombs go one step further and simply refer to notional dedications of 'many thousands of vessels', illustrate colourful travertine and hardstone examples, or depict vessel workshop scenes. Despite severe looting, it is clear that these claims were never backed up with commensurate levels of real grave goods.

These developments are visible in the Memphite courtly cemeteries but are even more pronounced in provincial tombs. The occasional wealthy burial includes full-sized vessels reflecting the power of a very few provincial bureaucrats (Garstang 1903: 30, pl. xxxvi; Bernard 1966–1967: 121–2, fig. 26; Baer 1960), but most local elites did not have these aspirations. For example, at Balat, the mastabas of the high-ranking govenors of the Dakhla oasis contain some very fine travertine containers, along with a few bowls and hardstone heirlooms, but only perhaps 10–20% of the burials placed around these monuments are equipped with such items (Minault-Gout 1986; Valloggia 1986, 1998; Castel and Pantalacci 2005). The wealth visible in late OK provincial cemeteries varies considerably, but the burials at Qau and Badari offer a similar picture of these lower and subelite groups (Figure 5.5). The vast majority of vessels were small travertine pots (E123-6, 130-131, 139-141), found with other cosmetic equipment such as grinders, lumps of galena and ochre, shells, pots of grease, and mirrors. Again, these came from ca. 15% of the excavated late OK-earlier FIP graves and are found with both sexes, but if early osteoarchaeological identifications can be believed, more commonly with women (e.g. Brunton 1927: 54–5). Furthermore, taking a revised tomb chronology based on assemblage seriation (Seidlmayer 1990: 124–210), the prevalence of stone vessels in tombs peaks in the mid-6th Dynasty and then declines dramatically and FIP to early MK tombs are generally poorer in the number of stone vessels they contain [Figures 5.5(c) and (d)], possibly reflecting the impact of a period in which Egypt is thought to have suffered from famine, political disunity, and low Nile floods (Hassan 1997).[10]

This section on third-millennium Egyptian stone vessels has necessarily covered a lot of ground, and it is now worth summarising the main points. The first major industry appears in Lower Egypt in the fourth millennium and these objects are thereafter taken up as prestige goods in Upper Egypt and made in a greater variety of shapes and materials. Well before the beginning of the Dynastic period, Upper Egyptian-style material culture had become dominant throughout Egypt and stone vessels are found in huge quantities in Dynasties 0–1 royal graves and are a ubiquitous feature in elite burial assemblages. Travertine becomes by far the most popular material, but a wide range of harder stones are exploited and, along with more complex vessel shapes and finer finishing, these highlight growing technical skill. However, in the early years of the Old Kingdom, this spiralling investment in stone vessel display falters and then collapses. The first indication is probably a slow decrease in shape and material diversity during the 2nd–3rd Dynasties and a decline in their presence in lower elite tombs. The Netjerikhet complex represents our last visible consumption of quantities of vessels on the scale of the ED and the 4th Dynasty signals the emergence of pyramid cemeteries, statuary, and sarcophagi as alternative stone-based status markers. Metal vessels are probably implicated as well, both promoting virtuoso display in the rival medium of stone during the ED and hastening its decline thereafter. By the 5th–6th Dynasties the role of stone vessels is very different: ritual sets, models, and notional dedications replace real vessels in many elite graves and there is a stronger emphasis on small cosmetic containers.

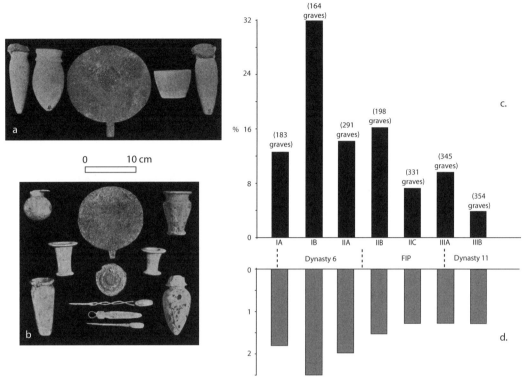

FIGURE 5.5. The late OK-FIP cemeteries at Qau and Badari: (a) Stone vessels and some of the other contents from tomb 462. Note the mud seals for the pots. (b) Stone vessels and some of the other wealthy contents from tomb 5009. The anorthosite gneiss pot is likely to be reused or an heirloom. (c) The percentage of graves with stone vessels for each of Seidlmayer's *stufen* (the stated grave totals include both those with and without stone vessels). (d) The average number of vessels per grave for those with such items (Seidlmayer 1990: figs. 47–8; Brunton 1927: 54–55, pl. xlix).

Overall, this suggests the final stages of a profound transformation in the way stone vessels were being valued, dividing the logics visible in the period of Egyptian state formation and pyramid-building from the different ones that exist throughout the rest of the Bronze Age.

## The Levant

### The Pre-Third Millennium Background

Groundstone vessels have a long history in the Levant, with the use of mortars and bowls (including some highly decorated examples) for crushing wild seeds in semisedentary Natufian settlements, and more obvious still as local communities began to take up cereal agriculture (Wright 1993, 2000). By the Chalcolithic period, large basalt (and occasionally a similar looking stone known as phosphorite) vessels are found in both tombs and settlements in the southern Levant and are one of the few object types that persist in the altered socioeconomic circumstances of EBI (Amiran and Porat 1984; Braun 1990; Rowan 1998; Philip and Williams-Thorpe 2000). The simplest EBI form is a flaring bowl, but more complex vessels add handles or elaborate fenestrated stands (L1-4), all of which have parallels in contemporary pottery. The earlier and thinner-walled Chalcolithic basalt vessel types may well be related to extremely rare hammered sheet metal versions (Philip and Rehren 1996), but such links seem less likely for the thicker EBI forms.

Perhaps the best window on the use of these vessels comes from EBIA communal shaft tombs at Bab edh-Dhra (Schaub 2006) which have been plausibly identified as belonging to family burying groups from semipastoralist communities living on the Kerak plateau. Some 50 basalt bowls were found within ca. 106 chambers in cemetery A, compared to nearly five times as much pottery (which included imitations of basalt types). No chamber had more than one or two basalt vessels, suggesting that while these may have been prestige items, their mortuary use was not marking out a very steep social hierarchy. Basalt is plentiful in the southern Levant but both stylistic and petrographic analysis reveal a relatively complex pattern of specialised manufacture and distribution (at Bab edh-Dhra and perhaps Beth Shan: Braun 2004: 57–8), rather than a simple picture of local procurement, suggesting that these items were important in forging or maintaining social networks over some distance (Philip and Williams-Thorpe 2000). More broadly, these fourth-millennium objects were part of a wider basalt vessel-making zone extending throughout the southern Levant and Lower Egypt. The cross-cultural parallels for this type of industry are addressed in Chapter 8, but the huge size, limited number of shapes, simple decoration and concentration on one stone-type suggest that these artefacts were balancing their emphasis on prestige display with a degree of social restraint.

## Egyptian Vessels

Earlier Predynastic contacts between Egypt and the southern Levant were probably driven by the copper trade (Bard 1994: 278–9) but encouraged the exchange of a variety of other objects as well. Several flaring basalt bowls found at Maadi are likely imports from the southern Levant (Rizkana and Seeher 1988: type 5D) and, in return, there is one problematic Egyptian jar fragment from the site of Ein Gedi, an apparent shrine on the margins of more settled areas (Ussishkin 1980: fig. 12).[11] By the late Nagada–early 1st Dynasty, much stronger links are visible and well-connected Levantine sites obtain an array of Egyptian material, including stone vessels. These sites suggest not only local acquisition and emulation strategies but also the possible presence of resident Egyptians (van den Brink and Braun 2003). Thereafter during EBII-III, overall evidence for such interaction declines but Egyptian stone vessels continue to be found at southern Levantine sites such as Tel Yarmuth (primarily bowls; Sowada 2002). However, by far our most informative window is a cache of nine travertine vessels found in a shrine at Ai (Amiran 1970). The assemblage probably evokes the logistics and the socioeconomic impact of overland Sinai trade, including a two-piece travertine jar (with a carved feature on the side that probably copies Levantine transport jars), an imitation waterskin, an oil container, and a series of bowls that could be stacked together for easy overland transport. At both Yarmuth and Ai, vessel styles often have their best parallels with Dynasty 1–3 assemblages, raising the possibility that some originally arrived in EBII and were curated locally (Sowada, personal communication).

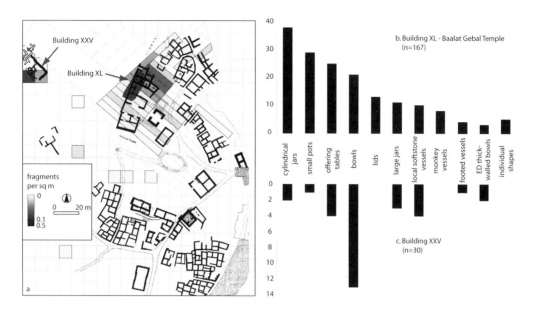

FIGURE 5.6. Stone vessels from late–third-millennium Byblos (for further details see Appendix 2): (a) approximate densities of OK-style stone vessels. This figure includes Montet's irregular *Temple Syrien* sounding, Dunand's elongated trenches and later excavation grid. The structures shown here are those attributed to Saghieh's phase KIV (after Montet 1928: pl. xxii; Dunand 1939: pls. ccvi–ix; Saghieh 1983: plan 1). (b) Vessel shapes from Building XL; (c) vessel shapes from Building XXV.

At some point after the 1st Dynasty, however, and certainly by the Old Kingdom, there is a clear shift in Egyptian interest northwards in favour of Byblos and away from the southern Levant. Thereafter, Byblos becomes utterly preeminent in the range and quantity of its Egyptian imports, with stone vessels comprising much of the surviving material. OK stone vessels are concentrated in two main areas at Byblos (Figure 5.6): Building XL (Montet 1928; Dunand 1939: 288–308; Saghieh 1983: 40–5, fig. 13) and Building XXV (Dunand 1958: 899–900; Saghieh 1983: 36–7, fig. 12a). There are examples of earlier shapes, but both deposits were probably closed in the late OK on the basis of style, material, and inscriptions. Building XL was almost certainly the main temple of Baalat Gebal, who was linked with the Egyptian divinity Hathor (Espinel 2002). The large number of oil jars, offering tables and cosmetic pots from this context were probably part of the temple's ritual equipment [Figure 5.6(b)]. These appear to be products of both a few high-level exchanges and some more humble and idiosyncratic dedications. In the former category are the inscribed cylindrical jars and offering tables with *sed* festival inscriptions. In the latter, however, are the large numbers of collared cosmetic pots that, in Egypt, are overwhelmingly associated with the personal property of provincial elites. They may have been placed in the temple by lesser Egyptian personnel passing through Byblos or by locals who acquired Egyptian imports through subroyal trade.

The second, much smaller, concentration of OK stone vessels was found in Building XXV on the burnt floor of a large hall constructed in orthostatic masonry (Dunand 1958: 899; Saghieh 1983: 37). This was probably a palace or upper elite residence and there is a far greater proportion of bowls and tables than at the Baalat Gebal temple [Figure 5.6(c)]. This emphasis finds parallels at Ebla, the only other northern Levantine site to reveal Egyptian stone vessels at this time. Over 200 OK vessel fragments were concentrated in one part of Palace G at Ebla (Scandone-Matthiae 1981, 1988)[12] and most of the identifiable fragments are bowls and lamps, suggesting that these items were for domestic display rather than for personal grooming or use in a specific ritual.

In fact, both the Ebla Palace G and Byblos Building XXV assemblages look distinctly like the results of specific exchanges (e.g. greeting or wedding gifts) between Egyptian and northern Levantine royal households. The bowls and lamps, along with the high proportion of anorthosite gneiss vessels,[13] match well the tableware we see amongst the funerary equipment of the OK Egyptian royal family (e.g. Jéquier 1934; Firth and Quibell 1935: 132). Royal diplomacy in the form of deliberate temple dedications, greeting gifts or marriage transfers are familiar ways in which the Egyptian state forged close economic and political ties in later periods, and it is not hard to see why these two sites were now singled out for particular attention. Ebla held a favoured position along the contemporary caravan route bringing lapis lazuli from further east (also perhaps silver, obsidian, and textiles), while Byblos was the maritime port through which the same materials might be shipped to Egypt, along with local coniferous woods and oils.

## Non-Egyptian Vessels

The spectacle of foreign contacts offered by the Egyptian stone vessels at Byblos and Ebla has tended to obscure the fact that a few other vessels from these deposits were possibly produced in one or more contemporary northern Levantine softstone traditions (L5, 6, 7). One typological group, with some intriguing long-distance connections, is suggested by a series of chloritite or steatite bowls found at Byblos and Hama [Figures 5.7(a)–(f)]. Most of the fragments are carved with concentric rows of herringbone pattern applied to the tops and sides of the rim and the same motif appears on a lid fitted with a separate bovine-shaped handle.[14] These decoration-intensive designs and carved forms had a common prototype in basketry and woodcarving traditions where such techniques are usually at home, but, given their deep shape, undecorated lower halves, heat-resistant material, and fitted covers, suggest they may also have been cooking vessels. The striking thing about these vessels is that they have relatively close and contemporary parallels at sites in lowland Mesopotamia, as well as on the Omani peninsula, in south-central Iran and as far east as Bactria-Margiana (Potts 2003). The issue of where these vessels were actually made is further complicated by the fact that suitable ophiolitic deposits of chloritite/steatite exist in all of these regions (except for Mesopotamia). The latter three areas were indeed producing a large number of contemporary chloritite vessels, but this type is only a minority component (see Chapter 8). Hence, these objects remain difficult to place: they may well be exotic imports at the northern Levantine sites, reflecting, for example, important flows of metal from further east via Mesopotamia, but the lack of other eastern chloritite products (e.g. Figurative-style) from west of Mari and Tell Brak (David 2007), leaves open the possibility that they are actually a local tradition more loosely inspired by long distance links and Mesopotamian consumption patterns.

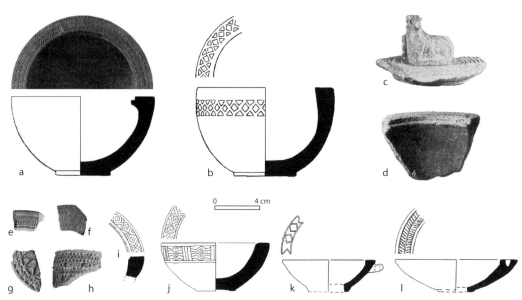

FIGURE 5.7. EBA softstone vessels from the northern Levant: (a)–(g) chloritite (or steatite) from Byblos (after Montet 1928: fig. 30, pl. xlvi; Dunand 1939: fig. 270, pls. cxlv–cxlvi; Money-Coutts 1936); (h) chloritite (or steatite) from Hama (after Ingholt 1992: pl. xv.4); (i) soft white stone from Byblos (after Dunand 1939: fig. 229); (j) soft white stone from Hama (after Pinnock 1981: fig. B3); (k) and (l) soft white stone from Ebla (after Pinnock 1981: figs. A1, B4).

A second related style is suggested by chloritite or steatite fragments with all-over red and white inlay [Figures 5.7(g) and (h)]. The dense added decoration meant that similar-looking products could be made in a variety of materials, and comparable pieces are also found in pottery and painted on white stone at Mari (Dunand 1939: pl. cxlv; Parrot 1956: pl. L). A third and final tradition is indicated by a group of vessels found at Ebla (Pinnock 1981). These were made in a soft white stone and are decorated with incised geometric designs [Figures 5.7(i) and (l); L7]. Some stylistic overlap with the chloritite vessels is visible in the location of the decorative bands (top and below rim) and in certain rhomboid patterns. These vessels are found only in northern Levantine temples and high-status residences, but we find the same decoration on a gold bowl from a royal grave at Ur (Pinnock 1981: fig. A1; Woolley 1955b: pl. 162), again suggesting that these motifs also fitted into a wider northern Levantine–Mesopotamian style zone.

## Cyprus and Central Anatolia

Cyprus and Anatolia both have long histories of stone vessel manufacture: Aceramic Neolithic communities on Cyprus made a wide range of vessels in soft chalk/limestone and coarse volcanic stones (Dikaios 1953: 232–64, 441, pls. xli–lix; Manen 2003; Jackson 2003) and production in Anatolia also stretches back to at least as early as the eighth millennium BC (Moorey 1994: 38; also see Takaoğlu 2006 with further references).[15] Despite this early period of prolific local manufacture, neither region subsequently makes many vessels of third millennium date. One Cypriot Philia culture tomb has produced a group of gypsum/travertine vessels, some of which may well have been rare but local products.[16] In Anatolia, there is patchy evidence for the imported Cycladic marble vessels both of Grotta-Pelos type at Iasos and of later Keros-Syros or Kastri group type around the Izmir Bay and inland from it (see below and Takaoğlu 2004). Local stone vessels are also rare if widespread finds, but our only informative window on their use is at Beycesultan, where small stone bowls and pestles were found togther in an apparent ritual context and were probably used for grinding pigments.[17] This extremely patchy pattern of use in both EBA Cyprus and Anatolia no doubt reflects the dominance of metal-based prestige strategies. In Anatolia especially, contemporary eating and drinking practices were more suited to flashier, lighter, more repairable metal vessels (or less production-intensive ones such as pottery). Indeed, as will become clear, when these Anatolian mainland ways of expressing status became extensively adopted in the Cyclades and western Aegean littoral in late EB2-3, indigenous stone vessel industries in these areas also suffered.

## The Aegean

### The Pre-Third Millennium Background

Neolithic stone vessel finds in the Aegean are part of the same patchy but widespread pattern visible throughout Anatolia and the Balkans, but in several instances hint at relatively specialised manufacturing from a very early stage (Perles 2001: 221–3, 285–7). By the FN phase, there is evidence for more intensive insular colonisation, and in the Cyclades, we see the gradual disappearance of the village-based communities of the fifth to fourth millennia BC and the emergence of more dispersed settlement and cemetery pattern typical of the third (Broodbank 1999, 2000: 117ff). It is in this area, and later in Crete, that we see a major stone vessel tradition emerge during the EBA.

### The Grotta-Pelos Phase

Detailed analysis of Cycladic society and its material culture is hampered by recent Western esteem for vessels and figurines as art objects (Gill and Chippindale 1993; Broodbank 2000: 58–65). Severe looting and the lack of contextual data for many Cycladic artefacts makes it hard to derive meaningful patterns from the limited archaeological record that remains. Our evidence is sufficient, however, to show that marble vessels become more visible in Grotta-Pelos assemblages, occur in substantial numbers in Keros-Syros contexts, and cease to be used almost completely after the Kastri group phase. Marble vessels are usually found in cemeteries, in perhaps 10–20% of graves at the larger sites (Tsountas 1898, 1899; Doumas 1977; Hekman 2003), but there are a few settlement finds and signs of wear, breakage, and repair indicate that they were probably also used by the living.

There are four main Grotta-Pelos shapes in marble: footed jars known conventionally as *kandiles*, beakers, shallow bowls, and palettes (Cyc1-4). All four have suspension holes and show signs of wear and repair, indicating that these were more than just decorative features (Sherratt 2000: 110). Their distribution is concentrated heavily on Naxos and Paros, where the best sources of white marble are found (Figure 5.8; Higgins and Higgins 1996: 170–95). They never accumulate in vast quantities in any one grave and their large size, limited number of shapes, simple decoration, and single material all imply they filled a relatively circumscribed set of social roles. In other words, such objects may have accompanied the ephemeral claims

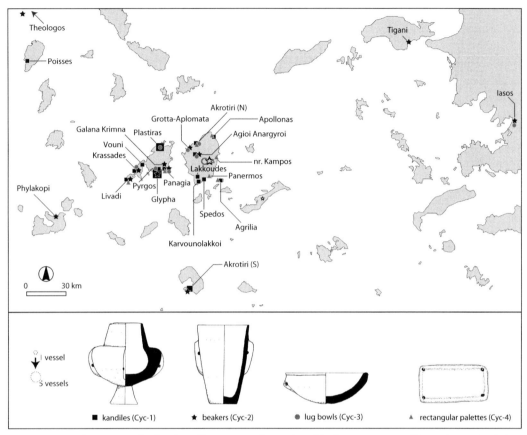

FIGURE 5.8. Distribution map of archaeologically provenanced examples of the four main ECI marble vessel types. Symbols in outline refer to examples for which only a general island location is known.

of more powerful local individuals, but they are unlikely to have expressed more enduring levels of social stratification. However, these same conservative characteristics also made them emblematic durables, well-suited to forging a common cultural identity amongst a potentially fragile demographic network of Naxian and Parian communities (Broodbank 2000: 183ff).

A closer glance at these shapes offers some important insights into their likely uses. For example, *kandiles* are not only the most common marble type but also the shortest lived, first appearing in stone during this period and disappearing at the end of it.[18] They are undecorated, moderately polished, and occasionally lop-sided artefacts but perhaps engender limited value distinctions based on size and weight. They can be very large and heavy (up to ca. 20 kg; Getz-Gentle 1996: n. 35, 245, 251) and show the greatest size variability of almost any Cycladic marble form.[19] Sometimes the interiors were only partially removed and while this may have saved time on manufacture, it also created a noticeably weighty object. More broadly, the *kandila* fits into a modest quantifying logic influencing those few prestigious graves with a range of other goods, and marble vessels in such contexts needed to be unusually large or heaped together in small groups (Doumas 1977: pl. xi.d–f). The *kandila* was not a pouring or drinking vessel and at least some of the time, may have been hung, precarious and upright, by its four lugs. Residue analysis has suggested the presence of grain in one example, either as part of a solid or suspended in a liquid such as beer (Rottländer 1990). While it remains difficult to offer any firm evidence for the shape's actual function, its globular body and restricted neck are a good design to enhance the aroma of any liquid contents and both its size and smell would be emphasised if the vessel was suspended at certain times.

In contrast to kandiles, palettes are a type that continues into the succeeding Keros–Syros phase. Many of these objects preserve traces of cinnabar-rich red pigments on their upper surface, where lumps of the material were crushed using a pestle (Tsountas 1898: pl. 10.13). This practice reflects a Cycladic emphasis on aspects of bodily adornment and modification that is present in the Grotta Pelos phase but becomes particularly pronounced later (depilation, tattooing, body painting, dress- or hair-pins and jewelery, Broodbank 2000: 247–9). These palettes are also the only vessel type whose distribution is confined to the Grotta-Pelos core area (Figure 5.8). This would be unsurprising if the distinctions of physical appearance that palettes helped to create were also used to mark out Naxian and Parian islanders from their neighbours. On a smaller scale, however, such tatooing and body-painting could potentially forge distinct family or community identities as well.

In contrast to palettes, Grotta-Pelos beakers are implicated in much more conservative, longer-range traditions. These vessels were probably drinking cups and an example from Iasos shows one tilted up to the mouth of the deceased Figure 5.9(a)]. They are the only shape with an earlier fifth- and fourth millennium ancestry and the most geographically promiscuous, with ca. 40% found some way beyond the Grotta-Pelos core region (Figure 5.8). A closer look at these vessels emphasises their possible association with women. One FN beaker was found in a multiple burial including several women and another with an adult female (Coleman 1977: 64–5, 86). ECI examples from well-documented tombs are found with schematic figurines and this is the only ECI shape occasionally decorated with female genitalia and hands grasping breasts (Doumas 1977: fig. 46; Getz-Gentle 1996: 47–9; Coleman 1999). The beaker's wide distribution is especially interesting and an even more extensive spatial pattern is true of pointed marble beakers from the preceding FN/Chalcolithic period, which are

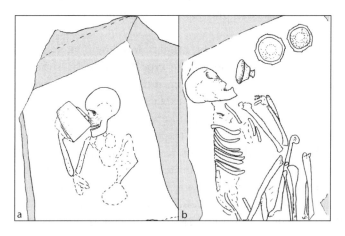

FIGURE 5.9. Marble vessels and body position in EBA graves: (a) a beaker in Iasos tomb 81 (after Pecorella 1984: fig. 93), and (b) two bowls and a cup in Chalandriani tomb 408 (after Tsountas 1899: pl. 88).

found across western Anatolia, the Aegean islands and in one instance as far north as Bulgaria (Takaoğlu 2005: 41–2). It would not be surprising if only a few specialist communities were actually involved in making such items (as seems likely for the Chalcolithic examples based on the evidence from Kulaksızlar), but one possible explanation of the subsequent dispersal of these items and their apparent gendering is that they were linked in some manner to the movement of women, perhaps as part of a tradition of long-distance exogamous networks between LN-FN villages (Broodbank 2000: 160–74), and survived as a traditional practice into ECI, despite the other demographic changes implied by the different Grotta-Pelos settlement patterns.

## The Keros-Syros Phase

Significant changes occur to Cycladic material culture at the end of the Grotta-Pelos phase and in Kampos-group assemblages (Doumas 1977: 18–20; Renfrew 1984). Marble *kandiles* and beakers occur in small numbers and plain bowls are also found, but far more important is the increased prominence of two activities: metallurgy and body decoration. These phenomena are contextually linked in Kampos group graves, probably indicating the emerging status of a few individuals with specialist knowledge in one or both of these domains (Broodbank 2000: 249). For example, miniature vessels and other artefacts are now made in a translucent light green stone, and most of these have possible tattooing and/or metallurgical associations. A rare excavated example from Agioi Anargyroi is probably a model crucible, but needle handles and ring bowls (for applying pigments?) are also known (Doumas 1977: pl. xxxv; Getz-Gentle 1996: 185–90).

In the following Keros-Syros phase, marble bowls and palettes remain common, but the overall range of shapes (and to a lesser extent materials) diversifies dramatically (Cyc5-20). Suspension lugs become less common, while footed forms suggest that display on flat surfaces such as tables was increasingly important. A new class of stone vessel also appears: these were carved out chlorite-rich stones into spherical and hut-shaped boxes and their hatch and spiral designs are also found on contemporary Cycladic pottery and Cretan chloritite vessels (see below). The increased availability of copper and bronze tools (e.g. Renfrew 1972: 326–32, fig. 17.2), which made softstone more straighforward to work, may be one technical factor behind these new softstone traditions. The increased impact of metal objects also affects the style of Cycladic marble vessels and some pottery forms, which are now given sharp inset rims, carinations, flaring shapes, vertical grooves, tubular spouts, and fake rivets. All of these features probably refer to metal vessels and the techniques used to make them (Broodbank 2000: 269–70). The striking links amongst traditional carved designs, softstone vessels, and metalworking are explored in greater detail in Chapter 8.

Unlike Grotta-Pelos artefacts, the collection of material culture that has been labelled as Keros-Syros extends over the entire Cyclades and to the coastal fringes of Attica, Euboea, and northern Crete (e.g. Broodbank 2000: figs. 87, 100). However, larger numbers of such objects are concentrated at a few key sites and it is worth comparing two of these, Chalandriani-Kastri and Daskaleio-Kavos, for how their assemblages reflect this period of intense regional interaction. Neither of these two communities would intuitively seem like prime locations for a prosperous site, but both established impressive interisland contacts, probably based on longboat voyaging (Broodbank 2000: 183ff). In terms of their stone vessels, the two sites are quite different. At Chalandriani, Hekman's recent synthesis (2003) of the find inventories and tomb groups allows us to make much firmer interpretations than before. For example, there are 122 stone vessels from all known tombs at the site, representing ca. 14% of the overall recorded number of grave goods. From Tsountas' excavations, we can also suggest that perhaps 10% of the ca. 540 tombs (mostly single burials) contained stone vessels and no single tomb more than five. In other words, only a limited section of the population was able or willing to use these objects for their funerary rites, part of a wider, skewed distribution of grave goods, in which many tombs had few if any objects and only a small number contained a larger assemblage.

This suggests some degree of status differentiation through mortuary practice, but Renfrew's further suggestion (1972: 373–5) that there was a degree of separation and exclusivity at Chalandriani, with the use of marble for richer graves and pottery for poorer ones, no longer seems so clear-cut. Instead, cluster analysis of the better preserved tomb inventories has been used to suggest some general (but by no means absolute) artefact groupings within the cemetery (Hekman 2003: 182–7): (1) pottery bowls, stone palettes, pestles, and frying pans, mainly found in circular tombs; (2) footed biconical pottery jars, stone bowls, obsidian blades, metal tweezers, metal scrapers, bone pins, and bone tubes; (3) pottery cups, metal pins, needles, punches, spatulas, shell necklaces, and stone figurines, mainly found in rectangular tombs; and (4) footed pottery bowls, cups and goblets, spherical jars, and short-necked jugs. It is certainly possible, as Heckman suggests, that the first and third clusters reflect gendered differences in burial assemblage and tomb form, while the second is associated with particular tattooing practices, for which the stone bowls seem to have been used to prepare pigments (e.g. tomb 242). The stone vessels themselves are almost all made of white marble (over 80%), with a much smaller group of grey banded marble, and only two of chloritite/steatite. The main shapes are rim-lug bowls (Cyc7, ca. 35%), plain bowls (Cyc5, ca. 23%), flaring cups (Cyc11, ca. 22%), palettes (Cyc4B, ca. 10%), and spouted bowls (Cyc6, ca. 9%). The bowls are frequently 8–12 cm in diameter, with the rim-lugged versions found in especially consistent dimensions, perhaps suggesting that function (e.g. as handheld pigment bowls) or sumptuary law (e.g. encouraging equivalence) was acting as a constraining factor on their size.[20]

At Dhaskaleio-Kavos, white marble bowls are extremely common finds, but the overall range of vessel shapes, sizes, materials, and decoration seems much greater, even if it is difficult to avoid the sample biases introduced by intensive looting. Most stone vessel finds come from the probable cemetery area in the north of the site and almost the entire range of Keros-Syros vessel types are present.[21] The majority are made of white marble, but some of these have painted or incised patterns and others are made of banded grey marble, chloritites, and various coloured limestones. These alternative materials and added decorative elements suggest at least an occasional emphasis on visual distinctiveness that is missing at many other Cycladic cemeteries. The range of vessel sizes is also impressive and parallels the large figurines from the site (e.g. Zapheiropoulou 1968a: fig. 1). As Cyprian Broodbank has argued (2000: 223–41), four factors combine to promote the levels of crafting virtuosity and prestige competition visible at Dhaskaleio-Kavos: (1) the proximity of excellent local marble sources, (2) an intense ECII network of interisland contacts in the southern Aegean, (3) the potential fragility of Dhaskaleio-Kavos' unusual status in this world, and (4) the increasing importance of metal artefacts and metallurgy. The first of these factors meant that there was no natural check to the size or quantity of artefacts that might be produced. The second reflects Keros' nodal location within both a smaller island cluster and a larger one (Naxos-Erimonisia-Amorgos). This position made Daskaleio-Kavos a place to visit or pass through as much as a point of departure. However, the island is agriculturally poor and one of many possible locations that might serve as a hub of interaction within the Erimonisia (e.g. Agrilia in the earlier Kampos-group phase). Its stone vessels certainly emphasise a level of material prosperity, but these distinctive prestige goods, of various sizes, shapes materials and designs, also probably indicate the importance of competitive display both within and beyond the community.

Finally, Dhaskaleio-Kavos also reveals good evidence for on-site metallurgical activity, pointing to a complementary avenue for manufacturing effort and prestige consumption. However, with hindsight, we might identify a tension between traditional marble-based display and metal-based alternatives (including rare examples of metal vessels from the EBA Aegean) that marked not just a series of different object types, but potentially also a wider set of Aegean cultural alignments and modes of behaviour. More precisely, the competitive distinctions visible in the stone vessels from Dhaskaleio-Kavos and the relative segregation of stone and metal at Chalandriani may be early signs of a transformation in Aegean prestige logics that sees the complete disappearance of the Cycladic stone vessel industry, and a similar decline in Cycladic figurines (Broodbank 2000: 316). With the disappearance of these objects also goes any sense in which marble was a prestige material *per se*.

Thereafter the consumption logics of the late EB2-3 Aegean were heavily inspired by Anatolian practices that, overall, put heavy emphasis on metal but very little on stone (e.g. Nakou 1997: 639–42).[22] The demographic conditions that made stone vessels important connective items in ECI-II, were also changing as a more nucleated settlement pattern emerged by the beginning of the MBA (e.g. Wagstaff and Cherry 1982: 139). At or beyond the edge of the Anatolianising zone, we encounter the odd late stone vessel (e.g. one with a rough 'depas' cup form: Caskey 1956: fig. 4), but such efforts were rare and it is unsurprising that we now see a new stone vessel tradition and new sources of exotic imitation emerging on Crete for a quite different set of reasons.

## EMIIA Crete

Unlike Cycladic marble vessels with a long ancestry, the first indigenous stone vessels in Crete appear relatively suddenly in EMIIA (Warren 1965, 1969: 182-3). These vessels are a series of box shapes and spouted bowls (C23A, 33A, 33D, 33F, 37A) carved out of chloritite and decorated with running spirals and hatched triangles. They have a wide distribution across Crete, but the consistency of their decoration and shape suggests a limited number of workshops, for which perhaps the most likely location is the southern Mesara-Asterousia region, where there are important chloritite deposits (Figure 5.10; Becker 1976: 364–5, fig. 1 no. 3). There are very few archaeological assemblages that offer us any further idea into how these objects were being used, but a little insight is provided by a group of EMIIA finds, in an apparent primary context on the tomb floor, from the southwestern part of the round tomb at Lebena Papoura Ib, which comprised an EMIIA-style chloritite

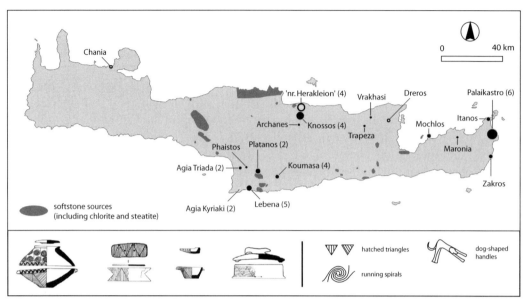

FIGURE 5.10. The distribution of EMIIA-style chloritite vessels, along with known softstone sources on Crete (open symbol implies uncertain findspot).

spouted bowl, an incised grey-burnished ceramic pyxis and a marble figurine (Alexiou and Warren 2004: 54). Indeed, there are strong decorative, technical, and petrological links between the EMIIA chloritite vessels, local stamp seals, and incised grey burnished pottery, which represent a suite of local prestige objects produced by communities in this region and, to varying extents, traded across most of the central and eastern parts of the island.[23] Indeed, the odd vessel traveled further still, a neat indication of which is a marble lid from Aplomata on Naxos which crudely evokes the dog-shaped handle of a Cretan chloritite lid (Figure 5.11).

Even if we might suspect that they are the craft products of only a few dedicated communities, the designs on these early chloritite vessels fit into a wider, incised-style zone across much of the Cyclades and Crete. For example, the two groups of Cretan and Cycladic chloritite vessels represent distinct manufacturing traditions with separate spatial distributions, but share some common decorative motifs, which also appear on contemporary pottery. Many of the chloritite vessels possess internal partition walls, blocky shapes, sawn-off square edges, and incised decoration that suggest links with wood-based forms. The toolkits used to carve softstone are virtually identical to those used for wood and it is no accident that both the Cycladic and Cretan chloritite industries suddenly appear in a period during which we also have evidence for the increased availability of metal tools that made them easier to carve. A more detailed discussion of what these multimedia links imply is offered in Chapter 8.

### Later Prepalatial Crete

From EMIIB onwards, at about the same time as stone vessels all but disappear in the neighbouring Cyclades, we see a significant shift in the Cretan industry as well. Chloritite

FIGURE 5.11. Circular boxes with dog-handles: (a) an EMIIA chloritite lid from Mochlos (see also Plate 3) (Getz-Gentle 1996: pl. 111a) and (b) a marble copy from Aplomata (after Marangou 1990: 132 no. 136).

vessels become a rare component of the overall tradition, which now places more emphasis on harder stones and a wider variety of vessel forms. Unfortunately our assessment of these developments, during a key period of increasing differentiation in social structure, settlement patterning, and perhaps also political articulation across the island, is severely hampered by generally poor levels of chronological resolution. The very late third millennium is a period of apparent demographic and environmental disruption, as well as poor archaeological visibility, not only in Crete but throughout much of the eastern Mediterranean. In Crete, the pottery styles that are most diagnostic of EMIIB-III mainly come from the eastern and northern part of the island, making it difficult to assess whether the presence or absence of such objects implies real fluctuations in the fortunes of different areas or merely a geographic bias in our archaeological indicators (e.g. Watrous and Hadzi-Vallianou 2004: 251–2). Furthermore, some of the best stone vessel assemblages come from long-lived communal tombs, with little vertical stratigraphy and, in most cases, unfortunate histories of looting or incomplete publication. For example, there is definite variation in stone vessel sizes, shapes, and materials in different tombs across the island, but it is not always clear whether these reflect differences in the intensity of tomb use over time or contemporary patterns of production and consumption. Sometimes it is possible to suggest earlier (EMIIB-III), middle (EMIII-MMIA), and later (MMI-II) components, but such chronological insight is patchy. Finally, communal contexts are also potentially deceptive about scales of consumption, with long aggregate histories of multiple funerary events and associated community ceremonies often combining to create the mirage of a large and rich burial or smearing out the impact of a single rich interment.

The most striking evidence for EMIIB-MMI stone vessel use comes from two distinct areas: (1) the east Cretan site of Mochlos and (2) a range of communities in the Mesara plain and Asterousia moutains of south-central Crete. The following discussion addresses both regions in turn before considering the evidence for trading networks within and beyond the island. Finds from communal tombs on the islet of Mochlos provide us with our best window on the EMIIB-III period, and these objects suggest two main developments in the stone vessel tradition after EMIIA. The first is the production a range of miniature pots, cups, and spouted bowls (C17A1, 28, 29; Seager 1909: pl. viii.2), some of which may have been containers for small amounts of oil or a thicker unguent. Many of these are made of steatite, a locally available softstone whose use here we might see as a straightforward extension of the existing EMIIA logic of carving a geologically related softstone, chloritite.[24] These vessels often copy larger pottery forms and may sometimes have been used as funerary tokens but were also found in EMIIB levels of the Mochlos settlement (Seager 1909: 288–9, pl. viii.2). Despite steatite's softness, some were now drilled using shaped grinding stones and small tubular bits (which at this stage might have conceivably been made either of reeds or copper; Warren 1969: 161, D199, D264, D279) and overall, these EMIIB-III small, plain, drilled steatite pots contrast strongly with their larger, highly decorated, carved, boxlike chloritite EMIIA predecessors. Moreover, in addition to this variation on a softstone theme, we also now find larger and/or more unusually shaped EMIIB-III vessels (C8A-D, 17A3, 22A, 22D, 41A, 41D, 42A), being drilled from distinctive local travertines, breccias, dolomitic, or banded marbles and limestones.

How do we characterise this use of stone vessels at Mochlos? The largest numbers of such objects cluster in the most architecturally impressive tombs towards the upper northwestern edge of the cemetery (e.g. tombs IV–VI), which we might link to the most influential and wealthy families at the site, while evidence for a contemporary manufacturing locale has recently been found within the settlement area (Soles 2005: 13). Mochlos seems to have been a late example of an EB2 trading community with links to the Aegean islands, and occasionally further afield (Phillips 1996; Whitelaw 2004: 242–4). An interesting contrast can be drawn, however, between the abundance of certain imported raw materials such as gold, copper, and obsidian and the stone vessels themselves which, while often evoking an awareness of both late EB2 Cycladic and thereafter late OK Egyptian stone vessel traditions, do not provide clear evidence for many actual imports (see below for further discussion). It is also difficult to place Mochlos in its wider regional context. Similar stone vessels are found in a variety of funerary and cave contexts in northeastern Crete, but a few vessels have been found in contemporary east Cretan settlements, confirming the fact that stone vessels were not just funerary items (Seager 1909: 288–9, pl. viii.2; Warren 1972: 236–7, nos. 208–10, fig. 104; possibly Seager 1905: 219, 1907: 123). For example, at Myrtos Phournou Koriphi, a spouted bowl was found with an assortment of small objects in the innermost room of one of the apparent households suggesting that it was a personal possession, in contrast to the limestone kernoi found in more public areas of the Myrtos hamlet (Warren 1972: 230–1; Whitelaw 1983: 326).

In contrast to Mochlos, our evidence from the Mesara and Asterousia mountains comes from a wider range of communities. In EMI-II, this southern Cretan landscape gradually filled up with tiny farms and the odd slightly bigger hamlet (only Phaistos appears to have had a larger population of a few hundred; Watrous and Hadzi-Vallianou 2004). Small communal round-tombs were increasingly common features, often associated with a nearby settlement and often implying a contributing population of just one or two families. EMIIA stone vessels were part of a wider Mesara burial set placed in these tombs, which also included pottery, obsidian blades, sealstones, daggers, and stone figurines. By MMIA, the settlement pattern is much changed, with evidence for increasing settlement nucleation, and a corresponding decrease in the the overall number, and increase in the apparent size and elaboration, of the associated round tombs (Watrous 2004). We can therefore paint a picture of the Mesara as a relatively disconnected and culturally conservative locale until MMI, when developments such as the expansion of Phaistos and the use of sailing ships appear to have connected it with a much wider world (see also Carinci 2000). For the period in between the EMIIA and MMIA phases, field survey and excavation results, along with the suggestion of a break in burial activity at some tombs, possibly indicate regional decline, but the picture is made far more obscure by the rather poor level of local EMIIB-III diagnostic artefacts in the Mesara and indeed by the fact that some of the stone vessels have clear parallels with EMIIB-III products at Mochlos and elsewhere (e.g. all those at Lebena Papoura I, Alexiou and Warren 2004: 40, fig. 8, pls. 15F-G, 17C).

Despite some chronological problems associated with communal tomb use, the round-tombs from south-central Crete offer a slightly better picture than Mochlos of how quantities and types of stone vessels were related to individual interment events. For example, several of the Archanes tombs confirm that, within the burial chamber, stone vessels were deposited as the funerary possessions of individual people (e.g. Maggidis 1998: 91–2, fig. 6.5). However, apparent prestige objects such as stone vessels, sealstones and daggers were buried alongside only a limited number of individuals within any given tomb. For instance, Voros A produced an estimated 55–65 burials, perhaps representing the contribution of a couple of nuclear families over a few hundred years but only seven stone vessels (Marinatos 1930–31; Branigan 1993: 90–2). The evidence from both of these sites tentatively suggests that less than one fifth of the funerary community were being buried with stone vessels, and a similar fraction, if not necessarily the same group, is implied by the numbers of sealstones and daggers (Whitelaw 1983; Murphy 1998: 37). Such objects certainly do indicate the wealth and ostentation of a few people, but given the scale of the communities involved for any one tomb context, they are most likely to have expressed distinctions of age, gender, and status *within* families, such as the identity of household heads, rather than more elaborate vertical social hierarchies.

So we distort the scale of display implied by these long-lived ossuaries if we imbue them with the same level of sociopolitical ostentation as, say, late Predynastic tombs in Egypt, both of which we might otherwise wish to tie into our narratives of local state formation in conveniently similar ways, as signs of increasing social stratification. Even so, some limited *intra*community competition was probably occurring within larger Mesara settlements such as Platanos, Koumasa, and Agia Triada (also by implication Phaistos), each of which possessed several, larger round-tombs by MMIA. In addition, there is noticeable variation between the stone vessel assemblages of such sites, despite the fact that they are relatively close to one another. For example, Banti pointed out that the vessels from the Agia Triada Tholos A were smaller than those from Platanos (1930–1931: 243) and they seem to have made more use of dolomitic limestone and less of chloritite. Likewise, while the neighbouring communities at Koumasa, Platanos, and Porti all buried many chloritite vessels, reflecting their proximity to local outcrops of this material, the Porti round-tomb has produced more stick-handled cups (C17A) and few of the bird's nest bowls (C3) found in such large numbers at the other two sites (Warren 1969: 117–23; also Gerontakou 2003). This may partly reflect preservation bias, or very different intensities of tomb use for these three communities over the EMII-MMI period, but it may also be part of a wider array of site-specific differences in funerary material culture (e.g. seals) related to the construction of distinct village identities.

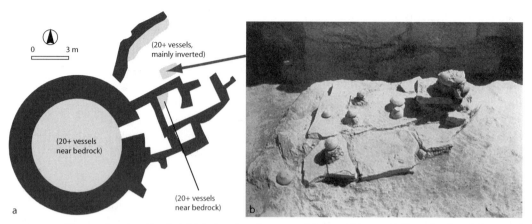

FIGURE 5.12. The round-tomb at Kamilari: (a) the location of stone vessel finds and (b) stone bird's nest bowls and clay conical cups placed upside down on a paved area (Levi 1961–1962: fig. 106).

The spatial distribution of vessels in and around the tomb also gives us some insight into these intra- and intervillage scale interactions. For example, at the Kamilari and Apesokari round-tombs, we find bird's nest bowls placed in three main areas: the burial chamber, one of the annexes, and external paved spaces (Figure 5.12; Schörgendorfer 1951). The first location confirms that these items were sometimes placed in the tomb with the deceased, and the second appears to reflect storage either in the form of funerary equipment ready for use or of redeposited bones and artefacts removed from the main chamber. The third indicates the mortuary observances of a wider group in the open places outside of the tomb. Pottery conical cups also appear in large numbers in tomb contexts from MMIA onwards (Hamilakis 1998: 123–5, tables 1–3), and the use of both types of artefact as all-purpose offering containers seems likely (though a more specific use to hold small amounts of food and drink at funerary ceremonies is possible: Branigan 1993: 129; Hamilakis 1998). At Kamilari, both vessel types were inverted on the ground in the external open areas and similar practices have been noted elsewhere [Figure 5.12(b); Sakellarakis 1968: fig. 4; Branigan 1993: 78]. Such spaces encouraged the participation of larger numbers of people, more frequently, than the narrow, cramped, and presumably rarely opened annexes and burial chamber. More generally, we should probably see annexes, open spaces, bird's nest bowls, and conical cups, as the regularisation of particular tomb rites and offerings out of an earlier more diverse set of practices (e.g. Hamilakis 1998: 123–5; Murphy 1998: 37–8).

**Trade within Crete**    The following discussion takes the later Prepalatial period as a whole to consider first a case study of internal trade and then the evidence for off-island influences on the Cretan industry. As is already obvious, some of the patterns described below continue into the second millennium, but greater chronological resolution is often difficult and therefore they are treated together in this chapter and highlighted again briefly in the following one, where MMI-II changes in stone vessel use are explored more fully. The lack of accurate stone provenancing, quarry prospection, or many published colour photographs makes it difficult to trace patterns of stone vessel exchange within Crete. Individual stone vessel imports can often be identified as outliers in specific site assemblages, but overall patterns are hard to discern. This problem becomes even worse in later periods where the suite of shapes is more regular across the island. For the very late Prepalatial (and perhaps the early Protopalatial), the best window on internal Cretan trade is provided by two groups of decorated chloritite vessels [Figure 5.13(a) and (b)]: (1) with incised lines, hatching, and inlay cutouts and (2) with vertical or diagonal incised nicks. Both groups were probably made by communities living near the chloritite sources of the southern Mesara–Asterousia region. It is tempting to see them as developing out of the EMIIA chloritite tradition, but well-dated examples usually come from MMI deposits, and decorative parallels are found on EMIII light-on-dark pottery and MMIA seals (Betancourt 1985: figs. 37–8; Sbonias 1995: 113–18).

The hatch-and-inlay group is more heavily decorated and more widely distributed across the island than the incised-nick group. Both are found throughout central Crete, probably reflecting a land-based distribution network around the Mesara and northwards to Archanes and Knossos. However, the hatch-and-inlay vessels also appear to have benefited from a second, probably seaborne, trade which brought them to coastal sites around the island. Overall, the spatial pattern is almost exactly the same as earlier EMIIA chloritite vessels (Figure 5.10), suggesting that the trading networks responsible for their movement around the island may not have changed all that much. Furthermore, the hatch-and-inlay vessels are more heavily decorated than the incised-nick group and might be seen as craft products that were explicitly branded as exotic and from a particular Mesara tradition. Wooden prototypes may have existed, but unlike in EMIIA, the chloritite versions were no longer carved but drilled, reflecting the dominance of this technique for the contemporary stone vessel industry as a whole. Finally, if we look at the regional distribution of hatch-and-inlay shapes (Figure 5.14), the greatest diversity of types is found at Platanos, which may have been the centre of production or very close to it. The strongest difference is visible for the north and east Cretan sites, particularly those for which a seaborne trade has been suggested, where only the kernos and more rarely the bird's nest bowl are found, along with their lids. This indicates an increasingly selective package of shapes, motifs, and associated practices as we move away from the source area for these products.

Chloritite vessels were just one part of a wider industry on the northern margins of the Asterousia which also produced amulets, beads, and sealstones in local steatite, chloritite, and bone (e.g. Xanthoudides 1924: 88–125). One group of MMIA seals which looks strongly linked to the hatch-and-inlay stone vessel tradition is the so-called white-pieces group. These seals share many of the same designs (e.g. hatched triangles, olive-leaf decoration, sun/star motif) as the vessels and similar distribution (though surviving in greatest numbers at Odigitria and Kali Limenes rather than Platanos). They were probably made from glazed and/or fire-hardened steatite (Pini 1990; Sbonias 1995: 113–8)[25] and hence drew on the same general softstone source area as the chloritite vessels. The same material was also used to make local imitations of Egyptian hippopotamus ivory scarabs, due to its white appearance and because it allowed a finer level of incised decoration than ordinary softstone (Pini 2000; Krzyszkowska 2005: 72–4).[26] Indeed, the link between these softstone workshops, Egyptianising practices, and burgeoning maritime trade are evoked nicely by two unique objects found at Platanos. The first is a bird's nest bowl in soft white stone carved into the shape of a scarab beetle in

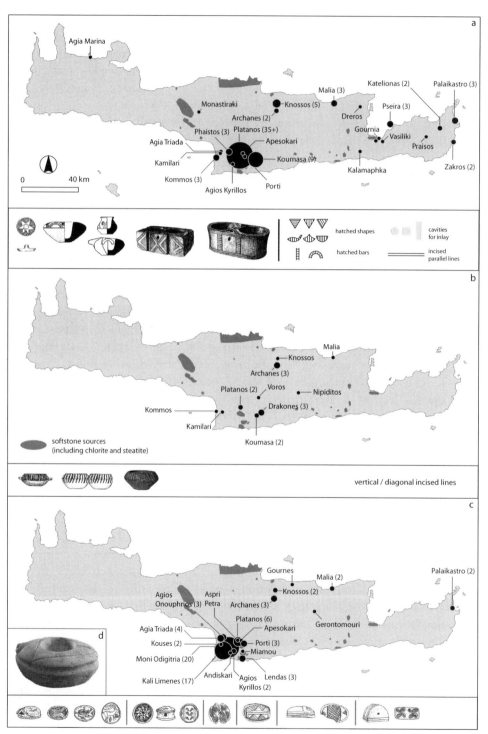

FIGURE 5.13. The distribution of three EMIII-MMI softstone artefact types from the southern Mesara–Asterousia region: (a) hatch-and-inlay vessels, (b) incised nick vessels, and (c) 'white pieces' seals (after Warren 1969; Becker 1976; Sbonias 1995: 113–18), with limited additions.

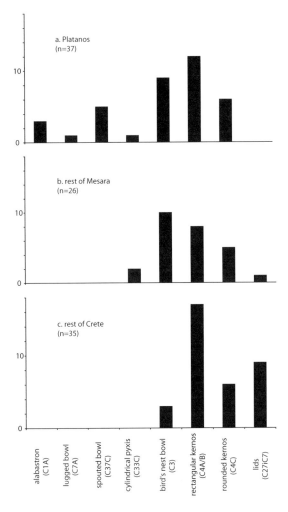

FIGURE 5.14. Chloritite vessels decorated with hatch-and-inlay designs from (a) Platanos, (b) the rest of the Mesara, and (c) the rest of Crete. The diversity of shapes decreases further away from a probable production zone near Platanos.

similar fashion to the much smaller scarab seal imitations [Figure 5.13(d); though a depiction of the local Cretan horned beetle also remains a possibility: Phillips 2005b: 44].[27] The second is a 'white pieces' seal with three faces decorated, respectively, with hatched designs, a goat(?), and a sailing ship [Figure 5.13 bottom left; Figure 8.2(c)]. The interplay of local and nonlocal both these objects is striking and implies maritime contact with Egypt in some form. This may conceivably have included direct southward journeys from the Mesara, with a return voyage presumably via the Levantine coast (see Chapter 3), but the dominance of *imitations* in the Mesara is suggestive of rather limited access to Egyptian goods that may well have been arriving in greater quantity elsewhere on the island (e.g. the north-central coast).

## Trade Beyond Crete

The discussion of this local southern Mesara-Asterousia industry and its intriguing combination of indigenous and imported values leads us to the question of Crete's off-island contacts in the late Prepalatial period. For earlier EB2, the connections between Crete and the Cyclades suggested by parallel chloritite vessel traditions have already been described above. Marble vessels of Kampos or Keros-Syros type have also been found at a number of Cretan sites (Warren 1969: P458, P459; 1981: fig. 2; Papadatos 2005: pl. 20.D1). The most impressive context so far uncovered is the cemetery at Agia Photia (Davaras and Betancourt 2004), a group of nearly 300 tombs which probably included as much as twice that many interments and is striking for the almost entirely Cycladic character of the ca. 1800 artefacts recovered from it. Indeed the similarities in material culture and tomb type between it and the Kampos-group cemetery at Ano Kouphonisi have led to the suggestion that this represented a discrete colony (Day et al. 1998). Interestingly, despite this, only three marble bowls and one palette were found in the cemetery. This might reflect the isolation of the community from Cycladic marble-working centres or, given the strong evidence for continued contact with the Cyclades suggested by the pottery, it may simply be an indicator of slightly reduced importance of marble vessels in the Kampos group phase. In later EB2-3, the north Cretan links with the Cyclades are less extensive. Later at Mochlos, we see a similarly ambiguous pattern with regard to Cycladic exchange: there is plenty of evidence for Melian obsidian, but no imported Cycladic stone vessels. Instead, we find less straightforward signs of Cycladic influence in three clear Cycladic imitations, a flaring cup and footed jar both made of white translucent travertine and a footed bowl of grey banded marble (Warren 1969: P516, P569, P571). These materials were available locally in the Mirabello region and were chosen to imitate the white marble and rarer banded grey marble used for Cycladic vessels.[28] One of these Mochlos vessels is especially interesting because it seems to be a rough copy of a Cycladic *kandila*. Such vessels are much earlier Cycladic objects, though they do occasionally turn up in later graves as heirlooms (e.g. Doumas 1977: fig. 49), and the Mochlos artisan who made the imitation must have been copying an antique and adopting a deliberately archaising style. Apart from these three vessels, Mochlos along with other northern and eastern Cretan sites continue to produce lugged bowls (C10A, 37A) similar in style (if not always material) to late Keros-Syros and Kastri-group marble types (Cyc6i, 7). Again the impression is that these links are relatively indirect, reflecting the fact that EMIIB-III (probably the peak period of Mochlos' prosperity) overlaps only briefly with the later Keros-Syros phase.

During this period and certainly by MMIA, we see the replacement of these oblique and occasionally ancestral references to Cycladic–Cretan relations, with Egyptian influences on the Cretan stone vessel tradition. Unfortunately, poor provenances, secondary stratigraphic contexts, and uncertain identifications mean that our interpretation of these early Egyptian contacts swims in something of an interpretative soup. Generally speaking, tiny amounts of Near Eastern material *may* have reached the Aegean during the earlier third millennium, via extended down-the-line circuits, but the vast majority of the evidence points to greater contact with Crete during EMIIB-MMI, and a particular concentration of finds in the MMIA period. Following Phillips (1996), we can break this evidence for early Egyptian links into four categories of declining cultural immediacy and, for us, increasing interpretative risk: (1) actual imports, (2) raw material, (3) import imitations, and (4) technical and ideological influence. With respect to stone vessels, the first three of these categories all raise interpretative challenges, but as we shall see below, there are several possible or probable early Egyptian imports from late Prepalatial contexts, an important group of local imitations, but no signs of imported raw blocks of stone at this stage. In addition, the use of tubular drill-bits and shaped grinding stones is a new development which might also be linked to the advanced Egyptian know-how in this domain, but the leap from other forms of drilling and grinding, for which we have good indigenous evidence from earlier periods, is not necessarily so great as to demand an exogenous explanation of this kind. In terms of a wider transmission of ideas, we might identify the appearance of miniature pots and flasks in EMIIB-III as matching the cosmetic priorities of the contemporary late Old Kingdom stone vessel tradition, but these patterns are not necessarily so directly linked. By MMI, there are also a few hints, such as some vessels from Agia Triada that are discussed below, that a wider set of Egyptian-inspired ablutionary habits were being adopted, but in the end these remain frustratingly inconclusive. Likewise, we can suggest on the basis of a range of circumstantial evidence that preservation bias has denied us a proper picture of this phenomenon at Knossos, where, judging by its likely size in EMIII-MMIA, we might have expected any higher-level exchanges to have occurred.

We can consider the physical evidence that we do possess in four subgroups, arguably in order of increasing relevance: (1) some highly equivocal LN-EMIIA pieces; (2) a 'floating' group of Egyptian stone vessels from Knossos and elsewhere that are Predynastic–Old King-dom in style, but found in undocumented, mixed, or late stratigraphic contexts; (3) a handful of more plausible imports from EMIIB-MMI/II contexts; and (4) local imitations. In the first category, there are three fragments from Late Neolithic levels at Knossos that, for one reason or another, make extremely unlikely identifications (Bevan 2004: 111). In addition, there is a tiny obsidian fragment (about a centimetre in length) from EMIIA Knossos (Warren 1981: 633–4, fig. 5) which might coincide with broader hints that a trickle of Near Eastern objects and raw materials were beginning to reach the Aegean at this time. The piece might be from the rim of an imported Egyptian vessel, but given its size, lack of clear diagnostic features (apart from the suggestion of a bevelled edge), findspot (an area also containing ordinary obsidian debitage), and mismatch between the date of its context and the most plausible Egyptian parent vessels (Dynasty 0–1), it remains only a slight possibility.

In the second category, there are a large number of Egyptian imports of definite Predynastic–Old Kingdom style that could indicate early contact, but are either unprove-nanced or found in later contexts (Bevan 2003: 62–9; 2004: 113–20). A few of these vessels make plausible indicators of early high-level contacts between an elite group at later Prepala-tial Knossos and royal courts in the northern Levant or Egypt. For example, a series of anorthosite gneiss bowl fragments of the type found in the 6th Dynasty burials of Pepi and Neit, as well as in the temple and palace contexts at Byblos and Ebla (see above), have been found at Knossos as well and may conceivably been part of similar late third millennium royal or upper elite exchanges with Crete. However, none of the Knossos anorthosite gneiss bowls come from definite early contexts and, more importantly, they are clearly copied much later on in the Neopalatial period (see Chapter 6), implying that at least some were acquired in the mid-second millennium or kept as heirlooms. More generally, antique Egyptian stone vessels are found in much later MB-LBA contexts throughout the Mediterranean and may well be associated with SIP-18th Dynasty tomb-robbing in Egypt (Phillips 1992; see Chapter 6).

What remains in the third category is a handful of more likely EMIIB-MMI/II imports. However, the most striking feature of this small, remaining group is how odd and eccentric a collection it is. The majority of the pieces are not the most common ones found in contemporary Egypt (late Old Kingdom–12th Dynasty). There is one definite import from Agia Triada and several plausible candidates from EMIIB-MMI deposits at Knossos. The Agia Triada jar is made of anorthosite gneiss and hence clearly identifiable as Egyptian, but it has only one known shape parallel in Egypt (Cairo M. 18419). There is only one possible cylindrical jar import, and no examples of collared pots or everted rim jars which together represent by far the three most common contemporary Egyptian vessel forms. Furthermore, neither the dated contexts nor the vessel styles allow us to pin down, on their own, when within a period of some four or five centuries these objects might be arriving. Crucially for any wider interpretation, this range also covers the centuries immediately before and after the important watershed represented by the appearance of the first Cretan palaces.

Should this rather frustrating set of evidence surprise us? As we saw earlier, much clearer evidence for imported Egyptian stone vessels does appear in contemporary contexts in the Levant, but there we find it in upper elite domestic contexts, not tombs, and at two extremely well-connected and important centres. This suggests not only that foreign access to Egyptian stone vessels was very circumscribed but also that the status (or political legitimacy) conferred by the best examples (e.g. large, inscribed, and/or in anorthosite gneiss) often made them too valuable to dispose of casually. What is therefore clear, when we turn to Crete, is that not only were equivalent sociopolitical hierarchies only just emerging on the island at this time, making it difficult to know whether comparable high-level political contacts would have been viable, but also that we lack undisturbed elite residential contexts from plausibly large urban centres such as late Prepalatial Knossos to compare like with like effectively. Indeed, there are out-of-context vessels of the right date and type at Knossos that can do no more than raise our suspicions about what we might be missing (e.g. carinated Egyptian bowls and cylindrical jars). Instead, we are left with evidence drawn mainly from smaller, sometimes marginal, Cretan hamlets and villages in the Mirabello and the Mesara. Such communities may have acquired exotica in ingenious ways, but were by no means well connected to the Near Eastern world.[29] What all of this implies is that we might explain the strangeness of the early Egyptian stone vessel evidence from Crete as the result of its having been refracted in two key ways: first because we cannot observe the centre of the phenomenon clearly but only its regional margins and, second, because it is quite possible that such contacts were being filtered through Byblos, a coastal centre which was heavily implicated in early eastern Mediterranean sailing voyages and has the clearest evidence for substantial Egyptian interaction in this period.

Given these idiosyncrasies, it is the fourth category of stone vessel evidence, a group of contemporary Cretan imitations, which are perhaps the most revealing (Figure 5.15). There are five interesting features to notice about these local imitations (see Bevan 2004: 112–3). Firstly, they are made of several varieties of local travertine[30] and dolomitic limestone that probably copy the whiteness and banding of Egyptian travertine or the dark flecks and white matrix of anorthosite gneiss. Secondly, they are miniaturised versions of Egyptian originals found in a greater range of sizes, implying that their contents were relatively precious (presumably an oil or unguent) and/or that their role was partly symbolic. Thirdly, and in

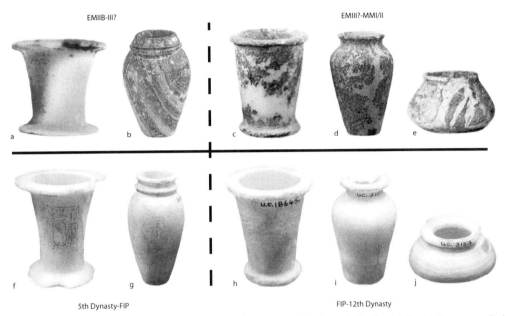

EMIIB-III?    EMIII?-MMI/II

5th Dynasty-FIP    FIP-12th Dynasty

FIGURE 5.15. Late Prepalatial Cretan imitations (a)–(e) of Egyptian OK-MK vessels (f)–(j): (a) dolomitic limestone cylindrical jar (ht. 4.2 cm, Soles 1992: pl. 30), (b) 'banded tufa' collared jar (ht. 7 cm, Karetsou 2000: no. 14), (c) dolomitic limestone cylindrical jar (ht. 5.3 cm, Karetsou 2000: no. 25h), (d) dolomitic limestone everted rim jar (ht. 5.8 cm, Karetsou 2000: no. 19a), (e) breccia alabastron (ht. 4.4 cm; Warren 1969: P4). (f) travertine cylindrical jar (UC 15791, ht. 14.7 cm), (g) travertine collared jar (UC 41356, ht. 11.8 cm), (h) travertine cylindrical jar (UC 18645, ht. 5.8 cm), (i) travertine everted rim jar (UC 31519), (j) travertine alabastron (UC 31518). Note that the confidence with which these Cretan and Egyptian forms can be correlated varies and is particularly uncertain for (e) and (j).

contrast to our small and rather eclectic sample of actual Egyptian imports, the imitations copy the most common contemporary Egyptian container shapes. This suggests we have a gap in our evidence that there were imported models for these copies that have not survived in our existing Cretan contexts (except for one cylindrical jar). Fourthly, these imitations have not so far been found at Knossos (even unstratified), perhaps implying that the Mochlos and Mesara imitations say more about the sometimes frustrated aspirations of powerful local families in these areas than about their concrete long–distance contacts. Finally, the smaller details of these imitative shapes suggest two chronological groups, comprising a few EMIIB–III vessels, most visible at Mochlos and similar to those styles common in late OK to FIP Egypt, and a larger number of MMI vessels associated with the Mesara tombs, and similar in style to Egyptian vessels found in later FIP-12 Dynasty contexts (Figure 5.15; Bevan 2004: 112–3). This suggests the increasing reach of Egyptian influence in the early part of the second millennium, linked to the appearance of sailing ships in the Aegean and the increasing importance of major agricultural regions on Crete such as the MMI Mesara.

The findspots of these Egyptian and Egyptianising stone vessels in communal tombs offer very few clues as to what value or meaning was ascribed to them in the local Cretan arena. They were particularly exotic examples of a much wider group of prestige durables, usually concentrating in the larger and wealthier Mesara tombs but also present in smaller burials on the south coast as well. However, the relatively limited number of sealstones and vessels,

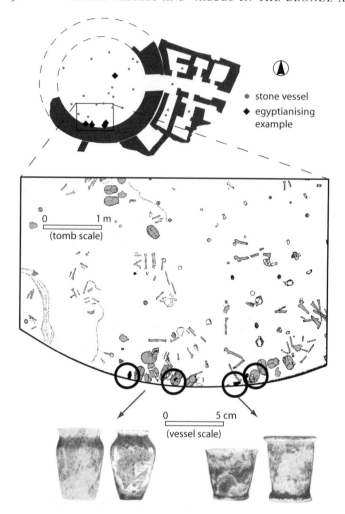

FIGURE 5.16. The distribution of Egyptianising stone vessels from Agia Triada Tholos A (after Banti 1930–1931: figs. 2, 4–5, 50c–f).

alongside the demographic scale of activity represented by EMII-MMI communal tombs, suggests that, in general, these items were marking out specific figures within family or multiple family groups, rather than a whole elite class. In other words, apart from a very few larger villages, we should be looking for evidence for competitive display and ranking between tombs and settlements rather than within them. Only one round-tomb at Agia Triada adds any further contextual detail to this picture (Figure 5.16). This EMII-MMI context provides the clearest early import, the jar made of anorthosite gneiss discussed above. As we have seen, this stone was ascribed high status in late third millennium Egypt, Byblos, and Ebla, and it is therefore unfortunate that the vessel's exact location in the tomb was not recorded and that its shape is extremely unusual and hence that we have few clues as to its function or meaning in either place. However, round-tomb A also produced the largest amount of Egyptianising material from a single context of this period, and at least four Egyptian vessel imitations cluster amongst a disturbed group of longbones and skulls, swept into the southern corner of the main burial chamber (admittedly amongst perhaps two hundred individuals in the tomb overall; see also Phillips 2005b: 43). These four vessels are made of dolomitic limestone, perhaps imitating Egyptian anorthosite gneiss, and seem to be in pairs of smaller and larger versions of the same shape. In contemporary Egypt, these vessel shapes held oils and ointments, were mainly used by women, and were deployed singly, in pairs and in sets of seven [e.g. Figure 5.5(b)]. The Agia Triada context hints that some of these roles may have continued to be important in Crete, but unfortunately provides no truly conclusive details.

To summarise, stone vessels have an important story to tell about significant social and cultural changes occurring in the Aegean during the third millennium BC, but their relevance is often narrower that hitherto assumed, contributing more to our understanding of regional trajectories, for example, in the Cyclades, eastern Crete, and the Mesara, than they do to any overall synthetic narrative. The earlier marble (and limestone) stone vessels are linked strongly to long-lived Neolithic and west Anatolian Chalcolithic traditions, and their persistence into the Bronze Age might well indicate that certain traditional social relationships survived along with them. By EB2, a separate class of highly decorated softstone vessels appears, with links to both probable soft media designs and emergent metallurgy that are considered again in Chapter 8. Thereafter, it is only the industry on Crete which continues to expand and diversify, becoming the second most prolific and enduring tradition in the Bronze Age eastern Mediterranean after Egypt and producing a wide range of bowls, pouring vessels, and small pots in a variety of materials. The influence first of the Cycladic marble tradition and thereafter of the Egyptian industry is clear, even if the number of definite imports is tiny and the timing, extent, and character of such contacts hard to discern. Despite patchy evidence, local Cretan vessels seem to be traded widely around the island during the EMII-MMI period. By MMIA, we can point to new sets of social priorities behind the growing size of a few urban centres and marked shifts in the funerary sphere. Existing stone vessel display becomes more standardised and a whole new set of stone vessel practices emerge which will dominate the MMI-II Cretan industry, particularly the growing popularity of certain bowl shapes and of serpentinite. These new forms and emphases then persist with only small alterations right through the Protopalatial period and are described fully in the following chapter.

# 6
# The Earlier Second Millennium

𝖑𝖌𝖑𝖌𝖑𝖌𝖑

*Chapter 5 charted the production and consumption of stone vessels in a rapidly changing* environment in which new production methods, luxury materials, and transport technologies were all becoming available. The very end of this period is notable for the low fidelity of our surviving material record across the entire region and for the impression of socioeconomic dislocation in many areas. Despite this apparent discontinuity, many of the patterns we observe in the later third millennium persist into the second: metal remained the dominant, high-value material and we can see the effects of its preeminence in the skeuomorphic character of other media and in the altered ways in which stone vessels adapted to a wider suite of prestige products. The eastern Mediterranean was now firmly tied together by long-range maritime and land-based routes that encouraged an intensified exchange of ideas as well as goods.

In the Levant, the reemergence of stone vessel use at Byblos and elsewhere followed a pattern established in the EBA, changing into something recognisably different only later on. In the northern Levant and Anatolia, we glimpse some intriguing practices and patterns associated with the very upper levels of society and driven by an increasingly shared set of prestige markers. In the Aegean, the earlier second millennium marked the appearance of palaces, writing and a highly stratified society on Crete. This complex palatial world was responsible for the second most elaborate and diverse stone vessel tradition in our region, and, unlike Egypt, one to whose meanings we have no textual shortcut.

## Egypt

### The Middle Kingdom
Middle Kingdom Egypt reveals both a degree of continuity in the social roles established for stone vessels during the later OK and some significant departures. The importance of cosmetic containers is even more pronounced than before, but tableware such as bowls and pouring vessels were now extremely rare, even in royal and upper elite contexts. We see the first appearance of some well-known Egyptian vessel shapes such as the alabastron and the everted rim jar (E135,145-7), but cylindrical jars and kohl pots were by far the most commonly used vessel types, both in courtly and provincial tombs (E36,154-8). Kohl was an Egyptian eye makeup with a much older Egyptian ancestry, but now given a highly recognisable receptacle, distinct from other cosmetic containers. Travertine continued to be the most common material, but anorthosite gneiss is now extremely rare. Instead, a range of local and foreign stones such as anhydrite, carnelian, hematite, lapis lazuli, obsidian, and steatite were used both by royal and nonroyal workshops (Aston 1994: 51–73).

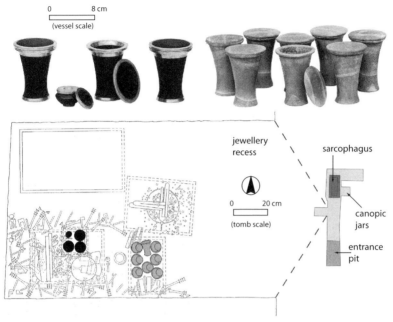

FIGURE 6.1. Obsidian vessels and a sacred oil set from the tomb of Sithhathor-yunet (after Winlock 1934: figs. 1–2, pl. xvi).

Our best view of stone vessel use within the royal family is offered by the burials of royal princesses at Lahun and Dahshur. In the tomb of Sithhathor-yunet, stone vessels were kept in two separate boxes in a side chamber containing her personal possessions (Figure 6.1). One box held a sacred oil set of travertine cylindrical jars and the other a smaller set of obsidian jars and a kohl pot, all capped with thick gold sheet. Similar stone vessels were placed in the tombs of other Middle Kingdom princesses and were also found abroad at Byblos (De Morgan 1894: figs. 136–7, pls. xix, xxv; figs. 6.2a–c). The careful finish and identical size of the cylindrical jars in particular indicate increasingly standardised royal products, no doubt containing exact quantities of oil. Stylistic consistency is a feature of royal workshops in many periods, but it is particularly pronounced here.

Further down the social scale, vessel size and style are much more varied and in many ways, the patterns of stone vessel use remain similar to those described in Chapter 5 for late OK provincial cemeteries. For example, the Haraga cemetery near the pyramid town of Kahun contained nearly 300 burials made over a century or so during the late Middle Kingdom and about 13% of these were furnished with stone vessels (Engelbach 1923; see also Seidlmayer 1990: 234–46). Kohl pots and cylindrical jars predominate and are found with both sexes but appear more common among females. Only the richest tombs contained more than one or two vessels and these also marked out their wealth with gold, bead jewellery, quantities of pottery, and scarabs.

## The Second Intermediate Period and Early 18th Dynasty

The SIP was a period of political upheaval and its material culture suggests a degree of regionalism which emerged from the division of Egypt into separate areas of Hyksos and

Theban political control. Contemporary stone vessels are made in a relatively conservative range of shapes: oil containers continue to be important, but the vast majority of vessels are kohl pots. Some of the latter are in new styles (E159-161), but there is also good evidence for the mobilisation of heirlooms and looted artefacts at a variety of social levels as a substitute for extensive contemporary production (see also Verbovsek 2006 for a wider perspective). Stone vessels from SIP contexts are frequently worn, chipped, mismatched with their lids, and/or of clear ED-MK style and may have been curated items or looted from earlier tombs (e.g. Petrie 1909: 6–10; Grajetzki 2003: fig. 78). There are also wider indications that the SIP to early 18th Dynasty sees unusually intense looting activities, creating an increased circulation of antique Egyptian stone vessels throughout the eastern Mediterranean (see below).

The Hyksos rulers continue to inscribe stone vessels as equipment for princesses and perhaps as gifts to foreign courts (e.g. Lilyquist 1995: figs. 12–5, 123–6), but some of this consumption may also have been sustained by the redeployment of older vessels. For example, the Aswan granite and anorthosite gneiss used for two elaborate Hyksos jars comes from quarries beyond the main area of Hyksos administration. Aswan granite was also primarily an OK stone and there is no obvious quarrying activity of anorthosite gneiss at Gebel el-Asr after the MK (Shaw and Bloxam 1999: 16). So these jars were probably made from either stores of raw stone or reused blocks from larger monuments or were reinscribed MK pieces.

Among less wealthy Egyptian groups, stone vessels seem less common in Lower Egyptian burials than they are in Upper Egypt. In the Delta, only a few vessels occur in Hyksos period graves, while in cemeteries from the Fayum southwards, on average ca. 15% of SIP graves possess these items, which is very similar to the proportion of the community using these items in the OK-MK.[1]

At the beginning of the 18th Dynasty, the most popular shapes are cylindrical jars, baggy alabastra, and kohl pots (E34, 162–6, 185), all of which are relatively common as royally inscribed objects, from lower elite tombs, and in colourful tomb paintings (Lilyquist 1995: figs. 6, 24, 51, 59–68). An altogether new shape is the squat jar with collared neck (E173), which becomes the template body shape behind a range of more complex 18th–19th Dynasty jars. None of these details involve particularly dramatic changes but are worth isolating here because they are relevant to the dating and reception of Egyptian imports in neighbouring regions of the eastern Mediterranean.

## The Levant

### Egyptian-Style Vessels

The end of the third millennium in the Levant is a relatively obscure period for which there is evidence of more mobile communities and a period of socioeconomic disruption (e.g. Dever 1995). Stone vessels do not seem to have been an important part of local material culture, and while limited contact between Egypt and Byblos probably continued (see Chapter 3), no imported Egyptian stone vessels can be attributed to this time. Urbanism, elite display, and interregional contact gradually reappear during MBIIA and high-level exchanges between Egypt and the northern Levant are evident again in a series of impressive MK imports from royal or upper elite tombs at Byblos and Ebla (Figure 6.2; Scandone-Matthiae 1988: pl. xiii).[2]

FIGURE 6.2. MK stone vessels from the Byblos tombs: (a) an obsidian cylindrical jar inscribed for Amenemhat III, (b) an obsidian jewellery chest inscribed for Amenemhat IV, (c) an anorthosite gneiss jar inscribed for an unknown 12th–13th Dynasty ruler, (d) a travertine fragment inscribed for a local figure of authority at Byblos, 'the prince/mayor, Yantin', and (e) a large travertine alabastron (Montet 1928: pls. lxxxviii, xci, cxxii, cxxvii).

As in the third millennium, certain features mark out these Egyptian finds as plausible greeting or marriage gifts between royal households. For example, at Byblos, a cylindrical jar and jewellery chest of obsidian have clear parallels in the burials of 12th Dynasty Egyptian princesses [e.g. Figure 6.1(a)] and a large anorthosite gneiss jar represents a rare post-OK use of this stone for a vessel. Two travertine alabastra from the tombs are also exceptionally large examples of their type [e.g. Figure 6.2(e)]. This high-level attention is also visible in the stone vessels and other objects inscribed in Egyptian and crediting local Byblites with MK political titles (Lilyquist 1993: 41–4 with references). Such official Egyptian titles emphasise the strongly Egyptianising flavour of local rule but are also deeply ambiguous about Byblos' status in relation to Egypt. The terms may well have been deliberately chosen by 12th and 13th Dynasty Egyptian rulers to be flattering to an external Levantine audience, but imply that Byblos was a vassal to an internal Egyptian one. Such flexibility of political meaning is a salient feature of later Egyptian foreign policy in the Amarna letters (see Chapter 3).

These high-status objects in the northern Levant suggest the continuity of late-third-millennium channels of upper elite exchange, but by later MBIIA this pattern alters dramatically. Stone vessels, scarabs, and other Egyptian material culture appear at a range of southern Levantine sites as well (Marcus 2002b) and this contact is probably linked to the increasing importance of southern Levantine groups in Egypt's eastern Delta (Bietak 1996). Apparent immigration westwards into Egypt created something of an Egypto-Levantine cultural continuum, spanning the southern Levant, Sinai, and Delta regions. The political culmination of this process was the accession to power in Egypt itself of a southern Levantine Hyksos dynasty, but the same strong cultural links exist throughout the broader MBIIB-LBIA phase,

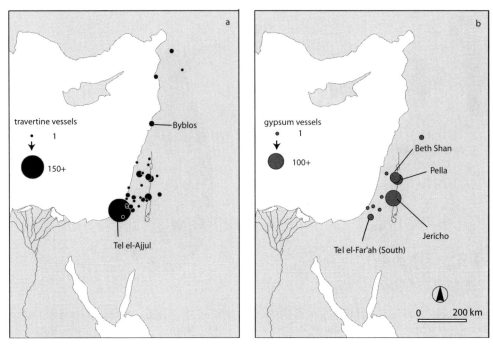

FIGURE 6.3. The distribution of (a) travertine and (b) gypsum vessels in the MBIIB-LBIA Levant (counts from Sparks 2007, with minor additions).

persisting after the collapse of Hyksos rule and right up until the Levantine campaigns of Thutmosis III.

If the earlier links between the northern Levant and Egypt suggest relatively unproblematic acceptance of Egyptian upper elite forms, these later southern Levantine contacts have a wider social impact but produce a more complicated range of local responses (for a comprehensive recent study, albeit with slightly different conclusions, see Sparks 2007). Southern Levantine sites attract the majority of travertine vessels in MBIIB-LBIA [Figure 6.3(a)], but while these are similar to the shapes found in contemporary Egypt, some differences do exist (Lilyquist 1996). Distinctive Levantine features include copies of local pottery forms such as dipper juglets and Egyptian forms that are unusually elongated in profile or oval in plan. Such indiosyncratic details could reflect three possible crafting scenarios: (1) production in Egypt tailored for an export market in the Levant (Ben-Dor 1945: 101), (2) manufacture in the Levant by itinerant Egyptian artisans, (3) a purely local Egyptianising tradition. The failure of these artefacts to fit easily into one unequivocally Egyptian group is not unsurprising given the apparent fragmentation of Egyptian territory at this time into a core Hyksos area around the eastern Delta, Bitter Lakes, and Wadi Tumilat (Bietak 1984), a slightly different zone in the rest of the Delta and lower Nile valley, and yet another in Upper Egypt. In any case, because the travertine vessels consumed by southern Levantine communities cannot simply be labelled generic Egyptian imports, we must at least explore the possibility that some form of deliberate cultural mediation was at work.

This debate over imports versus local products has tended to get side-tracked by issues of manufacturing technique and material provenance, neither of which really contribute much insight. As we shall see, there is a contemporary Levantine tradition of gypsum vessels that were carved products, in contrast to travertine vessels that were drilled. However, rather than this being a useful signature of contrasting Levantine and Egyptian techniques, it is mainly an indication of the two stones' relative hardness (see Chapter 4). Likewise, while the majority of travertine objects in the eastern Mediterranean were probably made of stone from Egyptian quarries, we would be unwise to attribute all travertine vessels to Egyptian production on the basis of their material alone. Other travertine sources do exist in the eastern Mediterranean area (though none of these were definitely used during this period) and the raw stone was traded widely to the extent that we find raw lumps of both local and imported Egyptian travertine being used in contemporary Cretan vessel workshops (see below).[3]

**Stone Vessel Use at Tel el-Ajjul** In summary, travertine vessels from the Levant are often slightly different from their counterparts in Egypt, but we struggle to pin down the source of this variation. In fact, the most likely explanation is that Tell el-Ajjul was a manufacturing centre for these Egypto-Levantine products. This site may have been the

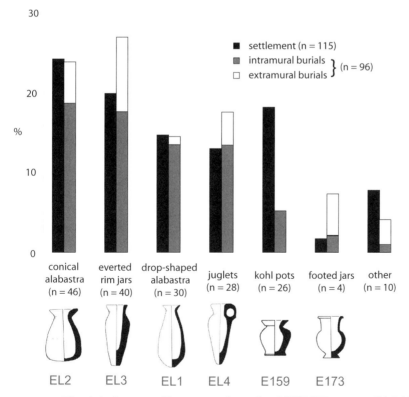

FIGURE 6.4. The relative frequency of five stone vessel types from MBIIB–LBI contexts at Tel el-Ajjul (Sparks 2007 and personal documentation).

FIGURE 6.5. Loop-handled jugs from (a) Tel el-Ajjul (traver-tine, after Petrie 1934: pl. xl.109), (b) Megiddo (traver-tine, Courtesy of the Oriental Institute of the University of Chicago.), (c) el Lisht (ceramic, Courtesy of the Metropoli-tan Museum of Art, 22.1.95), and (d) Knossos (travertine, Warren 1969: P623).

capital of the kingdom of Sharuhen attested in written sources and an important urban centre (Kempinski 1974). It lay at one end of the coastal trade route linking the north-east Egyptian and southern Levantine worlds and is relatively close to suggested sources of travertine in the Sinai and Negev (Lucas and Harris 1962: 59–60). Two drill cores provide direct evidence for on-site working and Ajjul is already heavily implicated in the production of other culturally synthetic products such as gold jewellery (Petrie 1934: 12, pl. xli.129, 131). Nearly 300 Egyptian-style stone vessels come from Ajjul, the vast majority of which are made of travertine (Petrie 1931, 1932, 1933, 1934; MacKay and Murray 1952; Sparks 2007: section 6.1.3). This assemblage provides some of the clearest known examples of Levantine stylistic influences: for example, elongated everted rim jars, juglets, and oval-plan conical alabastra are all common (Figure 6.4). A rare stone shape that picks out the complex range of cultural influences at play is a fragmentary loop-handled jug [Figure 6.5(a)]. There are only two other known travertine parallels and the shape copies a southern Levantine pottery form. The most famous and interculturally resonant ceramic example is one painted with possible Cretan-style dolphins and found at el-Lisht in Egypt but whose fabric is petrographically compatible with the Ajjul area (McGovern et al. 1994; Bourriau 1996).

The combination of settlement exposures and excavated cemeteries at Ajjul affords a privileged view of a complicated response to Egyptian cultural practices and the following discussion considers the evidence of the stone vessels in more detail. Most travertine shapes are found in similar proportions in both settlement and cemetery contexts at Ajjul, but there is a significant difference in the relative importance of kohl pots (Figure 6.4). This shape was extremely popular in MK-SIP Egypt but very rare in the Levant and so far unknown in the Aegean (see also Sparks 2007: section 3.1.17). Kohl was both an Egyptian method of personal beautification and a preventative treatment for Nilotic eye diseases. It may not have been so medically useful further north in the Mediterranean, but the contrast between Ajjul's settlement and tombs indicates either that a temporarily resident and nonburying Egyptian

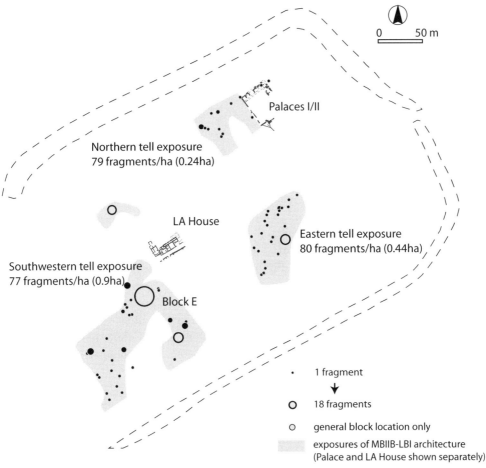

FIGURE 6.6. Settlement exposures at Tell el-Ajjul and the distribution of Egyptian-style stone vessels from nonfunerary contexts. (Sources: Petrie 1931, 1932, 1933, 1934; MacKay and Murray 1952; Sparks 2007, with minor modifications.)

population existed at the site or that this distinctly foreign mode of cosmetic enhancement was experimented with in everyday life but avoided in more normative mortuary practice.

Further insights are possible if we consider the spatial distribution of finds from the tell and tombs separately. Looking first at the tell, 130 vessels from nonfunerary contexts have sufficient provenance for us to plot them either by room or block (Figure 6.6). The three main exposures of MB-LBI settlement produce very similar densities (ca. 80 fragments per hectare) and a slight concentration around Block E is interesting because this area produced the two known drill cores, suggesting that workshop activity occurred nearby. The otherwise uniform artefact density also stands in sharp contrast with the two most impressive buildings at Ajjul (Palaces I/II and the LA House) whose domestic contexts have produced few, if any, Egyptian-style stone vessels. This is all the more intriguing for two reasons: firstly, because at other Levantine Bronze Age sites stone vessels from nonfunerary contexts are usually found in temples and palaces and are otherwise rare. Secondly, it contrasts with the distribution of another foreign vessel class, Cypriot ceramics, which were found in large numbers within the palace (Robertson 1999: 317).

The exact status of the 'palace' and the LA House are not clear, but consecutively through MBIIB-LBI, they may have been the residences of the local ruler. Their lack of stone vessels suggests either very different patterns of postdestruction looting than the rest of the settlement or, more likely, the especially charged nature of Egyptianising material for upper elite or royal groups living right on the edge of the Egyptian state. Daily use of travertine oil containers by less important groups in Ajjul society was probably a sign of cultural sophistication (e.g. knowledge of Egyptian-style cosmetics), but for those at the very top of the social and political hierarchy it may also have implied cultural subservience and so was avoided.

Turning to burial contexts, over 600 MBII-LBI tombs are known from a range of cemetery areas at Ajjul (Gonen 1992; Robertson 1999).[4] Both intramural and extramural burial was practised, with the latter becoming increasingly popular by LBI and dominant thereafter. Stone vessels are found in one or two burials that can be dated to late MBIIA, but become more common from MBIIB onwards. Figure 6.7 shows the distribution of MBIIB-LBI graves with and without stone vessels from the site and while certain burial grounds were slightly wealthier than others (in agreement with the impression given by other grave goods), the spatial distribution is still relatively even. About 10% of the burying community were interred with at least one of these travertine oil containers and no contemporary tomb has more than four (Petrie 1934: pl. lix), suggesting that on their own, these artefacts were not meant to map out more than a very flat social hierarchy.[5]

## Levantine Vessels

**Jordan Valley Gypsum Vessels**    While this interesting range of Egyptianising customs was being practiced on the coast, inland at least three Jordan valley centres were making their own stone vessels in MBIIB-LBIA: Jericho, Beth Shan, and Pella [Figure 6.3(b)]. Their products imitate some travertine shapes but are all made from local gypsum (L12-15; Sparks 2001: fig. 6.9). Gypsum is soft enough to be carved and these vessels could therefore be made more quickly but with greater risk of breakage than travertine, and some discarded blanks from Beth Shan are a good signature of the increased waste often involved (Ben-Dor 1945: pl. xxiii.5-7). These vessels also display other idiosyncrasies typical of softstone carving, including chisel and compass marks, sharper carinations, incised patterns, relief decoration, and less undercutting.

The site of Jericho provides the largest assemblage from the Jordan valley and its earliest gypsum vessel comes from a late MBIIA/early MBIIB context (Sparks 2001: 99). Thereafter, gypsum vessels occur in similar frequencies throughout MBIIB-LBIA and are one of a limited suite of artefact types, including toggle pins and scarabs, that seem to have been prestige markers. The practice of communal burial makes it difficult to know who was using these items for funerary display, but two pieces of proxy evidence suggest that it was a fairly small section of the community. Firstly, one gypsum or travertine vessel is found for every four to five bodies in the Jericho graves, and the actual proportion will have been lower than this because some people were buried with more than one vessel (Yasur-Landau 1992;

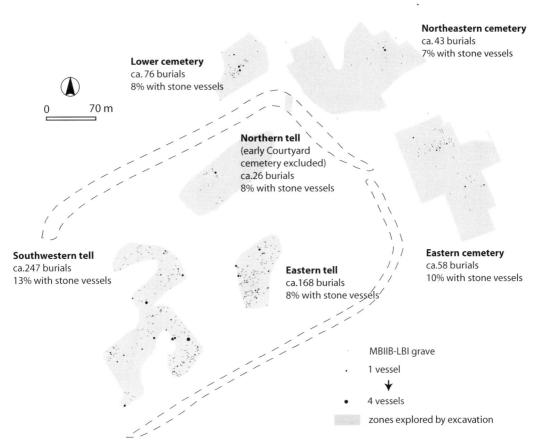

**Northeastern cemetery**
ca. 43 burials
7% with stone vessels

**Lower cemetery**
ca. 76 burials
8% with stone vessels

0        70 m

**Northern tell**
(early Courtyard
cemetery excluded)
ca. 26 burials
8% with stone vessels

**Southwestern tell**
ca. 247 burials
13% with stone vessels

**Eastern tell**
ca. 168 burials
8% with stone vessels

**Eastern cemetery**
ca. 58 burials
10% with stone vessels

MBIIB-LBI grave

·        1 vessel

↓

•        4 vessels

        zones explored by excavation

FIGURE 6.7. The distribution of MBIIB-LBI burials and accompanying stone vessels at Tel el-Ajjul. Graves and stone vessel finds are plotted wherever detailed locations were published (ca. 85% of the cases), but the accompanying calculations use all the known data for each area. The primarily EBA cemetery to the north of the site is not shown. (Sources: Petrie 1931, 1932, 1933, 1934; MacKay and Murray 1952; Robertson 1999; Gonen 1992; Sparks 2007, with minor modifications.)

Rosen 1995). Secondly, stone vessels make up one fifth of the overall assemblage of cosmetic containers from the site and, again, this is likely to be an overestimate because ivory and wood examples were not as well preserved as pottery and stone (Sparks 2007: fig. 80). So while we cannot be precise, the inland group deploying stone vessels at Jericho is not much larger than the coastal one observed at Tell el-Ajjul.

Tomb H6 offers a good impression of how gypsum vessels were being used in mortuary practice at Jericho (Figure 6.8). Here, a bowl with lugs in the form of rams' heads was found at the waist of the central adult skeleton, in contrast to gypsum juglets and alabastra that were placed next to the body in baskets with other articles for bodily grooming. In only two other surviving burials are vessels placed on the abdomen and both cases these are also gypsum rams head bowls. The practice does not seem to be age or gender specific but associated with important individuals who were also singled out for special treatment in other ways (e.g. placed on mud-brick platforms, Kenyon 1965: 576).

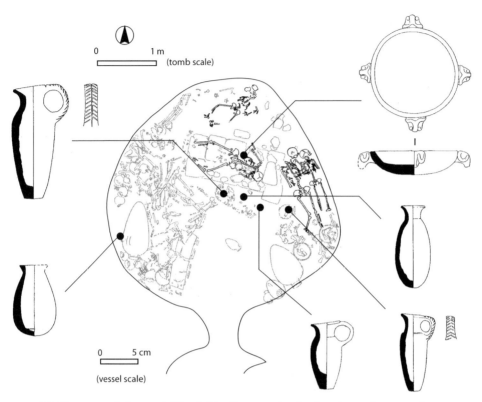

FIGURE 6.8. Gypsum vessels from tomb H6 at Jericho (Kenyon 1960: after figs. 187.5–7, 8–9, 11, 193).

While gypsum vessels sometimes copied Egypto-Levantine travertine shapes, they also expressed both regional and workshop-specific, local identities within the Jordan valley. For example, despite using the same material, adopting similar manufacturing techniques and being inspired by the same general range of forms, the Jericho, Pella, and, to a lesser extent, the Beth Shan communities specialised in certain shapes or added their own particular stylistic features. Jericho appears to have made most of the ram's head bowls and defined the neck area of its alabastra and juglets particularly carefully. Pella decorated its baggy alabastra with line-and-dot motifs, while Beth Shan made juglets, globular flasks, and everted rim jars but with fewer identifiably local details (L14–17, Sparks 2007: section 1.2.1). Some of these minor variations reflect chronological differences or stylistic drift in the products of different workshops, but more recognizable features branded them as coming from specific producers and in the case of the flasks, perhaps also evoked subtle differences in the oil recipes they contained.

**Other Levantine Workshops**  So far we have explored two probable Levantine stone vessel industries. The first may have been based at Tel el-Ajjul and produced vessels in a synthetic Egypto-Levantine style, while the other was an inland tradition which drew some inspiration from travertine vessels, but made its own products in local gypsum. Shallow bowls and mortars in much coarser stones are also found in the Levant at this time and were probably used for grinding cereals and other domestic activities (Buchholz 1963; Sparks 2007: section 3.3). In addition to these, we can pick out at least two more traditions, both from the northern Levant, but each with very different distributions and social contexts: (1) a group of vessels in chlorite-rich stones from Ugarit and (2) some very high-status vessels with upper elite associations as far afield as Anatolia and Mesopotamia.

The first of these comprises a series of fairly simple chloritite vessels at Ugarit (Eliot 1991; Sparks 2007: section 3.2.3). This was a localised, small-scale, and highly opportunistic industry that is most visible in the MBA soundings, but probably continues into the LBA as well. Chloritite is common among the small finds at Ugarit and found in the Baer-Bassit ophiolitic formations occurring in the hinterland north of the site. It is unclear whether copper ores are present or missing from the ophiolite sequence in this area (De Jesus 1980: 395, map 19; Chanut 2000), but there is a probable link between the use of chloritite for vessels and the metal industry, which Chapter 8 discusses in greater detail. For example, chloritite is admirably heat resistant and was also made into casting moulds and tuyère nozzles at Ugarit (Eliot 1991: 49–53). Several LBA Ugaritan letters mention a dark rock called *algabašu*, which is probably chloritite/steatite (or possibly basalt) and was sold for the cheap price of a shekel of silver (ca. 9. 4 g) for a talent of stone (ca. 28.2 kg, i.e. a 1:3,000 exchange rate by weight; Chanut 2000: 170–3).

The second tradition is wholly unlike the previous one in coming from a restricted range of upper elite contexts and using a variety of exotic stones. These vessels are either one-off virtuoso products or fit into a wide style zone which covers much of the northern Levant, northern Mesopotamia, and Anatolia and manifests itself in multiple luxury media such as metal, stone, and ivory. This regional pattern of exclusive upper elite manufacture and

FIGURE 6.9. Globular flasks in a northern Levantine and/or northern Mesopotamian tradition: (a) in sardonyx from the Tomb of the Princess, Ebla (Matthiae et al. 1995: no. 466), (b) in bronze from a votive jar deposit in the temple of Baalat Gebal, Byblos (Montet 1928: pl. lxxi.608), (c) in bronze from a Kültepe burial (Özgüç 1986: pl. 126.3), (d) a full-size statue of a goddess with globular flask from Zimri-Lim's palace at Mari. The statue was constructed so that water could flow into the back and out of the top of the vessel (Kohlmeyer et al. 1982: no. 82).

consumption continues into the LBA and differs from Egypt or Crete where these types of extravagant product fit into a much broader-based stone vessel tradition.

Our two best windows on this phenomenon come from royal tombs at Ebla and from palace and workshop contexts at Alalakh (Tel Atchana). At Ebla, flasks in sardonyx and white limestone were found in the Tomb of the Princess and have exact parallels in bronze from Ebla, Kültepe, and Byblos (Figure 6.9; Matthiae 1979: 161, fig. 62a–b; Matthiae et al. 1995: 502). The Akkadian name for this vessel shape is probably *hegallu* and it is typically held by gods in Mesopotamian art, with water (and sometimes fish) flowing out of it, suggesting an association with abundance or fertility (Black and Green 1992: 184; also Huot 1989). Its most obvious appearance in the contemporary northern Levant is with a large statue, probably of Ishtar-Innana, from the royal antechamber of the palace at Mari, which was perforated so that liquid can be made to flow from the back of the statue out through the vessel's mouth [Figure 6.9(d)]. The burial of the Ebla stone flask with a woman of royal status and the presence of a bronze flask in the temple precinct of Baalat Gebal at Byblos reinforces this local high-status female association.[6]

Alalakh provides further evidence of the same stylistically synthetic and multimedia vessel tradition. Several carinated bowls from the palace probably copy the shape of metal versions such as a silver bowl from Byblos (L8–9; Montet 1928: pl. lxxi). They are made of a serpentinite which appears different from the most common varieties used in Egypt (though a more precise analysis is clearly necessary), but finds parallels in several other vessels from the Levant and Crete (Figure 6.10). Alalakh also provides the clearest example of contemporary workshop activity. In one room of the town, four unfinished obsidian vessels, a granite jar, and many raw obsidian lumps were found alongside a male skeleton (Woolley 1955a: 109, 293–4; Sparks 2001: 94–7). The obsidian probably came from Anatolian sources to

a

b

c

d

0    5 cm

FIGURE 6.10. Possible Levantine stone vessels made of distinctively veined serpentinites from (a) Alalakh (BM 1939.6-13.111), (b) Tel el-Ajjul (UCL E.XIII.84/3), (c) central Crete (AM AE 384; note this is not a common Cretan style or material), (d) Megiddo (Loud 1948: pl. 231.2).

FIGURE 6.11. Semicircular Levantine boxes: (a) obsidian from Alalakh (Woolley 1955a: pl. lxxxiii) (b) obsidian from Tel el-Ajjul (Petrie 1934: pl. xxiii); (c) serpentinite from Tel el-Farah (UCL EVI.33/2); (d) serpentinite from Tel el-Farah (UCL EVII.182/9); (e) chloritite from Ugarit (Caubet 1991: pl. xii.11); (f) ivory with gold nails from Byblos (Montet 1928: pl. cvi).

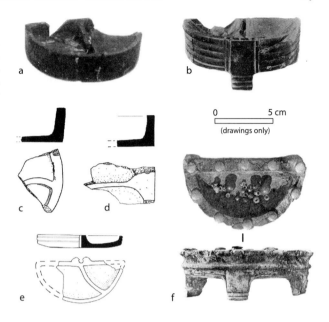

the north and the vessels reference a variety of cultural forms, including a tripod mortar of the type used throughout the northeastern Mediterranean and a semicircular cosmetic box with multimedia parallels from the Levant and Egypt (Figure 6.11; Vandier d'Abbadie 1972: no.131).

## Anatolia

Given these interregional links connecting the northern Levant with its terrestrial and maritime neighbours, it is unsurprising that some Anatolian stone vessels document a similar pattern of both small-scale softstone carving and hypercrafted, upper-elite products. As usual, some Anatolian finds remain frustratingly isolated from any broader geographical context (e.g. Mellaart and Murray 1995: 121–44, 245, 259 fig. O26–9), but two sites on the central plateau, Acemhöyük and Kültepe, give us a startling glimpse at both of these two types of industry and how they fitted into the complex intercultural relations of the Old Assyrian Colony period.

Acemhöyük and Kültepe were both part of a large trading system responsible for the exchange of metals and a few manufactured items, linking northern Mesopotamian cities such as Assur with various central Anatolia kingdoms (see Chapter 3). Carved softstone and highly crafted hardstone vessels are found at these sites in association with both local inhabitants and resident Assyrians. At Kültepe, two small zoomorphic boxes and a raptor-headed cup are carved out of chloritite and/or steatite (A5-6), but local pottery versions of both shapes are far more common. The boxes appear to be cosmetic containers and were found in female burials (Özgüç 1959: 109, though it is unclear on what basis the graves were sexed), while the cup was found in the merchant quarter (karum), next to an archive identifying the place as the home of a rich Assyrian trader (Özgüç 1986: pl. 133.4, 136.2).

FIGURE 6.12. Stone vessels from the Acemhöyük palace (after Özten 1988: pls. 3, 5, 14, 20a, 21b): (a) an obsidian bowl, (b) a radiolarite bowl and stand, (c) and (d) quartz crystal flasks, (e) an obsidian flask repaired with gold thread, (f) a decorated obsidian vessel, (g) a fluted obsidian flask with animal head handles, and (h) a plan of the palace with stone vessel findspots shown in light grey.

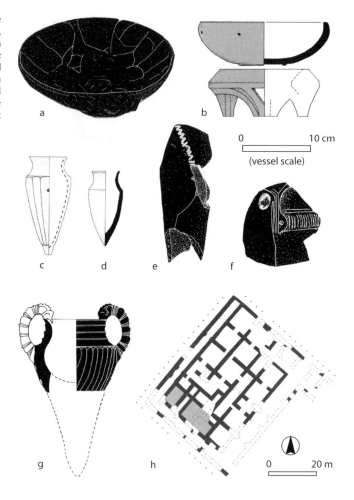

Later Hittite texts refer to similar animal-shaped drinking cups (*BIBRU*) made of metal, wood, and a bluish-coloured stone like this one and by then the tradition is clearly an older one linked to Assyrian trade, because the texts use Akkadian/Sumerian logograms to refer to these objects (Carruba 1967). Such cups emphasise the importance of drinking as a means of social interaction, not least between locals and Assyrians.

Kültepe has also produced fragments of obsidian and quartz crystal that were part of elaborate two-handled drinking flasks (Özgüç 1986: 50–1, pls. 67.2–4, 95.7, 96.3). These are also more commonly found in pottery, but the fluted decoration suggests metal prototypes for both. A whole group of such vessels have also been found at Acemhöyük, along with obsidian and radiolarite bowls (Figure 6.12). They appear to have been stored exclusively for the ruling family with other luxury goods in two rooms of the palace, while only vessels in softer, coarser, or otherwise less impressive stones are found in the adjacent town (Özten 1988). Substantial obsidian sources and possible quartz crystal exist on the central plateau (Rova 1987; Özten 1988: 394; Cauvin 1998), but written and archaeological evidence highlights both the extremely high value accorded these materials and the rich cosmology that might be woven around them. For example, one of the obsidian flasks from the Acemhöyük palace had been broken in antiquity and very carefully repaired with gold thread (Figure 6.12(e)]. Similarly, a letter from Mari reveals the king, Yamsh-Addu, offering his father what must have been an unusually large block of quartz crystal in exchange for 3,000 sheep and 60 male slaves (Michel 1992). The Mari texts also make it clear that ruling groups stockpiled their own supply of precious stones and at Kültepe, two tons of obsidian were stored in heaped blocks within the palace complex (Özgüç 1986: pl. 97.1–6).

Textual, contextual, and stylistic evidence link this rare and elaborate stone vessels with precious metal counterparts, but they were probably far more resistant to commodification than either metal or decorated pottery (e.g. in terms of convertible metal weight or by extension, commonly agreed exchange value). As such they were a luxurious and economically uncompromised medium in which to make more ideological statements and their storage together at Acemhöyük suggests an important role in local palace ritual. As we have seen, obsidian and quartz crystal were considered dark and light-coloured versions of the same substance in OK Egypt and were used as ritual opposites in opening-of-the-mouth sets. The same lexical link between these stones exists in Akkadian, the langauge of the Assyrian traders (*surru*-stone, André-Salvini 1995: 79), and it is extremely likely that similar binary associations either already existed in Anatolia or were adopted by local dynasts. Therefore, the vessel group at Acemhöyük and similar objects at Kültepe were probably employed in periodic palace ceremonies as metonyms, reminding participants of a more complex local cosmology and the ruler's place in it.

## The Aegean

### Protopalatial Crete

Most of the stone vessels from the second millennium Aegean were either made in Crete or are closely linked to Cretan ways of living. As we saw in Chapter 5, the stone vessel tradition began back in EMIIA with a very specific group of chloritite vessels, but by the later third millennium, a more diverse range of shapes and materials was employed, driven in part by the demands of contemporary mortuary practices. With a few notable exceptions, Prepalatial communities were small scale and their use of such objects indicate only relatively simple social distinctions rather than any dramatic level of elite competition that we might associate with processes of state formation. In contrast, the end of the third millennium and beginning of the second millennium marks a far more critical phase of sociopolitical transformation, during which we see larger urban centres, palaces, and writing all emerge within a couple of centuries. As these processes unfolded, three related developments in stone vessel use can be observed: (1) funerary display with these items became increasingly uniform (MMIA) and declined thereafter (MMIB-II); (2) stone vessels became a more pervasive feature of the Cretan household, associated with the daily storage, processing, and consumption of food and drink; and (3) an elite ritual dimension to stone vessel use emerged.

The previous chapter discussed many aspects of EMIII-MMI stone vessel use that are hard to define with any greater chronological precision and hence remain very relevant here. For example, bird's nest bowls from the Mesara are just one of several similar thick-walled bowl forms that develop out of a more diverse EMIIB-III tradition and become common in MMI tombs (C3,6,8,12). Many of these vessels were now undercut using a shaped grinder and the decision to bother with this labour-intensive process is a good indication of increased scales of production and some minute distinctions in relative value engendered by slightly more competitive production and consumption strategies. Thick-walled bowls were used in settlements as well, but a range of other types are much more closely linked to domestic activities. For example, there are now large numbers of cups for drinking, jugs for pouring, bucket-jars for storing liquids such as oil, lamps for lighting and open bowls for fine grinding, mixing, and serving. As this suite of domestic stone equipment emerged, serpentinite became the dominant material, used for ca. 70–90% of the repertoire. As with travertine in Egypt, it was well-suited to be a baseline material, above and below which other stones could be ordered. For example, it is just hard enough to encourage the use of a drill to make it into a vessel but not so intractable that it required outrageous amounts of time or scarce resources such as emery to work: a medium-sized bowl could probably be made in 2-3 person-days (Chapter 4). Serpentinite outcrops are found in widespread green schist facies throughout Crete (Becker 1976) but are not so commonplace that they could be accessed by everyone. The great variation in the appearance and texture of serpentinites encourages value distinctions and helps to mark out the products of particular workshops.

One of the most impressive aspects of this Protopalatial industry is its presence at all levels of the settlement hierarchy, from palaces and large towns to rural villages and farms (see below). Indeed, over the next five centuries, these objects reach a greater slice of the population than almost any other stone vessel industry in the Bronze Age eastern Mediterranean. The following sections begin by exploring stone vessel manufacture and use within palatial centres, then consider less ostentatious contexts and finally address the limited evidence for Cretan imports and exports.

At Knossos, the Protopalatial deposits have been heavily disturbed, but still offer an impression of the shapes and materials in use around the first palace. Plain and lugged open bowls and bucket jars are common, along with straight-sided jars and carinated cups. About 80% of the finished vessels are serpentinite, but several more colourful breccias, travertines, and banded limestones/marbles are also present. The latter stones often come from the same geological formations on Crete and worked lumps are relatively common at Knossos. These should be seen as a family of fancier materials whose higher value was deliberately emphasised at this time and imitated in MMIB-II decorated ceramics (Warren 1969: 173).[7]

As these material distinctions are established, a few palatial centres also stand out in making more elaborate and idiosyncratic shapes. For example, the three best known centres all experiment with larger, tablelike forms probably associated with feasting and ritual offering, but each produces distinctive regional types: a series of low, flat tables are visible at Knossos, lamps and libation tables at Phaistos, and footed dishes at Malia.[8]

Another highly recognisable stone shape made at late Protopalatial to early Neopalatial Knossos is the bridge-spouted jar. There are two main groups of these: the first was made out of chloritite decorated with horizontal grooves and circular white shell inlays [C13A, Figure 6.13(a)] and both the material and style suggest a fairly short and intensive episode of manufacture sometime in MMII-IIIA. The other was plain but made of a highly distinctive

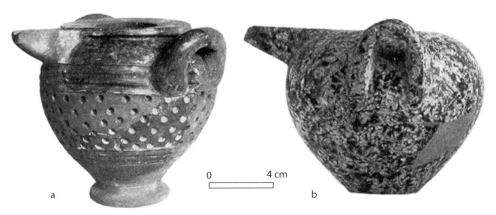

FIGURE 6.13. Knossian bridge-spouted jars: (a) chloritite with horizontal grooves and white inlay (Warren 1969: P187) and (b) gabbro from Mycenae (Xenaki-Sakellariou 1985: pl. 141).

variety of gabbro with massed white phenocrysts [C13B, Figure 6.13(b)]. This particular stone is deployed in small amounts at various Protopalatial sites and is the hardest material used for vessels at this time (ca. Mohs 5). It crafting into vessels is symptomatic of an increased concern with technical virtuosity, and these jars involved a relatively complex manufacturing sequence in which the vessel was repositioned several times and drilled with both tubular bits and several shaped grinders.[9] One of these gabbro jars was given a short Linear A inscription which on other stone vessel forms probably suggests the batch leader of a larger group deployed together (Tsountas and Manatt 1897: figs. 138–9; Schoep 1994). The bridge-spouted jar is a highly recognisable Cretan shape and was made even more so by such inscriptions, inlay decoration, and/or the use of distinctive stones, so we should probably think of these Knossian products as being deliberately emblematic of palace workshop production and hence well-suited to be high-level gifts or instruments of patronage.

A slightly different crafting and consumption environment is visible in Quartier Mu at Malia where the late Protopalatial levels of the town are particularly well preserved (Figure 6.14). Here, over 240 vessels are spread relatively evenly across two large buildings, with no clear differences in the distribution of specific shapes or materials. There is no unequivocal evidence for a stone vessel workshop in the excavated area, but isolated drill cores and slotted cobbles suggest one existed nearby. Evidence for other crafts, however, is extremely well-preserved in this quarter, where there seem to have been a cluster of multipurpose workshops whose proximity to each other engendered experimentation in multimedia techniques and styles. For example, pottery skeuomorphs of stone, basketry, and metal are all present (Détournay 1981: Figs. 6 and 7; also Poursat and Knappett 2005). These buildings may have had some administrative functions but were not part of the palace and it is unclear the degree to which we should see them as attached specialists working for an elite household, to a particular palatial agenda, or an entirely autonomous craft quarter.

One particularly intriguing context at Mu comprises a series of connected rooms in block V, Building B (Figures 6.14(a) and (b); Détournay 1981; Poursat 1981). Figurines, sealstones, faience, and a ceremonial dagger came from the upper floor, while a serpentinite jug, libation

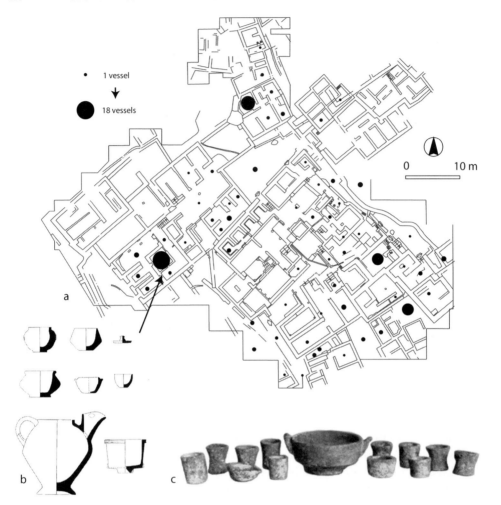

FIGURE 6.14. Quartier Mu and possible ritual vessel groups from two late Protopalatial contexts: (a) the distribution of stone vessels at Quartier Mu, (b) vessels from block V, Building B (after Détournay 1981: figs. 13, 16, 24, 34, 55, 59, 65, 82), (c) a set of jars and a bowl from Phaistos Room LI (Warren 1969: P254).

table, and a group of stone bowls came from the the basement rooms beneath. This was probably a shrine area and this collection of shapes may have been used to make solid and liquid dedications. We find a more carefully articulated ritual group in Room LI of the palace at Phaistos. Here, there was a miniature set of 11 cylindrical jars and a two-handled bowl on which small amounts of gold leaf were still adhering [Figure 6.14(c); Warren 1969: 45]. This practice of gilding, the use of fancier shapes and materials and the evidence for ritual vessel groups becomes far more obvious in the Neopalatial period, but these examples from Malia and Phaistos suggest ways in which palatial centres were distinguishing themselves even at this earlier stage.[10]

Beyond the palatial centres, experimentation and elaboration is much rarer. Even tiny sites such as Cheiromandres have produced the odd MM-style stone vessel (Tzedakis et al.

1990: 55, fig. 10 right), but perhaps our best view of the rural consumption of these objects is at Myrtos Pyrgos, an MM village on the south coast of Crete (Hankey 1972). The vast majority of the Protopalatial vessels from here were discarded in secondary dumps on the side of the hill, but even so, the limited range of shapes and failure to use many exotic stones suggests that those who displayed their status by such items at Myrtos did so in a relatively stable local arena, interrupted only infrequently by the more elaborate regimes of the palaces. Two visually distinguishable varieties of serpentinite predominate, probably from a limited number of local outcrops. There are a few more elaborate flaring jars and carinated cups, but also an unusually large number of plain or lugged bowls and the general impression is one of a highly conservative, local repertoire. A few stone imports do make it to Myrtos, some of which suggest connections with Malia to the north and and thereby dovetail with some of the pottery evidence from the site (Knappett 1999a), but these contacts are not strongly advertised in terms of decoration or shape variation.[11]

**Protopalatial Trade Beyond Crete**   A few Protopalatial stone vessels have been found in the Argolid and at island sites beyond Crete (Warren 1969: 184–5; also Benzi 1984), but they appear to have been a relatively minor feature of the first Cretan palaces' engagement with a wider Aegean world. MMI-II bowl fragments from Kastri on Kythera highlight the unusually precocious Cretan affiliations of this island and provide a wider context for early possible imports of *rosso antico* from the Mani to Crete, but the site stands out as an unusual case of an early Minoanising centre beyond Crete, rather than being typical of a wider pattern.[12]

While there is also good Protopalatial evidence in other media for Cretan interaction with Egypt and the wider eastern Mediterranean (e.g. Warren 2005), there is not a single imported Egyptian vessel that we can definitely attribute to trade during this period (Bevan 2003: 65–6). This absence is no doubt real in part, reflecting, for example, an apparent Cretan dislike for the most popular contemporary Egyptian shape, the kohl pot. However, a variety of problems obscure our understanding of this possible pattern. First, there is a tendency to interpret EMII-MMI/II imports and imitations as a late Prepalatial phenomenon associated with state formation rather than one which begins or continues in its aftermath. The imitations do appear to suit FIP-earlier 12th Dynasty styles better than later 12th–13th Dynasty ones, but the shapes are not always sufficiently diagnostic to be sure. Secondly, the unusual destruction and preservation history of Knossos leaves an information gap where we might expect to find many of these imports. Finally, there are a few MK ridge-necked alabastra in later contexts and we cannot be certain when they first arrived in Crete.

## The Neopalatial Period

The construction of new palatial buildings after MMIIB-IIIA provides a convenient if potentially misleading narrative break for studying Cretan material culture. In fact, many material developments make more sense either as amplifying trends first visible in the late Protopalatial or as more sudden phenomena occurring in later LMI. Much of the difficulty is avoided by distinguishing the fast stylistic turnover, hot-house experimentation, and highly competitive arena of the Neopalatial palace workshops from the far more stable and enduring regimes of stone vessel use in other contexts. The following section begins by looking at the overall patterns of stone vessel shapes, materials, and distribution before stratifying these by different levels of the social and settlement hierarchy. Discussion then moves to consider first the elaborate ritual vessels and foreign materials deployed in the palaces at this time and then the peculiarly strong links between Egypt and Crete. There is also substantial evidence for Neopalatial stone vessels in the wider Aegean area and we consider the variety of ways in which such Cretan practices were adopted, imposed, or resisted beyond Crete. The chapter ends by considering possible chronological distinctions within the Neopalatial period and what they might imply.

A few Protopalatial shapes disappear after MMII (C1A,6-8), and the style of the rest was altered quite heavily, but many of the domestic functions these vessels fulfilled continued. Assemblages are dominated by open bowls and high-shouldered bowls, decorated cylindrical jars, large bucket-jars, and lamps (C3i,5,9,14,24,25,31–2,40). Some of the bowls and jars were used in tombs, probably as containers for solid offerings, but the Neopalatial funerary record is so limited that we cannot really explore these roles in detail. The vast majority of vessels are still made in serpentinite but tend to be larger and heavier items than in the Protopalatial, suggesting that the scale of production had increased slightly, and that some value was assigned to relative vessel size. Curation of these objects for several generations was probably commonplace and so it is often difficult to pick out diachronic trends, but there are signs of steadily increasing elaboration throughout the period. For example, lamp and libation shapes were very simple in MMI-II, are slightly more elaborate in MMIII-LMIA, and occur in a much wider range of shapes, sizes, and decoration in LMIB-IIIA (C24). Some lamps, pithoi, and bucket jars were also now sufficiently unwieldy that they must have been relatively static household furniture.

Beyond this basic group of serpentinite vessels, the use of more elaborate shapes and materials is heavily concentrated in the larger towns, and particularly the palaces (see below). A relatively large proportion of the Cretan population seems to have lived in these urban centres and the overall distribution of Neopalatial vessels across the island is heavily dominated by the bigger towns and a few cult sites.[13] Levels of investigation and publication vary from region to region, but Neopalatial stone vessels appear to have been most popular in the northern and eastern parts of the island.

In the Prepalatial, tombs such as Voros and Archanes suggest a group of no more than a fifth of the interred population accompanied by such objects, but we struggle to discern whether they expressed social distinctions between genders, in families, and/or within the wider social hierarchy. By MMI-II, they appear to be reaching most of the materially visible levels of society. This widespread use continues in the Neopalatial and ordinary serpentinite vessels are preserved in the rubbish and collapse of a sufficiently diverse range of farms and townhouses to suggest that many people used such objects at least occasionally. However, alongside this popularity of stone vessels in general, we also see greater numbers and more varied shapes and materials as we get closer to the top rung of townhouses and the more important centres in the regional settlement hierarchy.

The Mirabello region has been particularly intensively investigated and offers an opportunity to look at these patterns in much more detail. Even farmsteads in this area such as

Chalinomouri and Chrysokamino have produced stone vessels and/or slotted cobbles that might be associated with their manufacture (Carter 2004: 90, pl. 21; Floyd 2000: fig. 78). Likewise, a scatter of such objects are also found across many buildings in the nearby towns of Mochlos, Pseira, and Gournia (Boyd Hawes et al. 1908: 22–3; Soles et al. 2004; Floyd 1998). A typical townhouse such as Ff at Gournia preserves a couple of thick-walled serpentinite bowls in one all-purpose ground floor workroom and a jar from the upper floor. There is also workshop evidence from a wide range of locales, including drill cores, slotted cobbles, and unfinished vessels (e.g. Carter 2004). Each of the three main towns seems to have drawn on one or two different local serpentinite outcrops but also used fancier local travertines, breccias, and purple or banded grey limestones for a few more elaborate shapes such as drinking cups, rhyta, and lamps. These more impressive vessels tend to cluster in the larger buildings, suggesting they helped to mark out the lifestyles of the most important local families.

The stone vessel repertoires from the Mirabello area offer a rich picture of production and consumption permeating almost every visible level of local life. However, they are equally notable for what they are lacking. As we shall see in the next section, one of the most dramatic changes in the Neopalatial period is the appearance of a range of extremely elaborate stone vessel products associated with a limited number of palatial elite activities. However, there is only one possible vessel of foreign stone from this region (a rhyton from the Gournia central building that might be made of *rosso antico*, Warren 1969: P468) no imported Egyptian vessels, no examples inscribed with Linear A and none with relief carving. The Mirabello region was certainly connected to wider Aegean trading regimes, as the quantities of bronze objects from Mochlos and possible Knossian features at Pseira for example attest (e.g. Betancourt 2004), but it is interesting that it almost never acquires the kinds of upper elite stone vessels found at other sites such as Archanes, Knossos, Myrtos Pyrgos, Palaikastro, and Zakros.

**Ritual Groups and Imported Materials**  One of the most striking aspects of the Neopalatial stone vessel industry is the crafting of a few extremely elaborate shapes in exotic materials that were important components of highly choreographed rituals performed at the palaces and a few key shrines. The artisans that produced them appear to have worked in or adjacent to the palaces (e.g. Warren 1969: 159–60; Platon 1971: 210–22) and near a range of other craft specialists. These people were the most technically innovative (and probably the most hot-housed) in a spectrum of stone-workers on Crete that probably also included people working in provincial town workshops and perhaps migrant masons. A key difference between the earlier and later palaces is that even the most elaborate Protopalatial stone vessels were products in local materials that most artisans could probably make given the time. By the later Protopalatial there are indications, such as the ostentatious use of gabbro and gilding, that some workshops at the palace centres were becoming more exclusive in their ambitions. In the Neopalatial, this process escalates dramatically and, while we see experimentation with more complex shapes in a wide range of social contexts, the highest levels of elaboration occur in exotic materials unattainable to all but a few and produced by artisans working in immediate proximity to the palace itself, using advanced tools and multimedia techniques. As we shall see, this restriction of the knowledge and equipment necessary to create the most elaborate vessels was just one of several similar ways in which the upper elite defined a more exclusive arena for prestige display.

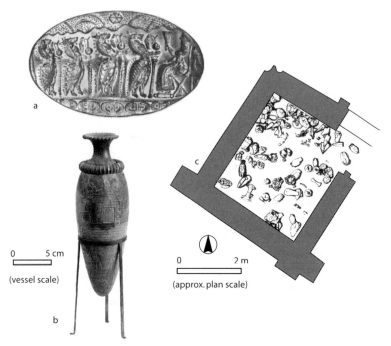

FIGURE 6.15. Neopalatial ritual vessels: (a) reversed image from a gold ring showing the use of Neopalatial-style jugs and a footed goblet in a supernatural scene (found in a later context at Tiryns; l.5.6 cm; Krzyszkowska 2005: fig. 457a), (b) a chloritite rhyton with relief decoration of a probable peak sanctuary (fragments of gold foil adhering to the neck and rim; ht. 31.1 cm without neck, courtesy of Herakleion Museum), (c) stone vessels in storage with other ritual paraphernalia in room XXV of the Zakros palace (after Platon 1971: 132).

The most common Neopalatial ritual shapes were rhyta, footed goblets, ewers, and jugs (C15,19,22,34,39), a suite of objects that could interact in elaborate ways over the pouring, straining, sprinkling, and drinking of liquids. A vivid iconography featuring these vessels occurs on gold rings, seals, wall paintings, and decorated chloritite vessels where they are depicted being carried in procession or used by probable goddess figures and fantastical beasts [Figure 6.15(a); also Baurain and Darcque 1983]. Though the cosmological details behind these scenes elude us, it seems clear from the shapes, decoration, and occasional inscription that such vessels were material mediators between a privileged upper elite group and the divine world. Exotic stones were just one medium through which such links were forged, and most of the stone ritual shapes have counterparts of comparable value in precious metal. Decorated chloritite vessels are a good example of the entanglement of these media at the top of the object value scale [Figure 6.15(b)]. Such vessels are probably an LMI phenomenon, appear to have been covered in gold foil, and may have been a cheaper and more robust way of making what looked like a solid gold vessel with *repoussé* decoration.[14] This ideologically charged, multimedia environment has some similarities with the way hypercrafted stone vessels were also used in the northern Levant and Anatolia, only here these efforts potentially carried even greater impact because they stood out so obviously from a wider stone vessel tradition.

Another way in which the broad class of elaborate ritual vessels was marked out was through the systematic use of exotic imported materials (Plate 2). The Protopalatial emphasis on a few higher value local stones continues in many towns, and a few of the polychrome marbles and limestones used for ritual vessels may also have a Cretan provenance, but the palace centres clearly embrace the added aura of foreignness. In a sense, this is a reflection of the Neopalatial ruling elite's increased engagement with the wider Aegean and eastern Mediterranean, and raw stone was imported from a host of different sources (Plate 2). There are examples of one-off use (e.g. Evans 1935: 933, fig. 905), but some stones such as travertine, quartz crystal, and Anatolian obsidian were acquired more often, whether as gifts from royal courts or through trading ventures, while others such as obsidian from Giali and *lapis lacedaemonius* or *rosso antico* from the Peloponnese may well have been collected directly (Waterhouse and Hope Simpson 1961: 119–21; Warren 1969: 126; Warren 1992; Betancourt 1997).[15]

These artefacts also have a very circumscribed distribution, linked explicitly to the palaces or a few other upper elite contexts where we might expect their political influence. We also find them stored together in groups of ritual objects and presumably only brought out periodically. The best example of this kind of storage area is the treasury in the west wing of the palace at Zakros [Figure 6.15(c)], though other candidates exist and there are early parallels in the ritual groups from Malia and Phaistos described above.[16] However, not all vessels with ritual associations were stored this way. Libation tables, for example, are found in large numbers outside of the palace centres, at peak, spring, and cave sanctuaries, suggesting their closer association with cult activity in the natural world (Metaxa-Muhly 1981). Likewise, bull's head rhyta and relief-decorated vessels made of chloritite and steatite are not usually found in storage contexts but (where not obviously in secondary dumps) on their own, fallen from upper floors and/or broken into particularly small pieces, suggesting a very different social life which perhaps involved display in more visible locations within the palace complex.[17] In this regard, they were part of a wider scheme of iconography-in-relief produced in real metal versions with repoussé decoration, but also at a more personal and repeatable scale on seals and gold finger rings, and at a larger, more permanent one on frescoes. These artistic products offered such visually rich symbols that they made for effective palatial propaganda, especially given the possible political connotations of bull imagery (Hallager and Hallager 1995). The links are strongest with Knossos in terms of number of finds and subject matter and these may all be part of a concerted artistic program by this one centre. Indeed, for most of these finds, the combination of restricted contexts of use and ostentatious upper elite branding (with a possible exception being the libation tables) fits neatly with similar patterns visible in palace architecture (e.g. narrow and labyrinthine entrances, defined processional routes, particular fresco imagery such as bull scenes) and on peak sanctuaries (e.g. the reduced overall numbers and increased wealth of finds), suggesting these were probably all ways in which certain palaces were redefining the chief ideological components of Cretan society on their own circumscribed terms.

**Egyptian-Style Vessels**   In addition to raw stone imports, the palatial centres also acquired impressive numbers of finished stone vessels from abroad. A handful of these are Anatolian,

Cypriot, Levantine, and/or Mesopotamian, but the vast majority are Egyptian.[18] These are just a highly recognisable and archaeologically robust indicator of a much larger range of Egyptian objects and influences arriving during the Neopalatial period (Warren 1989, 1995). Egyptian imports make up as much as 10% of the stone vessel assemblages from wealthier contexts around the Knossos palace,[19] but are exceedingly rare elsewhere. Part of the value of these artefacts no doubt resided in their ability to suggest familiarity with a geographically distant, culturally sophisticated, and diplomatically influential place. However, a closer look at them reveals a fascinating combination of fetishistic and iconoclastic responses to Egyptian material culture which involved three separate but overlapping behaviours: (1) the use of contemporary Egyptian oil containers, (2) an apparent reverence for and imitation of Egyptian antiques, and (3) the conversion of either of the first two into unequivocally Cretan shapes.

The first of these, brought significant numbers of SIP-early 18th Dynasty Egypt travertine vessels to Crete, and particularly to Knossos. Many of the fragments come from secondary deposits, but the LMI-II period stands out and is probably contemporary with the appearance of Cretan people and objects on the walls of several NK tombs, suggesting a period of heightened contact (Wachsmann 1987; Phillips 2001).[20] The Cretan upper elite were being highly selective in acquiring these items (also Phillips 2006): a far greater proportion are baggy alabastra (over 40%) than in contemporary Egypt or the Levant, and because this shape was never associated with a specific Egyptian oil, its popularity probably reflects the marketing of a specific container-style and/or Cretan preferences for how an Egyptian oil flask should look.[21] In contrast, there seems to have been no interest in kohl pots, one of the most popular shapes in Egypt.

The second phenomenon worth exploring is the consumption of Egyptian antiques and/or antiquities. A range of later PD to early OK vessels are found throughout the MB-LB Aegean but again cluster at Neopalatial Knossos. These were only a selection of the Egyptian vessels from this period and express a clear preference for hardstone bowls and jars.[22] There is limited independent evidence for links with late OK-early MK Egypt during the EMIIB-MMI period of Cretan state formation, and some of the PD-OK vessels may have arrived as early as the last centuries of the third millennium (Chapter 5; Bevan 2004). However, many of the vessels are of even earlier PD-ED style and are so widespread across the MB-LB Mediterranean that some recirculation through SIP-early NK tomb-robbing seems likely (Pomerance 1980; Phillips 1992).[23] Particularly evocative, if hard to pin down entirely, are hints that such reuse of older Egyptian material was sometimes officially sanctioned: for example, Amenhotep III seems to have been one of the rulers who built or added to a shrine (or perceived tomb) of Osiris at Abydos, thereby cutting through the tomb of Djer and providing one possible explanation for why a late Predynastic palette was found at Amarna, reinscribed for Amenhotep III and Ty (Petrie 1901b: 8, 16–7, 37; Aldred 1975: 52; Phillips 1992: 162).[24]

These old vessels were also imitated in hard Cretan stones such as gabbro, Giali obsidian, and quartz crystal, even to the extent of copying the drilled depression in the interior base of the heart-shaped bowls (C30A-C; Bevan 2003: 66–9), which implies strongly that Cretan consumers were interested in the original antiquity for their own sake rather than merely as an attractive, hard raw material. In contrast, no contemporary Egyptian vessels

such as alabastra are imitated in this way (though they are occasionally copied in ceramic: e.g. Boyd Hawes et al. 1908: pl. vii.15). In addition, while, on the one hand, the original imported antiquities have a relatively tight distribution within Crete (primarily the Knossos and Zakros palaces) but are also found in other upper elite contexts throughout the Aegean and eastern Mediterranean, on the other, the imitations have a more extensive distribution on Crete but have been found neither within the palaces themselves nor anywhere beyond the island (also Phillips 2006: 298). For Crete therefore, this suggests (1) that the supply of real antiques was insufficient or too socially restricted to satisfy the demands of those wished to display such goods and (2) that possession of these objects held a specific social cachet, more relevant to the claims of a broad elite group on Crete than elsewhere and distinct from the use of contemporary Egyptian vessels and raw travertine. Views have tended to support either the early arrival and curation of antiquities in Prepalatial Crete or their later Neopalatial acquisition as a result of tomb-robbing, but a third possibility involves a combination of the two: later imported antiquities and their imitations were used by the Cretan elite, in the knowledge or memory of a few real heirlooms from earlier Egypt–Crete links, to construct fictitious ancestral lineages or otherwise lay claim to status and legitimacy, during a period when such links were again important social and political capital.

The third interesting behaviour with regard to imported Egyptian stone vessels in Crete involves deliberate acts of conversion made in palatial workshops (Warren 1996; Bevan 2003: 69; Phillips in press: Chapter 4, Appendix B). Both contemporary alabastra and antique heart-shaped bowls were cut down, perforated, and/or given new attachments to transform them into a few highly recognisable Cretan shapes such as bridge-spouted jars, jugs with flaring handles, or rhyta. Whole examples, fragmentary handles, and spout attachments make it clear that these conversions were relatively common, especially in elite contexts around the Knossos palace. This reinvention of Egyptian objects as Cretan ones involved a complex web of associations, the best example being the technical processes and prestige logics linking the acquisition and conversion of PD-OK heart-shaped bowls, with the use of Cretan gabbro to imitate Egyptian porphyritic rocks and the manufacture of Cretan bridge-spouted jars (Figure 6.16).

**Cretan-Style Stone Vessels Beyond Crete**   During the Neopalatial period, Cretan cultural influence is far more prevalent beyond the island and in the wider eastern Mediterranean, perhaps evoked most obviously by the presence of Aegean-style wall-paintings at a number of Levantine and Egyptian sites (e.g. Niemeier and Niemeier 2000). Within the Aegean, Cretan-style stone vessels are found in relatively large numbers beyond the island itself, but by contrast, such objects are extremely rare in the wider eastern Mediterreanean and even the limited number of Neopalatial exports that have been identified so far is heavily exaggerated. Perhaps the best candidate is a blossom bowl from Byblos (see below), but we lack clear information about when exactly it arrived at the site. One, or possibly two, lamps with shell decoration from Ugarit and another more elaborate example from Alalakh are of definite Aegean style, but not only do these come from later LBA contexts, but their shape and decoration fall into a broad LMI-IIIA range, suggesting they may be post-Neopalatial products (see Chapter 7). A tall basalt lamp from a MBIIC temple context at Alalakh may conceivably have been influenced by Neopalatial columnar lamps, especially in view of the

FIGURE 6.16. Antiques, imitations, and conversions: (a) a Dynasty 0–1 heart-shaped bowl of andesite porphyry, with roll handles removed and a Cretan spout added. The latter is cut with inlay holes to imitate the Egyptian stone's phenocrysts (Karetsou 2000: no. 208), (b) a Cretan gabbro imitation of a heart-shaped bowl in the process of being converted to a bridge-spouted jar, by drilling a spout-role in the shoulder (Karetsou 2000: no. 214), (c) a late Protopalatial or early Neopalatial bridge-spouted jar in gabbro (Xenaki-Sakellariou 1985: pl. 141), (d) a Dynasty 3–4 heart-shaped bowl (Warren 1969: P592), (e) a Cretan gabbro imitation of a heart-shaped bowl (Warren 1969: P398).

contemporary evidence for Cretan-style wall-paintings at the site, but neither the material (basalt) nor the stylistic detail (e.g. no wick-cuttings) of this example identifies it unequivocally as a Cretan product and local manufacture remains a distinct possibility (Woolley 1955a: pl. LXXVIIIq). Some limestone fragments from the Amman airport site were initially identified as Cretan rhyta but are almost certainly parts of Egyptian-style jars and their separate stands (Hankey 1974: S44–S49). A variety of other small fragments have been identified as Cretan, but none of these are at all convincing (Sparks 2007: section 1.1, figs. 1.2–6). In particular, the chloritite pieces from Ugarit clearly fit into a local MB–LB tradition in this stone (see above and Chapter 7). Finally, a fragment of a large jar from Lachish has some inscribed signs that are similar to Linear A syllabograms, but this piece seems to be a local product from the very end of the Bronze Age rather than anything to do with the Cretan Neopalatial (Finkelberg et al. 1996).

Within the Aegean itself, Cretan-style stone vessels offer some important insights into patterns of social and political influence for a variety of reasons. First, they seem to occupy a middle range of value between metal and pottery vessels and, used in combination with this other evidence, may well expose a much wider social spectrum of Cretan cultural

emulation. Second, there is no other major stone vessel industry in the Aegean during the MB-LBA and, therefore, unlike some pottery styles, Cretan stone vessels could not be 'grafted' onto native material culture in any easy way. The techniques necessary for drilling stone vessels could be learned but, like wheel-throwing pottery, were a highly skilled endeavour that usually involved a period of apprenticeship (see Chapter 4). Evidence of on-site manufacture therefore should indicate individuals with a profoundly Cretan cultural and technical background who either were locally resident or travelled around with their stone-working skills.

Cretan-style stone vessels are found at a range of sites in the Aegean islands, as well as from sites along the southwestern Anatolian and Peloponnesian coasts. Most of these objects are open or thick-walled bowls, jars, and lamps, but many are from mixed LB1-3 deposits or limited exposures and thus remain difficult to put into context.[25] The following sections look in more detail, first at two of the closer islands to Crete, Thera, and Kythera, that both show very strong Cretan links but whose archaeological records offer very different perspectives on local stone vessel use. As an antidote to the extreme Minoanisation of these two sites, discussion then moves to consider briefly Phylakopi on Melos and Agia Irini on Kea where adoption of Cretan cultural traits was far more selective. Finally, we consider the Shaft Graves at Mycenae and the quite different behaviour they reveal.

The unique volcanic preservation conditions at Akrotiri often produce stone vessels apparently still resting in the places where they were being stored or used rather than in secondary deposits. However, the destruction context is far from pristine and says a lot about what the inhabitants who left after the initial earthquake chose to remove (e.g. most of the metal objects whose value was more convertible) and what they chose to leave. Drill cores, raw stone lumps, and unfinished pieces indicate local production, of both polished Cretan-style stone vessels and mortars and lamps in local volcanic stone (Warren 1978, 1979; Michailidou 1990: fig. 18). Most of the former group are the same basic domestic suite of thick-walled bowls, lamps, and bucket jars as on Crete (Warren 1979; Devetzi 2000). These are found in both impressively frescoed rooms and more mundane activity spaces throughout the site and are depicted in at least two wall paintings (e.g. Doumas 1992: no. 64). The excavated quarter is relatively wealthy and much closer to the prosperous houses known at Knossos or Palaikastro than to the smaller structures common in many other Cretan settlements.

Despite this general prosperity, Building Δ stands out from the rest for its large numbers of stone vessels, elaborate shapes, exotic materials, and probable imports. Most of these were gathered together in room 16 and it is unclear whether this was a temporary collection made after the earthquake or the type of deliberate ritual store found on Crete, especially given the ostrich-egg rhyta, bronze vessels, and triton shells found in the same deposit. There are many ritual shapes gathered together here, but perhaps the most interesting feature is the number of white-coloured vessels, made mainly of marble and limestone, but also Egyptian travertine and gypsum. For example, three of the four footed goblets are made of white marble and the high value of these objects is obvious from the fact that (a) one was repaired with silver rivets (Warren 1979: pl. 20a–b) and (b) there are several white-painted, pottery imitations from the same context (Marinatos 1974: pl. 61b). This stone was worked on site and these were probably local products (Devetzi 2000: 138 no. 83). Such elaborate vessels indicate a close familiarity with Cretan ritual practice, but their unusual emphasis on white stone also expresses a distinct island identity.

Akrotiri represents such an unusual preservation scenario that it is often hard to make it mesh with the archaeological record from the rest of the Aegean. A good point of comparison is another highly Minoanised harbour site at Kastri on Kythera. This island sustained a large population and an almost entirely Cretan material culture during the Neopalatial (Coldstream and Huxley 1972; Sakellarakis 1996; Banou 2002; Broodbank 2004), and excavation of the settlement, its tombs, and adjacent peak santuary, along with an intensive survey of Kythera's interior, provide a dramatically different set of archaeological perspectives than Akrotiri. Almost all of the vessels from known contexts on the island come from Kastri or its nearby peak sanctuary, though the large numbers of Minoanised farmsteads in the interior may also have had access to these items.[26]

The Kastri assemblage reveals a curious mixture of glut and scarcity. On the one hand, a relatively large number of vessels (ca. 20) came from a small sounding into two or three houses of the Neopalatial settlement. In addition, thick-walled bowls, jars, lamps, and even a couple of eastern Mediterranean antiquities come from the large number of multichambered tombs along the Kastri ridge or are chance finds from this area. Raw lumps of *rosso antico* and *lapis lacedaemonius* as well as at least one finished vessel in the latter stone have been found on the peak sanctuary (Sakellarakis 1996), and similar raw material has been identified during field survey of the settlement (KIP site 60). The dedication of raw stone on the peak sanctuary, along with the number of bronze figurines, suggests strongly that Kastri was the trading node through which Peloponnesian raw materials flowed to Crete. However, while there was almost certainly some local production,[27] the apparent lack of serpentinite outcrops on Kythera meant that this stone had to come from an off-island source (Crete or the Peloponnese). The relative scarcity of this material at Kastri is suggested, first, by the much higher level of repair (ca. 10%) found here than elsewhere and, second, by the frequent imitation of stone vessels in local dark-slipped pottery (Bevan et al. 2002: 77–9, figs. 13.3, 13.8, 17.145, 20.246–8).[28] The latter is a practice that is also found nearby at Agios Stephanos (Rutter 1979) but is rare elsewhere. As such, there seems to have been a division between the wealthiest groups at the site who benefitted from long distance trading networks of which Kythera was a part, and ordinary inhabitants who actively aspired to but sometimes struggled to get access to this particular component of Cretan material culture.

In contrast to Akrotiri and Kastri, Agia Irini on Kea shows more limited signs of stone vessel use and Phylakopi on Melos even less (Bosanquet and Welch 1904: 196–7, figs. 165–9; Renfrew and Cherry 1985: 342–7, fig. 8.11). Both sites produce similar numbers of vessel fragments from settlement contexts as Kastri but across much larger horizontal exposures. Instead of the array of wealthy Minoanised buildings at Akrotiri, we can point to only one or two households with such evidence at either of these sites (Whitelaw 2005: 53–60). Only in House A at Agia Irini do we find definite evidence for local manufacture, and a wider array of materials and exotic shapes (Cummer and Schofield 1984).

On the mainland, nine stone vessels are found amongst the unprecedented wealth interred in the Mycenae Shaft Graves and these contexts offer a completely different picture to those visible on the Aegean islands (Figure 6.17; Karo 1930–1933; Mylonas 1973). Vessels occur

FIGURE 6.17. Stone vessels from the Shaft Graves at Mycenae: (a) an ECII white marble pyxis from Grave N (Mylonas 1973: pl. 154d), (b) a duck-shaped bowl of quartz crystal from Grave O (Mylonas 1973: pl. 183), (c) a white gypsum ladle in the form of two cupped hands from Grave III (Karo 1930–1933: pl. cxxxviii.164), (d) a travertine jug from Grave IV (Karo 1930–1933: 1930–1933: pl. cxl.592), (e) a white marble/limestone footed goblet from Grave IV (Karo 1930–1933: pl. cxxxviii.600), (f) a white marble/limestone bowl of quatrefoil shape with three elaborate flaring handles from Grave IV (Karo 1930–1933: pl. cxxxviii.389), (g) a white marble/limestone footed goblet from Grave V (Karo 1930–1933: pl. cxxxviii.854), (h) an Egyptian travertine alabastron converted into a gilded, bridge-spouted jar from Grave V (spout missing; Karo 1930–1933: pl. cxxxvii.829), (i) a white stone bowl from Grave III (Karo 1930–1933: pl. clxvi.165).

in both Grave Circles and with the burials of both men and women. What is really strange about this assemblage, however, is the fact that it includes none of the common Cretan thick-walled bowls, lamps, or jars but rather a far more eclectic collection of vessels, many of which do not fit into the known Neopalatial crafting tradition in a straightforward manner. For example, the earliest dated grave with a stone vessel is tomb N, but it contained an antiquity, an Early Cycladic II marble spool pyxis, which was at least five centuries old by the time it was buried here, alongside an older adult male (or possibly with the previous male interment) and an array of pottery and weaponry [Figure 6.17(a)]. The only other stone vessel from Grave Circle B is a duck-shaped quartz crystal bowl from burial O which was found in association with an adult female, and alongside an array of pottery, quartz crystal, amber, and ivory jewellery [Figure 6.17(b)]. Cretan artisans were technically capable of producing this duck bowl and certainly worked quartz crystal at this stage, but it is nonetheless a strange piece that may be foreign, given that there are no obvious matches for it in the Aegean and broad stylistic parallels in MB-LBA vessels and weights from Egypt, the Levant, and Mesopotamia (e.g. E189-90).

Overall, the wealth buried in the later Grave Circle A is more substantial than Circle B and there are also more stone vessels, but the same pattern of unusual shapes persists. For example, while the flaring handles of the extremely elaborate, white marble quatrefoil bowl from Grave IV [Figure 6.17(f)] have clear parallels in Cretan ritual vessels, the best match for style and material comes from another unplundered shaft grave on Skopelos (NM 9074, Platon 1949: 551). In fact, perhaps the most important feature about the vessels in both Grave Circles is that they are all made of white-coloured stones (travertine, marble, limestone, gypsum, and quartz crystal). Such a preference is much closer to the tastes seen at Akrotiri [especially the two white marble/limestone footed goblets; Figures 6.17(e) and (g)] than those suggested by the overall suite of stone vessels from Crete and reinforces the general impression of strong Cycladic links in the Shaft Graves (e.g. Graziadio 1991: 417–8; Panagiotakopoulou et al. 1997). To summarise, there is very little about these stone vessels that implies slavish imitation of Cretan practice (and see below with respect to the unusual interment of a Cretan ladle). Instead, they combine well with the evidence from other Shaft Grave objects (e.g. weapons, drinking vessels, grave stelae, jewellery) to suggest the eclectic, aggressively independent, and occasionally antiquarian tastes of a warrior elite, whose amassed wealth probably came from raiding and trading within a wider Aegean, Balkan, and Mediterranean sphere.

Furthermore, what these case studies from Akrotiri, Kastri, and Mycenae show is that the impact of Cretan palatial society beyond Crete cannot really be accessed by a checklist or bald description of object types but requires us to grapple more closely with how Cretan culture encouraged patterns of both emulation and resistance (Broodbank 2004: 48). The final sections of this chapter therefore explore two vessel shapes that evoke such deeper meaning in interesting ways but have quite different stories to tell about the reception of Cretan culture abroad. The first study briefly considers blossom bowls, one of the most common and emblematic of Cretan vessel shapes, with a wide geographic distribution and a continuing popularity after the Neopalatial period. The second considers some shallow pouring vessels called ladles, with a shorter history and a much tighter spatial distribution, whose dissemination was probably part of a wider political agenda.

Over 150 blossom bowls are known from archaeological contexts and these are widely distributed in both settlements and tombs throughout Crete, the Aegean and as far afield as Byblos and Troy (Warren 1969: 14–7). These vessels are most popular during the Neopalatial, but first appear slightly earlier and remain in use over a period of some four to five centuries. They are usually made of serpentinite and carved with a decoration of six broad petals, each with a midrib (Figure 6.18).[29] Ceramic copies are rare on Crete but are also found at sites on or beyond the edges of Cretan palatial influence (Bevan et al. 2002: 79, no. 38).

Such a consistent design suggests that a specific flower was being shown and the best candidate by far is the saffron crocus, which is native to Crete and has six broad petals (pale

FIGURE 6.18. (a) *Crocus sativus* (photo courtesy of Gernot Katzer) and (b) a blossom bowl (Warren 1979: pl. 18).

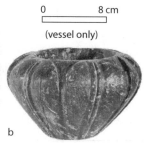

0 ⸻ 8 cm
(vessel only)

pink to purple) with a double midrib of more intense colour in their centre. This flower is commonly depicted in Cretan wall-paintings and is a pictographic sign in Cretan writing (Morgan 1988: 29–32; Negbi and Negbi 2002). Saffron has a vast array of possibly uses, as a colorant and flavouring for food, a textile dye, a medicine, and/or an ingredient for perfume (e.g. Martlew 2004: 125). The most dramatic perspective on its importance is offered by the Saffron-Gatherer fresco at Akrotiri which depicts the harvesting of this plant as a significant ritual event and possibly part of female maturation rites (Rehak 2004). The appearance of crocus images on female dresses and jewellery reinforces this association with women and it would not be surprising if blossom bowls were gendered possessions too, though at this stage we lack sufficient evidence (e.g. preferential association with female skeletons in graves) to really know. In any case, if blossom bowls make relatively emblematic Cretan vessels by virtue of their distinctive shape alone, a possible link to the smell, flavour, and colour of saffron as well as the formal dress, jewellery, perfume, and diet of women would mean that they were even more central to the construction of Cretan identity.

In contrast to the extensive temporal and contextual distribution of the blossom bowls, ladles are restricted to cult contexts at a limited number of Neopalatial sites [Figure 6.19(f)]. The majority come from the peak sanctuary on Mt. Juktas or from nearby Knossos and Archanes. Beyond Crete, they are found at definite and probable peak sanctuaries on Kythera and Kea, respectively, in a possible ritual cave on Kalymnos and in two tombs at Mycenae.[30] Three further pieces of evidence implicate these vessels in ritual offerings linking towns and, in particular, their neighbouring peak sanctuaries. Ladles are one of a very few Neopalatial shapes that were made as votive miniatures or sometimes inscribed in Linear A. If we assume Linear B phonetic values, these inscribed examples suggest short dedicatory formulae to one or more divine females (Schoep 1994; Sakellarakis and Olivier 1994) and may have been batch leaders in large-scale dedications of the vessels or their contents. A decorated chloritite rhyton fragment also shows them being carried by two males in what may be a procession [Figure 6.19(d)].

So a variety of evidence suggests that ladles were used in a specific ceremony by groups of worshippers (it would be interesting to know if this was also a male-gendered activity), perhaps processing from town to peak. They were held out in front of the participants, cupped in the palm of both hands, and their use is closely linked to Juktas and its neighbouring settlements. When we see ladles elsewhere we must therefore wonder whether they are not promoting a particular Knossian ideology. It is probably no accident that ladles are otherwise found only in cult contexts at a few major Cretan settlements or abroad at peak or cave sanctuaries close to nodal sites for access routes to important raw materials such as metal and prestige stone. Only at Mycenae, far beyond the Cretan cultural orbit, is their meaning altered more dramatically by their use in funerary deposits.

As usual, such meaning is difficult to clarify further, though the ladles' trilobal shape offers some clues. These vessels have been described as heart-shaped in the past (Warren 1969: 48) and the form is otherwise used only for Cretan amulets suspended on the chest (Effinger 1996: 47–8). Their stylised outline does resemble the atria/aorta region of the heart and a more lifelike version may be depicted on the interior base of a ladle from Palaikastro [Figure 6.19(b)]. The Egyptian hieroglyphic sign for the heart (*ib*) was also trilobal and it was likewise a stylistic template for stone jars, scarabs, and amulets [Figure 6.19(e)]. This cardiac

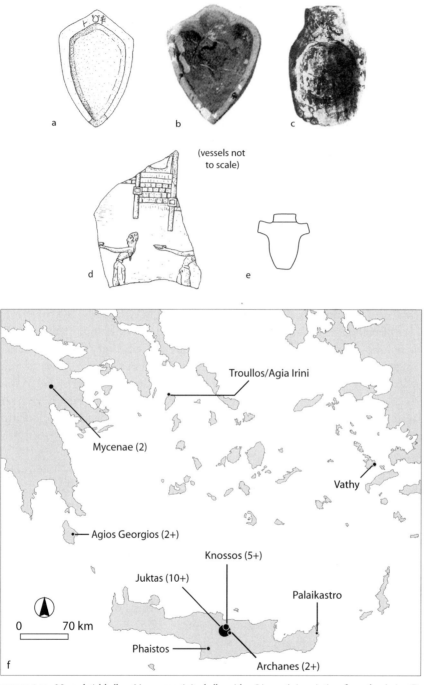

FIGURE 6.19. Neopalatial ladles: (a) a serpentinite ladle with a Linear A inscription from the Agios Georgios peak sanctuary on Kythera (after Sakellarakis and Olivier 1994: fig. 4), (b) a serpentinite ladle with a carved design in its interior base from Palaikastro (Bosanquet and Dawkins 1908: pl. xxx.c2), (c) a gypsum ladle in the shape of cupped hands from Mycenae (Karo 1930–1933: pl. clxvi), (d) a chloritite rhyton fragment decorated with a procession of males holding ladles, (e) the Egyptian hieroglyph for the heart, (f) the distribution of ladles throughout the Aegean.

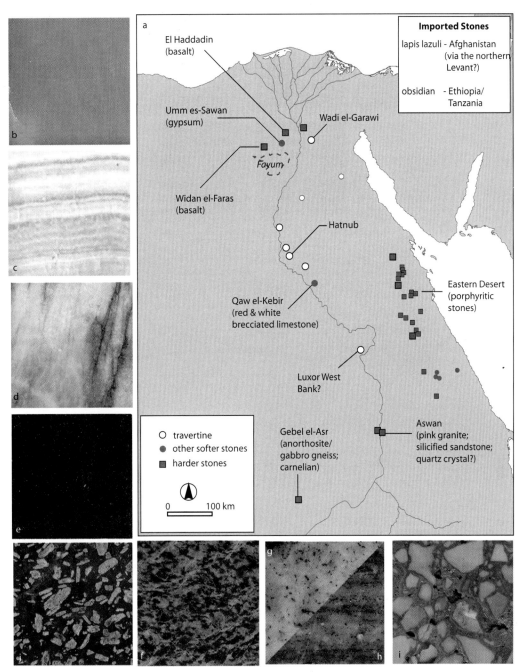

PLATE I. A resource landscape for Egyptian stone vessels: (a) a map of some important stone quarries in Egypt, (b) travertine from Hatnub, (c) banded travertine (unknown source), (d) gypsum from Umm es-Sawan, (e) basalt from Widan el-Faras, (f) andesite porphyry from Wadi Umm Towat, (g) serpentinite from Wadi Umm Esh, (h) red and white breccia from Qaw el-Kebir, (h–i) anorthosite and gabbro gneiss from near Gebel el-Asr, N.B. A smaller symbol is used on the map for a quarry with no evidence for PD-NK activity. The andesite porphyry and serpentinite slab sections come from quarries where no Pharaonic activity is known and are shown as examples of the general material only. Sources: Aston et al. 2000; Klemm and Klemm 1993; Mallory-Greenough et al. 1999; slab section courtesy of www.geology.utoledo.edu.

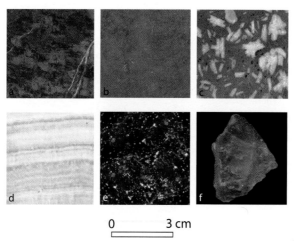

0 ——— 3 cm

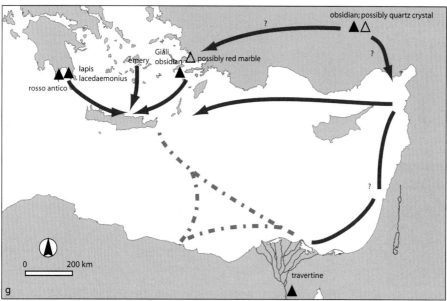

PLATE 2. Neopalatial use of imported materials: (a) serpentinite (not obviously imported but the most common material for vessels, this example from Kroton-Miamou), (b) *rosso antico*, (c) *lapis lacedaemonius*, (d) Egyptian travertine, (e) Giali obsidian, (f) quartz crystal, (g) distribution map.

connection might indicate that Cretan ladles held token offerings of blood, especially given the evidence for animal and possible human sacrifice at Knossos (Warren 1984; Sakellarakis and Sapouna-Sakellaraki 1997: 269–311). Their use in a blood-letting ritual linking palace and peak also provides a plausible reason for why they might make such ideologically charged objects beyond the Knossos area.

To summarise, Cretan vessels go through a number of distinct changes from MMI to LMI. The range of shapes and materials found in the EMII-MMI tombs gradually disappears, replaced by a greater emphasis on one or two shapes. At the same time, other forms emerge that were more suitable for household use and serpentinite becomes the dominant baseline material. At certain Protopalatial centres, experimentation is visible in lamps, libation tables, bridge-spouted jars, and harder materials and/or surface treatments such as gilding. There are occasional instances of vessels stored together, apparently for ritual use, prefiguring a practice that becomes more visible later on. Outside these centres, stone vessels seem to be relatively common items in use throughout most levels of the settlement hierarchy. Fancier versions tend to be marked out by their use of several specific, more colourful Cretan stones. In the Neopalatial period, serpentinite remains the dominant material and vessels continue to be found in a wide range of social contexts. Beyond Crete, these stone vessels were caught up in the varied ways in which other Aegean communities responded to the spread of Cretan palatial influence. At the upper elite end of the spectrum, production and consumption practices became increasingly elaborate and both ritual shapes and Egyptian imports appeared to be linked strongly to the specific political and social discourse associated with the palaces. Looking ahead, it is therefore not very surprising that such objects were a tradition that did not long outlive them.

# 7
## The Later Second Millennium

🔲🔲🔲🔲🔲🔲

*Chapters 5 and 6 explored the social roles that stone vessels played over the third and earlier* second millennia, a time in which different regions of the eastern Mediterranean were brought into increasingly frequent contact. Such entanglement became even more intense in the later LBA as privileged groups consumed a range of international exotica that were contextualised differently in different communities but nevertheless possessed a widespread currency as status markers. Two major developments at either end of the geographic zone under consideration here provide particularly relevant background to the following discussion. First, the campaigns of Thutmosis III brought large areas of the Levant under Egyptian control or influence. Ideologically, these conquests were part of a long tradition of smiting the 'amu, but this time their political and cultural impact was far more profound. The material result was a more permanent Egyptian political interest in the Levantine kingdoms, a flood of war booty into Egypt and, more gradually, an increased demand for and sensitivity to a range of foreign material culture. The second, roughly contemporary development was the destruction of most of the Cretan palaces and with them the disappearance of many of the chief components of Neopalatial material culture. At Knossos, an important palatial centre persisted after these destructions and continued to produce stone vessels, challenging us to makes sense of evidence for both continuity and disjuncture. Indeed, whatever the exact political events, most of the Aegean falls into the cultural orbit of the Mycenaean palace centres, producing a much altered local socioeconomic world, with important repercussions for its interaction with the rest of the eastern Mediterranean.

Stone vessels were affected in different ways by such developments. We see the emergence of a number of smaller traditions that did not exist before and the major established Cretan and Egyptian industries are much altered. This chapter follows the same anticlockwise geographic sequence as the last two, beginning with the Egyptian stone vessel industry which, as in the earlier second millennium, boasts the widest eastern Mediterranean impact. Occasionally, the discussion of vessel traditions continues into the earliest part of the Iron Age wherever the end of the second millennium BC seems too arbitrary an interpretative division.

## Egypt

### The Mid-18th Dynasty
While there is no sharp break to overall stone vessel styles in the reign of Thutmosis III, significant changes gradually set in around this time. Cylindrical jars and alabastra (E34, 185–7) continue, but both are rarer. The kohl tube appears and, by the Amarna period,

replaces the kohl pot as the preferred receptacle for eye makeup (E168–9, 163–6). Two other new forms are the lentoid flask and *tazza* (E170-1, 194). The former has stylistic links with a broad range of small pottery flasks from the contemporary eastern Mediterranean (e.g. Furumark 1941: types 187, 190; Amiran 1969: 166–7, pl. 51) and reflects not only the great popularity of foreign oils and their containers,[1] but also the increased prominence of pottery storage jars and flasks that drew on Levantine prototypes but were a locally made feature of an Egyptian wine industry that seems to have been expanding since the beginning of the 18th Dynasty (Bourriau 2004). The thin-walled, ribbed *tazza* shape is probably inspired by metal versions and footed dishes of this kind seem to have been used to hold more solid cosmetics. Several contemporary tomb paintings show these and other vessels being offered to both men and women, for bodily grooming (balsam cones for the head and oils for the lower arms and neck) and as part of the proper expression of hospitality before and during banquets. The same scenes also emphasise the important part played by freshly cut lotus blossoms and neck garlands during such occasions, and explains why these two items became the two most common designs painted or incised on stone vessels (Davies 1973: pls. lxiii-vii; Freed 1981: figs. 2, 30, 76).

Such depictions suggest a key role for stone and metal vessels in private and public grooming, as well as more broadly with eating and drinking. One important development in upper elite production and consumption is the increased levels of functional distinction, separating (1) smaller cosmetic containers, (2) larger jars for storing oil mixtures, and (3) possible wine sets. Contemporary royal burials at Thebes reveal at least the first two of these: smaller pots are gilded and made in a variety of exotic materials such as anhydrite, haematite, hornblende diorite, serpentinite, and travertine (e.g. Winlock 1948: pl. xxx; Lilyquist 2003: 139–40, 203–19). In contrast, there are also groups of larger travertine and serpentinite jars. They each contained ca. 2L of ointment mixture presumably used for basic bodily cleansing, and each royal wife may have been furnished with a group of about 10 (Winlock 1948; Lilyquist 2003: especially 139–40).

Many of these developments reflect deliberate changes by royal workshops or even direct royal intervention. For example, there are significant numbers of inscribed vessels of Hatshepsut and Thutmosis III, and several texts claim such items were made 'according to the design of the king's own heart' (Breasted 1907: passages 164, 545, 775; Lilyquist 1995: 3). In addition, these vessels are extremely standardised products and, for the first time, liquid measures in *hin* are sometimes inscribed on their exteriors (Figure 7.1, also Sobhy 1924).[2]

FIGURE 7.1. Measurement and standardisation during the reign of Thutmosis III: (a) travertine vessels inscribed for General Djehuty (Lilyquist 1995: fig. 155), (b) travertine alabastron with 16.25 *hin* capacity (ca. 7.6 L; Lilyquist 1995: fig. 85), (c) travertine jar with 14.5 *hin* capacity (ca. 6.8 L; Lilyquist 1995: fig. 94).

a                                    b                    c

These larger jar forms were all created around the same basic shape, comprising a globular (and later ovoid) body with a collared neck and square rim. This form first occurs in the early 18th Dynasty as a simple jar (E173), and one practical implication of its adoption as a template for larger royal products was the standard manufacturing sequence it engendered across the wider Egyptian repertoire. Such vessels almost always possess a depression in the interior base which suggests a central tapering cavity was drilled first and undercutting proceeded afterwards. This body shape is also highly symbolic: the globular version evoked the hieroglyphic sign for the stomach and windpipe (*nefer*), while the ovoid form referred to the lungs and trachea (*sema*, Wilkinson 1994: 78–81).

A variety of handle shapes were added to this template, driven by the popularity of Levantine, Cypriot, and possibly Aegean jars. Travertine vessels of this style first appear in the reigns of Hatshepsut and Thutmosis III and might have loop handles on the shoulder,[3] vertical handles of Canaanite jar style, or Cypriot base-ring features (hereafter BR, E174-5,181-2, Lilyquist 1995: fig. 90-1). As with many other innovations in the Egyptian stone vessel industry, these appear to be top-down changes driven by the tastes of the royal court. For example, BR pottery imports are common in Egypt in the 18th Dynasty, but the real prototypes for the travertine vessels were probably of precious metal and copied first in royal workshops. For example, BR-style travertine jugs appear at least as early as, if not before, the main arrival of Cypriot BR pottery in Egypt (Aston 1994: 151). Metal BR-style jugs are shown on the Thutmosis III Karnak relief (Figure 7.2) and the handle terminus of the stone versions are carved into a scroll design, which is not found in pottery and may skeuomorph a metal attachment. Finally, the vast majority of BR pottery imported to Egypt are juglets rather than jugs (Bergoffen 1991: 69), while the opposite pattern is true in stone. It is unclear whether this reflects the storage of different contents in the jugs and juglets, respectively, or that they were meant to express different scales of consumption.

From Thutmosis III onwards, we can also turn to a range of important written documents and depictions that are explicit about the value regimes surrounding stone vessels and other objects, at least as seen through the eyes of royal propaganda or correspondence. On pylon VI of the Karnak temple in Thebes, Thutmosis III recorded the annals of his Levantine campaigns and depicted the vast proceeds that he subsequently dedicated to the temple (Figure 7.2). This depiction offers a startling taxonomy of Egyptian high culture, which rated gold at the top of its value hierarchy and pottery not even worthy of mention (Sherratt and Sherratt 1991: 361). We have stone vessels at two different levels in this scale: first and less numerous are cylindrical jars, jugs, amphorae, lotus cups, footed jars, and alabastra in lapis lazuli and 'of costly stone, made according to the design of the king's own heart'. As we have seen, this fits into other suggestions, rhetorical or not, that the pharaoh was intervening directly in the process of creating such hypercrafted objects, but makes it difficult to see how such vessels could themselves have been Levantine tribute. Separated from these by bronze objects are large numbers of travertine oil jars 'as annual dues (*ḥtr*)'.[4] Unfortunately, the circumstances surrounding the dedication of these vessels are obscure: travertine vessels would make surprising annual dues from Levantine communities and perhaps the reference is to annual gifts of Levantine oils made by the pharaoh to the Karnak temple. In any case, the alabastra, cylindrical jars, and flasks are familiar and entirely consistent with what we know of contemporary elite vessels. The loop-handled amphorae

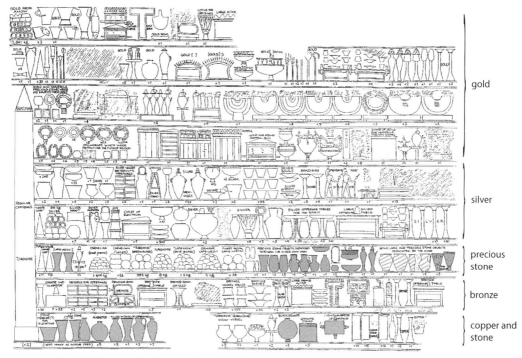

FIGURE 7.2. A relief from Karnak showing the spoils dedicated to the temple from Thutmosis III's Levantine campaigns in order of relative value (after Sherratt and Sherratt 1991: fig. 2; stone vessels in this depiction are shaded grey and those that may combine stone with other media are hatched).

and the three-ridged precious stone cup (along with the metal *tazze*) are shapes which the archaeological record also suggests appear at this time.

So the Karnak relief gives us a wonderful schematic of the Egyptian upper elite value scale, and the types and quantities of exotic objects it depicts can wreak havoc with our sense of archaeological scale. As we shall see, the Amarna letters confirm that the issues of scale raised here are not easily avoided and provide a good indication that basic elements of this value scheme were well established, even if we also find evidence for later attempts at modifying their details. Before looking more closely at the Amarna correspondence, the following paragraphs return to the archaeological record and explore the role of stone vessels further down the Egyptian social hierarchy.

An excellent indicator of the sharp gradient of the New Kingdom social pyramid is a series of well-made ceramic imitations of travertine and hornblende diorite vessels. These come from the tomb of Akhenaton's parents and from burials of lesser royal wives in the Valley of the Queens and hence are curious for being found in wealthy burials not poor ones (Bourriau 1981: 39,117; Holthoer 1994). Their use suggests that stone products made by the royal workshops were available in quantity only to the immediate royal family and the pharaoh's closest advisors. The allure of this inner royal circle was such, however, that, for less well-connected members of the upper elite or perhaps merely when insufficient stores of stone examples existed, it was clearly worth using lower-value ceramic copies, perhaps still containing the best quality oils, to knowingly reference a specific ultraelite practice (royal workshop production and royal cosmetics) rather than to use ordinary travertine vessels and thereby be incorporated implicitly into a wider wealthy class.

This wider privileged class was made up of individuals such as Nakht from Assasif who was buried with a wide range of toilet articles, weapons, tools, and vessels, including a serpentinite kohl pot, a PD-OK antiquity, and two jars in other exotic stones (Lansing 1917: 22; Lilyquist 1995: 62). Sacred oil sets were also used by members of this social group: one contemporary example was found in the tomb of the architect Kha (Schiaparelli 1927), and another is listed on a discarded tomb inventory, along with boxes of clothes, jars of wine, oil and honey, copper vessels, and different bits of furniture (Raisman 1985). However, the general absence of both exotic small oil containers and the larger unguent jars found in the Tomb of the Foreign Wives, or of their imitations in pottery, is a key feature of such contexts, reflecting the point in the social scale at which such articles of royal production were no longer directly relevant to the competitive regimes of the lower elite.

Unfortunately, although we can be relatively precise about the types of people deploying stone vessels in this way (professional scribes, government servants, mainly those around the capital), these examples are difficult to place in a satisfactory wider context, because after the early NK we have few, if any, large-scale cemetery exposures. The impression remains that a similar proportion of people were burying such items as in the MK-SIP. An apparently typical example of stone vessel use amongst a lower provincial elite are the two females, one male and a child buried with baskets containing travertine oil flasks and kohl pots, some gold jewellery, and some BR pottery juglets (Merrillees 1974).

## The Amarna Age

During the Amarna period, some existing shapes, such as *tazze*, continue to be popular, but there are also several new vessels with stylistic links to Mycenaean pottery, such as lentoid flasks, stirrup jars, ring-handle jugs, and kraters (E176,178–9,196; Furumark 1941: types 226, 279; Hankey 1995). These reflect the prevalence of LHIIIA2-B oil containers not only in Egypt but throughout the eastern Mediterranean (Van Wijngaarden 2002). Unfortunately, as before, the absence of discrete cemetery groups limits our ability to characterise the use of stone vessels across the whole Egyptian social spectrum. At Amarna, a few travertine *tazze*, shallow dishes, and bowls are found in the larger private houses, along with the occasional heirloom or antiquity, but seem overshadowed by the popularity of the glass and faience industries (E171,212; Frankfort and Pendlebury 1933; Shortland et al. 2001). In contrast to this paucity of general cemetery evidence, we benefit from the chance preservation of two spectacular glimpses, the tomb of Tutankhamun and the Amarna letters, at how stone vessels were being used by the ruler himself, and in both cases, we can recognise major changes from what went before in the logic by which these vessels were deployed.

To take the archaeological evidence first, the vast majority of vessels from Tutankhamun's funerary assemblage are made of travertine and hence involve no visible effort to express higher value through harder or more colourful materials (El-Khouli 1993). These vessels fall into three categories: (1) smaller models and vessel sets, (2) enormous inscribed oil or wine jars, and (3) elaborate display vessels. The first of these were found in one or two boxes in the antechamber and probably include a sacred oil set. The second category of oil jars

FIGURE 7.3. Elaborate travertine vessels from the tomb of Tutankhamun: (a) a *sema*-shaped vessel with Hapi figures, papyrus, and lily (Edwards 1979: 88, 99); (b) a lamp with the royal family depicted within the walls of the goblet. (Courtesy of the Cairo Museum.)

are impressive for their size (often over 30 cm high) and the telling fact that the contents, but not the containers, were robbed during antiquity. At least some of these were inscribed in earlier reigns and were heirlooms by now. Vessels in the third category are hypercrafted objects, invested with gold, glass, lapis, and obsidian inlay and cached together within the antechamber or the nested set of funerary shrines. They were clearly made to highlight virtuoso carving skill and are invested with cosmologically charged designs: one set of vessels adopts the hieroglyph for the lungs and oesophagus (*sema*) as a basic form around which are placed two Hapis, representing the fertility of the Nile and Upper and Lower Egypt (Edwards 1979). The union of the latter is also symbolised by the entwining of papyrus and lily plants. The vulture on the lid is either Mut or Nekhbet and was meant to protect the perfume [Figure 7.3(a)]. Several of the lamps are also extremely elaborate products: on one lotus-shaped example are depictions of the god of eternity, Heh. The vessel also has an interior lining on which was painted a scene showing the king and queen. Sandwiched between layers of travertine, this image could be seen only when the lamp was lighted [Figure 7.3(b)].

The almost exclusive use of travertine as the core material for these products, in the absence of any vessels in ultrahigh value stones, is a striking contrast to the Thutmosis III dedication pylon. This overhaul of the traditional values within which stone vessels were conceived at the upper elite end of the scale was made from the top down. It probably fits into the religious iconoclasm of Tutankhamun's father Akhenaton and the massive changes we see in royal art during his reign. The dominance of travertine was no doubt encouraged by the presence of numerous quarries in the vicinity of the new capital but may also have been favoured because it was not strongly associated with any traditional deity and had potentially luminescent properties (e.g. the lamp). It was thus very appropriate to the regime's new religious agenda which was heavily concerned with solar worship and an ideology of light (Aufrère 1991: xxiii, 148, 696–8). The amount of gold in Tutankhamun's tomb is hard to compare with the plundered assemblages from other reigns but may also have been imbued with extra importance during the reign of his father, as a direct manifestation of Aten.

Turning to the evidence of the Amarna letters, to what extent do they support the picture provided by the Tutankhamun finds? In fact, our understanding of stone vessel value regimes throughout the Near East is profoundly improved by the survival of this diplomatic correspondence. Four letters mention stone vessels, all of them in connection with the transfer of huge numbers of prestige items as gifts and counter gifts during royal marriages between Akhenaton or Tutankhamun and Babylonian or Mitannian royal daughters (Moran 1987: EA 13, 14, 22, 25). As we shall see, in each of the letters—Babylonian, Mitannian, and Egyptian—stone vessels are valued in markedly different ways.

The gifts accompanying the daughters of foreign rulers include only a few stone vessels. The Babylonian king sends gilded flasks (*mušalu*) of lapis lazuli and *dušû*-stone at the end of his lists of gold, silver, and bronze vessels. The king of Mitanni sends gilded flasks, *kunninu* bowls, and helmet-shaped vessels of marble, inlaid with lapis lazuli, malachite, *marḫallu*, and *ḫulalu* stones, as well as a few other partially or wholly stone vessels within multimedia sets (Moran 1987: EA 13, 22, 25; Postgate 1997). In the latter's gift list, such vessels are given fairly heterogeneous groupings, arranged more clearly by theme (equestrian equipment, clothes, weapons, jewellery, oils) than by material or value. The emphasis on harder precious stones, gilding, and sometimes inlay, and their association with sets of precious metal vessels, suggests exactly the kinds of high-profile upper elite contexts and explicit multimedia matches that we encountered archaeologically for stone vessels from the coastal northern Levant and Anatolia in the earlier second millennium.

In contrast, the Egyptian countergift to Tushratta, king of Mitanni, mentions significantly larger numbers of stone vessels than the foreign letters:

1 stone *ḫattu*-jar, full of 'sweet oil', (called) *azida*.
19 stone jars, full of 'sweet oil'; *kubu* is its name
20 stone jars (called) *akūnu*, which are full of 'sweet oil'.
9 *kukkubu*-containers, of stone, full of 'sweet oil'; *namša* is its name.
1 'cucumber', of stone, full of 'sweet oil'
6 very large stone vessels, full of 'sweet oil'
[x] *kukkubu*-containers of stone, full of 'sweet oil'; *maṣiqta* is its name.
[x] jugs of stone, full of 'sweet oil'; *kuba* is its name.
[x] *kukkubu*-containers of stone, full of 'sweet oil'; *kuba-puwanaḫ* is its name.
[x] *kukkubu*-containers of stone, full of 'sweet oil'; *kuiḫku* is its name.
[x] [j]ars full of 'sweet oil'; *ašša* is its name.
[the t]otal of the stone vessels full of 'sweet oil':
[x] 000 and 7 vessels.

[x] em[pty] boxes, of stone, [...].
[1] *kukkubu*-container, of stone; *našša* is its name, [and] 1 small one just li[ke i]t.
[x] onagers, of stone, [and] 1 sm[all one] just like it.

[x] *galdu*, of stone, ...is its name.

[and *x* sm]all ones ju[st li]ke them; 35 *ḫaragabaš* of stone.

[1] lar[ge...]..., of stone; its name....

[and *x* smal]l ones, of stone; vessels...and 2....

[x] [...with] their stands; its name *sabnakû*.

[...]; its name *kuiḫku*

[...o]f stone.

[...]; its name...

and 1 sma[ll one].

21 female figurines, of stone,...[...].

1 cripple, of stone, with a jar in its hand.

1 *kukkubu*-container, of stone; *šuibta* is its name.

3 jars of stone; 2 large goblets, of stone, the *hin*.

3 pails, of stone; 1 sieve, of stone.

1 tall stand, of stone.

2 *agannu*-jars, of stone; 38 *išqillatu*-vessels, of stone.

1 container of oil; *wadḫa* is its name.

3 *kukkubu*-containers, of stone; *namša* is its name.

2 headrests, of stone.

1 headrest, of *dušû*-stone

1 bowl, of white stone; its name *ṣillihta*.

9 containers of oil, of white stone; its name *wadḫa*.

The total of empty stone vessels:

160 and 3.

(Conchavi-Rainey 1999: EA14: 34–73)

So, these gifts are broken up into a larger group of stone oil jars and a smaller one of empty vessels, all of which follow jewellery, gold, silver, bronze, and fine textiles in the catalogue but precede ebony and ivory goods. Note that the order roughly parallels the kinds of distinction that we encountered in the Thutmosis III Karnak relief, with stone vessels as one of the less important classes of prestige product (and again pottery is not mentioned). Many of the vessel names can be plausibly identified and suggest common types such as cylindrical jars (*namša* or *nmst* in Egyptian), large bowls (*agannu*), and two-handled amphorae (*akūnu* or *ikn* in Egyptian; Conchavi-Rainey 1999: 226–8, also Horowitz and Oshima 2002). Moreover, 'a cripple with a jar in his hand' is probably a Bes figure holding a footed jar and a stone sieve may well be the type of wine strainer found with Tutankhamun (Caubet 1991: pl. ii.14; Conchavi-Rainey 1999: pl. 2; El-Khouli 1993: pls. 25a-b). These specific labels given to vessel shapes, stones, and specific oils communicated an entire taxonomy along with the gifts themselves. Also of interest is the way in which larger and smaller empty vessels are described in pairs: 'a *kukkubu*-container...and a small one just like it.' Travertine is very likely to be the default stone referred to in this list, and while a few other white-coloured stones are also mentioned, no effort is made to distinguish harder or more precious rocks.

To summarise, a consistent pattern in the Mitannian and Babylonian lists is the production of a range of ultrahigh value vessels, generally gilded and in harder stones or inlaid combinations. This is exactly the emphasis we find in second millennium products from these regions, and in the upper rank of semiprecious vessels in Thutmosis III's Karnak inscription. At times, we can recognise stone names that possessed intense mytho-ideological connotations (Aufrère 1991; André-Salvini 1995; Postgate 1997), but the Babylonian list still places them at the bottom of the metallic scale, while the Mitannian list makes less effort to position them in such an explicit hierarchy. In contrast, the lack of obvious hardstone vessels, the probable dominance of travertine, and the separation of vast numbers of oil jars from a few more elaborate empty vessels mirrors the taxonomy we observe archaeologically in Tutankhamun's tomb. In other words, text and material remains alike suggest that the upper Amarna elite retained much of the overall scale of values from its predecessors but, for stone vessels in particular, had departed from older established logics and was forging something new.

**The 19th Dynasty**
The extent to which these new regimes were continued in the ensuing Ramesside period is unclear, mainly because we have neither the evidence of royal correspondence nor the well-preserved tomb assemblages to assist us. An emphasis on extremely large vessels certainly continues. Body forms now tend to be ovoid rather than globular and this fits into a tendency, visible in all media, to elongate 18th Dynasty shapes (e.g. lentoid flasks, E195). A highly recognisable new jar form has carved gazelle heads for handles and a range of round-bottomed vessels also now appear (E183,192-3,197). Incised or painted decoration of these large jars becomes more common, appearing on most jar shapes and their accompanying lids (E198). We lack the necessary undisturbed royal contexts to decide if such changes were begun in the royal workshops, but the continued crafting of elaborate travertine vessels is shown by a lentoid flask that is gilded in gold, provided with a sheet silver base, and inscribed for Ramses II and Nefertari (Petrie 1937: 14, pl. xxxvi.917). Lapis lazuli vessels are also amongst the tribute of Retenu arriving in Egypt during the reign of Seti I (Breasted 1907: passage 106).

As is the case throughout the NK, it is difficult to get a view of how stone vessels were being deployed across society in general. Nevertheless, further textual evidence is helpful, but this time, from ostraca and with reference to the world beyond the upper elite. At Deir el-Medina in the reign of Seti I, the workman Pashedu made a will for his family before a witness and allotted possessions and food allowances to his children, including a mirror, frying pan, and greenstone (serpentinite?) vessels for his daughter Isis (Kitchen 1993: 409:1). Similarly, a 19th Dynasty limestone block from the Valley of the Kings lists travertine vessels amongst the objects given to a woman, Khaysheb, by a number of other people. The vessels were transferred along with basketry, woodwork, faience, metalwork, foodstuffs, and clothing (Cerny 1935: 57, 77–8, pl. lxxv). Isolated examples though they are, these ostraca provide rare glimpses of the use of stone vessels in daily life, including their movement and curation from person to person.

After the 19th Dynasty, stone vessel use is even more difficult to assess because of the limited number of relevant deposits, but few if any of the very large vessels are now found. The TIP corpus is made up of shallow cosmetic dishes, lugged bowls, and various flask shapes (Aston 1994: types 203–214). An interesting development, returned to briefly in Chapter 9, is the appearance of a range of round-bottomed lugged jars which, by the Late Period at least, reflect both deliberate antiquarianism and a renewed emphasis on suspension.

## The Levant

Despite the important geopolitical changes besetting this region during the later second millennium, some of the broad MBA patterns continue. A range of sites consume Egyptian-style travertine vessels, and, again, there is the suspicion that some of these were either made or modified locally. Likewise, an inland tradition of gypsum vessel manufacture continues in the Jordan valley. A closer look at the details of this picture, however, reveals that many things had also changed. The following sections consider first the Egyptian-style vessels from the Levant, focusing on a few key sites that exemplify the wider patterns of production and consumption in which these objects were embedded. Discussion then turns to the gypsum industry to explore the increasingly independent trajectory that this tradition was following at the end of the Late Bronze Age and through into the early Iron Age.

### Egyptian-Style Vessels

The distribution of travertine vessels from LBIB-II contexts in the Levant is much changed from what went before. The relatively widespread popularity of these objects (and in many cases, probably their contents as well) continues, but Ugarit and Cyprus are now much more visible consumers (Figure 7.4, to compare with Figure 6.3): this may partly reflect a

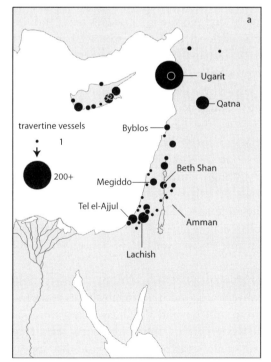
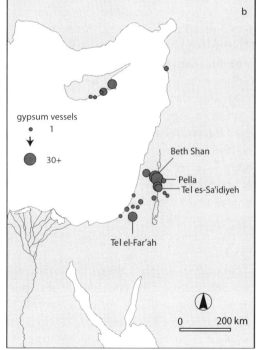

FIGURE 7.4. The distribution of (a) travertine and (b) gypsum vessels in the LBIB-II Levant (counts from Jacobsson 1994; Sparks 2007, Ahrens, personal communication, with additional minor modifications).

bias in our available sample which favours later Bronze Age deposits in these areas, but it also suggests a shift northwards of the zone where such intercultural display was being most intensively explored (see Ugarit and Cyprus below). In addition, there are also notably fewer vessels of this kind from sites along the central Levantine coast (e.g. Ashdod, Tel Abu Hawam, and Sarepta), especially given the relative abundance of other imported containers such as Mycenaean pottery at these sites (Van Wijngaarden 2002: map 7). In the light of fluctuating contemporary political allegiances in the area, this suggests that we might treat the patterns of stone vessel exchange and use pertaining to the southern Levant and those associated with Cyprus and the northern Levant as separate phenomena, with an ill-defined gap in between. In any case, many familiar MBA vessels such as alabastra, dipper juglets, and everted rim jars are no longer found in LBA Levantine contexts except as probable heirlooms or recycled material, and new forms such as collared pots, *tazze*, lentoid flasks, and large handled jars emerge, in line with their popularity in contemporary Egypt (E170-1,173-8,181-4,192–5). However, the production and consumption of Egyptian-style travertine vessels is far from a straightforward case of blanket importation. While no single argument is decisive, once again a wide range of clues suggest that several processes were at work, including the import of a selected group of Egyptian stone vessels, their local modification, and occasionally perhaps their complete substitution by local copies.

The evidence for this falls into three related categories. Firstly, some of the vessels in the Levant are in shapes, or have specific details, that are found extremely rarely in Egypt, if at all. For example, many of the collared pots and *tazze* from the Levant were made with a separate base which was attached to the body with a tenon join (Es4-5). These are rarely found in Egypt, where the most popular version was made in one piece with a deeper bowl and less pronounced foot (E170-1). A few vessels also copied local Levantine pottery shapes (Es6; Amiran 1969: pl. 27.14). Jars with stylised duck's-head shaped handles and stone BR juglets are both relatively common in the Levant and Cyprus but much less visible in Egypt (Es7-8). Some of the earliest examples of the stone BR juglets also come from Levantine contexts, suggesting they were a Cypro-Levantine innovation (e.g. Petrie 1931: pls. xx.15, xxii.23; 1932: xxii.26). Secondly, as Lilyquist suggests (1996), the Levantine examples sometimes used travertines and serpentinites that are not the common varieties found in Egypt. It is certainly possible to argue either way over macroscopic assessments of individual pieces, but taken as a group, the differences are relatively striking. Thirdly, a few vessels show signs of modification, using the basic body shape of an Egyptian-style jar to build new forms, such as flasks with duck-shaped lugs or Canaanite-style jars.[5] These conversions along with the separate pieces used to make *tazze* and collared pots suggest the careful husbanding of travertine or similar looking material that was not always available in convenient larger blocks.

So while we cannot always be confident in our attribution of individual pieces, we should probably envisage the coexistence of imports, conversions, and import substitutes at several larger Levantine and Cypriot centres, both within and beyond the areas under nominal Egyptian hegemony. In any case, it is important to recognise this ambiguity of manufacturing provenance, because it is a wider feature of the intercultural expressions of taste that appear repeatedly, with minor variations, in many Levantine and Cypriot assemblages. Three good examples are the mortuary complexes at Kamid el-Loz, Qatna, and Amman. Kamid el-Loz seems to have been an Egyptian administrative centre from the mid-18th Dynasty, and an impressive group of stone vessels was found in a probable funerary deposit at the Schatzhaus, alongside ivory cosmetic boxes and Cypriot and Mycenaean pottery (Miron 1990: 91-8; Adler 1996; Lilyquist 1996). The stone vessel assemblage stands out for several reasons. There are one or two Egyptian PD-OK antiquities, some MBA alabastra, several vessels of likely Levantine manufacture, one possible Assyrian import,[6] and no gypsum vessels. These spatial distributions of materials and shapes seems purposive, with most of the travertine and limestone vessels coming from room S, but a group of serpentinite jars present in room T, and the two Egyptian antiquities found around the doorway.

Good general parallels for the the stone vessel consumption habits revealed by the Schatzhaus group are the royal tomb at Qatna (Al-Maqdissi et al. 2003; also Novák and Pfälzner 2003: pl. 13; Ahrens 2006) and the longer-lived mortuary complex at Amman (Hankey 1974; Hennessy 1989). At Qatna, amongst a wealth of grave goods in gold, ivory, lapis lazuli, bronze, and pottery, there were also about 60 stone vessels (for what follows, also Ahrens, personal communication). Most were Egyptian-style vessels made of travertine, white marble/limestone, or occasionally serpentinite (again with indications that a few may not have been made in Egypt itself), but there were also a number of Egyptian ED antiquities and MK alabastra. The deposition of different types in different chambers of the tomb is again apparent. At Amman, stone vessels are found alongside Mycenaean and Cypriot pottery, ivory, and other valuables. Oil or wine serving vessels predominate and three striking features of these are (1) the relatively large proportion made of serpentinite (20–25%), (2) the number of vessels with Cypriot base-ring style designs (ca. 80%), and (3) the lack of gypsum vessels, despite the site's relative proximity to the Jordan valley. As at Kamid el-Loz, these features, along with the presence of a few eccentric vessel forms (e.g. a jar with relief decoration of a snake), some Egyptian PD-OK antiquities, and some MK-early 18th Dynasty-style pieces, suggest more than simply a bland picture of imported Egyptian objects or local manufacture but practices that were at once both more eclectic and more structured, reflecting a particular range of tastes found within the most privileged and well-connected Levantine elite groups, for which stone vessels are only some of the most robust archaeological indicators.

**Stone Vessel Use at Ugarit**   In Chapter 6, we explored the role of Tel el-Ajjul in making culturally synthetic products, including Egyptian-style stone vessels. Ajjul declines in importance in LBIB-II, but Ugarit was one of the main sites that takes on a similar role. This movement northwards of a key zone of Egyptianising and intercultural style coincides with the extension of Egypt's nominal frontier, from the Sinai to the northern Levant. Such environments on the edge of Egyptian political and cultural influence clearly encouraged the imitation and transformation of Egyptian material culture in distinctive ways. Just as Byblos and Tel el-Ajjul were used as Levantine case studies in earlier periods to consider the social and political discourse surrounding Egyptian-style practices, so the following section explores the use of stone vessels at Ugarit in greater detail.

Ugarit was one of the most significant of an array of LBA trading towns facing each other along the coasts of Cilicia, Cyprus, and the northern Levant. It was a highly cosmopolitan centre where trade and diplomacy were conducted by many different ethnic groups, speaking in multiple languages, writing in several different scripts and on a variety of media. The town and its adjacent port were contested spaces in terms of international politics, local trading rights, land holding, and cultural affiliation (Yon 2003). Ugarit's extensive archaeological and documentary evidence promote it as a case study, but require careful integration. The following discussion begins by considering what kinds of stone vessels are found at Ugarit and then looks comparatively at their local value, relative to another type of exotic vessel, Mycenaean-style pottery. It then focuses on several key archaeological contexts and what they tell us about stone vessel consumption in (1) temple and associated ritual spaces, (2) the royal palace, and (3) the houses and tombs of the upper elite. It ends by introducing a particular individual belonging to the latter group and suggests that the objects found in his house and tomb can help us chase similar personalities in other regions where our information is a lot less specific.

Stone vessels were a relatively minor component of the exotic containers used at LBA Ugarit, where there were also vessels in metal, ivory, decorated pottery, and no doubt various hardwoods. The main excavated deposits at the site are contemporary with the 19th Dynasty, but there are also several important Amarna Age contexts. While there are clear stylistic changes in the Egyptian stone vessel repertoire across these two periods, the same main functional groups are present throughout, with small cosmetic flasks, *tazze*, and large oil jars being the most common (Caubet 1991). Many of the stone vessels at Ugarit are definite imports from Egypt, and there are also no known tools or debris that provide unequivocal evidence for local manufacture. However, as with the Levant in general, a combination of style, material, and reworked pieces at Ugarit probably do implicate it or its immediate neighbours in some small-scale production. This picture fits well with the character of other foreign-style products such as Mycenaean pottery (e.g. Sherratt 1982), where we can chart more explicitly a gradual transition from selective importation of these objects to their later substitution with local imitations. Egyptian-style stone vessels follow this trajectory only so far because definite Egyptian imports continue to be important throughout. As we shall see, one reason for this is probably the different values of these two products, but it may also be because travertine was a more restricted raw material than clay and stone vessel-drilling a more restricted skill than potting.[7]

It is worth pursuing a comparison of these two highly recognisable cultural brands, from opposite ends of the eastern Mediterranean, a little further.[8] Both object classes were closely associated with the consumption of oil and wine at Ugarit, but remained exotic minority components of the available suite of vessels at the site. As such, they were important mechanisms for social display, particularly in the light of written evidence for important local oil and wine festivals (Lipinski 1988: 140–1). Figure 7.5 shows the approximate densities of Egyptian-style stone vessels and Mycenaean-style pottery recorded across different parts of the site and the harbour town at Minet el-Beida. These absolute numbers resist direct comparison because the excavation and recording histories of each zone vary, with, for example, the high densities in the Centre Ville reflecting more recent and intensive investigation. However, the *ratio* of stone vessels to Mycenaean pottery for each area should still offer a good index of their relative popularity. In most parts of the site, Mycenaean-style pottery is over three times more common than Egyptian-style stone vessels and it is only in two of the most prestigious zones, the Palais Royal and the Palais Sud, that we find this ratio approaching equity. These

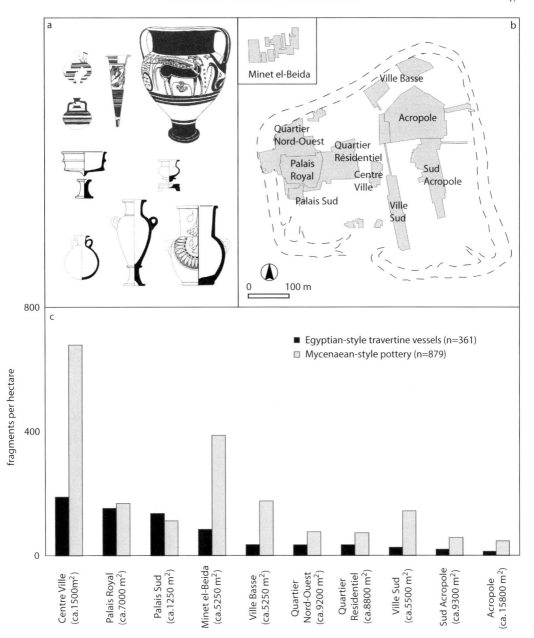

FIGURE 7.5. Two foreign-style vessel classes at Ugarit: (a) examples of Mycenaean-style pottery (above, van Wijngaarden 1999: figs. 5, 7, 9) and Egyptian-style travertine vessels (below, after Caubet 1991: pls. ix.1, 8, x.1, ix.1); neither are to scale. (b) Plan of the different excavation areas at Ugarit and (c) relative densities recorded for each excavation area.

proportions suggest that consumption of stone vessels was an elite behavior that tailed off far more rapidly down through the social hierarchy at Ugarit than Mycenaean pottery. Within each zone, this fact is also emphasised by the far more circumscribed contexts in which we find stone vessels, which tend to be only temples and the wealthiest houses or tombs. We could reasonably infer that this spatial distribution was matched by a correspondingly low frequency of use: put simply, stone vessels were deployed by fewer people, in fewer places, and probably on fewer occasions than their Mycenaean pottery counterparts.

Considering several of these areas in greater detail reveals not only how rich such contextual study can be but also how important it is to consider the formation processes behind individual deposits. The unusual nature of the Palais Royal and Palais Sud are obvious from both text and archaeology and are discussed again below, but the Centre Ville offers a good example of a more ordinary section of the settlement. A comparison with the finds in other media from this excavation suggests that stone vessels are concentrated in the same areas as Myceanean and Cypriot pottery but are not so closely associated with the findspots of bronze, faience, or glass. Over 20 vessel fragments are concentrated in and around the Temple aux Rhytons and a building across the street to the north (Mallet 1987; Mallet and Matoïan 2001). These objects have been identified as part of the ritual paraphernalia of this complex in its final phase, but several things make these two buildings difficult to interpret. Firstly, the identification of the complex as a temple rests on the number of Mycenaean-style rhyta and other possible cultic objects found in its vicinity but is troublesome because the building has neither an archive to identify it securely as a temple, nor the obvious architectural elaboration of the Acropolis temples. It may therefore be a less monumental ritual space similar to the Temple of the Hurrian Priest, but the travertine vessels found in and immediately around the building are mainly *tazze* and, on their own, do not really differentiate it from similar finds in ordinary houses.

In contrast, the travertine vessels found across the street (*fosse* 1237) to the north are more impressive, but grouping them with the others in the temple building to the south potentially conflates two phases of use. The *fosse* 1237 vessels are mainly small oil containers, found alongside Cypriot pottery and ivory duck-pyxides in a much later secondary context (Yon et al. 1982: 189). They are not incompatible with use during the final phase of the site, but they resemble more closely the types of objects found in deposit 213 at Minet el-Beida, which is Amarna period in date [Figure 7.6(a)], than the the final phase of the Temple aux Rhytons. Perhaps a better explanation for the presence of these vessels here is that they were a store or a refuse dump associated with the northern building in its previous incarnation as an olive oil processing workshop and possibly attached to an earlier phase of the temple to its south (Callot 1987). Indeed, this intriguingly complex connection between Ugaritan oil production and Egyptianising consumption has an important corollary in Canaanite-style jars found at Amarna which have been petrographically provenanced as coming from the Ugarit region but were marked in Egyptian hieratic as containing *nḥḥ* oil (probably olive, possibly sesame; Serpico 2004).

In contrast to the Centre Ville, the Palais Royal was a much more prestigious zone of the site, but also one of the least well-recorded. Despite this more obscure archaeological perspective, the palace clearly had greatest access to stone vessels and possessed the majority of examples in harder stones, more unusual shapes,[9] with incised rather than painted decoration or with royal Egyptian inscriptions. The latter inscribed vessels are associated primarily with the reigns of Amenhotep III and Ramses II and there is a general hiatus of inscriptions between them, during the period of Hittite control over Ugarit. This pattern, combined with a similar concentration in the fourteenth-to-thirteenth-century palace at Assur

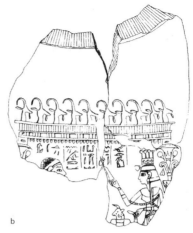

FIGURE 7.6. Travertine vessels from Ugarit: (a) travertine *tazze* and collared pots stored inside a pottery jar at Minet el-Beida (Schaeffer 1938: fig. 21), (b) a fragment inscribed with a scene featuring Niqmadu (after Wachsmann 1987: pl. lx.B).

(von Bissing 1940), and the almost complete lack of stone vessels with royal inscriptions from the Egyptian vassal regions in the southern Levant, makes a case for seeing such objects as good tracers for formal Egyptian diplomacy (Sparks 2003; except in cases of clear reuse). Further tantalising evidence at Ugarit is offered by a travertine jar fragment from the palace which portrays the Ugaritan king Niqmadu and a female in Egyptian dress [Figure 7.6(b), see also Feldman 2002]. The decorative scheme on this vessel retains a general Egyptian layout but includes a caprid frieze of probable Levantine inspiration. The context may be the celebration of a marriage similar to the ones that involved stone vessel wedding gifts in the Amarna letters. The synthetic style also reflects shared elite tastes and the probable impact of mobile craftspeople, and a good comparative example of mobile stonemasons and syncretic ritual at Ugarit is a plea by the last king of Ugarit, 'Ammurapi, for a sculptor to be sent from Egypt to make a statue of the pharaoh Merneptah for a local Ugaritan temple (Lackenbacher 1995).

Textual archives and archaeological remains also combine to identify a series of wealthy traders living in mansions within the town during its last phase. These people were at the top end of a merchant class whose lesser members also lived in the harbour town at Minet el-Beida, but the most powerful among them were particularly complex figures, with administrative or diplomatic responsibilities that cannot always be separated from their eclectic range of commercial activities.[10] If there is a certain ambivalence in the terminology of royal appointments, traders, and messengers in the earlier Amarna letters, then it is hardly surprising in light of these disparate roles. One of the most important of such people at Ugarit was Yabninu, who lived in a huge mansion (the Palais Sud) immediately to the south of the royal palace (Courtois 1990), with an archive composed of Ugaritan alphabetic, cuneiform, and Cypro-Minoan texts.

These texts suggest a man closely linked with palace administration but with a series of maritime commercial ventures along the Levantine coast and with a particular interest in trade between Egypt and Hatti (Courtois 1990: 111–2, 141). A large number of stone vessels also come from his house and tomb. Amongst these, the presence of harder stones, royal inscriptions, and incised rather than painted decoration are all features otherwise concentrated in the palace (Caubet 1991: RS 19.244, 21.130). The few Mycenaean ceramics from this context are also extremely fine: for example, one krater is decorated with a master-of-horses design and may well evoke Yabninu's membership of the *maryannu* class (Yon et al. 2000: fig. 7a). In other words, Yabninu cuts a striking figure: a multilingual trader and administrator, with close links to the palace and a connoisseur's knowledge of foreign exotica. The fortuitous coincidence of textual and archaeological evidence allows us this privileged glimpse of an upper elite trader and profiles what we might expect the domestic and funerary material signatures of such people to look like in other regions where our evidence is often less explicit.

## Southern Levantine Gypsum Vessels

A gypsum vessel industry based at inland communities in the Jordan valley was highly visible in the mid-second millennium and becomes prominent again at the end of the Bronze Age and beginning of the Iron Age. Even more striking than before is the limited size and often poor finish of these products, which suggests small-scale local manufacture catering for individual consumption needs and not necessarily with any role in official or upper elite display. The main gypsum shapes now include *tazze*, lugged flasks, and pyxides (L18–21), but the stylistic ties between this tradition and one making Egyptian-style travertine vessels are far less obvious than before. Both these shifts in vessel style and some stratigraphic evidence (e.g. Sparks 2007: fig. 75) also suggest a dip in production from the period after the conquests of Thutmosis III up until the beginning of the 19th Dynasty, and it is probably no accident that this manufacturing lull coincides with a period of particularly effective Egyptian military interference in local affairs. In contrast, peaks in production occur first in the Hyksos period and second during the sociopolitical upheaval at the end of the Bronze Age, and we might read local manufacture as reflecting the increased popularity of local craft goods and cosmetics at times when at least one group of people in the area were particularly interested in asserting an autonomous local identity (for background, see Hasel 1998).

In LBIIB, the Jordan valley continues to be a core area of manufacture, but the tradition expands to include communities such as Tel el-Far'ah to the southwest. As in the MBA, communities produce similar shapes, but also manage to make some distinctive local products. Beth Shan was a manufacturer of lugged pyxides and flasks that are found in various unfinished, footed, decorated, or unusually large versions at the site (L19–21; James 1966: figs. 1.3, 50.11, 54.10, 119.12; Yadin and Geva 1986: fig. 36.2). In contrast, *tazze* are the main shape found at Tel el-Far'ah, and these are notable for being poorly finished, with thick bases and sides. At Pella and Tel es-Saidiyeh, there are also several decorated and/or unusual forms (Figure 7.7; Bourke and Sparks 1995: figs. 7.12–4).

Tel es-Saidiyeh in particular offers an interesting picture of the way in which these objects were being used in a local funerary arena (Pritchard 1980; Tubb and Dorrell 1991). Most of the LBIIB-Iron I burials were single inhumations and 4–11% have stone vessels, but almost never more than one.[11] These vessels included *tazze*, lugged flasks, and pyxides along with a few unusual forms. However, their role as status indicators is patchy: they do not occur in all the richer graves, and in several that are poorly equipped with other goods. In addition,

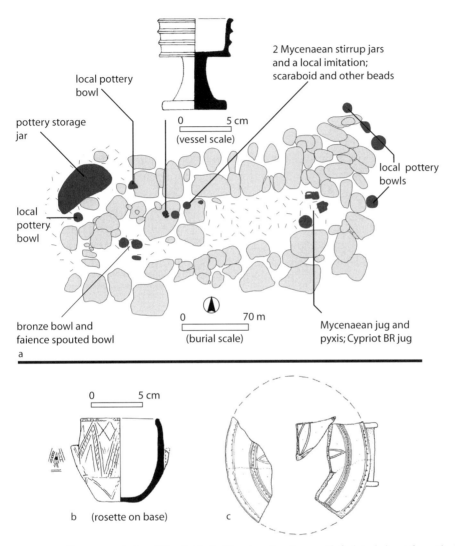

FIGURE 7.7. Gypsum vessels from Tel es-Saidiyeh: (a) a plan of tomb 117 with finds including a four-ridged gypsum *tazza*. A badly preserved primary burial was placed on top of a bed of stones and bitumen with its feet to the east (after Pritchard 1980: 21, fig. 21.17). (b) Incised gypsum vessels from tomb 389 (BM Western Asiatic).

there is a poor correlation between rich burials with weapons (e.g. tomb 102) and those with gypsum containers. This suggests that these objects were not merely expressing local elite status, but a horizontal social distinction as well, such as gender, ethnic group, or factional affiliation.

A few more elaborate graves offer insight on how gypsum vessels were (or were not) fitting into a wider range of grave goods. The graves richest in objects are often those invested with mudbrick or plaster lining and where the deceased was sometimes covered in bitumen, perhaps influenced by Egyptian mummification techniques. For example, tomb 389 was partially robbed but had such a lining and contained a single adult burial along with a silver finger-ring and two gypsum vessels [Figures 7.7(b) and (c); Tubb and Dorrell 1991: 86). The latter are densely decorated with incised rosettes, triangular nicks, and various linear designs. This level of surface investment is extremely rare in gypsum but has parallels in contemporary ivory or wood-carving. The vessels almost certainly are a pair made in the same workshop and, given gypsum vessels never occur here in large quantities or a wide range of sizes, dense added decoration was one appropriate way to be extravagant, while conforming to established consumption practices. Another example of such efforts is a *tazze* from tomb 117 which is unusual for having four moulded ribs instead of three [Figure 7.7(a)]. The tomb in which it was found was extremely wealthy, with a mud-brick lining and a floor of wadi stones. Its occupant was covered in bitumen and their accompanying equipment included local pottery, a large storage jar, Aegean and Cypriot imports, a bronze bowl, a faience spouted bowl, some beads, a silver ring, scarab of Amenhotep II, and the gypsum *tazza*. The spatial distribution of these items within the grave was carefully patterned into groups of objects with similar material, provenance, and function. The *tazze*'s location next to the miniature stirrup-jars and beads near the head of the burial suggests it retained its traditional association with personal grooming and adornment.

## Cyprus

### Egyptian-Style Vessels

After what appears to be a period of comparative isolation, Cyprus' engagement with a wider eastern Mediterranean world is increasingly obvious during the later second millennium, probably driven by the expansion of the Cypriot metal industry. One of the most obvious pieces of evidence is the growing presence of foreign objects in Cypriot tombs or, particularly towards the end of the period, their local imitation (Keswani 2004: 136–9). The first clear Egyptian stone vessel imports appear in LCypI-II,[12] but the vast majority are found in LCypIIA2-IIIA1 contexts contemporary with the Amarna period up to the end of the 19th Dynasty (Aström 1984: figs. 5a, 6; Jacobsson 1994: 9–20). The shapes involved reflect the peculiar predilections of local consumers rather than a simple cross section of Egyptian-style products: there are at least nine travertine BR-style jugs and juglets, 11 copies of Mycenaean-style kraters (E176), and a surprising number of vessels imitating the general shape of a Canaanite-style jar, often embellished with duck-shaped handles. As in the Levant, there is the suspicion that imports were being supplemented by local or Levantine versions as well.[13]

The distribution of travertine vessels favours Enkomi and other communities on the southern coast (Figure 7.4), and it is clear that elite families at these sites shared many of the same preoccupations as their Levantine neighbours. For example, Enkomi French Tomb 2 contained Cypriot and Mycenaean pottery, travertine footed jars and *tazze*, and a duck-headed bowl (Schaeffer 1952: 111–56), thereby evoking a very similar constellation of tastes as deposit 213 at Minet el-Beida, the Kamid el-Loz Schatzhaus, and many other Levantine contexts. Perhaps more interesting from a local perspective, however, are the stone vessels from Area I of the Enkomi settlement (Dikaios 1969: 195ff). In its later phases (levels IIIA-C), this area possessed an impressive ashlar building, including a probable cult area associated with metallurgy, containing a bronze hoard, ox skulls, a steatite/chloritite mould, and a bronze statue of a horned warrior or god. The stone vessels found across Area I evoke a telling blend of the local and the exotic. For example, a carved jug with imitation metal arcading and several whole and fragmentary chloritite vessels and mortars are local Cypriot products and possibly made at Enkomi. Less clear, however, are two Egyptian-style travertine vessels: the first is a ring-handled jug with many parallels elswhere in Cyprus and the eastern Mediterranean. It was decorated with an Egyptian-style festive garland and may have been used with an adjacent cache of BR pottery bowls for pouring and drinking ceremonies within the shrine area. The second travertine vessel (from a slightly earlier level) is a jar with separately attached duck-shaped lugs which fits into the group of Egyptian-style travertine vessels from Cypro-Levantine contexts, for which we might suspect either local manufacture or modification (see above).

## Local Cypriot Vessels

If the details of certain travertine vessels usually ascribed to the Egyptian industry at least raise a suspicion of limited local production and alteration, the evidence for the appearance of a small-scale local tradition on the island using gypsum and chloritite is much clearer [e.g. Figure 7.8(a)]. While the actual chronology is a little imprecise, the following sections address this industry in two phases, corresponding to Amarna Age and early 19th Dynasty products and then very late LBA and EIA vessels.

An arguably earlier group of gypsum vessels come mainly from Kition and Enkomi, though gypsum outcrops are widespread on the island. These comprise three main types: *tazze*, three-handled alabastra, and three-handled jars (Cyp1-3). The first of these copies travertine *tazze*, and while it was carved in one solid piece, it often imitates the high foot of the Egypto-Levantine versions (or their metal counterparts). As we have seen, similar gypsum *tazze* were being made at the same time in the southern Levant and share most of the same stylistic features and production marks (e.g. compass lines), making it difficult to know which of these areas was responsible for the occasional example found elsewhere at sites such as Ugarit or Knossos (e.g. Schaeffer 1949: figs. 64.5, 65.6; Warren 1969: P624). The other two Cypriot gypsum shapes, the three-handled alabastron and jar, copy LHIIIA2-B Mycenaean pottery (Furumark 1941: types 16–18, 34–5, 93–4).[14] The odd gypsum vessel copying local pottery forms such as BR or White-Shaved juglets are also found (Aström 1967: 70, no. 3; Jacobsson 1994: 77).[15] In its imitation of more exotic stone (travertine) and its mixed references to Egyptian, Mycenaean, and local material culture, the gypsum industry has much in common with Cypriot faience production, which drew inspiration from a range of different regions and sometimes imitated lapis lazuli, turquoise, or serpentinite (Peltenburg 1991a: 163–6). Perhaps our best window on the consumption of these objects is tomb V.6 from Kalavassos-*Mangia*, where the last three interments survive relatively intact and include one male adult, one female adult, and a child (McClennan 1988). Immediately to the southeast of the head of the female were placed a LHIIIB stirrup-jar, a gypsum alabastron, and a miniature stone mortar and pestle (the latter apparently in a box), all of which would appear to be components of a cosmetic set.

Cypriot artisans also carved local chlorite-rich rocks into vessels and there is at least one probable early example of a chloritite *tazza* (Myers et al. 1914: no. 1538).[16] However, by the end of the LBA, chloritite production expands to include a range of other shapes, while gypsum vessels become rarer (see below).[17] Most of these later chloritite products are

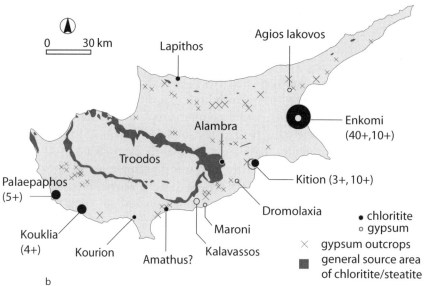

FIGURE 7.8. Cypriot stone vessels: (a) a representative selection of Egyptian-style, local chloritite, and gypsum vessels from Enkomi (Courtesy of the British Museum) (b) distribution map of chloritite and gypsum vessel findspots. The site totals are meant as a rough guide only and are unlikely to be comprehensive, given a series of unpublished examples that are known to exist.

miniaturised versions of Mycenaean-style pottery, ivory, or metal forms, including bowls, lugged tubes, amphorae, kraters, larnakes, and tripod mortars (Cyp4-11). The distribution of vessels is heavily dominated by Enkomi and an unfinished miniature amphora from the site confirms the impression that this was a production centre (Courtois 1984: no. 914, fig. 35.3, pl. xxii.14). Only the tripod mortars that may have been used to grind cosmetics seem to have been traded much beyond the island (e.g. Schaeffer 1949: fig. 62.16; Buchholz and Karageorghis 1973: no. 1159; Benzi 1992: T67/5).

The majority of these vessels were heavily decorated and such schemes fall into two main categories. Firstly, incised geometric motifs (hatched bands and triangles, compass-drawn spirals, dot-and-circle designs) reflect the types of decorative regimes encouraged by the working properties of this soft stone and have parallels in other soft media such as ivory, bone, and probably wood. Secondly, many of the miniature bowls, amphorae, and kraters have carinations, arcades, or handle attachments that skeuomorph full-sized metal versions (e.g. compare Karageorghis 1990: pl. xxiv.n66 with Buchholz and Karageorghis 1973: no. 1668). These metal shapes are all associated with eating and drinking display and the small, chloritite copies may have been used as model replacements (e.g. in tombs and rituals) or they may have been associated with a particular organic product and merely be evoking a wider Cypriot elite lifestyle. The link to metallurgy is emphasised by the fact that chloritite comes from the same broad upland zone in the Troodos mountains as Cypriot metals and because, as at Ugarit, it was also used for making jewellery moulds and possible tuyère nozzles because of its heat-resistant properties (Aström 1967: fig. 73; Bear 1963: 46; see also Chapter 8).[18]

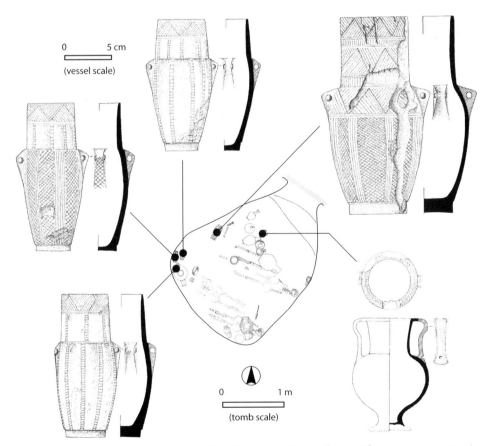

FIGURE 7.9. Gypsum vessels in burial chamber III at Kition (after Karageorghis 1960: figs. 12, 52, 58, 59, 61, 67).

A good example of the mortuary use of Cypriot softstone vessels is provided by an un-plundered LCypIII chamber tomb at Kition (Karageorghis 1960). Here, three adult skeletons were found surrounded by a grave assemblage, including four lugged gypsum jars, densely covered in incised decoration, and one other vessel, clearly skeuomorphing a metal jar [Figure 7.9(e)]. Three of the incised jars were cached together at the head of one burial, while the largest example and the metallicising vessel were found at the feet of another. The cross-media links with softer materials, such as ivory and bone, suggested by the vessels' incised decoration, is also reflected in the spatial association of the large jar and a similarly decorated, lugged bone tube. More generally, the emphasis on lugged vessels may reflect the need to suspend and agitate the contents—perhaps a perfumed oil or narcotic—to produce and disseminate their smell or effect.

## Anatolia

Hittite Anatolia presents the same methodological problems as the region did in earlier peri-ods. The distances between well-explored sites are often vast and such sparse understanding has a much greater negative impact on the study of stone vessels than on pottery, because the former survives in much smaller quantities. There is the general impression that, as before, stone vessels were not numerically important items and that metal and pottery dominate at either end of the display spectrum.

At Boğazköy, for example, there are several tantalising textual and archaeological clues but insufficient concrete evidence to take them very far and a suspicion that some stone vessel finds from LBA contexts were recycled objects or heirlooms by this time. Local and imported stone vessels have been found both in the palace area and the lower town. These include a few Egyptian vessels, but none of definite NK date. At least two are MK products, including an obsidian fragment inscribed for the Hyksos pharaoh Khian. It may have been a high-level gift a few centuries earlier, but neither the type of exchange nor the date when it occurred can really be established (Boehmer 1972: no. 2178-9, pl. lxxxii). Two other vessels are probably Egyptian but not chronologically diagnostic, and a third is much closer in shape to contemporary gypsum vessels from Assur, suggesting a possible continued overland link in this direction (Boehmer 1979: pl. xxxii-iii; Harper et al. 1995: 81–91). Even more intriguing is an isolated chloritite bottle from Hittite levels at Alişar Höyük that was almost certainly made during the later third or early second millennium in Bactria-Margiana much further east (von der Osten 1937: fig. 264.d1527; see David 2007).

Local stone vessel manufacture was almost certainly occurring on a small scale in Hittite Anatolia, and we find both finished vessels and Cretan-style slotted cobbles that were used as part of tubular drilling activities (Boehmer 1972: pls. lxxxii-iv, 1979: pls. xxxv-vi, though not necessarily for vessels: see Seeher 2005). Basalt tripod mortars and grinding bowls seem to have been particularly popular and are part of a wider northeastern Mediterranean zone that used similar looking grinding utensils (Boehmer 1972: pls. lxxxi-ii, 1979: pl. xxxii; Sparks 2007: section 3; Warren 1979: 83–6, pls. 15–16). The rest of the assemblage is difficult to put into any proper context: some obsidian vessel fragments may be elaborate contemporary products or the same type as those found at Kültepe and Acemhöyük and hence heirlooms (see Chapter 6). There are also several marble bowl fragments and it is just possible they are made of the same sort of white stone as Hatti is recorded sending to Thutmosis III (Breasted

1907: passages 485, 491, 509). Equally intriguing but unsatisfactory are hints offered by the mention of stone *BIBRU* cups in the Hittite texts (Carruba 1967). There is an earlier, carved chloritite example of such a vessel from Kültepe and several vessel fragments of other types from Boğazköy to suggest that this softstone tradition may have continued, but no definite Hittite versions. Beyond the capital, Hittite sites such as Alişar Höyük and Alaca Höyük produce hardly any vessels, but there are hints that the picture might be quite different in key areas such as the Cilician delta where contacts with the rest of the eastern Mediterranean were more intense (Goldman 1956: fig. 421; Heltzer 1977: 209; Archi 1984: 204).

## The Aegean

Stone vessels continue to be made after the Neopalatial period, but in smaller quantities and in a reduced range of shapes. Knossos apparently remained as a palace centre until LMIIIA2, and while its material culture took on some mainland attributes, it is often difficult to assess whether stone vessels in LMII–IIIA contexts represent (1) heirlooms, (2) artefacts looted during or after the LMIB destructions, or (3) continued production in Neopalatial styles. On the mainland, the selective consumption strategies that prompted such a restricted and selected range of types in the Shaft Graves disappeared and Neopalatial-style stone vessels occur relatively frequently in LHIIIA–B burials. Some vessel styles and techniques clearly indicate continued manufacture at Knossos in LMII–IIIA and then at Mycenae in LHIIIB1, but we risk overemphasising the degree of discontinuity by only considering these types and ignoring products that maintain an earlier tradition and are thus harder to disentangle from processes of curation and recirculation. To place this complex situation in a wider context, the following discussion first considers the foreign vessels reaching the Aegean, and especially the concentration of finds from the Knossos valley, where important socioeconomic changes were taking place. The focus then broadens to look at the implications of these changes, first for the rest of Crete and then the Aegean at large, before finally addressing the vessel tradition visible in the LHIIIB1 Ivory Houses at Mycenae.

### Egyptian, Cypriot, and Levantine Vessels

The later second millennium is a period in which Aegean pottery is commonplace in the rest of the Eastern Mediterranean and, in return, a wide variety of Near Eastern goods are found in post-Neopalatial Aegean contexts. These finds come from a number of different centres, but subdivision of the finds by finer date ranges (where possible) suggests that Knossos continued to play a prominent role in directing the flow of these goods until LMIIIA and that it is only in LHIIIA2–B that Mycenae becomes more centrally involved (Cline 1994: 85–93). Numerically speaking, the more than 60 Egyptian-style stone vessels that are part of this group of foreign trade goods in LB2–3 represent an impressive assemblage, but closer attention suggests a rather more complicated picture (Bevan 2003: 70–1), with the suspicion that, while a few special contexts imply continued acquisition of such items, some of the vessels originally arrived during the Neopalatial period (or soon thereafter in LMII) but sometimes only entered the archaeological record later on. For example, baggy alabastra are found in contexts as late as as LHIIIB (e.g. Warren 1969: 114), but no longer appear to have been as prominent part of the Egyptian tradition during the Amarna and Ramesside periods. Several other vessels suggest trade during the mid-18th Dynasty (e.g. Bosanquet

1904: pl. 14; Alexiou 1967: pl. 10), but very few are of Amarna period or Ramesside manufacture, despite the fact that potentially diagnostic vessel styles do exist (e.g. E176-98). Indeed, this is all the more interesting given the clear involvement of the Aegean in eastern Mediterranean pottery and oil trade at this time and the large numbers of Egyptian-style stone vessels found in contemporary contexts in Cyprus and at Ugarit. It suggests that we should interpret the pattern of foreign stone vessels in the Aegean as something closely linked to MMIII-LMII Crete (and the Knossos valley in particular) but smeared into a more extensive and chronologically enduring pattern by the continued deployment of curated or looted material.[19]

## LMII-III Knossos

In LMII, stone vessels are only one possible type of grave good amongst a range of funerary strategies (Preston 2001). They are rarely found in burials with lots of weapons or large of amounts of bronzework,[20] suggesting that such items were inappropriate to the mortuary claims of certain types of people. Burial customs seem to become more consistent but also to decline in overall wealth during LMIIIA-B (Preston 2004: table 2). Only a few of the burials at Mavro Spelio, Sellopoulo, and Zapher Papoura have stone vessels (perhaps 5% at the latter cemetery, though this is confused by disturbed and multiple burials). Those stone vessels that do occur in tombs can be separated into three distinct categories: (1) thick-walled serpentinite bowls which may either have continued to be made in this period or have been heirlooms, (2) fragments of elaborate Neopalatial shapes that also suggest tomb reuse or limited curation, and (3) foreign imports.

In fact there are unusual concentrations of foreign stone vessels in only a few important late-fifteenth- to early-fourteenth-century BC tombs. These seem to be using such objects to evoke a complicated but consistent set of values surrounding the appropriate use of both the palatial and the exotic, the old and the new. More specifically, they combine (1) Egyptian stone vessel imports, (2) products from Cretan palatial workshops, (3) Egyptian antiquities, (4) Egyptianising materials, and (5) Cypriot or Levantine vessels in various Egyptianising styles. This selection is drawn from a much wider set of possible choices, is therefore unlikely to be haphazard, and suggests deliberate connoisseurship. In all cases, we should probably see these surviving stone objects as archaeologically persistent tracers for a wider range of goods that have either been robbed for their convertible value (e.g. metals) or long since rotted away. Four tombs (three relatively unplundered, the other wholly empty) are worth addressing in more detail: Tomb B at Katsamba, the so-called Isopata Royal Tomb and Mycenae tombs *P* and 102. Three stone vessels come from Katsamba tomb B: the first is a travertine Canaanite-style jar with a cartouche of Thutmosis III which was an heirloom by the time it was finally buried here and may have arrived during Neopalatial times. The second is an Early Dynastic heart-shaped bowl. In Chapters 5 and 6 we considered that these out-of-time Egyptian vessels might have been used in Neopalatial Crete to claim ancestral links to foreign contact and local authority, and a similar statement may have been behind its interment with the owner of tomb B. The third vessel is a travertine bowl with distinctive lug handles for which there are no clear parallels in Egypt, but several more or less comparable pieces in the Levant (e.g. Macalister 1912: pl. lxxxix.14, L21; Callot and Calvet 2001).

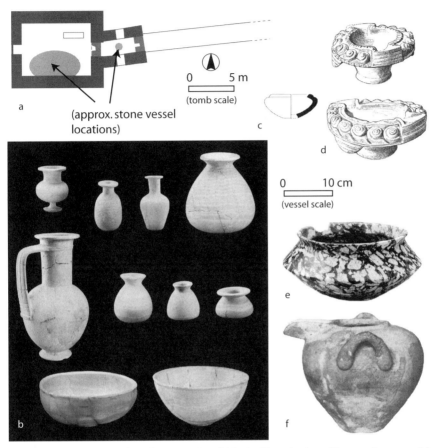

FIGURE 7.10. Stone vessels from the Isopata Royal Tomb: (a) tomb plan with approximate vessel locations; (b) Egyptian travertine vessels, including a possible oil set; (c) Early Dynastic collared diorite bowl; (d) two Cretan lamps with whorl decoration, (e) black and white porphyry bowl, (f) bridge-spouted jar in banded local travertine (after Evans 1906: figs. 126–8, pl. xciii; Warren 1969: P189; Karetsou 2000: nos. 232–9). In addition, the tomb group also included one small bowl in a local white travertine and several serpentinite lids.

These three vessels from tomb B at the port town of Knossos represent a curious range of exotica whose meanings are far from straightforward. However, further south along the valley route from the harbour town to the Knossos palace, there is an even more impressive tomb, built of monumental dressed stone blocks and with the largest assemblage of foreign stone vessels from any single Aegean deposit (the so-called Isopata Royal Tomb; Figure 7.10). Here, there are 10 travertine vessels, including two bowls, as well as a series of flasks that probably constitute an Egyptian sacred oil set similar to a contemporary example buried with Kha, an architect of Thutmosis IV (Bisset et al. 1996: fig. 1).[21] As we have seen in previous chapters, such sets have a long pharaonic history, dating back to at least the early Old Kingdom and were part of the rites performed so that the deceased could pass safely through the seven gates of the underworld (Gee 1998: table 7.5; Robinson 2003: 148–53). The presence of a full set at Isopata is therefore intriguing because it might have implied that the owner was knowledgeable about such practices but also frustrating because we lack sufficient contextual detail to really know. One of the two hardstone bowls from the tomb is also Egyptian, but an Early Dynastic antiquity [compare Figure 7.10(c) with E106, also Warren 1969: 110–111, P596-598]. The other is made of a porphyritic stone similar, if not identical to one used in 1st Dynasty Egypt [Plate 1(e); Aston 1994: 23], but its strongest parallels in terms of shape are with vessels from an upper elite northern Levantine tradition (e.g. L8-9, see discussion in Bevan 2003: 70–1). Additional stone vessels from this tomb include a bridge-spouted jar and a tiny bowl, both in local polychrome travertine, as well as two lamps with whorl-shell decoration.

The architecture, prominent location, and finds from the Isopata find impressive parallels in tombs *P* and 102 at Mycenae, as well as in the archaeological record at Ugarit. Tomb *P* is extremely unusual for being cut into the earlier Grave Circle B at the site, and its owner may conceivably have been asserting links to a previous ruling lineage at Mycenae. It was built in a very similar vaulted and niched ashlar design to Isopata, and convincing parallels and very good matches are found in the built tombs at Ugarit and its harbour town, suggesting that this may have been the source of this foreign mortuary style in the Aegean. Tomb 102, however, was of far less impressive rock-cut construction, but well-placed amongst a tiny cluster of other chamber tombs to the south of the Atreus tholos (Iakovidis and French 2003: E4:14). All three tomb assemblages probably included Palace-style storage jars. Tomb *P* was almost completely robbed but there were dumps nearby that were almost certainly associated with it which included an Egyptian scarab of lapis lazuli, a sealstone with a bull or deer image, and Palace-style jars (Mylonas 1973: 211–25, pl. 194–6).[22] The grave goods from 102 in particular offer further striking parallels for those at Isopata [Figure 7.11(a)], including not only more Palace-style jars and two matching stone lamps with whorl decoration but also a travertine BR jug, two gabbro bridge-spouted jars whose connection to late Protopalatial or early Neopalatial production at Knossos we have discussed in the previous chapter [Figures 6.13 and 6.16], and a Neopalatial ritual jug made in Egyptian travertine. With the exception of the lamps, the stones chosen for vessels in these two tombs are either Egyptian or have a history as local Egyptianising materials (gabbro, local polychrome travertines). Interestingly, Ugarit and its port town also provide good comparanda for many of these objects, including footed travertine jars, antique Egyptian stone bowls, travertine base-ring style jugs, and indeed examples of the same Cretan lamps with whorl decoration (Caubet 1991: pls. vii. 2, xii.10, probably also RS 16.022).[23]

What all of these tombs seem to express is a dual mortuary strategy which emphasised (1) the ability to acquire and display (perhaps also to consume correctly) a range of foreign or foreign-style products and (2) an emphasis on close palace connections (tomb location, whorl-shell lamps, palace-style jars, and at Isopata also masons' marks and a bull sealing). These are clearly the interments of powerful upper elite individuals who wish to describe a particular burial persona, one with close links to the ruling palatial authority and a connoisseur's familiarity with exotica. Such people may have been related to the royal family (or whatever palatial authority existed at Knossos) but especially at Mycenae are more likely close to but outside of the most circumscribed royal group (who buried themselves in tholoi). As such, they may have had similar combination of administrative and trading interests to the Ugaritan Yabninu introduced above, though they lived one or two centuries before him.

FIGURE 7.11. (a) Stone vessels from Mycenae chamber tomb 102 (after Bosanquet 1904: pl. xiv) and monumental vaulted funerary architecture of (b) Isopata Royal Tomb (Evans 1935: fig. 753) and (c) Tomb VI at Minet el-Beida (Evans 1935: fig. 751).

**LMII-IIIA Gypsum Vessels**   Another new development in LMII is the production at Knossos of a suite of softstone vessels, particularly in local gypsum.[24] Crete is dotted with many outcrops of the stone and a major deposit is Gypsades Hill at Knossos itself. Gypsum begins to be used for architectural features during the Protopalatial period but is employed far more intensively in the Neopalatial for floors, door jambs, and wall veneer, particularly at Knossos. However, the type of gypsum used for making vessels was a fine-grained alabastrine variety, rather than the shiny selenite gypsum often preferred for architecture (Chlouveraki 2002). As in LBA Cyprus, chlorite-rich stones were also occasionally used for the same types of vessels.[25] Known softstone shapes include large squat alabastra, cylindrical boxes, bowls, basins, libation tables, and pithoi (C1B, 2, 8K, 18B, 27iiC, 25, 26vi) and their distribution is heavily concentrated on Knossos and the coast immediately to its north, with other examples coming from eastern Crete and the mainland [Figure 7.12(c)].[26] Two possible gypsum vessel-making areas areas are known from within the palace: the upper floor 'Lapidary's Workshop' above the cache of *lapis lacedaemonius* blocks in the east wing of the palace, where two

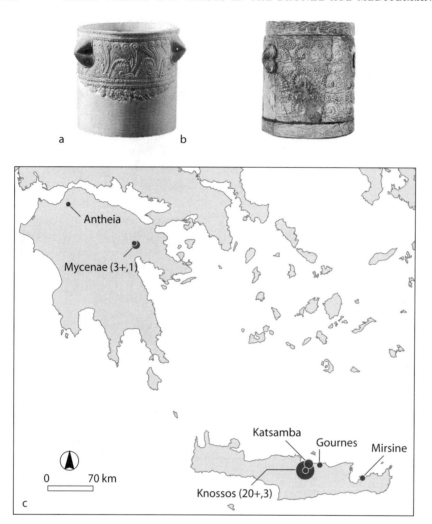

FIGURE 7.12.  LMII–IIIA gypsum vessels: (a) pyxis and lid from Antheia (ht. 7.5 cm, after Demakopoulou 1988: no. 43); (b) ivory parallel from a chamber tomb on the Acropolis, Athens (ht. 5 cm Shear 1940: fig. 31); (c) distribution map of Knossos-style gypsum vessels (shown in grey), as well as a few further examples of identical style in chloritite (shown in black).

unfinished banded gypsum amphorae were found (Evans 1935: 896–900, figs. 875–6) and an upper floor area in the west wing of the palace from which unfinished vessels, blanks, and waste pieces seem to have fallen (Warren 1967; Evely 1980).

Most of these gypsum and chloritite vessels are carved with detailed decorative schemes of whorl shells, shallow spirals, figure-of-eight shield handles, rosettes, corded bands, and even nautili. The closest stylistic parallels are found with the contemporary Aegean ivories [Figures 7.12(a) and (b)], and gypsum may have been used to copy this more exotic material, sometimes for vessels too large to have ever been made of real ivory. In any case, the same designs are found on a wide variety of other products probably made at the Knossos palace, including pottery and bronze weapons (Popham 1978: 183–4, pl. 25c; MacDonald 1987).

Many of these softstone vessels are preserved for us in grave contexts, but at least eight alabastra and three lids were also found in the so-called throne room at Knossos (Warren 1969: 5–6, 71; von Arbin 1984) and therefore seem to have been part of the ceremonies occurring in this room just before the destruction of the palace, perhaps in an annointing ritual by or for the person who sat on the throne (a ruler or a stand-in for a divinity are both plausible suggestions). Such a high-profile location, along with the palace workshop contexts and the vessels' highly recognisable decorative style, suggests that, found elswhere, these objects may have made very effective ideological projections of the Knossos centre.

**LB2–3 Beyond the Knossos Valley**     Across Crete, beyond the Knossos valley and its harbour zone, ca. 14% of published LMIII tombs (Löwe 1996) have been found with stone vessels. As at Knossos, many of these vessels were curated items, a good example being the cemetery at Elounda where thick-walled bowls are found alongside obvious heirlooms or looted objects from earlier periods (van Effenterre 1948: pls. xxi, xxxiv). LMII-III stone vessel use outside of the Knossos valley was quite conservative, prioritising a few shapes (thick-walled bowls, lamps, and a few metal skeuomorphs), and visible in the funerary display of a restricted proportion of the population.

A few Cretan stone vessels have been found at sites outside of the Aegean but rarely in well-published or stratified contexts (see also Chapter 6). Some of these are probably associated with Neopalatial period exchanges or people, but there are a few interesting examples that seem to reflect LB2–3 activity, contemporary with the peak period of overseas trade in Mycenaean-style products. Lamps decorated with a band of shells around the rim have been found at Ugarit and Enkomi (see above with respect to Isopata, also Dikaios 1969: 276, pls. 134.54, 164.15), but an extremely elaborate stone lamp made of purple marble/limestone (possibly *rosso antico*) was also found in a secondary refuse context at Alalakh (along with Mycenaean pottery, Woolley 1955a: 294, pl. lxxix). It seems to have been discarded unfinished, raising the intriguing possibility that it had either been traded as raw material or was the result of work by a locally resident Aegean stone mason. It was hollowed out by the use of adjacent small drillings, which is a manufacturing technique that has Neopalatial antecedents, but becomes the dominant method used in making LHIIIB1 Ivory Houses-style vessels (see below). The outside is decorated with a network of tricurved arches, which is typically LB2–3A in date (Warren 1969: 55–6). The material, design, and production technique suggest a late date and imply crafting knowledge and materials associated with workshops at Knossos and thereafter Mycenae during the LB2–3 period.

**Mycenae Ivory Houses–Style Vessels**
In addition to the continued presence of Cretan-style vessels in later-second-millennium Aegean contexts, some mainland manufacture is also visible by this time. The most obvious examples come from the LHIIIB1 Ivory Houses, down the slope from citadel at Mycenae (Tournavitou 1995: 213–36).[27] Here scattered through the rectangular building known as the House of Shields, with a smaller group in the adjacent House of Sphinxes, over a hundred whole and fragmentary vessels were found which have links to the styles and production techniques found before on Crete but also indicate a slightly different set of priorities. The range of shapes is relatively limited, consisting of various jars, alabastra, a rhyton, and a

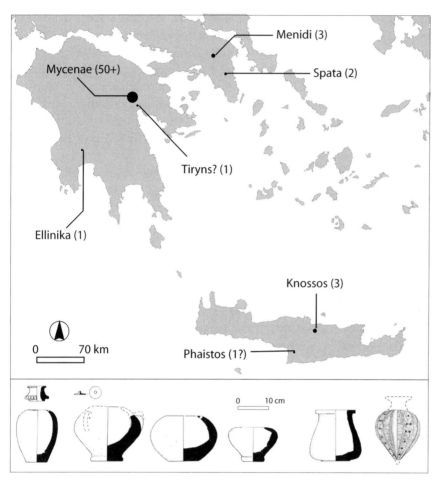

FIGURE 7.13. Distribution map of Ivory Houses-style vessels.

few more unusual pieces (M1-5), many of which have parallels in contemporary pottery. Serpentinite is the most common material, but conglomerate, breccia, bioclastic limestone, and *lapis lacedaemonius* are also present. Incised decoration, shallow carved designs, quartz crystal inlay, and possibly gold leaf were added to a small number of examples. However, the two most striking things about these vessels is (1) their construction in separate pieces and (2) the dominant use of small tubular drillings to hollow out the interior. These manufacturing decisions are telling, because they imply the survival of a limited set of the techniques used by palatial workshops in MMIII-LMIIIA Crete. For example, the assembly of vessels from multiple parts was used to create some of the most elaborate Neopalatial ritual vessels, but it was not something regularly done by most stone vessel producers. Likewise, the hollowing out the vessel interior using adjacent and diagonal small drillings was only one of a number of techniques deployed in Neopalatial period, but now became the exclusive method used. The latter feature also implies a more restricted toolkit, because the diameters of the drill cores are often similar, and there is no obvious use of shaped grinding stones for undercutting the shoulder. In other words, the artisans making the vessels were working within a technical tradition that developed out of the elite workshops of Cretan palatial centres but now used a more limited range of strategies and tools.

While the majority of vessels with this distinctive style have been found in the Ivory Houses, other examples come from tholoi and chamber tombs in Attica, the Argolid, and Messenia, as well as from settlement debris at Knossos and possibly Phaistos (Figure 7.13).[28] The composite shapes and rough interior finishing indicate a very different set of priorities than Cretan palatial vessels, despite an inherited technical tradition. The use of quartz crystal inlay, and possible gold leaf, suggests an emphasis on eye-catching decoration applied to elaborate but fragile composite vessels.

The same emphasis on showy kit-sets is seen in the faience and ivory objects stored within the Mycenae Ivory Houses. The presence of artefacts that were meant to be assembled from multiple parts and the absence of almost any primary manufacturing tools or debris suggest that these were places where such objects were brought together but not actually made. The Linear B texts from these houses also point to storage and assembly priorities rather than to production (Shelmerdine 1999: 569). This distributed orgnisation of palace labour was an efficient way of mobilising elaborate manufactured goods from craftspeople working on separate components in a variety of locations and may well be part of a broader *o-pa* system referred to in Linear B texts (see Bendall 2003). In other words, just as monumental tholoi imply a more complex economic relationship between the palace elite and a wider kingdom than the Shaft Grave burials (by virtue of the logistics and human resources necessary for their construction), so in a smaller way, these later stone vessels were also integrated into the structure of the Mycenaean economy in a more complex way than their Shaft Grave equivalents.

# 8

# The Rough and the Smooth: Stone Vessels from a Comparative Perspective

卍卍卍卍卍卍

*The preceding chapters have covered a large area and an extended period of time to make* some explanatory links across the whole Bronze Age eastern Mediterranean. This chapter takes such a comparative approach to its logical conclusion by considering, albeit rapidly, the roles played by stone vessel traditions across the world and throughout human history. In this regard, it is important to explore comparisons not only with other Mediterranean and Middle Eastern stone vessel industries but also with those in wholly separate parts of the world, so that we can distinguish patterns of convergent usage driven by similar conditions from those that are part of an inherited or diffused cultural tradition. In other words, while such a perspective cannot hope to be comprehensive, it aims to distinguish the smooth cross-cultural themes and those rougher idiosyncrasies specific to the cultural development of the Bronze Age eastern Mediterranean.

Figure 8.1 presents the result of a literature search on pre-twentieth century stone vessel industries across the world, ignoring simple mortars and palettes. No doubt, it is very far from complete and reflects a degree of investigative bias in favour of regions close to the eastern Mediterranean, but it nonetheless suggests that such objects have a very wide geographic distribution. Stone vessels have been made by communities living in the full range of global climatic conditions (arctic, boreal, temperate, semiarid, tropical rainforest, desert), by nonsedentary and sedentary populations, hunter-gatherers and agro-pastoralists, ceramic and nonceramic, pre- and postmechanised, precapitalist and capitalist. Moreover, they have also been deployed for a wide range of human activities, including food processing (grinding), preparation (cooking) and serving (tableware), inhaled or imbibed narcotics, smoke production (censers), storage (semipermanent installations), lighting (lamps), and various ritual performances (e.g. libations, shamanic ceremonies).

Amidst this impressive diversity, however, the eastern Mediterranean and Middle East stands out as an area that has consistently encouraged the largest number and widest range of traditions. Ultimately, we may wish to explain this high prevalence at a continental scale (e.g. following Diamond 1998). The intensity and variety of material culture found in this region, of which stone vessels are only one excellent example, is encouraged by Eurasia's heterogeneous geology, which provides diverse raw materials, and by its east–west axial orientation. The latter facilitates the movement of people, goods, and ideas through zones of broadly similar ecology, particularly in the Near East with its major riverine (Nile, Tigris, Euphrates) and maritime (Mediterranean, Red Sea/Persian Gulf) conduits. Geographical configuration has also, in premechanised times at least, repeatedly

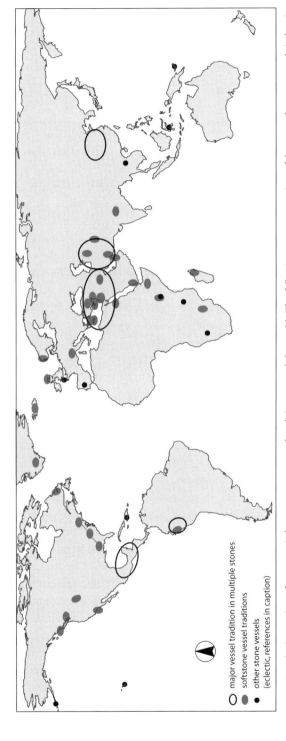

FIGURE 8.1. An impression of pre-twentieth-century stone vessel traditions around the world. The following sources are points of departure for stone vessels industries outside of the prehistoric eastern Mediterranean (not including quernstones and common mortars): Africa (Caton-Thompson 1929; Clark 1964; Curle 1937; Harrell and Max 2006; Merrick 1973; Morris 1991; Radimilahy 1998; Robertshaw 1990: 167–72; Whitemore 1912); the Americas (Adams 2005; Burger 1992; Drew and Wilson 1980; Duff 1980; Frison 1982; King 1977; McCartney 1970; McCawley 1996: 136–8; Rouse 1992: figs. 17a,c; Truncer 2004); Europe (Butler 1991; Hurtado 1997: 110, fig. 6.4; Mathiassen 1935; Paunier 1983; Pilo 1989; Quinnell 1993; Rutherford 1978; Rütimeyer 1924: 38–143), western and central Asia (Hallett 1990; Magen 2002; Phillips and Simpson 2007; Durrani 1964; Roosevelt 2006); southern and eastern Asia, the Pacific, and Australasia (Raven 1933; Corney 1920; Sherwin and Haddon 1933).

○ major vessel tradition in multiple stones

● softstone vessel traditions

• other stone vessels
(eclectic, references in caption)

encouraged the eastern Mediterranean and Middle East (at the centre of this east–west zone) to be made up of politically fragmented but economically interdependent units, prompting material and cultural experimentation but also making the results less likely to die out with the contingent fortunes of any single polity. A concentration of the right candidates for plant and animal domestication also enabled dense, sedentary, and socially stratified human populations, high consumer demand, substantial manufacturing capacity, and favourable conditions for product innovation.

These simple features go some way towards explaining why stone vessels traditions are common and highly varied in this area, but only offer satisfactory insights at a very gross scale. Beyond this, our understanding is greatly improved by building a more subtle comparative case. The following discussion therefore reconsiders the evidence of Chapters 3–7 alongside a brief selection of other case studies. It focuses on three different types of stone vessel phenomenon: the first addresses small-scale societies where stone vessels are associated with patterns of intensified foraging, early agriculture, and/or growing economic interdependence. The second considers vessels made from sub-Mohs scale 3 stones, a seemingly innocent physical threshold, but one responsible for geographically widespread and socially malleable forms of material culture. The third and final stone vessel phenomenon is one feature of the highly wrought expressions of elite taste that exist in early complex societies, who produced vessels in a range of different material and shapes and for whom these objects were just one of many possible avenues of status display. Such an analysis by no means exhausts the range of interesting questions that might be asked of stone vessels from a comparative perspective but nonetheless illuminates the study of the Bronze Age eastern Mediterranean traditions in useful ways.

## Stone Vessels in Small-Scale Societies

Traditionally, archaeologists have associated the development of groundstone technologies with the adoption of agriculture and a range of staple crops (cereals, rice, maize) that required milling before they could be converted into food. Certainly, sedentary agricultural life seems to be a precondition for the development of the most diverse and elaborate stone vessel industries (see below), not least because the latter have only ever really emerged in highly complex societies, with stratified urban populations and highly specialised craft skills. However, there is growing evidence for the presence of groundstone technologies in a range of preforming contexts throughout the world, and it may in fact be more appropriate to speak of the uptake of groundstone bowls, mortars, and querns at two general stages: (1) as part of a move towards more sedentary foraging and (2) during a transition to agriculture (e.g. Wright 1994: 240). These shifts occur at different times around the world, but the initial introduction of a broader spectrum diet, including seed processing, seems to have been particularly important. Some of the earliest evidence comes from Middle Palaeolithic Africa, where alongside these developing processing strategies, we also see similar objects used for grinding ochre, suggesting that they were simultaneously part of an expansion in representational behaviour associated with the development of modern humans (McBrearty and Brooks 2000: esp. 524–531; Ambrose 2001: 1751). Likewise, in the eastern Mediterranean, the use of querns to grind cereals certainly preceded the domestication of these plants (e.g. Wright 1991; Piperno et al. 2004), and we see impressive, decorated stone vessels being produced, for example, by prefarming Natufian communities in the southern Levant. Even so, the scale and character of groundstone vessel use does seem to change with the appearance of the first farming settlements, and we can trace the use of such objects across an extensive number of early Neolithic sites in the region. In this sense, although groundstone objects were by no means a novelty, we might still associate them with a Neolithic package of characteristic tools, ideologies, agricultural strategies, and culinary habits that spreads out of the Near East and into Europe (Wright 2000).

In theory, stone vessels are not very sensible forms of material culture for mobile groups because they offer a bad weight to capacity ratio and do not pack very well. When we find them used by hunter-gatherer populations, it is often by those groups that benefit from the richest wild food resources, experience the highest population densities, and are semisedentary, all of which seem to encourage increased levels of social ranking and craft specialisation (e.g. in the Jordan valley or along the North American Pacific coast). Moreover, stone vessels emerge in these areas most obviously when communities have moved towards increasing management of these wild resources, higher population densities, and greater sedentism. Ironically, these strategies often coincide with periods of apparent climatic stress, when the use of grinding stones for processing seeds or heat-resistant steatite pots for slower cooking may have helped extend the range of possible food. Even so, more mobile groups do sometimes use such items, particularly steatite cooking pots (see below), and in such cases may well cache them at important seasonal campsites, as the Beja tribes of the Egyptian eastern desert did during the nineteenth and early twentieth centuries AD (Whittemore 1912). In several north American cases as well, such behaviour would explain the rather odd range of archaeological contexts in which groups of steatite cooking vessels are sometimes found (e.g. Frison 1982; Truncer 2004).

So there is both an important role for stone vessels among pre- and nonagricultural groups, and a clear relationship between stone vessel production and the earliest phases of the eastern Mediterranean Neolithic, especially prior to the consistent use of pottery. Thereafter in the latter area, a low-intensity tradition of stone vessel manufacture seems to continue, though perhaps with a more restricted range of social roles and increasingly sharp distinction between those used for primary food-processing and those meant for other functions. By the Chalcolithic or its local equivalents, we see a range of industries exhibiting similar features throughout the eastern Mediterranean, such as those in the late fifth- and fourth-millennium BC Cyclades, the southern Levant, and Lower Egypt. These traditions reveal an extremely limited number of vessel shapes, only one or two stones (e.g. marble or basalt), comparatively large vessel dimensions, but simple decoration, and a relatively wide geographical distribution. These features suggest that such artefacts may have brought temporary prestige to a few individuals within fairly extended networks of economic and social interaction but that their use was socially conservative and most likely channeled into activities that reinforced community values.

## Softstone Industries

As we have seen in previous chapters, the term softstone can be used as crude but useful shorthand for a range of stones, including steatite, chloritite, gypsum, chalk, and some volcanic tuffs, that have a mineral hardness below Mohs scale 3 and hence are usually carved rather that drilled. This seemingly innocent working property has wider implications, however, encouraging ideological and technological links with other soft media such as wood, ivory, bone, and some soft artificial compounds. These links are visible in Europe as far back as 20,000–30,000 years ago in the technical and stylistic similarities between Palaeolithic figurines made of steatite/chloritite and those made of mammoth ivory (Mussi et al. 2000: 117-8). As was suggested in Chapter 4, the emphasis on carving vessels rather than drilling them also affects production rationales in more complex ways, facilitating speedier rates of manufacture but with greater risk of breakage, and often focusing skilled attention on the addition of fancy exterior decoration rather than on removal of the interior (see Chapter 4). We might make a further useful separation between darker-coloured, ultramafic softstones that usually come from quite specific ophiolite geologies (e.g. steatite, chloritite, and slightly harder serpentinites[1]) and lighter-coloured rocks (e.g. chalk, gypsum). The distinction is sharper still because ophiolite formations are part of broader orogenic environments that often also produce timber and metals (see below), while gypsum and chalk are formed (in different ways) in shallow water and hence are usually found in different environmental and economic contexts, close to coastal areas, estuaries, and brackish lakes (e.g. Prentice 1990: 187–91).

The following sections introduce a number of case studies in the manufacture, use, and deposition of both light and dark softstone vessels from other areas of the world, focusing on (1) chalk vessels from Second Temple period Judaea, (2) chloritite/steatite and argillite vessels from the North American west, and then drawing the discussion back round to the Bronze Age eastern Mediterranean and Middle East by considering (3) chloritite vessels from south-central Iran and the Omani peninsula. These examples should make it clear that, for a variety of important reasons, softstone vessels are a very sensitive tracer of wider socioeconomic and political change and hence have considerable analytical value.

## Light-Coloured Softstones

During the Jewish Second Temple Period (ca. 50 BC–70 AD), chalk vessels become suddenly and briefly popular in the Roman province of Judaea before vanishing almost completely after the Bar Kokhba revolt, an abrupt trajectory of use which is in sharp contrast to many other, more enduring, forms of Jewish material culture (for what follows, see Magen 2002). The consumption of these items began as quite a narrow fashion in the vicinity of Jerusalem but expanded into the Golan and Galilee to become a wider Palestinian Jewish custom for a time. The vessels' shapes, manufacture, and decoration reveal an intriguing contrast between extreme simplicity in many cases and reference to contemporary and more exotic Graeco-Roman styles and techniques in others. For example, some of the vessels imitate imported pottery, glass, and metal vessels, were given added decoration and/or were made on a horizontal lathe (itself likely to be a Graeco-Roman innovation). Others, however, were far more determinedly straightforward objects: for example, a very popular shape was the mug, which copied well-known local wooden prototypes, was undecorated, and continued to be made only by hand-carving (Magen 2002: 40). Moreover, we can see these stylistic and technical tensions expressed clearly in terms of normative social practice and Jewish ritual observance, because textual sources reveal that such vessels had important roles in the application of Jewish purity laws, especially the strict observance briefly favoured by the

Pharisees (Magen 2002: 138–47). Pottery, metal, and glass vessels were said to transmit human impurity and were proscribed from ritual use. In contrast, stone, dung, and earthenware vessels were said to be resistant to such pollution, with stone vessels in particular used for the purification of water and as containers for ointment (e.g. for New Testament examples, *John* 2:6; *Luke* 7:37–8).

Chalk vessels could be made fairly expediently, from a material usually found in the immediate vicinity, if not right under the feet of local Jewish communities, making them naturally occurring and symbolic markers of local Jewish identity in contrast to Romanised, artificially manipulated, and often imported materials such as metal, glass, and pottery. The use of an ultralocal white stone, the general conservatism but cross-media references of the chalk shapes, and their sanctioning by an established Jewish faction during a period of heightened political confrontation are all striking. Such vessels arguably expressed and exploited a concern about pollution by outside political domination, commercial influences, and alternative ranked prestige indicators, emphasising a cultural and ideological faultline amongst Pharisee, Saducee, and Roman world views.

How does this evocative, albeit textually illuminated, case study inform our perception of the use of softstone vessels in the Bronze Age? It suggests strongly that a combination of the natural, local, expediently carved, easily decorated character of such stones, along with their cross-media links, and distinct source areas might make them excellent material tracers for wider concerns, including short bursts of political faction or socioeconomic change. As the other case studies below and evidence from Chapters 5–7 should suggest, many such industries seem to be part of contact phenomena, appearing among communities that were being strongly influenced by sometimes attractive, sometimes repellent external forces.

Returning to the Bronze Age eastern Mediterranean, the archaeological evidence is inevitably less neatly presented than the Jewish textual sources, but again it suggests that these objects are often entangled in the expression of group identity, both within local communities and between them and a wider world. For example, gypsum vessels appear relatively suddenly in the Jordan valley during the MBA, almost certainly drawing on ultralocal stone sources. The vessel designs reference both exotic and foreign-style travertine vessels on the one hand and very indigenous products on the other. These vessels were not usually long-distance trade goods and their manufacture focuses on only a few sites. As with the Second Temple chalk vessels, such items arguably express a tension between foreign and local elements, and it is interesting that peak periods in their production coincide with fluctuations in the character of Egyptian political influence. The first MBIIB-C group is contemporary with a period of relative political instability in Hyksos Egypt. A second comes with an apparent change (and in many cases a decline) in Egyptian control at the end of the Bronze Age and early Iron Age. Between these two periods, Egyptian political and cultural influence on the area was arguably more extensive and the gypsum industry far less visible. Other gypsum vessel traditions in the Bronze Age eastern Mediterranean occur in broadly equivalent circumstances, though the details are often elusive. The industry that emerges suddenly at LMII-IIIA Knossos almost certainly draws on the large gypsum deposits in the immediate vicinity of the town and is a new feature of Cretan stone vessel production which does last for more than one or two centuries at most. It seems strongly tied to the workshops and consumption routines of the upper elite at the Knossos palace, during a period of apparent sociopolitical flux, when, in the mortuary record at least, different elite groups were experimenting with a range of new and traditional, Cretan and Mainland-style, Aegean and eastern behaviours. The Cypriot tradition of gypsum vessels that appears at the end of the Bronze Age also coincides with a period of rapid socioeconomic change on the island, drawing on a ubiquitous local resource, and mixing local designs with others strongly linked to Egyptian- or Mycenaean-style products.

## Dark-Coloured Softstones

If light-coloured softstones are potentially sensitive indicators of wider social patterning, then dark-coloured varieties are arguably even more so due to their particular geological provenance. Most of the latter are ultramafic rocks that come from wider ophiolite sequences that are thought to be fragments of ocean floor pushed upwards onto the land surface at points where major tectonic plates come together (Malpas 1992; Dilek 2003). A typical ophiolitic sequence includes a mixture of different sedimentary and metamorphic rocks, including peridotites, serpentinites and gabbros, extrusive pillow lavas, argillites, cherts, chloritites, limestones, and steatites, to name but a few. A variety of metal ores are associated with such formations, especially sulphidic copper. Not all ophiolite deposits are the same, but many of those in the eastern Mediterranean and Middle East are associated with obducted fragments from the same ancient oceanic crust (the Tethys Ocean), perhaps the most well-known manifestations of which are those in the Cypriot Troodos, the Syrian Baer-Bassit, and the Omani al-Hajjar mountains (Degnan and Robertson 1998; Koepke et al. 2002).

The dark stones from these ophiolite zones, and especially the softer varieties such as chloritite and steatite, provide one of the commonest sources of material for stone vessels throughout the world (Figure 8.1, Bevan 2007). For example, steatite/chloritite vessels were used for cooking throughout prehistoric eastern North America, drawing on widespread outcrops in the Appalachian mountains (Truncer 2004). There is evidence for patchy but persistent manufacture over a period of up to a thousand years, but with a comparatively short peak period of production towards the end of the Late Archaic (later second millennium BC), followed by a switch to the use of steatite-tempered pottery in the subsequent early Woodland period. Much later, on the Californian Pacific coast, Gabrielino communities were producing steatite/chloritite vessels for boiling water, cooking food, and use in shamanic rituals (Wlodarski 1979; McCawley 1996: 136–8). The raw material seems to have come primarily from sources on San Catalina island, but the resulting vessels were part of a wider set of trade goods that linked Channel Island and coastal communities of both the Gabrielino and Chumash tribes into networks of economic interdependence, also perhaps as a means of buffering subsistence risk. The specialisation of different communities in particular products such as softstone vessels, plant and animal products, or shell beads is notable, as is the fact that although steatite use begins much earlier, the production of vessels seems to peak from the seventeenth century onwards during a period of increasing contact with Europeans and a growing availability of metal tools (Wlodarski et al. 1984). A broadly similar pattern is apparent further north and east, in what is mostly modern-day western Wyoming, where the Sheepeater Shoshone were producing elongated steatite cooking pots (Frison 1982; Adams 2005). We have less contextual information for the social and economic context behind these products, but again, while the use of local steatite/chloritite outcrops seems to have had a long ancestry, vessel production appears to peak in the proto- and early historic period, with the use of metal tools apparent on many surviving examples.

Finally, further north along the Pacific coast, the Haida Gwaii made elaborately decorated vessels, pipes, and other objects out of argillite, a shiny black stone that was quarried from a single source on Queen Charlotte Islands (Drew and Wilson 1980: 159–84, 201–15, 229–33). There had been a prehistoric tradition of zoomorphic and anthropomorphic bowls made of steatite/chloritite along the Fraser River (e.g. Duff 1980: nos. 30–57), but the peak of argillite crafting occurred in the nineteenth century AD and was strongly influenced by European contact. Not only was the manufacture of such objects made easier by the appearance of metal tools, but the industry itself seems to have been oriented towards the consumption of curios, including pipes, plates, bowls, and boxes, by mariners, traders, and other Europeans who came to Haida Gwaii villages. Smoking was not indigenous to the northwest Pacific coast, but came in around the time of the Europeans and some argillite pipes mimic common nineteenth-century European clay versions, shipping tackle or reused gun barrels (also King 1977). Even so, such products were given added decorative elements in local styles that had a long ancestry in basketry and wood-carving, and in this sense were deliberately inserted into existing technical, artistic, and economic logics. These patterns therefore reflect one local response to the opportunities and disruptions brought by the arrival of the Europeans, during a period in which iron, copper, and steel replaces many tools and status goods previously made in wood, stone, bone, and shell. The wider effect such contact had on traditional patterns of prestige display and social cohesion are perhaps best documented in the historically contingent extravagance of the nineteenth-century potlatch ceremonies.

These North American examples, on a different continent and with no cultural connection to the Bronze Age eastern Mediterranean, emphasise some common features of vessels made from dark softstones. They tend to be associated with cooking and pipe-smoking, where heat resistance is important, and are often invested with carved designs, but also influenced by the increased prominence of metal tools and/or by the trading opportunities engendered by interregional contact. Such analogies remain rather loose, however, especially given the fact cooking vessels and pipes are not actually roles we see emphasised very strongly in the Bronze Age eastern Mediterranean (see below). In contrast, two clear examples of contact-period, *Metallshock* phenomena that offer a sharper and more contingently Old World focus. Well-known and related chloritite traditions are associated with the Bronze Age communities of both south-central Iran and northern Oman. These were two of three key areas that produced distinctively decorated chloritite vessels during this period, the other being Bactria, about which we we know far less (Hiebert 1994). All three were located in ophiolite zones and hence potential suppliers of a range of other mineral products, most critical of which was probably copper ore, to the more densely urbanised lowland Mesopotamian kingdoms (Beale 1973). In return, we can hypothesise an archaeologically obscure Mesopotamian trade in textiles, oils, leather, grain, and fish (Crawford 1973) as well as procurement by more direct and aggressive means such as military campaiging (e.g. visible in the 'booty of Elam' or 'booty of Makkan' vessels; Potts 1989).

Perhaps the most well-known chloritite vessels in the Near East are those carved in Figurative style (also known as Intercultural Style or *série ancienne*) and made by communities at places such as Tepe Yahya and near Jiroft in modern-day south-central Iran (de Miroschedji

1973; Lamberg-Karlovsky 1988; Madjidzadeh 2003). Textual sources suggest this region may have been the third millennium kingdom of Marhasi/Parashum and the related stone called *marḥasu* that was used for oil containers and bowls may refer to local chloritite (Steinkeller 1982: 251, but see also Moorey 1994: 50). The peak of vessel production seems to be in the mid-third millennium BC, at which time we see a take-off in manufacture at Tepe Yahya that Kohl (1977: 117) has firmly linked to (1) a matching increase in the popularity of incised grey burnished pottery, (2) increased use of metal tools, and (3) a switch from local production to one tailored for interregional exchange. The chloritite vessels from Tepe Yahya were primarily made with small metal punches and were heavily decorated with relief carving (fantastical beasts, ordinary animals, architectural motifs, mat-weave designs), some colouring, and occasional shell inlay. These dense decorative schemes were part of a broader 'trans-Elamite' style visible in sealstones, metal objects, and ceramics and no doubt also in perishable soft media such as basketry, textiles, or wood (Amiet 1986). Moreover, the figurative schemes reveal a relatively coherent grammar of motifs that straddles the ideologies of both the producing region and the elites of Susiana and lowland Mesopotamia who were consuming them (Lamberg-Karlovsky 1975: 362; also for metal see Francfort 2005).

A large number of these vessels have also been found, further north along the coast, on Tarut island (part of the area known as Dilmun in contemporary textual records; Zarins 1978), suggesting that a maritime network was responsible for the vessels' distribution up the Gulf to Mesopotamian urban centres. Indeed, the strong directionality of this trade is also suggested by the fact that in contrast, immediately to the north (Shahr-I Sokhta), east (Bampur), and south (Oman) of the production zone, Figurative-style vessels are less common and more frequently copied in incised, grey-burnished pottery (De Cardi 1970: 319–25, figs. 45–6; Méry 2000: 204–17). This provides an interesting backdrop to the fact that thereafter in the late third millennium, we see the appearance of a distinct new deco-rated chloritite tradition in one of these areas, the Oman peninsula (Umm an-Nar style or *série récente*). Textual sources identify this region as the kingdom of Makkan and mention its possession of a range of wood, metal, and stone resources (Vallat 1991). While a few small chloritite objects were made during earlier periods, drawing on the substantial outcrops of the the Semail ophiolite in the al-Hajjar mountains, the appearance of this vessel industry is relatively sudden (David 1996). Initially, it may have been inspired by the neighbour-ing Figurative-style products, but the designs are much simpler and less firmly linked to Mesopotamian ideologies. Likewise, while some examples did reach centres in the Dilmun area and lowland Mesopotamia, the distribution is less extensive than for Figurative-style and becomes even more restricted by the earlier second millennium (Wadi Suq style or *série tardive*; David 1996).

What should these comparative examples tell us about the nature of the ophiolitic softstone industries in the Bronze Age eastern Mediterranean? As we have seen, the light, often whitish appearance of chalk and alabastrine gypsum encouraged their aesthetic connection with ivory, bone, and harder travertine products. In contrast, the dark colour of ultramafic softstones, often in distinct greyish, brownish, bluish, reddish, or greenish hues, encouraged their association with both wood and metal products. The latter links are also reinforced by the fact that the source areas for chloritite, steatite, and serpentinite are the same broad ophiolite zones from which the eastern Mediterranean and Middle East drew most of its metal and many of its timber resources.

However, raw lumps or finished objects in chloritite and steatite were not simply piggy-backing on the trade in metals but also became an economic objective in their own right, primarily because they offered huge industrial advantages over other stones. For example, their broad heat-resistant and -insulating properties encourage their use as a temper for pottery (facilitating higher firing temperatures), as lamps or pipes, and as vessels for slow-cooking food or heating drinks.[2] Interestingly, although the last four of these roles are common elsewhere, they are not functions we see these materials playing in the Bronze Age eastern Mediterranean. Perhaps this indicates a greater emphasis on cold drinks, imbibed narcotics, and fried or roasted food rather than hot drinks, inhaled smoke, and broiled food.[3] The two roles that we do see such materials clearly playing are as cosmetic containers and metallurgical tools. Both chloritite and steatite have a natural association with cosmetics because they are organophilic (their surfaces have a particular affinity for organic compounds), and steatite in particular is soft and unctuous, which encourages its use to thicken and carry perfumes (e.g. as a container, additive, or powdered method of application). For metallurgy, these materials are even more useful because they (1) are soft and easy to carve into desired tool shapes; (2) are fine-grained and retain a lot of added detail (e.g. for jewellery moulds); (3) are durable and hence amenable to reuse (more so than clay), especially after undergoing limited dehydration during initial use; (4) have a low thermal expansion coefficient and hence will not shatter due to sudden contact with hot metal; (5) have a high thermal refractoriness and hence will not bloat or collapse under prolonged and intense heating (e.g. as blowpipe or tuyère nozzles); (6) have a low chemical reactivity with inorganics and hence maintain a sharp separation between metal and mould; and (7) are thermally insulating and hence relatively easy to handle when hot (Read 1957: 408–12; Engel and Wright 1960: 846–50; Martinón-Torres, personal communication).

Metals and softstones were not the only attractive resources associated with the ophiolite zone. The geological diversity of these special locales provides the highest floral biodiversity of any Mediterranean landscape, including a wide range of timber, tree products, and aromatic plants (Roberts and Proctor 1992).[4] In other words, the increased exploitation of ultramafic stones can be taken as an archaeologically robust tracer not only for intensified metal prospection, extraction, and exchange but also for a much wider commodification of the ophiolitic landscape. Such intensified patterns of exploitation usually link these upland landscapes with (1) lowland or maritime entrepots (e.g. Susa, Dilmun, Ugarit, Enkomi) and (2) larger neighbouring states or communities which provided a market for metals and thereafter also a range of other products. For example, a Gulf trade route in metals from south-central Iran (and beyond) via Dilmun is arguably the explanation behind the appearance and directional flow of Figurative- and Umm an-Nar-style chloritite vessels towards lowland Mesopotamia in the third millennium BC. Hence, in lowland Mesopotamia we find Omani/Dilmun-style softstone seals or their bitumen imitations being used to mark accounts between Dilmun merchants trading in copper and agricultural produce (probably in opposite directions; Hallo and Buchanan 1965; Lambert 1976). Likewise, the appearance of Umm an-Nar-style softstone vessels dovetails well with a possible switch from Iranian to Omani copper ores, for where lowland Mesopotamian centres were acquiring the bulk of their metals (Potts 1993: 387; see also Weeks 2003). Indeed, the distributions of softstone objects in several Mediterranean and Middle Eastern case studies concentrate on key transhipment points, at the foot of the mountains or on the coast (for later examples, see also Weir 2007; Magee et al. 2005). Unsurprisingly, of the wider group of ophiolite zones it is usually those that were particularly close to the sea, and the advantages they offered in terms of maritime transport, that encouraged this level of economic interest. Moreover, the relationship between upland settlements and these larger lowland or coastal trading centres was a fluid one, with economic incentives for traders at the latter both to move later stages of production out of the source area and also to explore various avenues for effective product substitution. The manufacture of a range of imitation vessels and seals at Susa or Dilmun from bitumen compound may well be an example of such opportunism (e.g. Potts 1999: pl. 6.5).

This complex pattern of product association is worth exploring further, not least because we should think of both organic and inorganic ophiolitic products as being some of the most obviously branded in Aegean and Near Eastern circulation, with highly recognisable materials and distinctive styles. Figure 8.2 tries to capture these repeated associations by presenting some of the more iconographically explicit chloritite/steatite products. For example, across several different traditions in the Aegean, Cyprus, Iran, and Oman, we see the use of ultramafic softstones (and artificial steatite compounds) for a common range of products, including vessels, moulds, blowpipe nozzles, sealstones, spindle whorls, and beads. In most cases, both the function and the iconography of these objects reveal strong links to woodworking, basketry, wool-spinning, and metallurgy. Sealstones are also often very visible and suggest the importance of commodity-marking and bureaucratic interest in the flows of these goods.[5] The vessel shapes are often boxes, cylinders, hut-shapes, and lugged jars that all arguably have soft media links but occasionally also include copies of metal vessels. Classic materials that either survive in the archaeological record or are evoked by decorative motifs include chloritite, steatite, serpentinite, steatite paste, grey-burnished ceramics, wood, basketry, coarse woolen textiles, and bone. It is also striking that incised grey-burnished pottery, itself usually fashioned from a local steatite-rich fabric, appears in tandem with the softstone vessels in a number of separate Cretan, Cycladic, Iranian, and Omani contexts. Nevertheless, the impact of metal value regimes is never entirely absent from such crafting traditions, and there are usually at least one or two metallicising shapes as well, with arcades, articulated handle attachments, rivets, and/or thin-walled carinations that copy features technically linked to metal vessels [e.g. Figure 8.2(g)]. Moreover, the more figurative designs also usually convey a synthetic iconography, with both clear local elements and an obvious awareness of the value regimes and ideologies of a wider market. For example, across a range of different softstone traditions, images of goats, mountains, indigenous architecture, hunting dogs, ingots, particular trees, and plants seem drawn from recognisable local landscapes and important local commodities, while some of the more elaborate scenes have a demonstrably wider elite currency. This might imply a variety of local opinions about how old traditions should coexist with new or foreign influences, as well as especially ambivalent attitudes about metals, whose acquisition, exchange, and consumption no doubt enriched a few but is also likely to have brought traumatic changes for upland communities.

FIGURE 8.2. Softstone products and imagery from four Bronze Age ophiolitic landscapes (the material is chloritite unless otherwise stated): ECI/II Cyclades and EMII-MMI Crete (third millennium BC): (a) box with multiple compartments and architectural design, ht. 9.5 cm (Getz-Gentle 1996: pl.110b), (b) circular box with dog-handled lid, d. 11 cm (Getz-Gentle 1996: pl. 111a), (c) three-faced stamp seal of burnt white steatite, with goat (?), sailing ship, and hatched design, l. 2.3 cm (Matz 1969: no. 287); LCypII-III Cyprus (late second millennium BC), (d) box with two compartments and incised hatched triangles, ht. 3.8 (Warren 1969: P49), (e) lugged tube, ht. 12.1 cm (BM 1897.4-1.1330), (f) cylinder seal probably showing a human figure with spear, oxhide ingots, a deer, a goat, a dog, and a bull, ht. 2.3 cm (BM 1897.4-1.361), (g) miniature krater similar to metal versions, ht. 10.2 cm (BM 1897.04-01.1424); south-central Iran (mid-third millennium BC): (h) footed cup carved in relief with goats and plants, ht. 16 cm (after Madjidzadeh 2003: 19), (i) box with two compartments, carved in relief with architectural and weave patterns, ht. 6.3 cm (de Miroschedji 1973: pl. v.c); Northern Oman (late third millennium BC): (j) box with two compartments, incised with dots and circles, ht. 7.7 (de Miroschedji 1973: pl. vii.h), (k) bowl with incised with dots and circles, ht. 6.8 cm (de Miroschedji 1973: pl. vi.f), (l) a seal in burnt white chloritite/steatite, with dot design, two goats and perhaps a bun ingot? d. 2.2 cm (Harper et al. 1992: no. 78), (m) bottle incised on all four sides with goats, a plant leaf and flower (perhaps from the caper family based on petal/leaf shape?), as well as an indication of mountainous terrain, ht. 8.7 cm (de Miroschedji 1973: fig. 10, pl. viii.d).

So a comparative analysis of several Bronze Age softstone vessel industries suggests important similarities in how they fit with a broader social, economic, and political world. Certainly not all the chloritite/steatite vessels reflect this set of relationships: for example, in Early Dynastic Egypt (excluding palettes for the moment) or Neopalatial Crete, chloritite is only used occasionally and for intensively decorated vessels that seem to have been covered in gold leaf. These products are closely associated with palatial or royal workshops and occur within extremely diverse and established stone vessel industries. In both cases, these may be attempts to counterfeit solid gold vessels, taking advantage of the ability of ultramafic stones to be carved with sharp detail. However, apart from these upper elite examples, the above model is very relevant to understanding the crafting logics, styles, and consumption patterns of the EB2 Aegean and LBA Cyprus (with the softstone vessel industries from the EB-LBA northern Levant at present too obscure to describe with any confidence).[6] The relatively sudden appearance of chloritite vessels and incised grey-burnished pottery traditions in the early EB2 Cyclades and Crete coincides with a period of increased metal exploitation and consumption (see Chapter 5). We can certainly contrast these products, whose decorative links were often to basketry, woodworking, or their hybrids [e.g. compare Figure 8.2(b) with Sentance 2001: 90 bottom right], with the subsequent late EB2-3 ceramic emphasis on imitating metal (e.g. Vasilike and Urfirnis wares). There is a strong intercultural dimension here too because while incised decoration had a local Aegean ancestry that we can occasionally glimpse, for example, in Neolithic pottery, the new metal-base values were associated with Anatolianising customs (e.g. of drinking and pouring). The relatively sudden appearance of chloritite vessels and incised grey-burnished pottery, during what appears to be a period of acute social and demographic change, may reflect one scale of response to the growing importance of partially foreign, metal-based value regimes. The chloritite vessels we find later in EMIII-MMIA are drilled products that were also part of a broader stone vessel tradition, but even so, there is iconographic and distributional evidence that this later use of ultramafic stones may itself reflect a new developments in the Mesara, including (1) settlement nucleation and the altered social and economic rationales this would imply for marginal communites in the Asterousia uplands, (2) possible exploitation of small local copper sources in the Asterousia (Faure 1966: 47–60; Branigan 1968: 51–2), and (3) increasing connectedness of the Aegean with the outside world as the result of sailing ships [e.g. figure 8.2(c), see also Chapter 5].

On Cyprus, we see the appearance of chloritite vessels towards the end of the Bronze Age, alongside an explosion in evidence for Cypriot metallurgy. As we saw in Chapter 7, these softstone vessels adopt either decorative schemes that are very similar to other local soft media designs (e.g. bone and presumably wood) or skeuomorph metal. Chloritite is also used for stamp and cylinder seals engraved with Common-style designs, for jewellery moulds, blowpipe or tuyère nozzles, spindle whorls, and beads. The patterns of chloritite use across the water at Ugarit begin slightly earlier in the MBA and may well be similar though we lack sufficient archaeological exposures to attempt further interpretation (see Chapter 6). Certainly, the accounts of Yabninu at LBA Ugarit suggest that he was consistently trading in the produce of the ophiolite hinterland to the north of the site, possibly including copper and iron, but most clearly seen in one account recording a large sale of timber (pine, cypress, juniper), turtle-doves, horses, wool, aromatic plants, walnuts, reeds and *algabašu*-stone, in total worth 600 shekels of silver (5.6 kg, Pardee 2000: 23–41). As we have seen, *algabašu*-stone probably refers to chloritite/steatite and appears in at least two other Ugaritan letters, including one from the king of Amurru to the king of Ugarit whose only subject is a delayed shipment of the stone (Chanut 2000: 170-3).[7]

## Complex Stone Vessel Traditions

The last two sections have discussed stone vessels that were produced in a variety of ecological and social contexts. However, examples of long-lived or recurrent traditions that make vessels in a range of hard and soft stones are found primarily amongst early complex societies from the midlatitudes, particularly in the eastern Mediterranean, Mesopotamia/highland Iran, China, and Mesoamerica. Indeed of the five or six near-pristine instances of the emergence of complex, stratified societies, stone vessels are an important, if sometimes quite specialised, component of elite material culture in all but one.[8] In such contexts, stone vessels fit nicely into a wider panoply of elite high culture that often includes prestige vessels made of other materials such as metal, decorated pottery, porcelain, glass, faience, bone, ivory, and wood. The skeuomorphic tendencies encouraged by such multimedia tastes are often extremely visible and different stones take their place within elaborate, cosmologically defined material hierarchies. The reproduction of these value cosmologies are usually a feature of key transformative or group-constitutive rituals and provide emblems for the vertical and horizontal distinctions made within the human social order as well (e.g. Saunders 2005). The complex quarrying, drilling, carving, and polishing operations associated with harder rocks, lengthy periods of craft apprenticeship, and a high degree of labour investment are all best suited to full-time specialists, though certain skills might be deployed across several different elite media by the same individual. Industries that draw on a combination of sedimentary, metamorphic, and igneous rocks also usually imply a large and established political territory or complex long-distance trading networks.

A key feature of these complex, premechanised societies is that they usually become heavily tradition bound, with ruling elites and their subordinates under great pressure not to tamper with a vocabulary of high culture that was often defined in the distant past (Baines and Yoffee 2000). These sunk-cost effects encourage periods of apparent stability in everything from agriculture to military strategies to status display, punctuated by sharp and often exogenous ideological ruptures (see Chapter 2). In many cases, the hierarchy of stone value seems to have been fairly robust over thousands of years. Cross-culturally, the definition and cosmological associations of stones and of colour categories are closely intertwined (e.g. Schafer 1963; Baines 1985; Saunders 2005). Green-coloured stones are repeatedly associated with fertility and rejuvenation, while white stones and black stones are regularly used to construct binary cosmological oppositions (see below). Furthermore, despite the fact that small fragments can sometimes circulate quite widely, the most exotic hardstones are often given roles that suggest they were deemed to resist commodification in ways that, for example, precious metal vessel could not due to their obvious bullion value. A few key stones (e.g. varying combinations of jade, quartz crystal, obsidian, and/or lapis lazuli depending on the area) were so strongly linked to elite ideology that we see them deliberately commingled with the human body in highly charged ways (e.g. their use for the eyes of divine statues, for models of human skulls, for teeth inlays, or as a powder additive for elixirs). The following discussion briefly compares four areas of the world where major vessel traditions, in multiple stones, have been found – Mesoamerica, China, Mesopotamia, and Egypt. Only the last two of these could be said to have been in significant contact with one other, although at certain times, long-distance links between the cultures of western Asia and China may have had an attenuated influence (see below).

The diversity of Mesoamerican stone vessel traditions is impressive given the absence of metal tools and, in particular, the tubular copper drills that were used for making such items in the eastern Mediterranean, the Middle East, and China (see below). Above and beyond the common occurrence of mortars for grinding maize (so-called *metates*), the published literature also reveals small numbers of other Olmec, Maya, and Aztec stone vessels, made from obsidian, jade, travertine, marble, gypsum, granite, and steatite/chlorite (e.g. Pasztory 1993: 236–60) and present from at least the first millennium BC up to the period of European conquest. Much further south, in Peru, stone vessels also appear with some of the earliest evidence for complex, stratified communities, alongside similarly decorated fine pottery and carved wooden vessels (e.g. Burger 1992: 89–90, 95–6, 107–8, 218, figs. 71, 82, 96–7, 241–2). However, amongst these New World industries, the Maya stone vessel traditions have received the most detailed analytical attention, and three related features about them are worth noting: (1) the extreme rarity of vessels in the hardest stones, (2) the lack of a particularly complex hierarchy of vessel materials, and (3) the elite connection between stone vessels and decorated ceramics. Taking the first point, despite the lack of metal tools, the rarity of Maya hardstone vessels is surprising, given the importance of jade and obsidian in Maya cosmology (Friedel 1993), and the overwhleming importance of the former as the prestige material for smaller objects (Garber et al. 1993). Two wooden vessels from upper elite burials at Tikal were given all-over jade mosaic coverings (Martin and Grube 2000: 46–8), but their superficial design and ultrahigh status findspots reinforce the impression that Maya artisans rarely if ever made solid vessels in such hard stones.

Second, and more generally, the hierarchy of stones and other materials used for Maya vessels seems far flatter than in the eastern Mediterranean or China with, for instance, no examples in metal or artificial compounds such as faience, lacquer, porcelain, or glass. Rather, among the Late Classic Maya in particular (ca. 600–900 AD), greater emphasis was placed on either decorated pottery or white-coloured stones such as marble, travertine, and gypsum (for what follows, see Luke 2002, 2006; Luke et al. 2006). Travertine in particular had powerful ideological and geological connections to ritual caves (it may often have been acquired in the form of speleotherms, Brady et al. 1997: 731ff) and to the ancestors. It also provided an ideal ground on which to add elaborate painted, carved, or incised texts and images, following the same elite iconographic canon found on other prestige objects and in stucco architecture. Three major Late Classic regional traditions of white stone vessel-carving stand out: in the Yucatan, the south-central Maya Lowlands, and the Ulua Valley. The Ulua vessels have been most intensively studied and were probably carved at Travesía, just to the south of the core Maya area, drawing on local outcrops of white or pinkish marble. All three industries produced cup and bowl shapes (often adorned with zoomorphic handles, ring bases, and/or tripod feet), and a few inscriptional hints suggest these may have held a cacao-rich beverage. Each regional tradition also had strong contextual, material, and stylistic links with local polychrome or relief-decorated ceramics, but the stone vessels were generally found in a far more restricted range of archaeological contexts (e.g. royal burials, ritual caves, and caches) than their pottery counterparts, suggesting that they were marking out only the upper portion of a wider elite group.

In China, jade (in most cases nephrite) was also the preeminent material for elite display and was acquired from a range of northern and southern sources at different times. Jade is an attractive, hard (Mohs 6–7), and particularly cohesive stone, but its aesthetic and material properties were invested with much wider Chinese symbolism, including a particular musical quality, an association with purity, wisdom, personal virtue, and, perhaps most importantly, immortality (Rawson 1995: 13–4). Its use for vessels seems to have been extremely rare in earlier periods (excluding *cong* tubes that are unlikely to have been vessel parts). During the Shang Dynasty, for example, cast bronzes were an extremely important elite symbol, while rare examples of jade (and marble) vessels were probably used only for special libation rituals (Rawson 1995: 385–412, also Laufer 1912: 315–23). Nonetheless, the stone was clearly at the top of the material hierarchy and found only in an extremely limited number of upper elite contexts. We see this status more explicitly from the later first millennium BC onwards when attenuated links with western Asian elite lifestyles led to the introduction of new vessel shapes and materials such as inlaid bronze, silver, quartz crystal, and glass, but rare jade vessels still seem to be preeminent amongst these (Rawson 1995: 3912).

However, by far the most evocative evidence for jade vessels and their role comes from much later, in the sixteenth to seventeenth centuries AD (late Ming and Qing Dynasties), when royal concerns about the increasing affluence and competitiveness of a wider elite group led to a series of explicit sumptuary laws. These specified correspondences between the political and social hierarchy, on the one hand, and a matching hierarchy of things, on the other. This included instruction on what materials were appropriate for different people to use as tableware: jade vessels were thus reserved entirely for royalty (something which was not the case in practice), with gold, silver, pewter, porcelain, or lacquer vessels assigned by decreasing social rank (Clunas 2004: 149–50). The nature of elite aspirations in early modern China is also visible in the number of printed manuals on elite taste and in a connoisseurship for art objects, particularly antiques or antiquities. The latter included Neolithic and Bronze Age jades, but also a range of better and worse imitations, focusing in particular on objects and styles associated with an earlier period of Chinese political unification under the Han Dynasty. The curation or reexcavation of old objects, the production of forgeries, and the evidence for heated arguments over authenticity that were the result of these practices all arguably reflect the commodification of elite lineage at this time (Clunas 2004: 91–115) and provide an intriguing analogy for the way in which similar authenticity and legitimacy debates might have been played themselves out in an eastern Mediterranean context, for example, in the use and abuse of Egyptian stone vessel antiquities in Neopalatial Crete (see Chapter 6).

The last case study in this section compares Mesopotamian stone vessel traditions to their Egyptian neighbours and hence addresses patterns that might conceivably reflect both branching and blending processes of cultural transmission. Direct, long-distance links between Mesopotamia and Egypt certainly existed in the later Bronze Age (e.g. in the Amarna letters) and many commentators have suggested that indirect forms of Mesopotamian influence, via the Levant, were important for the form that Egyptian culinary and drinking habits, administrative practices, and elite political display eventually took during the later fourth millennium BC (most recently Wengrow 2006; also Moorey 1987). With respect to stone vessels, Mesopotamian traditions have a much longer and more substantial pre-Bronze Age ancestry, with such objects being made from at least the eighth millennium BC. From the sixth millennium onwards, there is also evidence for an impressive variety of vessel shapes, hard and soft stones, and manufacturing methods (Moorey 1994: 36–59, e.g. Adams 1983). Indeed, some of these early Mesopotamian vessels were already being made using the distinctive type of figure-of-eight grinding stone (Moholy-Nagy 1983: fig. 132.7, 140.8; driven by a forked shaft and weighted drill) that we find later on in both Mesopotamian and Egyptian contexts (Figure 4.9; Eichmann 1987), suggesting that this specific technology spread from east to west sometime thereafter.

Despite the fact that the evidence is fairly patchy and difficult to interpret, it seems clear that some, albeit very indirect, links existed between these two areas by the later fourth millennium BC. Several commentators have also emphasised some limited shape parallels between Early Dynastic Egyptian and late Uruk stone vessels, though most these are fairly generic (e.g. travertine cylindrical jars, hardstone bowls; see Reisner 1931: 202–12). More interesting perhaps are a series of convergent patterns in the overall character of the stone vessel traditions in these two areas that suggests some degree of mutual awareness at an upper elite level and basic congruence in the roles required of such objects during a period of apparent political unification in both areas. More precisely, the popularity of Egyptian and Mesopotamian stone vessels as elite display items follow strikingly similar trajectories over perhaps a thousand years. In both areas, from the later fourth through into the first part of the third millennium (the Nagada IIC-Early Dynastic in Egypt and the Late Uruk to Early Dynastic periods in Mesopotamia), there is a peak in (1) the quantities of vessels being made, (2) their technical elaboration, (3) the combination of exotic and local stones, and (4) the prevalence of these objects in a range of social contexts. Thereafter, the number and variety of vessels in royal tombs continue to be impressive, but there are signs of change. For example, the Egyptian patterns of reuse, cruder production, and increased substitution from Netjerikhet-Djoser onwards (see Chapter 5) are mirrored by the sharp decline in the presence of exotic hardstone vessels in Early Dynastic III Mesopotamian graves and a general drop in prevalence of stone vessels in nonroyal burials (Moorey 1994: 43–5). Instead, this period sees both regions switch towards greater emphasis on cosmetic vessels rather than elite stone tableware. In Egypt, we have linked this to the increased importance of a range of other forms of stone-based display (e.g. pyramids, sarcophagi, statuary) as well as of precious metal vessels. In Mesopotamia, we can point to the appearance of Figurative-style softstone vessels in greater numbers at Mesopotamian sites, the latter being a phenomenon that may reflect the intensified flow of metals via similar routes. By the second millennium, Mesopotamian stone vessels arguably followed a similar pattern to those in the northern Levant and Anatolia, where a small scale of production is closely tied to the multimedia habits and attached workshops of a narrow upper elite group. In contrast, Egyptian stone vessels continue to be more prominent, mainly as cosmetic containers for a fairly wide elite group, both at court and in provincial centres right through until the first millennium BC.

In both Egypt and Mesopotamia, highly urbanised riverine centres provided the demand for stone vessels in the first place. The stone cosmologies that emerge in these two locales share some broad similarities, perhaps most obviously when it comes to what are perceived as the most important materials in the hierarchy (lapis lazuli, quartz crystal, obsidian), but are nonetheless separate elite constructions, albeit with incredibly long-lasting influences (Aufrère 1991; Harris 1961; Postgate 1997). The Mesopotamian myth of the stones is perhaps the most interesting definition of such a scheme, telling the tale of an unsuccessful revolt by various stones against the god Ninurta (van Dijk 1983). After their defeat, each stone was assigned its role in human society and its place in a value hierarchy, depending on how loyal it had been to Ninurta during the rebellion against him. The fall from grace was perhaps greatest for emery, an extremely hard stone (Mohs scale 8–9) that might otherwise have been seen as an exotic material but was thus consigned to a lowly, industrial function as an abrasive. This deliberate articulation of stone value is certainly present in Egypt but fair less specific in the surviving records, and one reason for this contrast may well be the very different geographies of acquisition that fed Egyptian and Mesopotamian consumption. The urban workshops of both regions were able to use local resources of gypsum, travertine, and limestone for some of their own products but also drew more exotic stones from distant upland areas. A key difference is that this more remote acquisition occurred within the political boundaries of the Egyptian state, while it often crossed over into neighbouring polities in Mesopotamia and included both raw materials and finished goods (Wengrow 2006). This made the Egyptian industry an almost entirely indigenous one, whose products were highly recognisable cultural markers, even when imitated elsewhere. In contrast, stone vessels found in Mesopotamia (and the same might said of metal objects), mapped out a more complex relationship between lowland Mesopotamian centres and their upland neighbours, the latter often being independent and relatively complex societies in their own right. In Egypt, the possession of harder stone vessels could make claims about access to products from royal expeditions, royal workshops, and occasionally production by other upper elite groups. In Mesopotamia, it was far more a signature of long-distance trade or plunder from military successes abroad.

This chapter has sought to draw on a wide range of comparative material to explore what patterns are present in the cross-cultural history of stone vessel manufacture, exchange, and consumption. It has emphasised that groundstone technologies are not an innovation of the first farmers but, in the Old World at least, emerge as one way of enhancing existing subsistence and representational strategies. The appearance of agriculture nonetheless placed greater emphasis on quernstone use and this domestic industry probably provided an early nursery for experiments with more elaborate shapes and less vesicular materials. Stone vessels are thereafter found in a relatively wide variety of small-scale societies, including some more complex hunter-gather groups, pastoralists, and sedentary farming communities, but in many cases, the very limited number of shapes, materials, and use-contexts suggest that certain social norms were in place that discouraged inappropriate levels of ostentation or experimentation. Softstone vessels are a type of material culture that seems particularly pervasive throughout the world, not least because the skillset and tools needed to work sub-Mohs 3 stones is so similar to other soft media. A further combination of appearance, geological provenance and geochemical properties encourage the soft, ultramafic stones found among ophiolite formations to be associated strongly with the flow of metals and other commodities, from upland to lowland zones and sometimes beyond. In contrast to the widespread nature of softstone vessels and other small-scale industries, the most complex stone vessel traditions come from a limited number of complex societies along the midlatitudes that have experienced high population densities and elite consumer demand—of these, those from the eastern Mediterranean and Middle East stand out as having produced the most consistently elaborate range of such material culture. With these insights in mind, the final chapter briefly revisits the theoretical agenda of Chapter 2 and explores the intriguing mix of culturally transmitted, historically contingent, and environmentally convergent factors that underpin the value of Bronze Age stone vessels in the eastern Mediterranean.

# 9
# Forging Value and Casting Stones

▣▣▣▣▣▣

*This short chapter draws together some interpretative loose ends raised by the preceding analyses* but more importantly revisits the wider issue of how we might use stone vessels to consider the ways in which objects are valued in Bronze Age eastern Mediterranean societies. It concludes the book by considering first what happens to the Bronze Age stone vessel traditions in the altered circumstances of the first millennium BC and then returns to some of the theoretical challenges raised in Chapter 2. Finally, it suggests some directions in which future research might lead.

## After the Bronze Age

The severe dislocation of existing elite power structures that occurred in most areas of the eastern Mediterranean at the end of the Bronze Age brought with it a decline, or in many cases the complete disappearance, of elite-sponsored crafts such as wall-painting, monument building, gold, faience, and ivory work (e.g. Peltenburg 2002; Sherratt 2003). Upper elite manufacture of stone vessels in exotic rocks also collapses, reappearing only much later in a Persian predilection for stone vessels to go alongside their precious metal tableware (Cahill 1985: 382–3; Amiet 1983). More broadly, however, different stone vessel industries responded in different ways to these disruptions, reflecting the varying points at which they had been inserted into the existing social and economic hierarchy. In the Aegean, such objects had continued to be a minority component of elite display after the Cretan Neopalatial period but disappeared entirely by the end of LHIIIB1, before the final demise of the Mycenaean palaces. Thereafter, it is only in the Classical period that we see a substantial indigenous stone vessel tradition reemerge, particularly with the Attic manufacture of marble cosmetic boxes (Rutherford 1978). Both the southern Levantine and Cypriot softstone traditions seem to continue for several centuries into the early part of the first millennium BC, suggesting that they were not so closely tied to the infrastructure of the Bronze Age palatial elites. An important exception to the overall pattern of complete political rupture is Egypt, whose stone vessel tradition also persists in reduced form throughout the TIP and Late Period. The Late Period vessels in particular suggest an increased emphasis on lugged shapes, including travertine alabastra, but also some imitations of ED-OK bowls and jars that reflect broader antiquarian tastes in contemporary political and social life (e.g. in tomb decoration, Davies 1902: pl. xxiv). Despite this evidence for limited continuity within Egypt, the production of Egyptian-style oil flasks collapses for several centuries after the end of the Bronze Age. After this hiatus, such items reappear again both within and outside of Egypt from the late eighth century BC onwards, and by the mid-first millennium travertine alabastra have become a truly Mediterranean-wide phenomenon (Roosevelt 2006). There are clear indications, however, that a number of regional centres such as western Anatolia were also making them, drawing on local travertine resources or similar-looking stones (e.g. Bruno 2002; Çolak and Lazzarini 2002).

Stone vessel traditions continue to be important in the Roman, Persian, and Islamic worlds and quartz crystal tableware in particular seem to have retained a position at the very top of the value scale (Vickers 1996). Even so, stone vessels never have the same overall importance that they do in the Bronze Age, probably because the sheer variety of other vessel materials and the ubiquity of metal plate discouraged their consistent use except in a few specific contexts.

## Vessels and Values

The title of this chapter invokes the increasing prominence of metals during the Bronze Age, both as materials for vessels and as standard units of exchange. Stone has a far deeper ancestry as a culturally modified material, but by the third millennium BC, stone vessels were clearly negotiating their place into a predominantly metal-based regime. Even so, the chapter title remains incongruous: stone is neither forged nor cast, and unlike metal, it can be worked as soon as it is quarried (indeed many softstones are easiest to handle in a perinatal state). If purification, convertibility, and recycling characterise metals, subtraction and idiosyncrasy are more relevant to stones, where sequential reduction from a large lump is the typical manufacturing pattern and each rock can have its own particular appearance and working properties (to the extent that many artisans express their work as a process of negotiation with each raw block). We might also contrast both of these materials with clay or artificial compounds such as faience or glass, for which additive experimentation with fabric recipes is an important feature. Ancient categories such as lapis-from-the-mountain (real lapis lazuli) and lapis-from-the-oven (Egyptian blue, faience, glass) may suggest superficial aesthetic links with natural stone, but the two were nonetheless careful demarcated and ranked in terms of their relative value.

These distinctions suggest that we can speak of a physical scaffolding for object value based on the nature of the material involved. Indeed, both the fractal decomposition of stone during human working and the agglomerative crystalline processes by which some rocks are formed lead to very skewed size distributions and hence large lumps are far more precious than the same weight in many pieces. A good example is the value of large diamonds in the modern Western world and the fact that such objects are often so singular that they are given individual titles (e.g. the Koh-i-Noor), displayed in isolation from other things, and/or installed in highly charged symbols of rank (crowns, sceptres, etc.). We should see the same principle behind the willingness of king Samsi-Addu of Assur to buy what was probably a large lump of quartz crystal from his son, Yamsh-Addu of Mari, for the seemingly exorbitant price of 3,000 sheep and 60 male slaves (Michel 1992). Indeed by comparison, small lumps of quartz crystal were relatively common and used for various industrial purposes (e.g. as burins).

The previous chapter also emphasised the convergent associations that might apply to stones as a result of their appearance, geochemical properties, or geographical provenance. Despite this, stone could also be malleable concept: for example, the Akkadian term for it (*abnu*) has a range of meanings beyond the scientific one we normally adopt and is unusual for being bigendered (Robson 2001: 40). So object value has both a physical scaffolding and a negotiable, polysemic quality. The former can sometimes elicit convergent responses in a range of different cultural situations, but the latter are far more contingently tied to a specific historical case. Unpicking the difference between these two types of influence should be a fundamental part of the agenda of material culture studies but is rarely addressed explicitly.

Part of the problem resides in our current interpretative habits. For example, many of the pictures in this book depict stone vessels against a blank background, a portrayal which is common throughout the archaeological literature. In catalogues and galleries, such depictions also facilitate the appreciation and revaluation of artefacts for the Western art market, where decontextualisation is both an invitation to postmodern reflection and a clever trick of the trade. However, while the simplicity of such an image is both attractive and analytically convenient, it is also misleading if used uncritically, because it suggests that an object is an independent observation, accessible to the modern viewer in a frictionless social space. Likewise, the exclusive study of a single object class such as stone vessels might be equally misleading if it assumed that the meaning behind one type of artefact was somehow isolatable. In fact, object value is temporally and spatially autocorrelated, dependent both on an inherited cultural tradition and on a nonrandom geographical, material, and social context. In formal terms, this would require that we address such nonstationary properties directly (e.g. by distinguishing branching from blending processes through cladistic analysis)—more prosaically, it suggests that synoptic studies are at best a first interpretative step and thereafter demand a wider comparative perspective.

Notions of purity, permanence, and essentialism are frequently projected onto stone due to its unprocessed, nonrecycleable, and nonbiodegradeable character. As a result, stone is often used for monumental building, statuary, cosmetic containers, ossuaries, or cremation urns, all contexts that reflect a human desire both to cheat the passage of time and to make carefully structured links with the natural world. It is also also an easy metaphorical platform from which to express abstract concepts in concrete terms or from which to make ideologies and narratives appear natural. For example, through careful combinations of stone objects, it is possible to express large-scale cosmological or geopolitical concepts within a single foundation deposit, burial, gift, or consumption event. Such objects can map out real territories by their assumed provenance (e.g. the corners of the known world), particular emotions because of their colour and texture, and/or evoke links to specific deities or mythical narratives.

One of the key social relationships behind stone vessel use that requires further attention is gender. At present, we know very little about whether men or women produced such items in the different Bronze Age eastern Mediterranean traditions—the least obscure case is probably late Old Kingdom Egypt where tomb reliefs assert that most stone masons were men or young boys. We might, however, expect such a situation to vary cross-culturally with the scale of the tradition and the materials involved, as it certainly does in other crafts. Well-grounded analysis of this topic is sorely lacking but requires a wider multidisciplinary perspective than could be achieved here. It should focus on the formal documentation of cases where gender roles correspond with specific artefact types and on interpretations that combine textual sources, iconography, and the osteoarchaeological record. For example, Egyptian–style travertine containers seem to have a long association with women, apparently more common in female graves during the late OK (see Chapter 5), associated with high status females in both the royal burials and marriage alliances of the Middle and New Kingdoms and shown predominantly with women in banquet scenes, but this association seems by no means absolute, and the same objects were owned and used by men as well. Sex- or gender-specific images are occasionally also visible on stone vessels themselves. The best examples are probably the gynomorphic marble beakers from the EBA Cyclades and 18th Dynasty travertine *gravidenflaschen* (see Chapter 5 and Brunner-Traut 1970). Explicitly male imagery is even rarer on stone vessels, with the possible exception of the chloritite relief vessels from Neopalatial Crete that as yet only show figures of men (Rehak 1995b: 453).

In contrast, one area that could receive significantly greater attention using existing datasets is cultural transmission. This topic has a long ancestry in archaeology, but quantitative evolutionary approaches to it now offer considerable further insight (see below), emphasising, for example, the important question of what constitutes the appropriate unit of replication on which cultural selection might operate. The default assumption is often that objects are the things which are passed on either between generations or between societies, but, of course, motifs, ideas, and motor habits can also have lives of their own. In many cases, it is also clear that we can talk about broader packages of goods, ideas, and practices that coalesce for a variety of reasons and effectively reproduce themselves as a group. In the last chapter, a lot of emphasis was placed on the common flows linking ultramafic softstone vessels and a wider suite of ophiolitic products, including metals. Another example of a cultural package is a seemingly disparate group of Cypriot- and Mycenaean-style ceramics, Egyptian-style travertine vessels, and ivory pyxides (to name but the most salient items) from a wide range of cultural origins which apparently coalesce as part of the proper expression of elite cosmetic behaviour across much of the LBA eastern Mediterranean. Not only were these objects often stored, shipped, and consumed together, but by the later LBA their manufacture was probably concentrated in the same major coastal entrepots as well.

Stone vessel drilling technologies have particularly interesting transmission histories. Device-aided drilling is a technique with very low-level craft roots, reflecting the almost ubiquitous skills used for bead perforation. Even so, the distribution of key groundstone tools and drilling strategies hint at important horizontal transmission episodes. For example, figure-of-eight grinders are found in Mesopotamia and later also in Egypt in such similar forms that it suggests diffusion of both the grinder and drill design from the former region to the latter, probably during the fifth or fourth millennium BC. In contrast, the grinders known from Chalcolithic Anatolia and Neopalatial Crete look slightly different. Likewise, it is only in the latter two regions that we find examples of amphibolite cobbles with tubular drilled slots, suggesting that some aspects of this western drilling tradition developed separately.

The complex decison-making involved in drilling with grinders and tubular drill-bits is also prone to transmission bottlenecks. In this respect, the disruption in most eastern Mediterranean hardstone vessel manufacture at the end of the Bronze Age probably reflects not just a decline in upper elite consumer demand but also a decline in the hot-house elite workshops where such specialist knowledge was reproduced. In fact, the reduction in the number of vessel-drilling strategies used by Aegean artisans, from many in LMI-IIIA Crete to just one at LHIIIB1 Mycenae, suggests a constriction of specialist knowledge sometime after the LMIB collapse of the Cretan palaces. Indeed, a similarly restricted transmission pattern, focused on limited continuity at LMII Knossos may be the context in which the Linear A script was adapted to write a narrow range of Mycenaean administrative documents in archaic Greek (e.g. Driessen and Schoep 1999).

In terms of who drove change and was responsible for key horizontal and vertical transmission episodes, the textual and iconographic sources from the Bronze Age eastern Mediterranean claim the overwhelming role of a few upper elite individuals in the process of material and ideological innovation (e.g. Imhotep, Thutmosis III, Akhenaton, Daedalus). While it is clear that, from a network theory or cultural selection perspective, such well-connected, superproducing, superconsuming, extensively-imitated people were of great importance as taste-makers, it is is often difficult to known how seriously to take claims of direct involvement in mundane issues such as object design. Such great figures also tend to have a centripetal effect on later narratives, inevitably promoting simplistic *ad hominen* explanations. In the case of Egypt, for example, we seem to have instances where rulers intervened directly in material culture innovation, but the same individuals also found it difficult to resist the inertia of established high culture. One of the duties of a good pharaoh was to return society to its initial pristine state (Hornung 1992: 164) and hence the widely innovative programme of an iconoclast such as Akhenaton was treated with great suspicion.

Beyond these unusual people, a broader elite group were primarily responsible for defining the value of stone vessels. For example, cemetery populations from Egypt, the Levant, and the Aegean show some variation over time and space but consistently suggest that some 10–20% of the burying population could afford to deploy these items in mortuary display. Others may have had access to such goods more occasionally but chose to retain rather than discard them. In any case, despite some important variation in the degree of skew in wealth distributions across different societies, the existence of a more wealthy elite group of approximately this size is fairly typical of many pre- and postcapitalist sedentary societies (see Chapter 2). What vary more obviously are both the overall levels of wealth displayed by a community as well as the presence or absence of supernova acts of consumption by the wealthiest few.

The only types of stone vessels that were regularly acquired by elites across the entire eastern Mediterranean were Egyptian in style, and an obvious question concerns why these products had such enduring popularity beyond the borders of the Egyptian state to the extent that they were exchanged in comparatively large numbers and/or copied locally, intermittently from at least the third millennium BC through to the first millennium AD. The medicinal and cosmetic qualities of Egyptian oils as well as their elaborate preparation may have been important and there are certainly signs that the contents were often more valuable than the vessels themselves. However, we know that many other regions successfully marketed their own complex oil recipes on an international stage and that some of these foreign products were even stored in Egyptian travertine vessels (e.g. in sacred oil sets). Various harder stones, such as marble, gypsum, or ultramafic rocks, were all potential alternatives to travertine as a stone medium for these containers and steatite in particular has a much closer technical affiliation with the perfume industry (see Chapter 8). Rather, the persistence of this object-material package must be explained as the result of Egypt's wider geopolitical influence over a long period, coupled with internal reasons why this stone was chosen by Egyptian elites in the first place.

Travertine was by far the dominant Egyptian vessels material, both at home and abroad. As suggested in Chapter 5, its persistent value as a baseline material within Egypt was affected by three main physical factors: first, it is just hard enough to discourage manufacture by carving and hence remained a medium that required a more involved crafting but was not so intractable that it could only be worked in special circumstances. Travertine takes an attractive polish and lends itself to perceived differences in quality (banding, colour, texture, provenance). Another key factor is arguably the spatial distribution of source outcrops that are fairly evenly spread from north to south, but not so obvious immediately beyond Egypt's borders. Travertine could therefore provide, from when it first appears in significant amounts during the period of state formation, a common but not commonplace emblem of unified Egyptian material culture. Moreover, it was incorporated into a set of core Egyptian objects and practices that was able to transmit itself over many generations and to other regions. Travertine containers were personal toiletry items whose contents had both a cosmetic and medicinal purpose. We see them deployed with a set of stylised gestures (offering, receiving, and applying) at some of the most important and intimate stages of Egyptian religious and social life, such as in rituals to purify and regenerate the body (opening of the mouth, anointing, passage through the gates of the underworld), or provided for guests at elite banquets as part of proper Egyptian hospitality. In other words, they were part of a whole panoply of living and dying activities associated with being Egyptian, responsible for the way a fairly wide elite group both in the provinces and at court might look, act, and smell. Abroad the role of such containers and their contents was validated by the fact that some were issued as gifts to neighbouring rulers and were important components in the Egyptian marriage transfers.

The fact that stone vessels were exchanged in this manner between elites, but were also used on a day-to-day basis, curated, bequeathed, and displayed, further emphasises their role in maintaining and forging relationships between people. As suggested in Chapter 2, it is useful to follow Alan Fiske in suggesting that people usually think about their relationships in terms of one or more basic logics which emphasise communal sharing, authority ranking, equivalence matching, or market pricing. Communal sharing is often reinforced by acts of food-sharing, emblematic body modification, physical intimacy, initiation rites, and purity taboos. Objects that are well-suited to cementing such relationships include important heirlooms, relics, and things that physically encourage shared acts and/or that have only limited size, material, and stylistic variation. In the Bronze Age eastern Mediterranean, some stone vessel shapes (e.g. open bowls, plates, or cups with several handles) may well have been part of food and drink sharing activities, but in most cases we lack sufficient contextual detail to be sure. More important perhaps is the frequent use of stone for cosmetic containers which links them naturally to concerns over purity. Perhaps the best examples in this respect are the later Jewish chalk vessels whose consumption certainly was an emblem of group membership and the result of ritual taboo. Certain Bronze Age softstone vessels also probably reinforced the social logics of a carefully defined community—for example, the limited range of shapes, materials, sizes, elaboration, and quantities (e.g. per tomb) of gypsum vessels from the MBA-early IA Jordan valley is in line with our expectations above about what material features might be selected for under this predominant logic. The use of stone palettes for grinding pigments used in body decoration involves these vessels in practices that, from a cross-cultural perspective, foreground the individual but usually initiate them into a clearly defined social group as well. Cycladic marble palettes, especially the Grotta-Pelos examples that have such a restricted distribution, are good examples of an object class that helped forge such social relationships, and they too show limited variability. More speculatively, if crocus-gathering by young Cretan girls has been correctly interpreted as an initiation rite, then it offers a context in which a strong sense of group identity and communal sharing is likely to have been forged. The regular shape, size, decoration, and material of blossom bowls is again entirely appropriate for reinforcing such social bonds, if indeed a link to saffron crocuses is valid.

Of course, in some of the above examples, the in-groups involved were also ranked above the rest of society by their use of such objects. Authority ranking logics are commonly constituted by a sort of social physics that emphasises people's relative position in hierarchies of space, time, size, number, and force (see Chapter 2). The most obvious way in which is this achieved for stone vessels is by clearly defined better and worse materials, a range of sizes and/or shape elaboration. Both the Cretan and Egyptian industries encouraged this sort of quality refinement by establishing baseline materials (serpentinite and travertine, respectively) above and below which a range of stones and materials might be arranged. Some vessels from these two traditions are indeed very large (e.g. storage jars), to the extent that they are likely to have been semipermanent installations. Raw quantities of stone may therefore be one rather crude way of expressing rank distinctions, but such a strategy seems to have been used far more for monumental architecture (e.g. ashlar blocks, stone panelling, stone floor tiles) than for vessels. Quantities of stone vessels, however, are quite often an expression of higher status, and we see such a logic taken to extremes in some of the late PD-early OK Egyptian royal tombs. A complementary or alternative strategy was to produce deliberately ostentatious, higher ranked versions of basic vessel shapes by the addition of inlays, complex handles, necks, spouts, and pedestal feet. By far the most ambitious example of this strategy are the vessels from the tomb of Tutankhamun where, instead of using a range of higher-value stones as was typical elite Egyptian practice, the travertine vessels were given fancy inlays and/or virtuoso carved elaborations on a basic hieroglyphic form.

The possession and conspicuous display of imported stone vessels, in contexts where others were using local versions, was another obvious way of expressing higher social ranking. Sometimes the material statements made by foreign objects seem fairly generic, merely advertising their owner's unusual ability to acquire exotica from abroad, while at other times they seem to be part of far more sophisticated elite statements. Indeed, exchange is a context that can lead to quite aggressive assertions of rank, for example, with certain types of gifts flowing downwards to subordinates and others (including tribute) flowing upwards. Within a given society, ranked exchange codes might be fairly transparent, but there was more room for ambivalence and outright deception when such transfers crossed political and cultural boundaries. For example, in Egypt many stone vessels were given written inscriptions, referring to the contents, to the producer, recipient, and/or occasion for which they were made. Painted versions were more common than inscribed ones and the latter were usually markers of upper elite production. Hence, inscribed vessels from OK-NK royal workshops were often used for royal propaganda and occasionally as rewards to subordinate officials. Abroad, however, the same vessels were rarely exchanged with vassal states (e.g. the LBA southern Levant) but were part of royal exchanges with supposed peers. Even so, the Amarna correspondence makes it clear that for an internal Egyptian audience, these exchanges could also be described as expressing Egyptian superiority, due to the way such objects were used inside the Egyptian state. Such diplomatic sleight-of-hand may also be behind the 6th Dynasty *heb sed* jars or the early MK vessels inscribed with potentially subservient Egyptian official titles, both of which were sent to Byblos during the late third and early second millennia. Likewise, the documented LBA cases of Egyptian royal marriage, in which large numbers of (probably inscribed) stone vessels were involved, suggest that for internal Egyptian audiences, the inflow of foreign brides was an expression of superiority, while in external diplomatic terms it assumed parity.

We can also contrast this Egyptian use of inscription with the way this practice developed in Neopalatial Crete. Unlike Egypt, writing was rarely used for display purposes in Crete but does appear on a restricted number of Neopalatial stone vessel shapes, especially ladles and libation tables. The inscriptions are short and often rather poorly executed and nothing about the material, manufacturing quality, or stylistic elaboration of the examples chosen for such treatment suggests that they were always higher value versions. On the contrary, while the sequential acts of procession and/or libation that these objects facilitated certainly left room for ranked distinctions based on the temporal or spatial ordering of participants, the primary logic seems to be one of equivalence matching. Cross-culturally, such relationships are usually constituted by transparently fair procedures such as turn-taking, random lotteries, overt matching of object sizes or quantities, and/or the use of physical place-holders as reminders of delayed reciprocal obligations. In comparison to the wider Neopalatial group of ritual stone vessels, the inscribed examples do not show conspicuous elaboration. They might also reflect categorical distinctions bases on group membership, but also seem to emphasise matched libationary contributions. This fits well with the lack of explicit ruler iconography in Neopalatial Crete, suggesting that whatever the actual distribution of political power, equivalence logics were often favoured over those that made authority ranks explicit, at least within a broadly defined elite group.

The fourth possible way of structuring social relationships is one based on measured ratios and market-style calculation logics. It is certainly clear that stone was bought and sold widely and that sealstones and stone weights were an important feature of propositional and quantifying economic logics. However, such features are less clearly manifest in the stone vessels themselves, unlike for metal plate whose bullion value was always a background consideration and in the Classical period encouraged the creation of vessels to a standard weight and purity (Vickers and Gill 1994: 46–54). Many of the products from ophiolite landscapes were probably caught up in such market-led calculations: ultramafic softstones are no exception in being linked to the economics of metals and metallurgy, but in some cases the vessels made from these materials may have been expressing a rather more ambivalent response to such commodification (see Chapter 8).

## Future Directions

The analysis in preceding chapters has raised as many questions as it has tried to answer. One major challenge has been the need to address stone vessel phenomena at a variety of scales from the broadly comparative to the highly contextual, without becoming disoriented by the experience. In this respect, four related avenues where future research might lead are (1) greater attention to the time-geographic paths of artefacts, (2) quantified comparison of related object classes, (3) more explicit analysis of skeuomorphism, and (4) more formal analysis of typological variation.

The first of these reflects the benefit of tracing out the typical paths by which certain types of object move through production, exchange, and consumption contexts, as well as through various human hands (female/male, old/young, local/foreign). The description of such a schematic trajectory makes it alarmingly obvious what we do not know or cannot say, but nonetheless allows us to identify artefactual outliers whose fortunes have been very different from the norm. In some sense, this agenda has always been a feature of material culture studies, but there are increasingly clear examples of how such joined-up thinking might be implemented. For example, even a small but careful surface collection of Chalcolithic marble figurine and vessel debris at Kulaksızlar in Anatolia, coupled with attention to the iconography of such objects and their wider distribution, provides considerable insight on early patterns of crafting and intervillage exchange. For later periods, it is clear that the time-geographic paths of products from ophiolite landscapes often coincide for much of their social lives or, by contrast, diverge in illuminating ways after their initial extraction and manufacture. The work currently being pursued on the economic life of Cypriot copper from mine to smelting village to entrepot to consumer, or similarly for a fancy stone such as Egyptian anorthosite gneiss, offers equally promising information about the scale, orientation, and impact of each industry. Continued attention to the issue of artefact provenance will also be necessary, primarily from the point of view of constituent raw material and the operational recipes involved in object manufacture.

This book has tried to create some comparative links between stone vessels and objects made in the same stones or vessels made in other materials. Further work is clearly necessary to establish a wider set of well-grounded comparisons between different artefact classes. Sampling bias is a spectre confronting most archaeological analysis to the extent that one of the most salient features of any artefact distribution map is usually the spatial pattern of how intensively people have looked. This patchy, uneven recovery can be addressed by designing alternative investigative strategies, but to some extent will always be a problem. An important way round the issue is to build up a sufficiently holistic impression of the density of different types of artefacts, coupled with an idea of the contextual differences between them. Once we can discuss patterns in terms of artefact densities or, more robust still, artefact ratios (e.g. of Mycenaean-style pottery to Egyptian-style travertine vessels, one juglet type to another, or one pottery fabric to another), rather than the mere collection of counts, our analyses will be on a far firmer footing.

In combination with such quantified comparison, more careful approaches to skeuomorphism are increasingly necessary if we are to sift out loose, multilateral stylistic allusions on objects from technically grounded and directional imitation or, indeed, deliberate fakes. Incidental technical details can be very important in this regard: for example, stone vessel makers in Early Dynastic Egypt chose to emphasise their use of a large tubular drill by leaving a sharply demarcated circular depression in the interior base of many vessels. This feature was copied (with an often crudely incised mark) not only by contemporary artisans working in softer materials but also by Cretan artisans 1,000 years later. It is the unusual presence of this interior drill-ring on the Neopalatial imitations that confirms Cretan craftspeople were not just reusing Egyptian antiquities for their fancy materials but were actually interested in the objects themselves. As Scott Ortman's work on basketry skeuomorphs in the American Southwest has suggested (2000), such formal frameworks also offer us a way to explore the preferred conceptual metaphors used by a particular society, despite the absence of textual sources and without resorting to wild speculation.

More formal approaches are also necessary to unpick typological variation. While sample size often confounds our assessment of relative material diversity, it is nonetheless clear that variation within object classes and between them can reflect important social and economic processes. For example, the range of objects that are exported from a core region or used by expatriate communities is often a carefully defined subset of the available range of products back home: this less diverse but better branded founding package is nonetheless better-suited to confronting the range of rival consumption strategies that exist abroad. More important perhaps is the potential for typology construction and testing to become not just a way of managing artefacts but also a way of explaining them. One of the most significant contributions of recent evolutionary approaches to cultural diversity has been the identification of the treelike patterns of stylistic descent that suggest indigenous cultural lineages through time or, by verifying their absence, the suggestion of alternative forms of cultural selection. There is potential for including emic classificatory systems here, too, especially in the eastern Mediterranean, by considering what appear to be the basic shape and material categories defined in language and iconography, and thereafter exploring what synchronic and diachronic variability exists around this idealised forms.

These suggestions are no doubt only one set of possible opportunities, but they are consistent in their emphasis on finding formal approaches to the complex ways in which material culture is thought about, produced, used, discarded, and/or passed on. Archaeology has a uniquely extensive perspective on such patterns and must vary the spatial and temporal magnification of its approaches if it is to explain them effectively. Studying stone vessels in a comparative context casts light on the changing value of these objects in Bronze Age eastern Mediterranean but also proposes routes by which future, more collaborative, research might proceed.

# Appendix
*Typological Guide*

᚛᚛᚛᚛᚛᚛

*This appendix offers rough stone vessel typologies for each region. Several of the typologies* have been directly transposed from existing published classifications and, where this occurs, the numbering system has been kept consistent with the original one but modified with a regional prefix (e.g. C20B refers to Cretan shape 20B from Warren's 1969 classification). For each shape, a brief description is given, along with an account of variation within the group, decoration (if any), and an estimated date range for the type. Type drawings are meant as a rough guide only: profiles are solid when taken from a specific example and otherwise dotted. A list of examples or reference to where such a list can be found within existing published catalogues is also provided but is not meant to be comprehensive. In the case of the very large Egyptian and Cretan traditions, the range of shapes is illustrated here, but the reader is referred to the original classifications for further details about individual types.

## Egypt (E-)
The numbered sequence of shapes has been borrowed from Aston (1994) with minor alterations. As with Warren's Cretan classification, Aston's individual types make distinctions at a slightly finer scale (e.g. for bowls) than the other typologies offered here and hence comparisons of type diversity should proceed cautiously. The earlier fourth millennium shapes in Aston's series (e.g. 1–24) have been omitted.

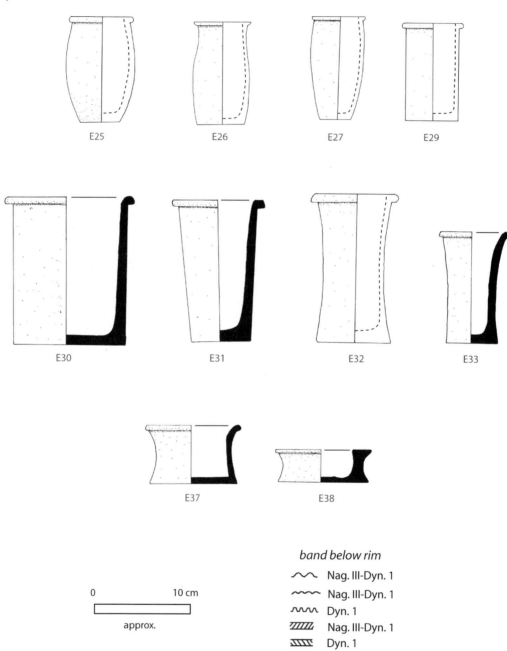

band below rim

∿∿ Nag. III-Dyn. 1
∼∼∼ Nag. III-Dyn. 1
ᴧᴧᴧ Dyn. 1
⬚⬚⬚ Nag. III-Dyn. 1
⬚⬚⬚ Dyn. 1
═══ Dyn. 1-3
▓▓▓ Dyn. 1

0            10 cm
approx.

1st–4th Dynasty cylindrical jars.

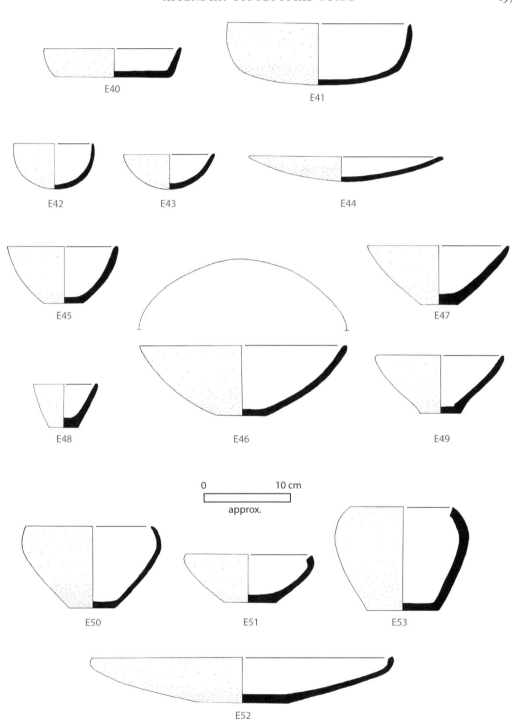

1st–4th Dynasty open bowls.

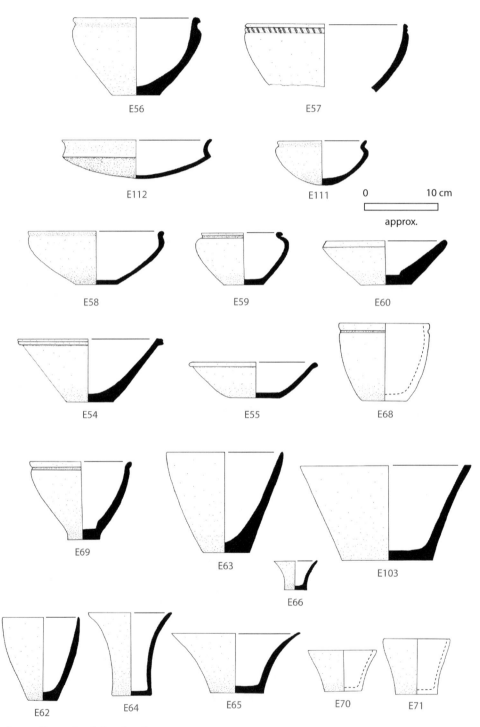

1st–4th open Dynasty bowls (continued).

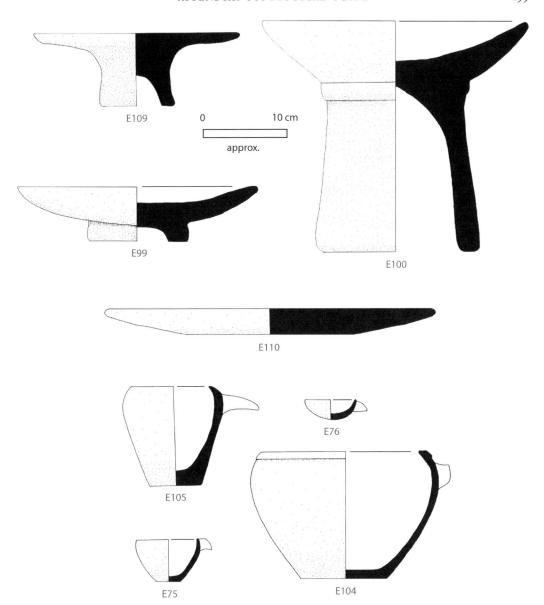

E109

0      10 cm

approx.

E99

E100

E110

E105

E76

E75

E104

1st–4th Dynasty tables and spouted bowls.

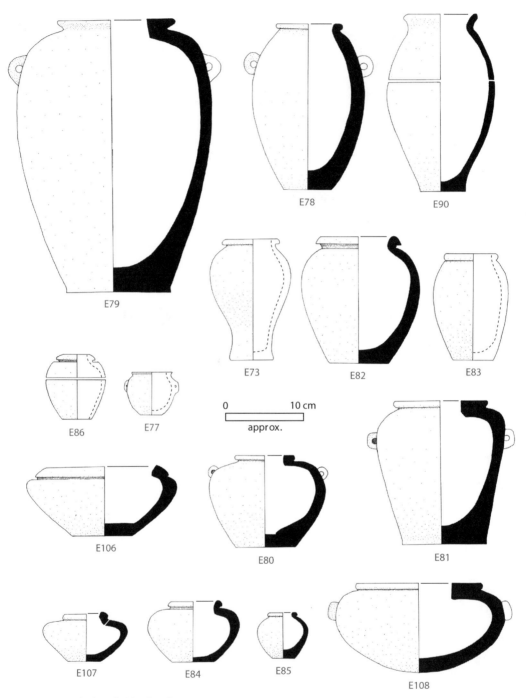

1st–4th Dynasty thick-walled bowls and jars.

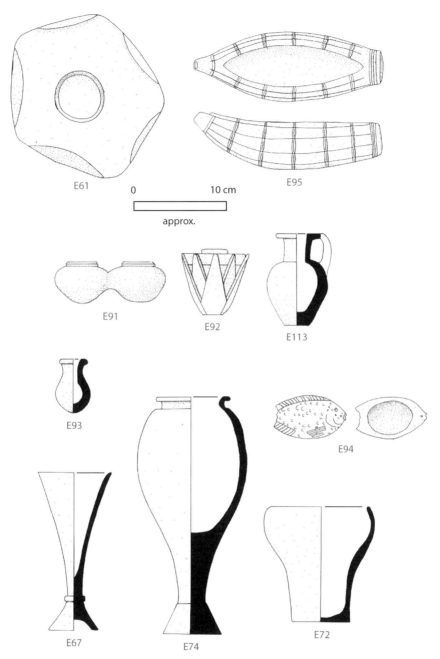

E61

0          10 cm

approx.

E95

E91

E92

E113

E93

E94

E67

E74

E72

1st–4th Dynasty miscellaneous vessels.

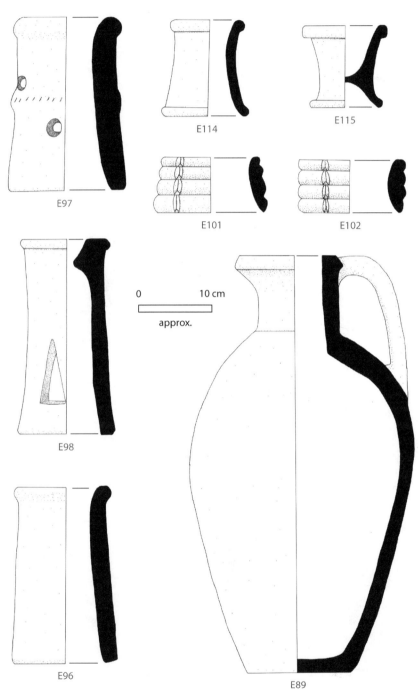

E114

E115

E97

E101

E102

E98

0          10 cm

approx.

E96

E89

1st–4th Dynasty jug and large stands.

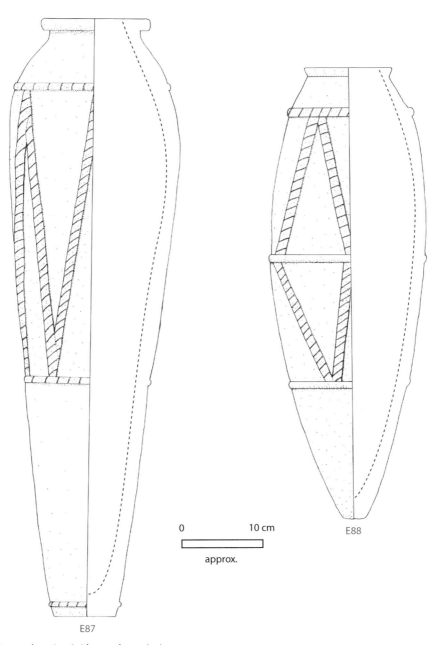

0    10 cm

approx.

E88

E87

1st–4th Dynasty large jars (with rope decoration).

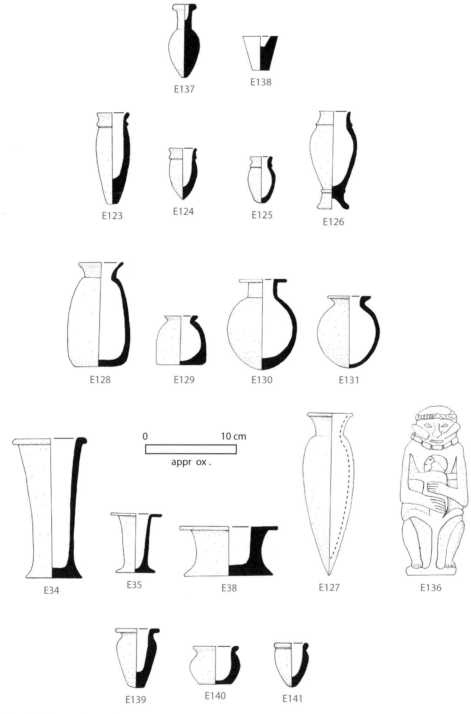

5th Dynasty, FIP cosmetic vessels.

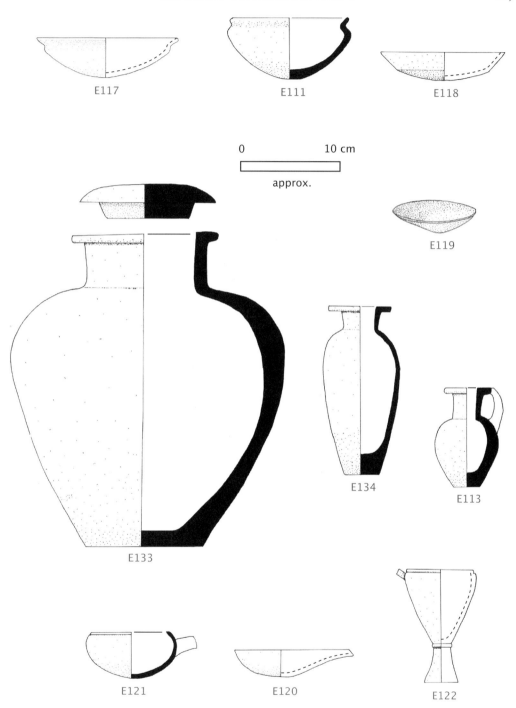

E117

E111

E118

0          10 cm

approx.

E119

E133

E134

E113

E121

E120

E122

5th–6th Dynasty miscellaneous vessels.

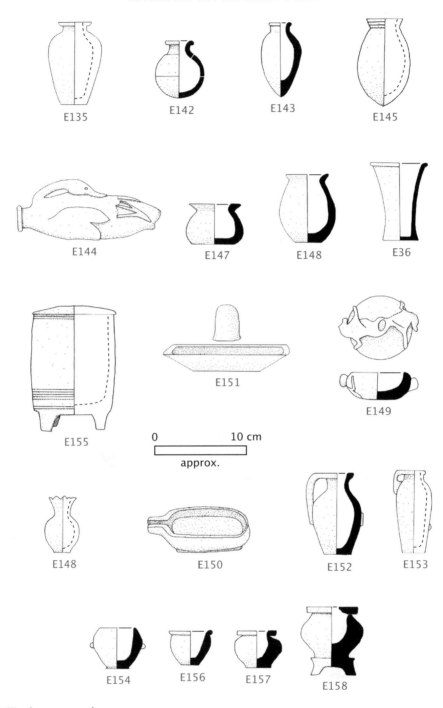

Middle Kingdom stone vessels.

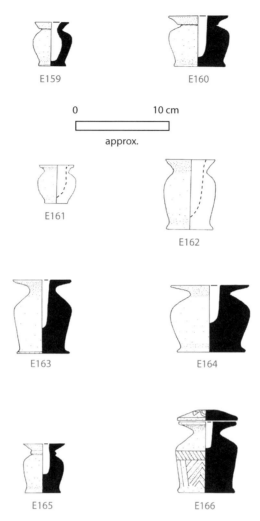

E159    E160

0                10 cm

approx.

E161

E162

E163    E164

E165    E166

SIP–early 18th Dynasty kohl pots.

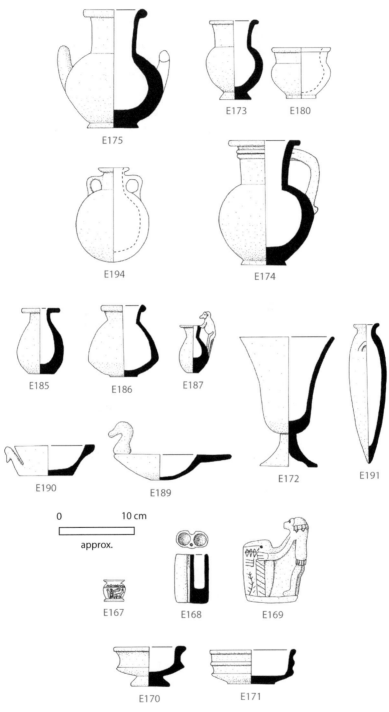

E175

E173    E180

E194    E174

E185    E186    E187    E172    E191

E190    E189

0        10 cm

approx.

E167    E168    E169

E170    E171

Thutmosis III–end of the 18th Dynasty.

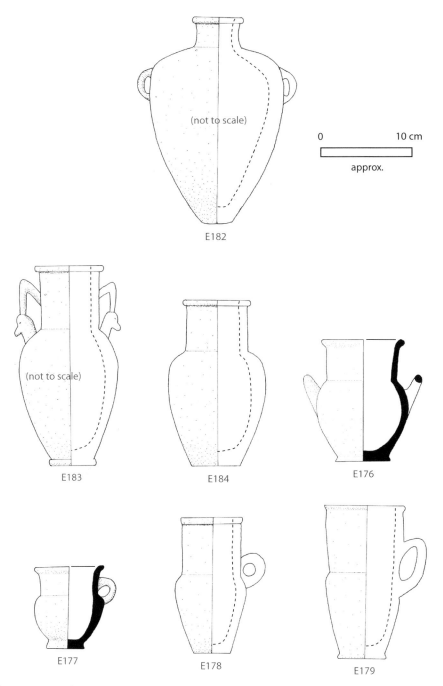

0                    10 cm

approx.

E182

E183                    E184                    E176

E177                    E178                    E179

Late 18th Dynasty onwards.

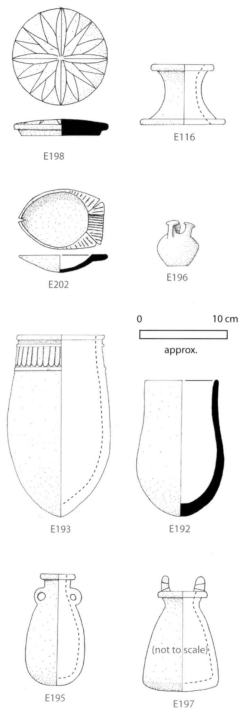

E198

E116

E202

E196

0                    10 cm

approx.

E193

E192

E195

E197

(not to scale)

Late 18th Dynasty onwards (continued).

## Egyptian-Style (Es-)

Those MBIIB–LBII travertine vessel shapes from the eastern Mediterranean that are often assumed to be Egyptian, but whose forms are often of mixed heritage and for which the source of manufacture still remains unclear have been given the prefix Es and have been separately numbered. This sequence is not meant to be comprehensive or to assert unequivocally that some Es vessels are not in fact of Egyptian provenance, but seeks to catch some of the eastern Mediterranean variation which is not as well represented by Aston's Egyptian typology. This also does not represent a number of larger stone jars found at Levantine sites, such as Kamid el-Loz and Qatna, whose place of manufacture is also debatable.

**Es1** – tall everted rim jar

| | |
|---|---|
| *Drawn:* | AM 1966.1812 |
| *Variations:* | n/a |
| *Decoration:* | n/a |
| *Date Range:* | MBIIB–LBIA |
| *Comments:* | Elongated version of MK Egyptian everted rim jar (E135). |
| *Examples:* | (Sparks 2007: 3.1.15) |

**Es2** – juglet

| | |
|---|---|
| *Drawn:* | AM 1949.34 |
| *Variations:* | flat base/rounded base |
| *Decoration:* | cord decoration on handle |
| *Date Range:* | MBIIB–LBIA |
| *Comments:* | Copies Levantine pottery juglets. |
| *Examples:* | (Sparks 2007: 3.9.1.1-2) |

**Es3** – collared jar with separate base

| | |
|---|---|
| *Drawn:* | (after Caubet 1991: pl. ix.8) |
| *Variations:* | square base/circular base |
| *Decoration:* | n/a |
| *Date Range:* | MBIIC–LBIIA? |
| *Comments:* | The shape is the same as E173, but the examples with a separate square base seem to be found mainly in the Levant. |
| *Examples:* | (Sparks 2007: 3.1.20.1) |

**Es4** – piriform jug

| | |
|---|---|
| *Drawn:* | (after Loud 1948: pl. 261.12) |
| *Variations:* | n/a |
| *Decoration:* | vertical grooves |
| *Date Range:* | MBIIC–LBI |
| *Comments:* | Copies Levantine pottery forms. |
| *Examples:* | Ajjul, Area T (Petrie 1934: pl. xl.109) |
| | Megiddo Tomb 5013J (Loud 1948: pls. 258.12, 261.12) |
| | Knossos Temple Tomb (Warren 1969: P623) |

**Es5** – footed cup or *tazza* with tenon join

| | |
|---|---|
| *Drawn:* | (after Caubet 1991: pl. ix.1) |
| *Variations:* | two ridges (i)/three-ridges (ii) |

*Decoration:*   n/a

*Date Range:*   LBI–II

*Comments:*   The shape is the same as E170-1, but Levantine examples frequently have a tenon join between body and foot.

*Examples:*   (see Clamer 1976: type L1-2; Sparks 2007: 3.1.6); however, also Lahun, Egypt (Petrie et al. 1923: pl. lxvi.13)

**Es6** – jar with stylised 'duck's head' lugs

*Drawn:*   (after Clamer 2002: no.245, figs. 2.152–3)

*Variations:*   lugs separate/modified/solid

tenon base

separate neck

*Decoration:*

*Date Range:*   LBI–II

*Comments:*   Varies in size, but broadly similar in shape to Canaanite-style transport jars and E182.

*Examples:*   Lachish (Tufnell 1958: pl. 26.46)

Tel Quasile (Mazar 1985: fig. 4.3)

Tel Dan (Clamer 2002: no. 245, figs. 2.152–3)

Kamid el-Loz (Lilyquist 1996: pl. 24.1-3)

Ugarit (at least two examples, Caubet 1991: pls. iv.9-10, xii.1-2)

Umm el-Marra (Curvers and Schwartz 1990: fig. 4)

Enkomi x2 (BM 1897.04-01.1090, 1285)

Semna, Nubia (Dunham and Janssen 1960: fig. 33, pl. 118a).

**Es7** – Base-ring-style juglet

*Drawn:*   (after Caubet 1991: pl. xii.16)

*Variations:*   n/a

*Decoration:*   petaliform rim

*Date Range:*   MBIIC–LBI

*Comments:*   The shape closely resembles a Cypriot pottery form. It is related to the stone BR jug (E174), but the juglets are found predominantly in the Levant and Cyprus.

*Examples:*   (Sparks 2007: 3.1.9.4; Clamer 1976: type E1a)

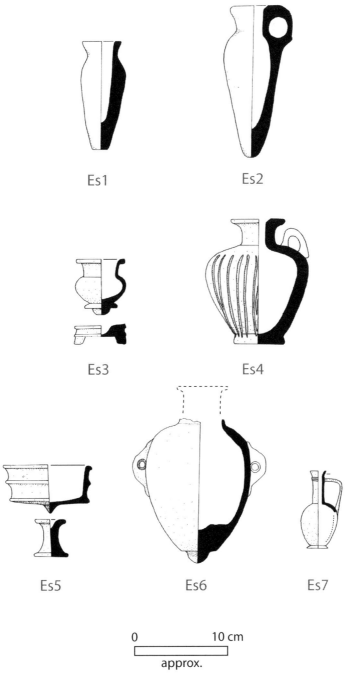

Vessels sometimes assumed to be Egyptian but of unclear provenance.

## Levant (L-)

This typology follows Ben-Dor (1945), Clamer (1976), and Sparks (2007) for later periods, but the numbering is new.

**L1** – flaring bowl

| | |
|---|---|
| *Drawn:* | (after Braun 1990: fig. 4) |
| *Variations:* | more pronounced flaring sides/less pronounced |
| | large and high/small and squat |
| | bevelled rim/tapered rim |
| *Decoration:* | single ring of relief decoration below rim |
| | double ring of relief decoration below rim |
| | rope decoration below rim |
| | cylindrical knobs below rim |
| *Date Range:* | EBI |
| *Comments:* | This shape is very similar to Chalcolithic flaring bowls, but the EBI versions have less pronounced flaring sides, thicker base and are often smaller. The rings of relief decoration seem to be a phenomenon mainly from the southern group of EBI sites. |
| *Examples:* | (see Braun 1990; Rowan 1998) |

**L2** – flaring bowl with handle

| | |
|---|---|
| *Drawn:* | (after Braun 1990: fig. 7) |
| *Variations:* | n/a |
| *Decoration:* | raised decoration in band below rim |
| | hornlike protrusions on handle |
| *Date Range:* | EBI |
| *Comments:* | Only two examples are known of this shape, both in basalt. |
| *Examples:* | (see Braun 1990; Rowan 1998) |

**L3** – flaring bowl with four vertical handles

| | |
|---|---|
| *Drawn:* | (after Braun 1990: fig. 7) |
| *Variations:* | solid handles/strap handles |
| *Decoration:* | n/a |
| *Date Range:* | late EBI(-early EBII?) |
| *Comments:* | The type seems to concentrate in the Beth Shan and Jezreel valleys. The finds contexts may suggest that the shape began to be produced in mid-late EBI. |
| *Examples:* | (see Braun 1990; Rowan 1998) |

**L4** – hemispherical bowl with protruding knobs below rim

| | |
|---|---|
| *Drawn:* | (after Braun 1990: fig. 4.3) |
| *Variations:* | fenestrated pedestal base/no pedestal ? |
| *Decoration:* | band of knobs below rim |
| *Date Range:* | late EBI? |
| *Comments:* | The shape has strong parallels in late EBI ceramics (Braun 1990: 94). |
| *Examples:* | (see Braun 1990; Rowan 1998) |

**L5** – incised lid with separate zoomorphic handle

| | |
|---|---|
| *Drawn:* | (after Money-Coutts 1936: pl. xxvii.a) |

*Variations:*     n/a

*Decoration:*     concentric rings of incised diagonal knicks

                     zoomorphic handle

*Date Range:*     EBII–III?/Byblos level KIV? (Saghieh 1983 for phasing)

*Comments:*       Only one example with a bull-shaped handle is known, from Byblos. Another fragment from this site with a slightly domed shape may be of this type. The stone used is chloritite/steatite. Lid was to cover L6.

*Examples:*       Byblos? bull-shaped handle (Money-Coutts 1936: pl. xxvii.a-b, d-e)

                     Byblos (Montet 1928: 80; Money-Coutts 1936: pl. xxviii.a)

**L6** – deep bowl with moulded base

*Drawn:*          (after Montet 1928: fig. 30)

*Variations:*     internal rim to fit lid

                     decorated on top of rim

                     decorated band below rim

*Decoration:*     concentric bands of incised herringbone pattern

                     incised diamonds and triangles

                     white and red inlay

*Date Range:*     EBII–III?/Byblos level KIV? (Saghieh 1983 for phasing)

*Comments:*       Associated with lid L5. The shape of the vessels with white (paste?) and red (stone) inlay may not be the same. Mostly made in chloritite/steatite, but a few are soft white limestone, gypsum, or less probably travertine. They may be local or possibly imports from much further east (Potts 2003).

*Examples:*       Byblos (Montet 1928: 80, fig. 30, pl. xlvi; Money-Coutts 1936: pl. xxviii)

                     Byblos? (Money-Coutts 1936: pl. xvii.c)

                     Ebla (Pinnock 1981: fig. B5)

                     Hama (Pinnock 1981:  fig. B.3c606)

**L7** – lugged bowl

*Drawn:*          (after Pinnock 1981: fig. b4)

*Variations:*     one lug/two lugs/fragmentary (no lugs)

*Decoration:*     incised rhomboids

                     zoomorphic lugs

                     hatched bands on rim and base

*Date Range:*     EBII–III?

*Comments:*       Found at Ebla and one found at Mari. The material is a soft white stone.

*Examples:*       (see Pinnock 1981)

**L8** – carinated bowl

*Drawn:*          BM 1951.1-3.42

*Variations:*     n/a

*Decoration:*     n/a

*Date Range:*     MBIIB–C

*Comments:*       Possibly copies metal shape.

*Examples:*       Alalakh × 2 (serpentinite, BM 1951.1-3.42, also Woolley 1955: 296)

**L9** – carinated lugged bowl/pyxis

*Drawn:*          BM 1939.6-13.111

*Variations:*    n/a
*Decoration:*    n/a
*Date Range:*    MBIIB-C
*Comments:*
*Examples:*      Alalakh (serpentinite, BM 1939.6-13.111)

**L10** – pierced lid
*Drawn:*         BM 1939.6-13.111
*Variations:*    n/a
*Decoration:*    n/a
*Date Range:*    MBIIB-C
*Comments:*      Lid for vessel of shape L9.
*Examples:*      Alalakh (serpentinite, BM 1939.6-13.111)
                 Amman (AM 1975.311-24)

**L11** – globular flask
*Drawn:*         (after Matthiae et al. 1995: no. 466)
*Variations:*    n/a
*Decoration:*    horizontal grooves on neck and above base
*Date Range:*    MBIIA-B?
*Comments:*      The shape has parallels in contemporary Anatolian/Levantine metalwork.
*Examples:*      Ebla (sardonyx and ?soft, white limestone, Matthiae 1979: 161, fig. 62a–b)

**L12** – drop-shaped alabastron
*Drawn:*         AM 1954.595
*Variations:*    articulated neck
*Decoration:*    n/a
*Date Range:*    MBIIB-LBIA
*Comments:*      Roughly copies E145.
*Examples:*      (see Ben-Dor 1945: type D; Sparks 2007: 1.1.7.1)

**L13** – baggy alabastron
*Drawn:*         (after Ben-Dor 1945: B4)
*Variations:*    handle/no handle
*Decoration:*    plain
                 dot-and-circle
                 rosette
*Date Range:*    MBIIB-?LBI
*Comments:*      Roughly copies E147-8. Most decorated examples come mainly from Pella.
*Examples:*      (see Ben-Dor 1945: type B; Sparks 2007: 1.1.7.2)

**L14** – everted rim jar
*Drawn:*         (after Ben-Dor 1945: C3)
*Variations:*    n/a
*Decoration:*    n/a
*Date Range:*    MBIIB-?LBI
*Comments:*      Copies E51 and E135. Most examples come from Beth Shan.
*Examples:*      (see Ben-Dor 1945: type C; Sparks 2007: 1.1.12)

**L15** – juglet

| | |
|---|---|
| *Drawn:* | AM 1954.594 |
| *Variations:* | strap handle/round handle |
| | plain base/disc base |
| | articulated shoulder |
| *Decoration:* | incised cord decoration on handle |
| *Date Range:* | MBIIB-?LBI |
| *Comments:* | All carved from gypsum. Often oval in plan view. |
| *Examples:* | (see Ben-Dor 1945: type A; Sparks 2007: 1.1.9) |

**L16** – globular pot

| | |
|---|---|
| *Drawn:* | (after Sparks 1998: fig. 47.2) |
| *Variations:* | n/a |
| *Decoration:* | n/a |
| *Date Range:* | MBII-LBI? |
| *Comments:* | All carved from gypsum. Most examples are from Beth Shan. |
| *Examples:* | (see Sparks 2007: 1.1.10) |

**L17** – ram's headed bowl

| | |
|---|---|
| *Drawn:* | BM (Jericho Tomb p-19) |
| *Variations:* | plain base/ring-base/disc base/stylised handles |
| *Decoration:* | incised zig-zag |
| *Date Range:* | MBIIB-C |
| *Comments:* | All carved from gypsum. Most examples are from Jericho. |
| *Examples:* | (see Sparks 2007: 1.1.2.4) |

**L18** – footed cup (*tazza*)

| | |
|---|---|
| *Drawn:* | (UCL E.vi.22/6; E.vi.23/8) |
| *Variations:* | three ridged/four ridged |
| | ridges pinched or moulded |
| | articulated top of foot |
| | thick, splayed foot |
| *Decoration:* | incised zig-zag |
| *Date Range:* | LBIB?-Iron I |
| *Comments:* | All carved from gypsum. Very similar to Cyp1. |
| *Examples:* | (see Ben-Dor 1945: type E; Clamer 1976: types L3a-d; Sparks 2007: 1.1.5) |

**L19** – lugged flask

| | |
|---|---|
| *Drawn:* | BM 1985.7-4.48 |
| *Variations:* | n/a |
| *Decoration:* | incised concentric circles |
| *Date Range:* | LBII-Iron I |
| *Comments:* | All carved from gypsum. Generally oval in plan view. Many examples are from Beth Shan. |
| *Examples:* | (Sparks 2007: 1.1.11) |

**L20** – lugged baggy jar

| | |
|---|---|
| *Drawn:* | BM Tomb 389.1, Tel es-Sa'idiyeh |
| *Variations:* | moulded rim/plain rim |

*Decoration:*   incised chevrons and ladder patterns
incised parallel lines and notches
plain

*Date Range:*   LBII–Iron I

*Comments:*   All carved from gypsum. Generally oval in plan view.

*Examples:*   (see Ben-Dor 1945: type F; Clamer 1976: type P4a; Sparks 2007: 1.1.14)

**L21** – lugged pyxis/bowl

*Drawn:*   BM 1990.3-3.143; BM tomb 379.2, Tel es-Sa'idiyeh

*Variations:*   flat base/low foot

*Decoration:*   incised concentric circles

*Date Range:*   LBII–Iron I

*Comments:*   All carved from gypsum. Most examples are from Beth Shan or Tel es-Sa'idiyeh.

*Examples:*   (see Sparks 2007: 1.1.4)

**L22** – bowl/dish

*Drawn:*   BM tomb 389.2, Tel es-Sa'idiyeh

*Variations:*   dish/bowl
single bar lug on rim
semicircular in plan

*Decoration:*   plain
incised rosette and ladder pattern

*Date Range:*   LBII–Iron I

*Comments:*   All carved from gypsum. Mainly from Tel es Sa'idiyeh and Pella.

*Examples:*   (Sparks 2007: 1.1.1-2)

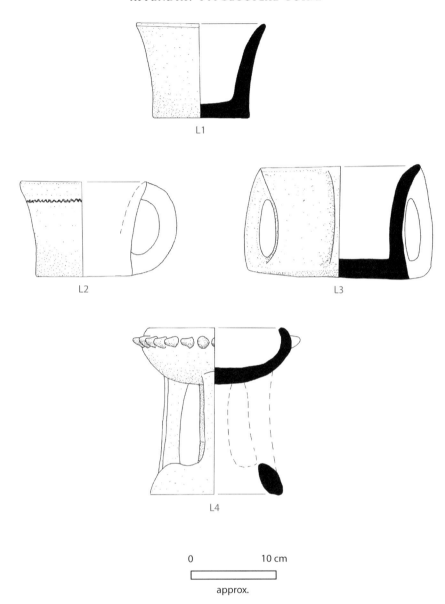

EBI basalt vessels.

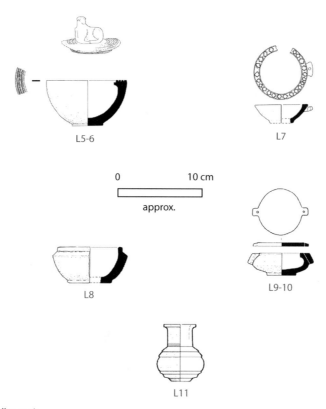

EB–MB vessels (miscellaneous).

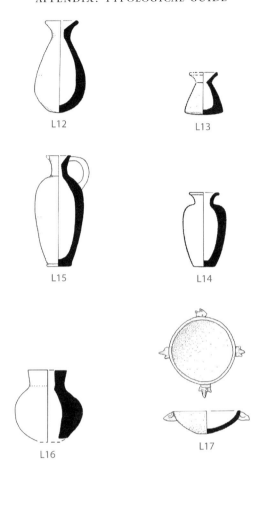

MBIIB–C gypsum vessels.

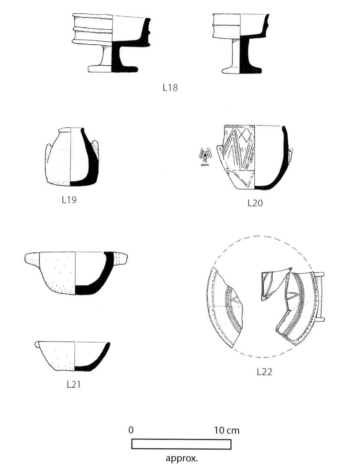

LBIB–Iron I gypsum vessels.

## Cyprus (Cyp-)

This typology is new. For possible Cypriot vessels made in Egyptian-style shapes, see the Es-numbers above.

**Cyp1** – footed cup (*tazza*)

| | |
|---|---|
| *Drawn:* | (after Aström 1967: 71.6; Karageorghis 1974: pls. lxvi.15, cxlix.15) |
| *Variations:* | internally partitioned into four |
| | two-ridged/three-ridged |
| *Decoration:* | concentric circles on base |
| *Date Range:* | LCypIIB-C |
| *Comments:* | Most are carved from gypsum. Very similar to L18. |
| *Examples:* | Kalavassos Mangia V.5, Larnaca M. (McClennan 1988: 218, fig. 8.33, pl. xxxiii.4) |
| | Kition T9, lower burial (Karageorghis 1974: 44, pls. lxvi.15, cxlix.15) |
| | Enkomi T11 (three examples, Schaeffer 1952: 130, 146, 151, fig. 60.9, pls. xxii.243, xxiii.2) |
| | Enkomi T66, BM 1897.4-1.1041 (Murray et al. 1900: fig. 63.1041) |
| | Cyp. M. 1934.iii-21.9 |
| | Cyp. M. 1962.vii-2.1 (two-ridged, concentric circles on base) |
| | Cyp. M. A207 (Aström 1967: 541, fig. 71.6) |
| | MMA Cesnola Coll. 1538 ('black steatite') |
| | MMA Cesnola Coll. 1637 |
| | Egypt (von Bissing 1907: pl. vii.18218) |

**Cyp2** – three-handled alabastron

| | |
|---|---|
| *Drawn:* | AM 1968.90 |
| *Variations:* | n/a |
| *Decoration:* | n/a |
| *Date Range:* | LCypII-III |
| *Comments:* | All carved from gypsum or travertine/limestone. The shape is similar to a Mycenean pottery form, although the neck is sometimes more elongated. |
| *Examples:* | Enkomi (Cyp. M. A208) |
| | Enkomi T94 (Cyp. M. A209, Dikaios 1971: 148 no. 3) |
| | Enkomi (Cyp. M. A210) |
| | Maroni T23 (Cyp. M. A212, Johnston 1980: 28 no. 189, pl. xxxviii) |
| | Maroni T25 (Cyp. M. A202, Johnston 1980: 30, pl. xli.205) |
| | Kalavassos-Mangia I.1 (Karageorghis 1976: 852) |
| | Kalavassos-Mangia V.5 (McClennan 1988: 220, fig. 9.56, pl. xxxiii) |
| | Dromolaxia (Cyp. M. A203B) |
| | Cyp. M. A208 |
| | AM 1968.90 |
| | AM 1968.91 |

**Cyp3** – three-handled jar

| | |
|---|---|
| *Drawn:* | (after Aström 1967: fig. 71.48) |

*Variations:*   flaring foot
*Decoration:*   n/a
*Date Range:*   LCypII-III
*Comments:*   All carved from gypsum or travertine/limestone. The shape is similar to a Mycenean pottery form.
*Examples:*   Agios Iakovos (Aström 1967: fig. 71.48)
Enkomi T66 (BM 1897.4–1.1316)
Enkomi Fr. T11 (Aström 1967)
Enkomi (Aström 1967: fig. 71.48)
Kition T9 upper burial (four examples, Karageorghis 1974: pl. lxxx)
Uppsala M. 412

**Cyp4** – small amphora with strap handles
*Drawn:*   (after Buchholz and Karageorghis 1973: no. 1669)
*Variations:*   n/a
*Decoration:*   fake rivet
bull's head design
*Date Range:*   LCypIII
*Comments:*   Shape probably copies larger-scale metal and ceramic kraters. Usually carved from chloritite.
*Examples:*   Alambra (Aström 1967: 71)
Enkomi (Courtois 1984: no. 898)
Enkomi (Courtois 1984: no. 914, fig. 35.3, pl. xxii.14)
Enkomi T406 (Buchholz and Karageorghis 1973: no. 1669)
Kition T3 (gypsum, Karageorghis 1960: figs. 66–7)
Kition (gypsum, Buchholz and Karageorghis 1973: no. 1667)
Kition (bull's head, Cyp.M. 1938.vi-23.5, Buchholz and Karageorghis 1973: no. 1668)
Kouklia T4 (Aström 1967: 71)
MMA Cesnola Coll. 1539 (Karageorghis 2000: no. 124)

**Cyp5** – small lugged amphora
*Drawn:*   BM 1897.4-1.915
*Variations:*   duck-shaped lugs
sharp horn lugs
*Decoration:*   (all incised)
hatched bands
hatched triangles
*Date Range:*   LCypIII
*Comments:*   Copies decoration on metal, ivory and bone vessels. Usually carved from chloritite.
*Examples:*   Enkomi (Stockholm M. 81, Aström (1967): 71)
Enkomi (Stockholm M. 83, Aström 1967: 71)
Enkomi (BM 1897.4-1.1330, Murray et al. 1900: fig. 44.1330)
Enkomi (Murray et al. 1900: fig. 45)
Enkomi Fr.T6 (Schaeffer 1936: fig. 41.45, 68, pls. xxxv.5, 3)

Enkomi T39 (BM 1897.4-1.915)

Enkomi (Courtois 1984: no. 911)

Enkomi (Louvre 84 AO 113, Courtois 1988: fig. 444)

Kition T3 (four examples in gypsum, Karageorghis 1960)

Kouklia (2 examples, Aström 1967: 71)

Lapithos T420 (Gjerstad et al. 1934: pls. liii.1:45, cliii.23)

Kourion T89 (BM 1896.2-1.96, Murray et al. 1900: 79)

Cyp. M. 1944.x-30.10

MMA Cesnola Coll. 1540 (three Archaic Phoenecian or Cypro-Minoan signs on base, Karageorghis 2000: no. 120)

MMA Cesnola Coll. 1542 (Karageorghis 2000: no. 119)

MMA Cesnola Coll. 1643 (gypsum, Karageorghis 2000: no. 116)

**Cyp6** – tall cylindrical jar (usually lugged)

| | |
|---|---|
| *Drawn:* | (after Schaeffer 1952: 235, fig. 88.7) |
| *Variations:* | lugged/not lugged |
| *Decoration:* | dot-and-circle |
| | hatched bands, horizontal grooves |
| *Date Range:* | LCypIII |
| *Comments:* | Parallels in ivory and bone. Usually carved from chloritite. |
| *Examples:* | Enkomi (Courtois 1984: no. 908, fig. 35.4) |
| | Enkomi T24 (BM 1897.4-1.886) |
| | Enkomi T35 (BM 1897.4-1.912) |
| | Enkomi Fr.T1 (Schaeffer 1952: 235, fig. 88.7) |

**Cyp7** – bowl

| | |
|---|---|
| *Drawn:* | (Courtois et al. 1986: pl. xxiii.9) |
| *Variations:* | moulded base/plain base |
| *Decoration:* | (all incised) |
| | arcades |
| | hatched bands |
| | handle |
| *Date Range:* | LCypIII |
| *Comments:* | Probably imitates metal versions. Usually carved from chloritite. |
| *Examples:* | Enkomi (Courtois 1984: no. 905) |
| | Enkomi (Courtois 1984: no. 913) |
| | Enkomi (Courtois 1984: no. 915, fig. 35.11) |
| | Enkomi (Aström 1967: fig. 71.47) |
| | Enkomi T38 (BM 1897.4-1.914) |
| | Enkomi T66 (BM 1897.4-1.1338) |
| | Palaepaphos × 3 (Elliott 1990: 133, one with handle) |

**Cyp8** – lugged bowl

| | |
|---|---|
| *Drawn:* | (after Courtois et al. 1986: pl. xxiii.10) |
| *Variations:* | one lug/two lugs |
| *Decoration:* | (all incised) |
| | running spirals |

                    dotted triangles

                    hatched bands

*Date Range:* LCypIII

*Comments:* Probably imitate metal versions. Usually carved from chloritite.

*Examples:* Enkomi (Courtois 1984: no. 909, fig. 35.10)

                Enkomi (Courtois 1984: no. 910, fig. 35.7)

                Cyp.M. W21 (Buchholz and Karageorghis 1973: no. 1670)

                MMA Cesnola Coll. 1539 (Karageorghis 2000: no. 124)

**Cyp9** – lid

*Drawn:* (not drawn)

*Variations:* n/a

*Decoration:* (all incised)

                    star pattern

                    dot-and-circle

                    arcs

*Date Range:* LCypIII

*Comments:* Similar designs also appear on spindle whorls. Usually carved from chloritite.

*Examples:* Enkomi (Courtois 1984: no. 907, fig. 35.6)

                Enkomi (BM 1897.4-1.1428)

                MMA Cesnola Coll. 1541

                MMA Cesnola Coll. 1553

                MMA Cesnola Coll. 1560

**Cyp10** – miniature larnax

*Drawn:* (after Aström 1967: fig. 71.43)

*Variations:* n/a

*Decoration:* plain

                    hatched triangles

*Date Range:* LCypIII

*Comments:* Copies larger-scale larnakes. Usually carved from chloritite.

*Examples:* Enkomi (Courtois 1984: no. 911)

                Enkomi (Dikaios 1971: pl. 147/8, 176.55)

                Enkomi (Aström 1967: fig. 71.43)

                Enkomi Fr. T1 (Schaeffer 1952: fig. 88.7)

                Enkomi (BM 1897.4-1.886)

                Kouklia (Kouklia M. KTAV 129)

                MMA Cesnola Coll. 1544 (Karageorghis 2000: no. 122)

**Cyp11** – miniature tripod mortar

*Drawn:* (after Courtois et al. 1986: pl. xxiii.16)

*Variations:* n/a

*Decoration:* incised lines

                    bull's head in relief

*Date Range:* LCypII-III

*Comments:* Copies larger-scale tripod mortars in volcanic stones. Usually in chloritite.

*Examples:* Enkomi × 6 (Schaeffer 1952: fig. 97 bottom, fig. 68.71)

Enkomi × 4 (Dikaios 1969: pl. 164.18, 172.18,21–22)

Enkomi × 3 (BM 1897.04-01.865,962,1332)

Enkomi × 2 (Courtois 1984: fig. 35.9; Courtois et al. 1986: pl. xxiii.16)

Palaepaphos (Elliott 1990: 132–3)

Ugarit (Schaeffer 1949: fig. 62.16)

Rhodes (Benzi 1992: T67/5) Cesnola Coll. 74.51.5025, 5139 (the latter of gypsum)

**Cyp12** – large plate with ring-base

*Drawn:* (after Schaeffer 1952: fig. 72.301)

*Variations:* n/a

*Decoration:* incised/plain

*Date Range:* LCypII-III

*Comments:* Often made of serpentinite. The shape is similar to basalt examples from the Levant (Sparks 2007: 3.1.1, pls. 1b).

*Examples:* Enkomi × 6 (Schaeffer 1952: figs. 66.10–11, 67.36, 68.91, 72.301, 304)

Enkomi × 2 (BM 1897.04-01.1338,1560)

Kition (Karageorghis 1960: fig. 73)

Byblos (Dunand 1958: fig. 707.13440)

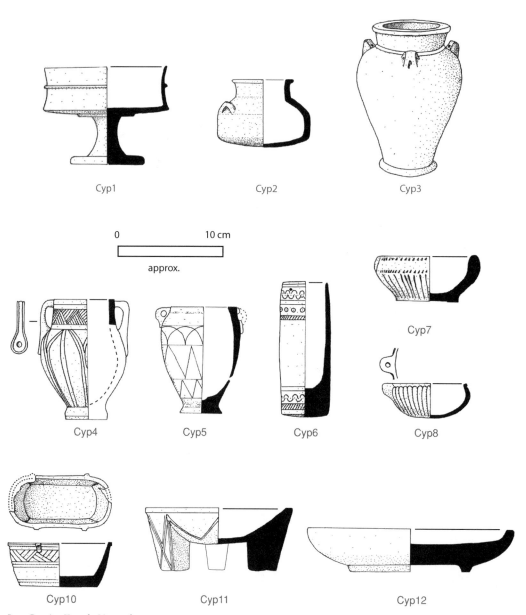

Cyp1                Cyp2                Cyp3

0          10 cm

approx.

Cyp4                Cyp5                Cyp6

Cyp7

Cyp8

Cyp10                Cyp11                Cyp12

Late Cypriot II–early IA vessels.

## Anatolia (A-)

The number of shapes is quite small and the typology is a new one (though drawing on Özten 1988). For the LBA, there is not enough evidence for stone vessels to make a classification of the existing shapes worthwhile at this stage.

**A1** – two-handled flask with pointed base
| | |
|---|---|
| *Drawn:* | (after Özgüç 1966: fig. 6) |
| *Variations:* | n/a |
| *Decoration:* | horizontal fluting on neck |
| | zoomorphic handles |
| | torsional fluting on body |
| *Date Range:* | Kültepe II (Acemhöyük III) |
| *Comments:* | Similar in shape to A2, so fragmentary examples could be from either one. There are many pottery examples, but both may be copying metal versions. |
| *Examples:* | Acemhöyük (Özten 1988) |
| | Kültepe (quartz crystal, Özgüç 1986: 51, pl. 96.3). |
| | Kültepe (Kayseri M. 82/917, obsidian, Özgüç 1986: 50, pl. 95.7) |

**A2** – flask with pointed base
| | |
|---|---|
| *Drawn:* | (after Özgüç 1966: figs. 4–5) |
| *Variations:* | fluted/unfluted |
| *Decoration:* | shallow vertical fluting |
| *Date Range:* | Kültepe II (Acemhöyük III) |
| *Comments:* | Similar shape to A1. |
| *Examples:* | (see Özten 1988) |

**A3** – shallow bowl
| | |
|---|---|
| *Drawn:* | (after Özten 1979: 385–6) |
| *Variations:* | base ring/plain |
| *Decoration:* | none |
| *Date Range:* | Acemhöyük III (Kültepe II) |
| *Comments:* | Several ceramic parallels. |
| *Examples:* | Acemhöyük (Ankara M., radiolarite, Özten 1979: pl. I) |
| | Acemhöyük (Ankara M. 158-11-67, obsidian, Özten 1979: pl. II-III). |

**A4** – three-footed stand
| | |
|---|---|
| *Drawn:* | (after Ankara M. photograph and Özten 1979: 385–6) |
| *Variations:* | n/a |
| *Decoration:* | none |
| *Date Range:* | Acemhöyük III (Kültepe II) |
| *Comments:* | Perforations in the feet suggest that the stand could have been made taller by the addition of another piece. |
| *Example:* | Acemhöyük (Ankara M., radiolarite, Özten 1979: 385–7, pl. II) |

**A5** – Zoomorphic box
| | |
|---|---|
| *Drawn:* | (after Özgüç 1959: pls. xxxv. 1–2, 1986: pl. 133.2) |
| *Variations:* | cow and boar shapes |

*Decoration:*    n/a
*Date Range:*   Kültepe Ib
*Comments:*     Many ceramic parallels.
*Examples:*     Kültepe (boar-shaped box, serpentinite/chloritite? Özgüç 1959: pls. xxxv.1–2)

Kültepe (cow/calf, serpentinite/chloritite?, Özgüç 1966: pl. 28.1; 1986: pl. 133.2)

**A6** – raptor-headed cup
*Drawn:*        (after Özgüç 1986: pl. 133.4)
*Variations:*   n/a
*Decoration:*   none
*Date Range:*   Kültepe Ib
*Comments:*     Only one stone example is known, but the shape has many ceramic parallels (e.g. Özgüç 1986: pls. 115.1–2).
*Example:*      Kültepe (Kayseri M. chloritite/steatite, Özgüç 1986: pl. 133.4)

Acemhöyük (attribution uncertain, obsidian, Özten 1988: pl. 21a–b, fig. 20)

**A7** – bowl with lug
*Drawn:*        (after Mellaart and Murray 1995: fig. 028)
*Variations:*   two small solid lugs/double button lug?
*Decoration:*   none
*Date Range:*   Beycesultan level V
*Comments:*     All from Beycesultan.
*Examples:*     Beycesultan (6 examples, chloritite?, Mellaart and Murray 1995: 121, 142–5)

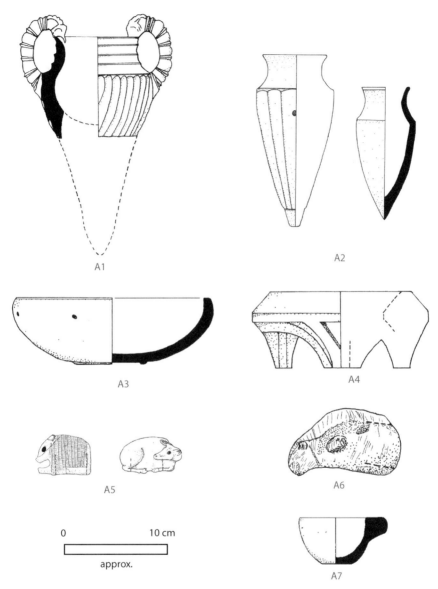

A1

A2

A3

A4

A5

A6

0   10 cm
approx.

A7

Anatolian MB stone vessels.

## Crete (C-)

The system of classification and numbering is taken from Warren (1969) with only minor alterations. As with Aston's Egyptian classification, Warren's individual types make distinctions at a slightly finer-scale (e.g. for bowls) than the other typologies offered here and hence comparisons of type diversity should proceed cautiously.

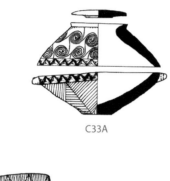

C33A

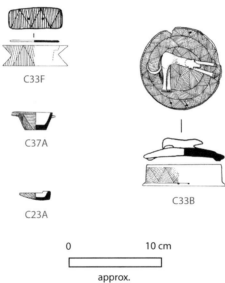

C33F

C37A

C23A

C33B

0          10 cm

approx.

EMIIA chloritite vessels.

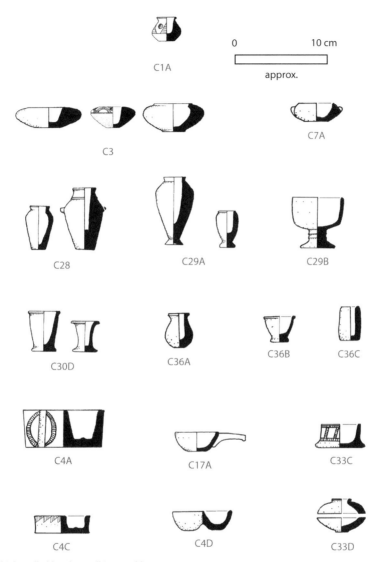

EMIIB–MMI thick-walled bowls, small jars, and boxes.

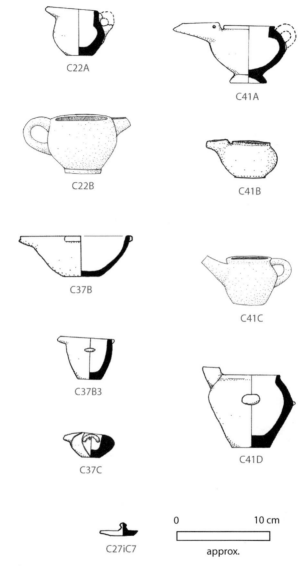

EMIIB–MMI spouted vessels.

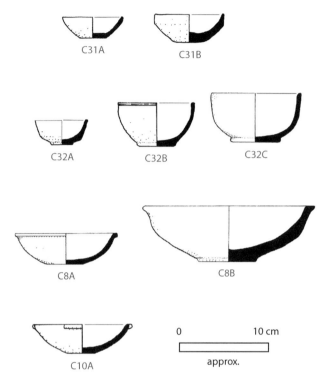

EMIIB–MMI open bowls.

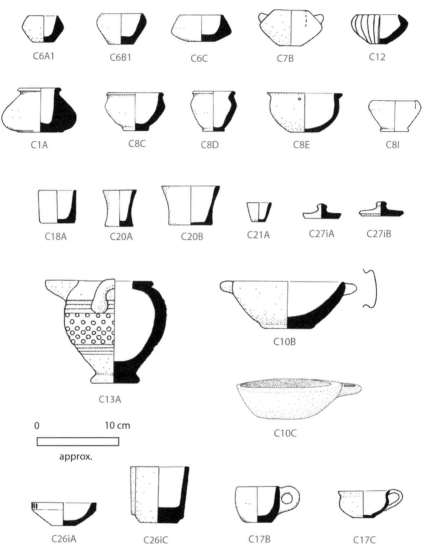

MMI–II vessels.

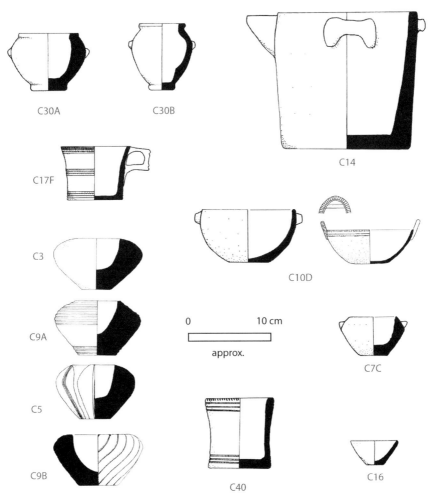

C30A

C30B

C14

C17F

C3

C10D

C9A

0        10 cm

approx.

C7C

C5

C9B

C40

C16

MMIII–LMI vessels.

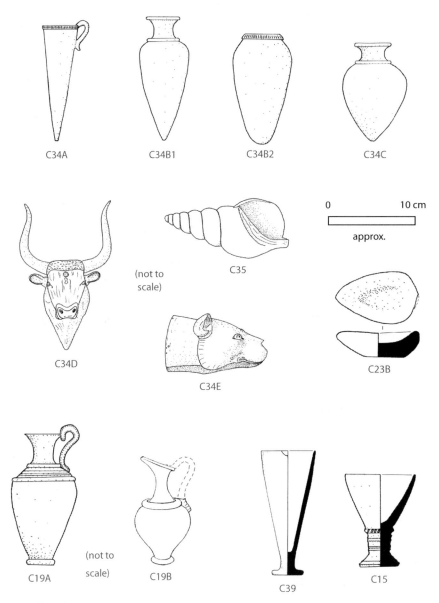

C34A          C34B1          C34B2          C34C

C34D

C35

(not to scale)

0                              10 cm

approx.

C34E

C23B

C19A          (not to scale)          C19B

C39

C15

MMIII–LMI ritual vessels.

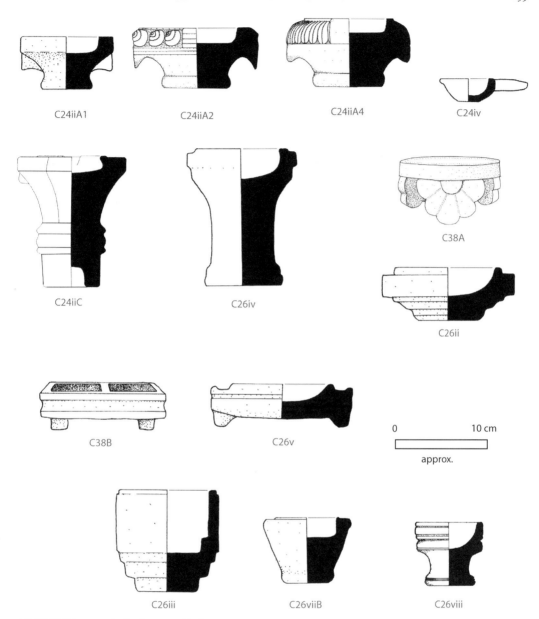

C24iiA1     C24iiA2     C24iiA4     C24iv

C24iiC     C26iv     C38A

C26ii

C38B     C26v

0          10 cm

approx.

C26iii     C26viiB     C26viii

MMIII-LMI lamps and miscellaneous table forms.

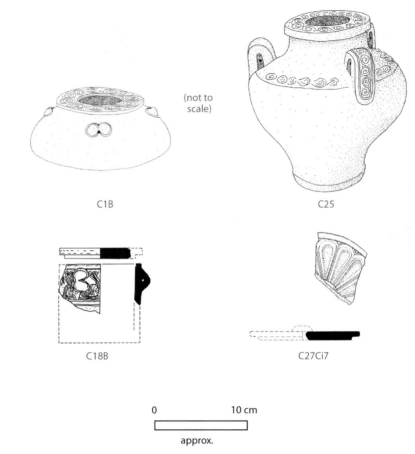

C1B

(not to scale)

C25

C18B

C27Ci7

0       10 cm

approx.

LMII–IIIA gypsum vessels.

## Mycenaean-Style Vessels (M-)

The numbering is new, but the identification of shapes roughly follows Tournavitou (1995) and Dickers (1995) with some alterations.

**M1** – lid

| | |
|---|---|
| *Drawn:* | (after Tournavitou 1995: fig. 35) |
| *Variations:* | usually a separate handle |
| *Decoration:* | n/a |
| *Date Range:* | LHIII(A2-)B1 |
| *Comments:* | Many of these seem to be made with separate pawn handles. |
| *Examples:* | Mycenae (Tournavitou 1995) |
| | Ellenika (Hatzi-Spiliopoulou 2000: pl. lxxi.g) |

**M2** – jar

| | |
|---|---|
| *Drawn:* | (after Tournavitou 1995: fig. 35, 36a) |
| *Variations:* | (a) neck-piece |
| | (b) globular (sometimes with moulded base) |
| | (c) tall, ovoid (sometimes moulded base, or slightly piriform) |
| | (d) squat, piriform (sometimes moulded base) |
| *Decoration:* | plain |
| | diagonal carved fluting |
| | metallicising neckpiece with diagonal fluting |
| *Date Range:* | LHIII(A2-)B1 |
| *Comments:* | Often fitted with a separate neck (M2a). Mainly from Mycenae. |
| *Examples:* | (a) Mycenae (Tournavitou 1995: IH 53/788; 54/403, 407) |
| | (a) Ellenika (Hatzi-Spiliopoulou 2000) |
| | (a) Knossos (KSM Evans box 1448) |
| | (b) Mycenae (Shear 1987: 123, pl. 38; Tournavitou 1995: IH 53/789; 54/402–3, 407, 410; 55/212) |
| | (c) Mycenae (Sakellarakis 1980: 178, pl. iii.6; Tournavitou 1995: IH 53/114; 54/401) |
| | (c) Menidi × 3 (Sakellarakis 1980: 183, pl. ix.25) |
| | (c) Phaistos (uncertain, Levi 1961–1962: fig. 122) |
| | (c) Ellenika (Hatzi-Spiliopoulou 2000) |
| | (d) Mycenae (Xenaki-Sakellariou 1985: 157, pl.56; Tournavitou 1995: IH 53/115, 788; 54/406) |

**M3** – alabastron

| | |
|---|---|
| *Drawn:* | (after Tournavitou 1995: fig. 38) |
| *Variations:* | n/a |
| *Decoration:* | n/a |
| *Date Range:* | LHIII(A2-)B1 |
| *Comments:* | Mainly from Mycenae. |
| *Examples:* | Mycenae (Tournavitou 1995: IH 54/351, 404, 412–3) |

**M4** – three-handled jar

| | |
|---|---|
| *Drawn:* | (after Tournavitou 1995: 678) |

| | |
|---|---|
| *Variations:* | n/a |
| *Decoration:* | n/a |
| *Date Range:* | LHIII(A2-)B1 |
| *Comments:* | These vessels may sometimes have had separate neck pieces, in which case they would have resembled Mycenaean three-handled pottery jars. |
| *Examples:* | Mainland Greece (Lilyquist 1996: pl. 11.1) |
| | Mycenae (Sakellarakis 1980: pl. iii.7; Tournavitou 1995: IH-53-414, 486, 491; Lilyquist 1996: pl. 11.3) |
| | Knossos (KSM Evans box 1891) |

**M5** – rhyton

| | |
|---|---|
| *Drawn:* | (after Sakellarakis 1980: pl. ix.29) |
| *Variations:* | n/a |
| *Decoration:* | rough incised herringbone pattern |
| | inlay holes |
| | vertical fluting |
| *Date Range:* | LHIII(A2-)B1 |
| *Comments:* | |
| *Examples:* | Mycenae (Sakellarakis 1980: pl. ix.29; Tournavitou 1995: fig. 41a) |
| | Mainland Greece (uncertain, Nauplion M. 69:16, Kaiser 1980: fig. 2) |
| | Knossos (KSM Evans box 1893) |

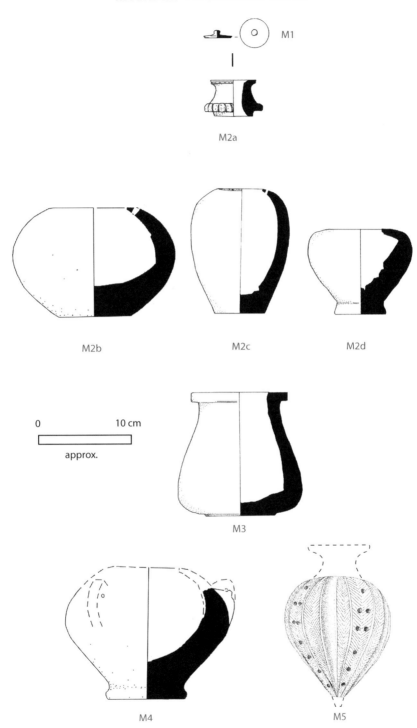

LHIIIB1 Ivory Houses style vessels.

## Cyclades (Cyc-)

The numbering for this typology is new, but the shapes follow the rough categories outlined in Getz-Gentle 1996.

**Cyc1** – collared neck jar with lugs (*kandile*)

| | |
|---|---|
| *Drawn:* | (after Getz-Gentle 1996: fig. 40) |
| *Variations:* | very large to very small |
| | short collar and short foot |
| | two small conjoined examples |
| *Decoration:* | n/a |
| *Date Range:* | ECI (Grotta-Pelos) |
| *Comments:* | |
| *Examples:* | (see Getz-Gentle 1996: 237-51, pls. I, 1–21) |

**Cyc2** – lugged beaker

| | |
|---|---|
| *Drawn:* | (after Getz-Gentle 1996: fig. 24b, pl. 29d) |
| *Variations:* | very large or very small |
| | large or small lugs |
| | horned lugs |
| | four lugs |
| | slightly everted rim |
| | gynopomorphic |
| *Decoration:* | gynoomorphic designs |
| *Date Range:* | ECI (Grotta-Pelos) |
| *Comments:* | |
| *Examples:* | (see Getz-Gentle 1996: 251–8, pls. 24–30) |

**Cyc3** – lugged bowl

| | |
|---|---|
| *Drawn:* | (after Getz-Gentle 1996: fig. 105) |
| *Variations:* | very large to very small |
| | two lugs |
| | groove below rim |
| | low foot/moulded base |
| | decorated/undecorated |
| *Decoration:* | band of incised triangles below rim |
| *Date Range:* | ECI (Grotta-Pelos) |
| *Comments:* | Often found with traces of ground pigment. |
| *Examples:* | (see Getz-Gentle 1996: 258–64, pls. 31–9) |

**Cyc4A** – rectangular perforated palette

| | |
|---|---|
| *Drawn:* | (after Getz-Gentle 1996: fig. 42f) |
| *Variations:* | very large or very small |
| | rectangular/slightly concave/slightly convex |
| | four perforations /less than four perforations |
| *Decoration:* | n/a |
| *Date Range:* | ECI (Grotta-Pelos) |

*Comments:*     Often found with traces of ground pigment.
*Examples:*     (see Getz-Gentle 1996: 264–6, figs. 42–3, pls. 40–2, 49)

**Cyc4B** – rectangular palette
*Drawn:*        (after Getz-Gentle 1996: fig. 46d)
*Variations:*   small to very large
*Decoration:*   n/a
*Date Range:*   ECI/II-II (Kampos and Keros-Syros)
*Comments:*
*Examples:*     (see Getz-Gentle 1996: 268–9)

**Cyc4C** – trough-shaped palette
*Drawn:*        (after Getz-Gentle 1996: fig. 47e)
*Variations:*   perforated/unperforated
*Decoration:*   n/a
*Date Range:*   ECI/II-II (Kampos and Keros-Syros)
*Comments:*     Often found with traces of ground pigment. Perhaps copying shape of
                palettes made from a split bone.
*Examples:*     (see Getz-Gentle 1996: 88–91, 269–71)

**Cyc5** – plain bowl
*Drawn:*        (after Getz-Gentle 1996: fig. 51a)
*Variations:*   very small to very large
*Decoration:*   occasionally painted?
*Date Range:*   ECI/II-II (Kampos and Keros-Syros)
*Comments:*
*Examples:*     (see Getz-Gentle 1996: 99–105, pls. v, 50–5)

**Cyc6** – spouted bowl
*Drawn:*        (after Getz-Gentle 1996: pl. 58c)
*Variations:*   spout and three rim lugs
                pedestal base
*Decoration:*   n/a
*Date Range:*   ECII (Keros-Syros)
*Comments:*
*Examples:*     (see Getz-Gentle 1996: 109–12, 273–4, figs. 55–6, 59, pls. 58–61)

**Cyc7** – lugged bowl
*Drawn:*        (after Getz-Gentle 1996: fig. 58)
*Variations:*   pedestal base
*Decoration:*   n/a
*Date Range:*   late ECII-III? (Keros-Syros and Kastri)
*Comments:*     Common at Chalandriani and imitated in Crete (C10A).
*Examples:*     (see Getz-Gentle 1996: 113–120, 275–8, pl. vii.c–d, pl. 63–9)

**Cyc8** – bowl with body lug
*Drawn:*        (after Getz-Gentle 1996: pl. 56b)
*Variations:*   rectangular/circular
*Decoration:*   n/a
*Date Range:*   ECII (Keros-Syros)

*Comments:*

*Examples:*    (see Getz-Gentle 1996: 105–7)

**Cyc9** – ring bowl

    *Drawn:*    (after Getz-Gentle 1996: fig. 104d)

    *Variations:*    spouted bowl on ring

                 marble/softstone

    *Decoration:*    n/a

    *Date Range:*    ECI/II (Kampos and Keros-Syros)

    *Comments:*    Possibly a receptacle for pigment.

    *Examples:*    (see Getz-Gentle 1996: 112–3, figs. 57, 104)

**Cyc10** – miniature bowl with attachment

    *Drawn:*    (after Getz-Gentle 1996: fig. 104c)

    *Variations:*    n/a

    *Decoration:*    silver gilding on rim

    *Date Range:*    ECI/II (Kampos and Keros-Syros)

    *Comments:*    Possibly a miniature crucible. Made in a translucent greenstone.

    *Examples:*    (see Getz-Gentle 1996: 107)

**Cyc11** – flaring cup

    *Drawn:*    FM GR 7b.1923

    *Variations:*    pedestal base

    *Decoration:*    n/a

    *Date Range:*    ECII (Keros-Syros)

    *Comments:*    The variety on a pedestal base is more common.

    *Examples:*    (see Getz-Gentle 1996: 120–3, 164–7, 278–9, 291–5, figs. 63, 94–5, pls. 91d, 98–101)

**Cyc12** – cup with vertical grooves

    *Drawn:*    (after Getz-Gentle 1996: fig. 52)

    *Variations:*    n/a

    *Decoration:*    n/a

    *Date Range:*    ECII? (Keros-Syros?)

    *Comments:*

    *Examples:*    (see Getz-Gentle 1996: 107–8, fig. 52)

**Cyc13** – spherical lugged pyxis

    *Drawn:*    (after Getz-Gentle 1996: fig. 70b)

    *Variations:*    pedestal base

                 double lugs/single lugs

                 marble/softstone

    *Decoration:*    incised vertical lines

                 incised hatched triangles

    *Date Range:*    ECII (Keros-Syros)

    *Comments:*    Common at Aplomata.

    *Examples:*    (see Getz-Gentle 1996: 129–36, 279–83, 295–6, figs. 70–1, pls. 10b, 72–7)

**Cyc14** – cylindrical pyxis

    *Drawn:*    (after Getz-Gentle 1996: fig. 80b)

*Variations:* n/a

*Decoration:* n/a

*Date Range:* ECII (Keros-Syros)

*Comments:*

*Examples:* (see Getz-Gentle 1996: 142–54, 284–7, figs. 78, 80–1, 85, pls. vii.b, 80–7)

**Cyc15** – hut-shaped pyxis

*Drawn:* (after Getz-Gentle 1996: figs. 88, 107)

*Variations:* circular/two cavities and figure-of-eight shape/multi-cavity and complex lugs/no lugs
internal partition

*Decoration:* incised spirals, lines, chevrons

*Date Range:* early (?) ECII (Keros-Syros)

*Comments:* Mainly carved from chloritite.

*Examples:* (see Getz-Gentle 1996: 192–9, figs. 107–9, pls. 108–14)

**Cyc16** – frying pan

*Drawn:* (after Getz-Gentle 1996: figs. 65a, 107c)

*Variations:* marble/softstone

*Decoration:* incised spirals

*Date Range:* ECII (Keros-Syros)

*Comments:*

*Examples:* (see Getz-Gentle 1996: 123–4)

**Cyc17** – dove tray

*Drawn:* (after Getz-Gentle 1996: pl. 71a)

*Variations:* n/a

*Decoration:* n/a

*Date Range:* ECII (Keros-Syros)

*Comments:*

*Examples:* (see Getz-Gentle 1996: 124–6)

**Cyc18** – lugged and collared jar

*Drawn:* (after Getz-Gentle 1996: pl. viii.a)

*Variations:* n/a

*Decoration:* n/a

*Date Range:* ECII (Keros-Syros)

*Comments:* Similar to decorated pottery forms.

*Examples:* (see Getz-Gentle 1996: 128–9)

**Cyc19** – zoomorphic vessel

*Drawn:* (after Getz-Gentle 1996: fig. 75b)

*Variations:* n/a

*Decoration:* incised lines on body

*Date Range:* ECI?-II (mainly Keros-Syros)

*Comments:* Known examples seem to be depicting a sheep (or less likely, a hedgehog or pig).

*Examples:* (see Getz-Gentle 1996: 136–42, figs. 73–5, pls. 78–9)

**Cyc20** – model lamp

*Drawn:*        (after Getz-Gentle 1996: fig. 97a)
*Variations:*   n/a
*Decoration:*   n/a
*Date Range:*   ECII
*Comments:*     Copies of working lamps?
*Examples:*     (see Getz-Gentle 1996: 168, figs. 97, 98b, pl. 102d)

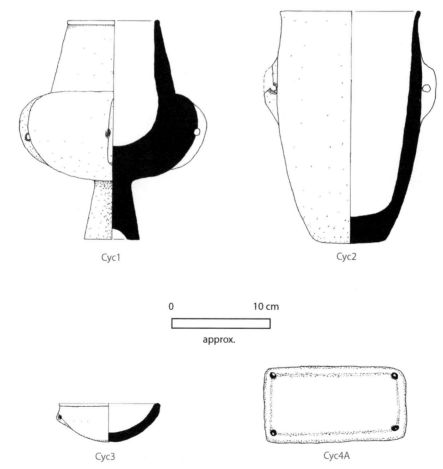

Grotta-Pelos marble vessels.

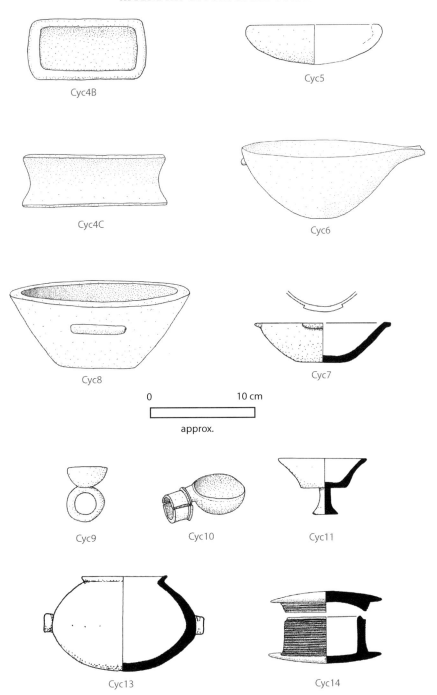

Kampos and Keros–Syros vessels in marble and softstone.

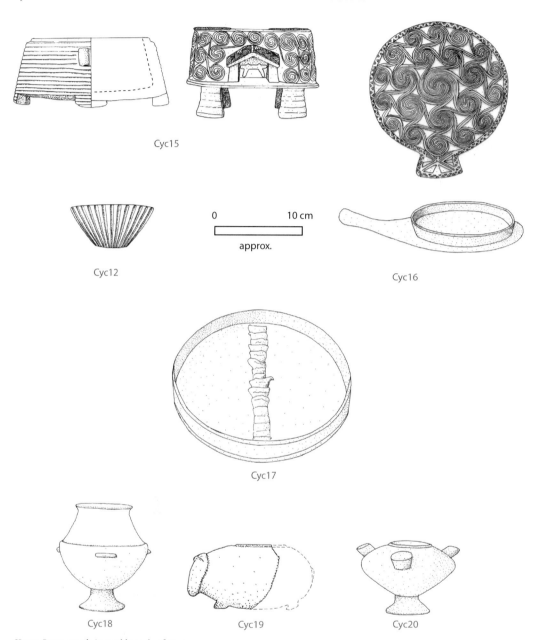

Cyc15

Cyc12

0          10 cm

approx.

Cyc16

Cyc17

Cyc18          Cyc19          Cyc20

Keros-Syros vessels in marble and softstone.

# Notes

菱菱菱菱菱菱菱

### Chapter 1 / Introduction

1. Statistical tests are not described in the text, but the term *significant* is used only when a pattern has been tested formally and a standard (no pattern) null hypothesis can be rejected with less than a 5% probability of error.
2. In contrast, actual steatite (talc) is more frequently used for beads and other small items than for vessels. There is certainly overlap in these terms, with serpentinised rocks often comprising some chlorite or steatite, but these three different stone names are both geologically acceptable and useful for most practical purposes.
3. The following are useful summaries of the regional evidence for social structure in the more complex, statelike societies of the Bronze Age eastern Mediterranean: Egypt (Baines 1995; Grajetski 2006), the Levant (Foster 1987; Vargyas 1988; Dalley 2002), Anatolia (Bryce 2002), Cyprus (Keswani 2004), and the Aegean (e.g. see Chadwick 1976: 61–83 and papers in Rehak 1995a). Palatial Crete is perhaps the complex, statelike society about whose social political system we are least certain, but the loose, threefold division suggested here remains useful and has the advantage of not assuming the nature of ultimate political control or territorial division on the island.

### Chapter 3 / Moving People, Objects, and Ideas

1. An intriguing exception to this is the evidence for the spread of early farming communities, across relatively large bodies of water, to places such as Cyprus, Crete, and the western Aegean. These colonisation episodes appear to have involved the wholesale movement of livestock, seed crop, equipment, and people (e.g. Broodbank and Strasser 1991: 239–42), suggesting that, in unusual circumstances, larger loads could be moved by a fleet of canoes. However, we should see this as an extremely involved and inherently risky strategy in terms of human, animal, and material resources, so unlikely to be the normal pattern of voyaging.
2. When there is clearly commercially motivated language in the Amarna correspondence, it comes from the ruler of Cyprus who, as a relative newcomer to the group of Great Kings, we might assume was still out of step with the way such international dealings were styled (Moran 1987: especially EA 35, 49–53).
3. The Karnak inscription suggest the dedication of 15 tons of gold and large amounts of other precious metals by Thutmosis III (Janssen 1975a). The Ulu Burun wreck also produced some 10 tons of copper and a ton of tin, and the extant Assur-Kültepe records indicate a trade of ca. 10 tons of silver and 100,000 textiles over a 40-year period (Larsen 1987: 51; Pulak 2006).
4. Prevailing current and winds combine to make a voyage from Crete to the Libyan coast comparatively short (perhaps four days under good conditions), while at the same time making a return voyage particularly hard. The latter voyage was occasionally made in later periods by large ships equipped with brailed sails (and keels) that allowed them to sail much closer to the wind, but such technology first becomes available only very late in the Bronze Age (Wachsmann 2000). It has also been suggested that the current beginning further west along the Libyan coast (linking the tip of classical Cyrenaica with Crete) might have carried ships north-eastwards towards the Aegean (Mantzourani and Theodorou 1989: fig. 8; Lambrou-Phillipson 1991: 12), but it is uncertain how important this could have been for any proposed direct Egypt-Crete route, given the wind conditions and the fact that this would first have involved a long journey from the Delta along the north African coast.

### Chapter 4 / Making Stone Vessels

1. In the Aegean, emery deposits occur on Naxos, Samos, and in parts of western Anatolia (Higgins and Higgins 1996: 179–80; Feenstra and Wunder 2003: figs. 2–3; Feenstra et al. 2002: 790–1, fig. 1). Lucas and Harris (1962) were sceptical about whether the Egyptians could acquire emery, but it may well have been an interregional trade item.
2. The references to these reliefs from the Old Kingdom onwards are as follows: the 5th Dynasty tombs of Sahure at Abusir (Borchardt 1910: 37, fig. 33) and Ty at Saqqara (Steindorff 1913: pl. 134); the 6th Dynasty tombs of Mereruka at Saqqara (Duell 1938: pl. 30) and Aba at Deir el Gebrawi (Davies 1902: pl. xiii); the 12th Dynasty tombs of Senbi (Blackman 1914: pl. v) and Pepionkh (Blackman 1953: pl. xvii) both at Meir; the 18th Dynasty tombs of Rekhmire (Davies 1973: pl. liv), Two Sculptors (Davies 1925: pl. xi), and Puyemre (Davies 1922: pl. xxiii), all three at Thebes, and, finally, the 26th Dynasty tomb of Aba at Thebes (Davies 1902: pl. xxiv). The latter is deliberately archaising, copying 5th–6th Dynasty reliefs, and should not be taken as an indication of Late Period production techniques.
3. These weights have been identified as a 'partially guided' cranking mechanism (their momentum, in swinging around the drill, removing some of the effort of rotating the tool, Sleeswyk 1981: 24ff), but this is not only unfeasible given their position on the drill as shown but would have placed unsustainable stresses on the vessel itself.
4. Goyon (1991) suggested that a cross-bar, which is often portrayed as sitting in the fork of the drill in hieroglyphic versions, was used to hold in place a cylindrical metal tubular drill, but it is far more likely that these representations show the shape in profile of a stone grinder.

5. Petrie suggested one drilling was as large as 70 cm in diameter (1901a: 19, though the estimate is based on the curve of a small fragment and may be exaggerated) and 11-cm-diameter tubular bits were definitely employed to drill Khufu's sarcophagus (Stocks 2001). Much smaller tubes were used to perforate vessel handles.
notes to pages 55–78

6. The use of a bow-drill is suggested by the presence of a possible drill capstone on the site (Takaoğlu 2005: pl. 24.156), but it remains unclear if this technology could really be used to drive a shaped abrading stone (e.g. Stocks 2003: 148–55). More likely perhaps, the shaped stones were placed between a forked stick and partially oscillated back and forth with a simpler drilling device akin to the one shown in later Old Kingdom Egyptian tomb reliefs, while lug handles and smaller items were perforated using a a bow-driven microdrill.

7. Getz-Gentle's suggestion (1996: 17–9, fig. 11) of a 'lathe-turning tool' that used a combination of a tiny obsidian or flint gouge and loose abrasive is implausible for two reasons. Firstly, thin chipped stone points such as the one she depicts can be used to drill small holes or for incising decoration but break under the pressure of gouging the interior of a vessel. Secondly when larger, thicker flint gouges are used to hollow out vessels (e.g. Figure 4.4), they work without loose abrasive.

8. They have been found at sites such as Chalinomouri, Chrysokamino, Gournia, Knossos, Kommos, Mochlos, Palaikastro, Pseira, and Zakros (Carter 2004: no. 33 with references; Platon 1978: 272). Similar tools are found as far away as Hittite Anatolia (e.g. Boehmer 1979: pls. xxxv–vi), though apparently not in the contemporary Levant and Egypt.

9. While the compass is deployed in a virtuoso fashion in much LB2-3 stonework, it was not a new tool (contra Warren 1969: 158–9; Evely 1993: 190). For example, it was used earlier for the design of MM-LM lids (e.g. KSM MP 73/54,125). Compass marks are more prominent on gypsum vessels because of the stone's softness.

## Chapter 5 / The Third Millennium

1. Its identification as a young female should be considered uncertain given the osteoarchaeological methods of the time.

2. The numbers of different stone vessel shapes and materials used in Figure 5.1 are taken from Aston 1994 and are meant as a proxy for the overall popularity of stone vessels as status markers, not as a comparative measure of shape and material diversity or richness. To assess the latter, these figures would need to be adjusted to account for variable sample size which is difficult because we do not really know actual quantities. Even so, the range of popular ED shapes and materials does indeed appear larger than in either the Predynastic or later OK. Figures for pyramid volume are taken from Kemp (1996: fig. 2.1). All three series have been standardised by subtracting the mean and dividing by the standard deviation.

3. Obsidian bowls have been found in Nagada III–Dynasty 1 contexts at Abydos (e.g. Petrie 1901b: nos. 87 and 106; El-Khouli 1978: nos. 3239, 4295, 5615–8; Dreyer 1992) and Nagada (e.g. DeMorgan 1897: figs. 625–7).

4. Connections have been made between cylindrical jars and a few other PD-ED shapes and those popular in Mesopotamia, but the stylistic links are very general and the connections they imply highly attenuated (see Chapter 8).

5. Its ancient Egyptian name was *mntt* (Harris 1961) and it is often called Cephren diorite by modern commentators, but there are in fact several recogniseable varieties found near Gebel el-Asr. All are made up primarily of plagioclase feldspar with greenish-black streaks or patches of hornblende (and a little biotite), but technically, the darker versions should be called diorite or gabbro gneisses (ca. 50% hornblende and biotite) and the lighter ones anorthosite gneisses (ca. 5% hornblende and biotite). The latter are more commonly used for stone vessels and therefore anorthosite gneiss is used as shorthand label throughout this book (Aston 1994: 62–4).

6. Another indication of this higher value is the fact that while inscriptions on harder stone vessels were inscribed, those on travertine in the Netjerikhet complex were usually written in ink (like pottery vessels elsewhere, Quibell 1934; Abou-Ghazi 1997: 3). Over 100 worked blocks of anorthosite gneiss were also found in Netjerikhet's complex, and may have belonged to a tessellated pavement (Firth and Quibell 1935: 20, 47, 126–7, pl. 93.5).

7. These shape-specific patterns include the use of anorthosite gneiss for open bowls, recrystallised limestone for high-shouldered jars and porphyritic stones for thick-walled, lugged bowls (Reisner 1931: figs. 53–8).

8. It remains unclear whether this was the actual location of her tomb or merely a deposit of funerary equipment in its immediate vicinity (Münch 2000).

9. Some stone vessels with inscriptions of Pepi I and his *heb sed*, found in much later contexts from Nubia and Deir el-Ballas were probably the result of SIP-early 18th Dynasty tomb-robbing (Lacovara 1991; see Chapter 6), but if any were actually heirlooms or robbed from the contents of local tombs, they would fit the pattern described here.

10. The poorly published but extensive cemetery at Kom el-Hisn on the edge of the western Delta, spanning perhaps a couple of centuries during the later FIP-11 Dynasty, is also a good indication of the low frequency of stone vessels at this time. Despite other evidence for relatively wealthy burials, such objects were only found in a few percent of the 879 graves excavated over the first four seasons at the site (see Orel 2000 for dating and full references to the preliminary reports).

11. The dominant occupation phase at this site appears to be Chalcolithic, but the stratigraphy is not clear-cut, and the vessel itself would perhaps be dated to the Early Dynastic on stylistic grounds (Ussishkin 1980: 23).

12. The fragments include inscriptions of Khafra and Pepi I. The palace archives suggest the building was in use ca. 2350–2250 BC and it is quite possible that the assemblage arrived as a group at this time, when the Khafra fragment was already an heirloom.

13. About one third of the vessel fragments from Ebla Palace G are made of this stone. Anorthosite gneiss is also present at Byblos though erratic published descriptions make it difficult to estimate quantities. Some stones that are described as *diorite*, *brèche grise noire*, or *tâchetée* are clearly anorthosite gneiss from the published photographs (e.g. Dunand 1958: no. 13566, pl. ccv and fig. 5.31bii).

14. This lid is in fact one of two unprovenanced pieces that were almost certainly looted from the Byblos deposits along with a group of OK stone vessels [Figure 5.7(c) and (d); Money-Coutts 1936]. One further possible example of this kind is a dark stone bowl with chain decoration from Abydos in Egypt (Amélineau 1905: pl. xxxi.8–9).

15. In particular, bowls and beakers of white marble are known from pre-third millennium Anatolian contexts at places such as Çatal Höyük, Domuztepe, Hacılar, Kulaksızlar, and Kum Tepe (Campbell 2000: 2; Mellaart 1964: 84, 1970a: 149ff, 1970b: 166–8, 439–46; Takaoğlu 2005; Sperling 1976: 311, 322 no. 139).

16. One or more of these vessels from Vasilia in the Cyprus Museum appear more likely to be made of gypsum, not travertine as previously suggested (Stewart 1962: figs. 104.8–9; Hennessy et al. 1988: figs. 48.3–4; though more formal analysis is clearly desirable). The provenance of the large, straight-sided bowl (this one perhaps more likely to be travertine or ordinary limestone) is unclear. It might conceivably be an Egyptian import (similar to E103), but could also be an extremely rare local product, or, less likely, from southern Anatolia (e.g. Goldman 1956: fig. 421) or Mesopotamia (Woolley 1955b: pl. 176.11818, pl. 242 types 15a–16c; Parrot 1956: 121). Alternatively, experimental use of local gypsum for some of these vessels would not be surprising, especially given the common Cypriot outcrops of this material and its later exploitation for vessels in the LBA (see Chapter 7). Very limited 4th and 3rd millennium use of chloritite and picrolite for one or two Cypriot vessels is also apparent (Vagnetti 1980: 49–50, pl. xix.107; Croft et al. 1998: 201, fig. 102.13, pl. 38.14).

17. Other Anatolian EBA sites with stone vessels include Tarsus (Goldman 1956: fig. 421), Aphrodisias (Joukowsky 1986: figs. 412.17, 413.8, 455.28, 472.24) and Troy (Blegen et al. 1958: 38, 46, 150, 159). This does not include the marble and obsidian vessels said to be from the Dorak treasure (Mellaart 1959: 754–7). The latter pieces have no known parallels in the third millennium Anatolian corpus, though obsidian vessels are known from Acemhöyük and Kültepe in the early second millennium (see Chapter 6).

18. Although, there are earlier ceramic parallels (e.g. Zachos 1990: no. 9) and some similarities with later footed jars.

19. For example, compared with the maximum dimensions of most other marble shapes listed in Getz-Gentle's checklists (1996), *kandiles* have a significantly larger coefficient of variation, whether or not unprovenanced examples are included.

20. More precisely, the diameters of rim-lugged bowls have a significantly lower coefficient of variation than either the diameters of plain bowls from the same cemetery or, for example, the heights of Grotta-Pelos vessels such as the beaker or kandila. Getz-Gentle also suggest that a distinctive local trait of the rim-lug bowls from Chalandriani is that the outside edges of their lugs follow the curve of the bowl's rim, rather than being squared-off (1996: 113–4), though it would be useful to have a broader and more formal basis for this comparison.

21. It has been suggested that the looted zone at Dhaskaleio-Kavos was a large pan-Cycladic sanctuary, but a cemetery seems far more likely (Broodbank 2000: 225–31). The published references for stone vessels are remarkably scattered (Zapheiropoulou 1968b: 100, figs. 5 and 6, 1968a: pl. 332, 1988: fig. 2, pl. 35; Marangou 1990: nos. 125, 135; Getz-Gentle 1996: 101–5, 107, 115, 118, 128, 161, 170, 203, n. 191, 211, 229, 248, 260, 274, 287, 301, 304, 339, 345, 350, 356, 411, pl. 112b, 113b; Broodbank 2000: fig. 69; Whitelaw 2006). A few worked fragments and lumps of emery were found on the surface of the site, but the extent to which manufacture occurred here remains unclear (T. Whitelaw, personal communication).

22. Some intriguing examples of possible late EB2 Cycladic contacts with the Izmir bay area include a possible marble sauceboat at Limantepe and the pithos burial from further inland, which included six copper weapons and tools, two rim-lug marble bowls of likely Cycladic type, a silver mirror, and pottery juglet (Takaoğlu 2004).

23. The seals were made of local chloritite/steatite, with some serpentinite, while the pottery is made in a fabric with inclusions from the same local ophiolitic complex (Wilson and Day 1994: group 1). Softstone beads and spindle whorls were also made locally though it is less clear how far these travelled. Decorative antecedents for the designs on these objects can be found in the painted motifs on local EMI dark-on-buff pottery and perhaps the best-documented collection of all of these products in the same context is from Lebena-Yerokambos II (Alexiou and Warren 2004: 125–40).

24. This does not imply that the EMIIA chloritite vessels were actually made in the Mirabello region (in fact they may well be Mesara-Asterousia products, as suggested above), just that steatite was a similar soft, green stone with which craftspeople from Mochlos could experiment. Steatite vessels were probably also made at other centres as well.

25. The pyrotechnic methods involved may well be similar to those suggested for white steatite beads in the Levantine Chalcolithic (Bar-Yosef Mayer et al. 2004) or for some Dilmun-style sealstones from the Persian Gulf (see Chapter 8).

26. Local Cretan seals made use of raw hippopotamus ivory as well, but these appear to be part of a more finely wrought tradition, using a separate iconographic scheme, to the extent that the use of powdered steatite by the manufacturers of the 'white-pieces' group, suggests an inability to access the imported raw material. However, Egyptian scarabs were also sometimes made of white steatite, so the copying may be more general.

27. There are about 30 vessels made of this material found at Platanos (Xanthoudides 1924).

28. A drill core of the white travertine has been found on the Mochlos town site (HM 1594).

29. The Egyptian scarabs from contexts on the south-central Cretan coast are interesting, but represent an incredibly portable, and hence contextually promiscuous, type of artefact. On their own, they cannot be used to prove regular contact between the Asterousia and Egypt. The former region would have made a good jumping off point for travelling south to Egypt but was not well placed for return voyages (see Chapter 3). A poorly published site on the edge of the western Delta that provides useful late FIP-11 Dynasty parallels for the Egyptianising stone vessels and scarabs in Crete is the cemetery at Kom el-Hisn (Hamada and Farid 1947a,b, 1948, 1950; and Orel 2000 for revised dating).

30. Three broad types of Cretan travertine can be distinguished macroscopically: (1) a polychrome 'banded tufa', (2) a patchy translucent brown and opaque white stone, and, more rarely, (3) a plain white variety. The first two stones appear together in faulted limestone formations, such as on Antikythera, Dia, central and eastern Crete, often alongside breccias (Warren

1969: 126–8, personal observation). They are chemically distinct from Egyptian travertines (Barbieri et al. 2002) and usually look very different. There is no sign of any use of raw Egyptian travertine in late Prepalatial stone vessel assemblages.

## Chapter 6 / The Earlier Second Millennium

1. Very few vessels are known from Tel el-Maskhuta (Holladay 1997: 196) or Tel el-Yahudiyeh (Petrie 1906; Lilyquist 1995: figs. 124–6) and only one or two from poststratum F graves at Tel el-Dab'a (Bietak 1991). The more southerly sites of Sedment, Mostagedda, Qau, and Badari were analysed for the percentage quoted here (Petrie and Brunton 1924; Brunton 1930, 1937).

2. A fragment with an inscription of Sesostris I was found in disturbed levels at Qatna (Roccati 2002), but given the lack of any good evidence for a palace building in the excavated area prior to MBIIB, and the recent finds of recycled stone vessels in the Qatna royal tomb, this piece may well have been a later MB-LB arrival (A. Ahrens, personal communication).

3. The Egyptian sources of the stone are clearly the most intensively exploited in this region (Klemm and Klemm 1993: 199–223; Aston et al. 2000), but unconfirmed outcrops of travertine are thought to exist in the Sinai and Negev (Lucas and Harris 1962: 59–60). Distinctive banded or mottled travertines are also known from Crete and were worked during the Bronze Age, but these usually look very different from the Egyptian varieties and have a different strontium isotope signature (Warren 1969: 124–56, Barbieri et al. 2002). Much closer to Egyptian stones in macroscopic appearance are the travertines from western Anatolian outcrops (Bruno 2002; Çolak and Lazzarini 2002), where there is evidence for Roman, but not yet any Bronze Age, exploitation. The travertine used for vessels found in Mesopotamia came from central highland Iran (Moorey 1994: 37). Christine Lilyquist has noted the presence of 'calcareous rocks' in the Levant, but there is as yet no definite evidence that these are anything but generic limestone formations (1996; also Sparks 2007: 9).

4. There are a further ca. 160 undatable graves with few if any accompanying grave goods. It is likely that many of these were also dug in MBII-LBI.

5. The most common grave type consisted of a simple pit, though a variety of more unusual types also existed. Of the latter, two of the three burnt 'Achan' deposits of bone and broken artefacts from the Lower cemetery contained stone vessels. However, within these extremely rich deposits, Egyptian-style vessels are only a limited part of a wider funerary display which emphasised a range of foreign contacts, including northern Levantine pottery, an obsidian dish, gold, silver, and ivory. In contrast, none of Petrie's five horse burials (mainly MBIIC-LBI from the Eastern cemetery) have stone vessels, suggesting that these objects did not fit the preferred funerary personas expressed by this practice (Wapnish 1997: 349–52).

6. There are several other vessels from the early MBA tombs at Ebla that do not fit happily into well-known eastern Mediterranean stone vessel traditions, but might be northern Levantine or Mesopotamian products. For example, a breccia jar from the Tomb of the Lord of Goats has been previously labelled an Egyptian PD-OK vessel, but both material and shape are rare if not unique (Scandone-Matthiae 1988: pl. xii.2). Likewise, a decorated white stone pyxis from the Tomb of the Cisterns and a loop-handled jar from the Tomb of the Princess are neither Cretan nor Egyptian (Matthiae et al. 1995: 501 no. 461; Lilyquist 1996: pls. 5.3, 10.3).

7. This analysis draws on published vessels and a full study of the unpublished finds from the KSM Evans boxes. There is a spread of likely Protopalatial material across much of the palace area, but also a concentration in the NW 'Kamares area'. Worked lumps of fancier stones come from boxes 30, 40, 46, and 1485, several of which have marks from saws and tubular drills.

8. The references for these are scattered (for Knossos, C38; KSM MUM 67/767, 72/152, Evans boxes 559, 1487, 1891, 1899, 1900; for Phaistos, C24i, C26i, Metaxa-Muhly 1981: 120–38; and for Malia, Warren 1969: P567).

9. Only a few of these vessels are published, but of the first inlaid group, there are over a dozen pieces in different museums (Warren 1969: 33, KSM Evans boxes 616, 1103, 1605, 1894; UCL 290). Of the gabbro vessels, there are four from Mycenae (Tsountas and Manatt 1897: figs. 138–9), and at least five diagnostic pieces, some body fragments as well as several drill cores from Knossos (KSM Evans boxes 472, 968, 1480b, 1893, 1894). Abrasion marks on the underside of the shoulder indicate undercutting with a series of shaped grinding stones inserted through the vessel's narrow mouth. Several handles have inverted small tubular drill rings, which make it clear that the vessel was turned upside down to work this area. The stone can be distinguished visually from the most common Egyptian gabbros and probably comes from south-central Crete, though no exact source is known (Warren 1969: 131).

10. In addition to gilding, incised pictorial decoration is another form of added surface treatment applied at MMII Phaistos (Warren 1969: P333). The vessels from block V, Building B at Mu may also have been deliberately heat-treated to make them red-coloured (Détournay 1981), but the presence of heavily vitrified ceramics from this area suggests rather that this part of the building was subject to abnormally high levels of heat during its destruction (C. Knappett, personal communication).

11. A small group of vessels at Myrtos are made in a light grey, tan, and bluish-black veined serpentinite (MP 70/46, 102, 148, 165, 167; 71/170, 207, 248, 254, 255; 73/1, 130) similar to one used at Malia (Warren 1969: 138–40). The best parallels for one bowl fragment with a band of incised decoration (MP/73/122) also come from MMI-II Malia (Chapouthier and Joly 1936: pl. xx.f; van Effenterre and van Effenterre 1963: pl. xxvi; Poursat 1966: fig. 40; Chevallier et al. 1975: pl. xxxii.1; but see also Benzi 1984: figs 17–8).

12. For example, an MMIA fragment was found alongside highly Minoanised pottery in deposit γ at Kastri; it was not originally published but is well labelled and also referred to in the excavation notebooks (no. 917, trench XII, level 6). The other fragment comes from deposit δ (Coldstream and Huxley 1972: fig. 59). Rosso antico may be the material of both an MMIA table from Knossos and a raw lump found underneath the Neopalatial palace at Malia (Chapoutier and Demargne 1942: 54, pl. lii.2c). However, the identifications remain uncertain and the main use of this stone is in the Neopalatial.

13. Many Neopalatial stone vessels remain unpublished, but a combination of Warren's catalogue (1969), more recent publications and estimates of Neopalatial stone vessel totals kindly supplied by those studying other assemblages, suggest the following very rough numbers: Knossos (500+); Palaikastro (ca. 200–300); Juktas, Malia, Mochlos, Pseira, Phaistos, Syme, Zakros (ca. 100–200); Agia Triada, Archanes, Gournia, Kommos, Myrtos Pyrgos (ca. 25–100). These are pretty meaningless numbers on their own, given the very different levels of investigation at each of these sites, but might be useful for comparsion with other material classes (e.g. as a background population with which to consider relative numbers of foreign imports). My thanks to Tristan Carter, Don Evely, and Orazio Palio for discussing these totals with me.

14. Gold leaf has to be applied to a relatively smooth and accurately finished surface. As a result, chloritite or steatite are ideal materials to make a core of this kind (see Chapter 8). Both stones would also be appropriate if the gilded vessel was also heated to produce a more seamless gold covering (e.g. in the more recent, mercury-aided process of fire-gilding). The earliest known context for them is LMIA, the majority from dated contexts are LMIB and the subject matter in several instances matches that of LMIB Marine-style ceramics (Hood 1961–1962: 29; Warren 1969: 162–3; Baurain and Darcque 1983; Logue 2004).

15. *Rosso antico* was only one of several red stones used in the Neopalatial. Most of the others are Cretan limestones and can usually be distinguished from it by eye, but red marble from Iasos requires petrographic and chemical analysis to distinguish it from *rosso antico* and may also have been exploited at this time (Lazzarini 2004). For no obvious reason, there was a significant preference for using these red-coloured stones for rhyta and lamps.

16. The main possible examples of storage areas are Zakros Shrine Treasury (Platon 1971: 133–48), the Knossos Central Treasury (Evans 1928: 820–4), the Palaikastro Block X hoard (Bosanquet and Dawkins 1908: 133–40, pl. xxx), and Akrotiri Delta Building, room 16 (Warren 1979: 105). The second of these is traditionally dated to the LMII-IIIA destruction (but may possibly be LMI: MacDonald 2002: 41) and the Akrotiri group could just be a temporary collection of objects made after the earthquake in the town.

17. It has also been suggested that both of these vessel types were deliberately broken during palace ceremonies and circulated as ritual tokens (Rehak 1995b), though this remains difficult to verify.

18. Only one or two alabastra are oval plan, Egypto-Levantine style products and could therefore be either from Egypt or from a centre such as Tel el-Ajjul (e.g. Lilyquist 1996: pl. 6.1, from Vapheio on the mainland); a zoomorphic softstone box may be Hittite (Evely 1999: no. 5), a small cup with a duck-head handle, carved in a soft white stone, might be Cypriot or Levantine (Benzi 1984: figs. 29–30) and there are several gypsum imports at Akrotiri that may be from the Jordan valley (e.g. Devetzi 2000: figs. 3,7, pl. 32b). However, at least one of the Akrotiri gypsum vessels is a small pot from a class of pottery and faience vessels whose main distribution concentrates in lower Mesopotamia (Devetzi 2000: 134, fig. 9, pl. 36d; E. Peltenburg, personal communication).

19. This estimate is based on a comparison between the number of finished Egyptian vessels and an overall estimate of MMIII-LMIIIA-style vessels. It may well be biased by a preferential recognition and recovery of such objects during excavation, but in reverse there is also a tendency for larger local vessels to break into many pieces and inflate their own numbers.

20. If the Aegean Long Chronology is accepted, however, most of the tomb paintings would be contemporary with LMII-IIIA1 in Aegean terms.

21. There are at least 65 baggy alabastra known from the island, including those counted by Warren (1989) and many further fragments in the KSM's Unexplored Mansion and Evans boxes.

22. The travertine bowls, lamps, cylindrical jars, and tables of the PD-OK period are sufficiently diagnostic that they are unlikely to have been missed in Cretan assemblages.

23. In Nubia and Egypt, such hardstone Egyptian antiquities have been found at Badari, Deir el Ballas, Kerma, Qau, Tel el-Amarna, and Thebes (Lacovara 1991; Phillips 1992: 169–71), but this list is certainly not comprehensive. In the Levant, they are known from Amman (Hankey 1974: fig. 1.1-2, pl. xxxii.a), Beth Shan (Rowe 1940: pl. 24.3, fig. 16, no. 398), Ains Shems (Grant 1932: pls. xlvii.3–4), Kamid el-Loz (Lilyquist 1996: pls. 28–29), Lachish (Tufnell 1958: pl. 26.10), Alalakh (Woolley 1955a: pl. lxxxi.9), Tel Beit Mirsim (Albright 1938: pl. 31.5), Qatna (Ahrens personal communication) and Ugarit (Caubet 1991: pls. i.1-2, viii.12). There is one example of heart-shaped jar made of Egyptian gabbro or hornblende diorite in the Cyprus Museum (CM 1963.x-17.1) and in the Aegean, they have been found at Archanes, Agia Triada, Asine, Kythera, Knossos (with by far the most examples), Kato Syme, Katsamba, Mycenae, Myrtos Pyrgos, Palaikastro, Pylos, and Zakros (Warren 1969: types 43A-E; Hankey 1972: 213, pl. 78-9; Karetsou 2000). While the term PD-OK is used here throughout to refer to these vessels, the vast majority are actually Early Dynastic to Old Kingdom in style.

24. By contrast, a Ramesside ostracon from Deir el-Medina provides one good example of the discovery, inventorying, and then resealing of a ruined old tomb by a series of officials, apparently without touching the contents which included stone vessels (Zonhoven 1969).

25. In addition to the sites discussed in the main text, relevant references include Warren 1969, Dickers 1995, Hiller 1993: 199; Niemeier and Niemeier 1997: fig. 72f-g; Matsas 1995: pl. xxxv.b; Monaco 1941: fig. 21.5,9; Morricone 1972: figs. 127a, 229c–d; Benzi 1984; 1993: pl. 36c bottom. There is at least one lamp without context from Iasos (N. Momigliano, personal communication).

26. The farmsteads were found by intensive surface survey and are therefore unlikely to have produced stone vessel evidence. One of these (KIP site 1), however, produced one slotted cobble which was used for tubular drilling activities, though whether for vessels or other objects remains unclear (see Chapter 4). One strange, undoubtedly much older, chloritite pyxis does come from an LMIB-IIIA tomb at Lioni, where the neighbouring settlement scatter suggests a farmstead or very small community (Coldstream and Huxley 1972: 263, pl. 84.1; Broodbank et al. 2005).

27. Perhaps the most obvious evidence for this is a large drill core from the Kastri excavations (d. 10.4 cm, Coldstream and Huxley 1972: pl. 61.345).

28. For example, this can be compared with large assemblages from Knossos, Pseira, and Myrtos Pyrgos, where in each case less than 1% of vessels have repair holes.

29. The earliest known example of this decoration is on a bowl from the EMII-MMI/II round-tomb at Koumasa and blossom bowls are found in LMIII tombs in sufficient quantities to suggest that they were either being curated in relatively large numbers or were still being made at that time. A very limited number of variants exist including one miniature bridge-spouted jar and a few bowls have more or fewer petals (Warren 1969: 14–7; Floyd 1998: pl. 18A).

30. Many of these ladles were catalogued by Warren (1969: 48–9), but others have since been found or identified at Juktas (published examples: Karetsou 1974: 236, pl. 179a; Karetsou 1975: fig. 4, pl. 265b; Karetsou 1978: 257, fig. 16.1), Vathy cave on Kalymnos (Benzi 1993: pl. 36c bottom), Agios Georgios (Sakellarakis 1996: 83–4) and Mycenae (Leinwand 1980). There are additional examples from Juktas and Knossos in the Ashmolean Museum (AM 1938.427, 1938.800, AE 769), Knossos Stratigraphical Museum (non-Evans unprovenanced stone boxes), and UCL collections (UCL 153).

## Chapter 7 / The Later Second Millennium

1. For example, the use of Cretan oil is possibly suggested by an ink inscription mentioning 'gift of Keftiu' (ḥst n kfti) amongst a series of other oils in stone jars from the tomb of Thutmosis IV (Lilyquist 1995: no. 110, fig. 122).

2. Ink inscriptions mentioning capacity may have also been present on some of the larger jars but have since faded or been washed off (e.g. Winlock 1948: 55; Lilyquist 2003: 139).

3. It is unclear where this design comes from, though there are some rare Cretan parallels (e.g. Levi 1961–1962: fig. 109) that are hard to place in a broader context.

4. One or more of the vessels is also said to be made of ḥsg-stone. This word is otherwise unattested in Egyptian but may be connected to the Akkadian aḫusigu, tentatively identified as amazonite (Harris 1961: 223).

5. Whole conversions and vessel parts have been found at Enkomi (Dikaios 1969: pls. 130.26a, 158.16; BM 1896.2-1.393; 1897.4-1.1090, 1285), Lachish (Tufnell 1958: pls. 26.35, 52.45), Megiddo (Loud 1948: fig. 260.30, pl. 261.30), Tel Dan (Clamer 2002: no. 245, figs. 2.152–3), and Ugarit (Margueron 1977: fig. 17, pl. ix.3; Caubet 1991: pl. xii.3, upside down; also Clamer 1986: 27–8, pl. IV.1). These involved reworking a typical travertine jar by adding an elongated neck and/or stylised duck-shaped lugs (the latter sometimes as separate pieces). Duck-shaped lug attachments were also used to convert ostrich eggs into vessels (e.g. Renfrew and Cherry 1985: 324, fig. 8.12.194, pl. 64c). A different conversion, into a pyxis, was found at Tel Beth Shemesh (Grant 1932: 157, no. 808).

6. The serpentinite jar with short loop handles on the shoulder is a rare, if not unknown, shape in Egypt but with exact matches in gypsum from Assur (Lilyquist 1996: pl. 27.1-3; Harper et al. 1995: no. 53).

7. A more complex case still is offered by vessels made in a variety of vitreous materials, the technical and stylistic details of which suggest a wide range of regional industries and mixed cultural affiliations, including local production of both Egyptian-style and Mycenaean-style faience vessels (Matoïan and Bouquillon 2003).

8. Egyptian stone vessels and Mycenaean pottery are both highly recognisable artefacts that have been keenly collected since excavations began. Both excavation notebooks and museum collections have been used in recent times to create relatively comprehensive catalogues (Caubet 1991; Van Wijngaarden 2002: 330–42; Yon et al. 2000). The measurements of excavation area used here are approximations from the published plans.

9. Relevant examples for hard stone and unusual shapes are RS 13.037, 14-21?, 15.[...], 15.160, 15.195, 15.209, 15.257, 15.330, 15.533, 15.544, 15.549, 16.012, 16.022, 16.058, 16.067, 17.[...], 18.[...] (zoomorphic), 18.151, 18.261, 20.334 (Caubet 1991). Note also that three anorthosite gneiss vessel fragments said to be from the Baltic (Caubet 1998: 106, pl. viii) are more likely to be Egyptian products, representing a rare use of stone from the Gebel el-Asr quarries after the MK.

10. Yabninu and the Palais Sud are considered here, but we might also include the houses of Urtenu, Sinaranu, and several others (De Conteson et al. 1974: 5–24).

11. This range reflects variation across different parts of the tell and the degree of looting. In the earlier excavations in the northern part of the tell, 5 of 45 graves had stone vessels (Pritchard 1980: 30ff). In the more recent excavations, 15 tombs had such items of ca. 400 graves, many of which were robbed, however (Tubb and Dorrell 1991).

12. The earliest might be a jar fragment with a cartouche of Ahmose from Kouklia-Teratsoudhia tomb 104, but the accompanying assemblage is of mixed date (Karageorghis 1990: pls. xx.1, lx.1). If this piece was not an heirloom when traded, then its arrival in Cyprus at this time would fit into the pattern of early Cypriot imports to Egypt in SIP and early 18th Dynasty contexts (see Chapter 3).

13. In addition to the discussion of this issue in the Levantine section above, a further hint that limited local Cypriot production in travertine-like stones was occurring is two examples of a Mycenaean-style pyxis (e.g. Cyp M. A212), a shape otherwise only made in gypsum in Cyprus (Cyp2, see below). Likewise, a larger Mycenaean-style jar is made of a cream-coloured limestone (BM 1897.04-01.1040), again emphasising that local Cypriot artisans occasionally exploited stones of this type.

14. Note the difference between the Cypriot gypsum alabastron, copying the three-handled Mycenaean pottery form, and the slightly later Levantine gypsum lugged pyxides (L20), copying the later and rarer two-handled Mycenaean version or its local Levantine imitations.

15. Although not seen by the author, the gypsum version of a White-Shaved juglet is especially intriguing because the pottery versions are not only similar to gypsum in colour and texture but made by carving down the exterior surface in a similar manner to the way gypsum is worked (Gittlen 1981: 51–4, esp. no. 19).

16. It is interesting that a *tazza* found at Tel el-Amarna has a higher foot and central division and appears to be made in one-piece of chloritite, all of which are found on Cypriot examples (Frankfort and Pendlebury 1933: 65, pl. xliv.8). The central division, use of softstone, and high foot are much rarer in Egypt, raising the curious possibility that this is a Cypriot import.

17. Serpentinite only really seems to have been used at this stage for a particular class of larger plate with ringbase (Cyp12) that have stylistic affinities with basalt plates from the Levant but were probably made in Cyprus (Sparks 2007: section 3.1.1, plates 1B).

18. Some commentators have suggested that the Cypriot ophiolites do not contain outcrops of this particular variety of chloritite (Elliott 1990: 140), but this issue is worth reconsidering, given that the geologically suitable area involved is so large, has such a history of intensive and potentially exhaustive exploitation, and that there are so many LCyp small finds such as biconical beads, pestles, spindle whorls, and stamp seals, made of chloritite and in local styles (Aström 1967: 59–68; Elliott 1990; Reyes 2001: 7–19).

19. Cypriot-made chloritite tripod mortars are known from Aegean contexts of this period (Buchholz and Karageorghis 1973: no. 1159; Benzi 1992: T67/5), but there are also a number of other shapes that might be Levantine or Cypriot products. For example, a gypsum three-handled jar from Mycenae (Sakellarakis 1980: pl. vi.6) is similar to Cypriot gypsum and limestone versions of this shape (Cyp3) but might also have been made at LMII–IIIA Knossos. A gypsum *tazza* from the Temple Tomb at Knossos was made either in the southern Levant or in Cyprus but it is difficult to say which. A jug from Mycenae's chamber tombs is similar to examples known from Kamid el-Loz and Amman (Lilyquist 1996: pls. 7.1, 17.1–4, fig. 7.17g–h).

20. One exception is a lugged bowl from Warrior Grave V (Hood and De Jong 1952: 275 v. 4, fig. 13, pl. 56b).

21. Sacred oil sets usually comprised seven vessels carrying the seven canonical oils and sometimes a further receptacle for eye paint.

22. The architectural connections between these tombs and those at Ugarit are impressive but specific problems or differences are worth noting: for example, the known Ugaritic tombs of this type are at least 50 years later in date and are placed within individual houses rather than outside the settlement (Schaeffer 1949: 90–2, figs. 78–89, pls. xvii–ix); Preston 1999: 137, also no. 39). Several similar built tombs have also been identified at Medeon, which was a centre well-placed for long-distance routes via the Gulf of Corinth (Müller 1999).

23. Another interesting unpublished find from Ugarit which may fit into a pattern of LBI–3 links, especially in view of the hoarded supplies of it found at LMII–IIIA Knossos, is a lump of Peloponnesian *lapis lacedaemonius* (Louvre M. 84 AO 503).

24. Only a few earlier vessels are known. Two gypsum lids come from the Vat Room deposit and could be either MMI or later kick-ups (Panagiotaki 1999: pl. 5c) and at least one large bird's nest bowl comes from Pseira (INSTAPEC PS 933).

25. These include a lid from Chamber tomb 17 at Mycenae (Warren 1969: 71), an unfinished bowl with moulded base and horizontal grooves from Knossos (Warren 1969: 80 P447), a rim fragment from Phaistos (Warren 1969: 40 P221), and decorated fragments from KSM Evans boxes 1452 (Little Palace), 1558 (House of the Sacrificed Oxen), 1893 (unprovenanced). Two others are of the same type but apparently made in serpentinite: an alabastron from Sellopoulo (Hood 1957: 25, pl. 2d) and a bowl with shallow spirals from Acropolis Hill, Knossos (Warren 1969: 25).

26. Gypsum vessels from beyond the Knossos valley but potentially linked to Knossian production include a libation table and two squat alabastra from Mycenae, a handle fragment from Thebes and a cylindrical pyxis from Antheia [Figures 7.12(a); Dickers 1995: pl. x.1; Xenaki-Sakellariou 1985: pls. 18, 56, 121]. In addition, two bowls from Mirsine and a footed box from the mainland are difficult to place within existing typologies (Warren 1969: 41; Sakellarakis 1980: pl. vii.18), while there are many fragments published as corroded 'alabaster' from mainland contexts that may in fact be gypsum (Frodin and Persson 1938: 167, 378; Persson 1931: 102; Kaiser 1980: M69: 25, 34–6, 39; Xenaki-Sakellariou 1985: pl. 141).

27. Other candidates for LHIIIA–B mainland manufacture include certain footed goblets and rhyta in *lapis lacedaemonius* (Kaiser 1980: fig. 2.23, pl. 6.1-2; Sakellarakis 1980: 181; Warren 1992: 293–5).

28. At least three fragments can be identified in the KSM Evans boxes at Knossos (KSM Evans boxes 1448, 1891, 1893). Each has characteristic rough, angled drillings visible on the interior. One is a rim fragment of a rhyton with incised decoration and possible attachment holes for a handle. The second is from a three-handled jar and its black and white mottled serpentinite is a good match for that used for some of the Mycenae jars (e.g. Demakopoulou 1988: no. 17). The only provenanced fragment is a neckpiece from the Little Palace in a bioclastic limestone similar to a jar from Mycenae and the lid from Ellenika (Wace 1955: pl. 24b; Hatzi-Spiliopoulou 2000: pl. lxxi.g). An ovoid jar of the right shape and material comes from Phaistos in Crete and is said to be unfinished, which may simply refer to the presence of rough drillings on its interior (Levi 1961–1962: fig. 122).

### Chapter 8 / The Rough and the Smooth: Stone Vessels from a Comparative Perspective

1. Serpentinite is sufficiently hard that it often is drilled rather than carved, leading to a less expedient and flexible pattern of exploitation, and it is therefore not discussed to any great extent in this section.

2. There is even some evidence that using steatite cooking pots can provide human consumers with a source of additional mineral nutrients (e.g. Quintaes et al. 2002).

3. One possible exception might be the deep chloritite bowls with fitted lids found in late third millennium BC northern Levantine contexts (Figure 5.7, Chapter 5). Their shape suggests a possible use in cooking, but there is no clear contextual evidence or published traces of surface burning.

4. The serpentinised zones present an especially challenging ecology, providing soils that are often thin, low-nutrient, and with a heavy metal content, and that stunt vegetation growth but also promote genetically adapted endemics. Other bedrock units in the ophiolite suite provide more friendly environments, however.

5. The lack of sealings to go with these sealstones in some contexts (e.g. LBA Cyprus) does not necessarily mean that their use was nonsphragistic, only that we lack suitable preservation contexts, either because sealings on wax were more common than clay or because sealed dockets were rarely stored in places where they would be burnt and survive.

6. Two further instances of an early connection between ophiolitic greenstones and metallurgy may be the use of picrolite in Chalcolithic Cyprus and of a similar light green stone in Cycladic Kampos group assemblages for miniature vessels, beads, and other small finds (but especially for cruciform figurines in Cyprus, see Chapter 5). Peltenburg has argued that the peak use of picrolite is a reflection of, and reaction to, increasing exploration of metal resources in the local ophiolite zone (1982; 1991b) and the same may well be true of the Cycladic stone (e.g. a possible model crucible in this material: Doumas 1977: pl. xxxv).

notes to pages 175–179

7. A less likely alternative identification of *algabašu* is basalt, which also would have come from the same broad ophiolite zone, but on balance a softstone seems more likely. Copper ores are certainly found among the adjacent southeastern Turkish and Cypriot ophiolites and De Jesus (1980: 395, map 19) claims that they are present in the Syrian Baer-Bassit zone, too, though this has been more recently questioned by Chanut (2000: 245–6).

8. The main exception being the Indus valley whose position on a vast alluvial plain may have discouraged this form of display.

# Bibliography

⌘⌘⌘⌘⌘⌘

Abou-Ghazi, D. (1997). Objects in the Egyptian Museum from the work of Jean-Philippe Lauer at Saqqara. In C. Berger and B. Mathieu (Eds.), *Etudes sur l'Ancien Empire et la Nécropole de Saqqara Dédiées à Jean-Philippe Lauer*, pp. 1–10. Montpelier: Orientalia Monspeliensia.

Adams, R. (2005). The Distribution of Soapstone Bowls and Bowl Fragments in the Rocky Mountain West: A Preliminary Report. Technical report, Office of the Wyoming State Archaeologist. http://wyoarchaeo.state.wy.us/pdf/steatite%20Distribution.pdf

Adams, R. M. (1983). The Jarmo Stone and Pottery Vessel Industries. In L. S. Braidwood, R. J. Braidwood, B. Howe, C. A. Reed, and P. J. Watson (Eds.), *Prehistoric Archaeology Along the Zagros Flanks*, pp. 209–232. Chicago: Oriental Institute.

Adler, W. (1996). Die Spätbronzezeitliche Pyxiden in Gestalt von Wasservögeln. In R. Hachmann (Ed.), *Kamid el-Loz 16. Schatzhaus Studien*, pp. 3–117. Bonn: Saarbrücker Beiträge Zur Altertumskunde.

Agouridis, C. (1997). Sea Routes and Navigation in the Third Millennium Aegean. *Oxford Journal of Archaeology 16.1*, 1–24.

Ahituv, S. (1996). Observations on Olive Oil in Ancient Egypt. In D. Eitam and M. Heltzer (Eds.), *Olive Oil in Antiquity*, pp. 41–44. Padua: Sargon.

Ahrens, A. (2006). A Journey's End—Two Egyptian Stone Vessels with Hieroglyphic Inscriptions from the Royal Tomb at Tell Mišrife/Qatna. *Ägypten und Levante 16*, 15–36.

Al-Maqdissi, M., H. Dohmann-Pfälzner, P. Pfälzner, and A. Suleiman (2003). Das königliche Hypogäum von Qatna. *Mitteilungen Des Deutschen Orient-Gesellschaft zu Berlin 135*, 189–218.

Albright, W. F. (1940). New Light on the History of Western Asia in the Second Millennium B.C. *Bulletin of the American Schools of Oriental Research 77*, 20–32.

Albright, W. F. (1949). *The Archaeology of Palestine*. London: Harmondsworth.

Albright, W. S. (1938). *The Excavation of Tell Beit Mirsim II: The Bronze Age*. Cambridge, MA: American Institute of Oriental Research.

Aldred, C. (1975). Egypt: the Amarna period and the End of the Eighteenth Dynasty. In I. E. S. Edwards, C. J. Gadd, N. G. L. Hammond, and E. Sollberger (Eds.), *The Cambridge Ancient History. Part 2—The Middle East and the Aegean Region, c.1380–1000 BC*, pp. 49–97. Cambridge: Cambridge University Press.

Alexiou, S. (1967). *Hysterominoikoi taphoi Limenos Knosou (Katsamba)*. Athens: Bibliotiki Archaiologikis Etaireias.

Alexiou, S., and P. Warren (2004). *The Early Minoan Tombs of Lebena, Southern Crete*. Sävedalen: Paul Åströms.

Algaze, G. (1993). *The Uruk World System. The Dynamics of Expansion of Early Mesopotamian Civilization*. Chicago: Chicago University Press.

Altenmüller, H., and A. M. Moussa (1977). *Das Grab des Nianchchnum und Chnumhotep*. Mainz: Philip von Zabern.

Ambrose, S. H. (2001). Paleolithic Technology and Human Evolution. *Science 291*, 1748–1753.

Amélineau, E. (1902). *Les Nouvelles Fouilles d'Abydos II*. Paris: Ernest Leroux.

Amélineau, E. (1905). *Les Nouvelles Fouilles d'Abydos V*. Paris: Ernest Leroux.

Amiet, P. (1983). Quelques épaves de la Vaisselle Royale Perse de Suse. In F. Vallat (Ed.), *Contributions à l'Histoire de l'Iran: Mélanges Offerts à Jean Perrot*, pp. 213–224. Paris: Editions Recherche sur les Civilisations.

Amiet, P. (1986). Antiquités Trans-élamites. *Revue d'Assyriologie et d'Archéologie Orientale 80*, 97–104.

Amiran, R. (1969). *Ancient Pottery of the Holy Land*. Jerusalem: Masada Press.

Amiran, R. (1970). The Egyptian Alabaster Vessels from Ai. *Israel Exploration Journal 20*, 170–179.

Amiran, R., and N. Porat (1984). The Basalt Vessels of the Chalcolithic Period and Early Bronze Age. *Tel Aviv 11*, 11–19.

259

André-Salvini, B. (1995). Les Pierres Précieuses dans les Sources écrites. In F. Tallon (Ed.), *Les Pierres Précieuses de l'Orient Ancien*. Paris: Réunion de Musées Nationaux.

Appadurai, A. (1986). Introduction: Commodities and the Politics of Value. In A. Appadurai (Ed.), *The Social Life of Things*, pp. 3–63. Cambridge: Cambridge University Press.

Appadurai, A. (2005). Materiality in the Future of Anthropology. In W. van Binsbergen and P. Geschiere (Eds.), *Commodification: Things, Agency, and Identities (The Social Life of Things Revisited)*, pp. 55–62. Münster: Lit.

Archi, A. (1984). Anatolia in the Second Millennium B.C. In A. Archi (Ed.), *Circulation of Goods in Non-Palatial Context in the Ancient Near East*, pp. 31–123. Rome: Edizioni dell'Atene.

Arkell, A. J. (1956). Stone Bowls of Khaaba (Third Dynasty). *Journal of Egyptian Archaeology 42*, 116.

Arnold, D. (1982). Keramikbearbeitung in Dahschur 1976–1981. *Mitteilungen Des Deutschen Archäologischen Instituts Abteilung Kairo 38*, 28–65.

Arnold, D. (1991). *Building in Egypt: Pharaonic Stone Masonry*. Oxford: Oxford University Press.

Arnold, D., F. F. Arnold, and S. Allen (1995). Canaanite Imports at Lisht, the Middle Kingdom Capital of Egypt. *Ägypten und Levante 5*, 13–32.

Artzy, M. (1997). Nomads of the Sea. In S. Swiny, R. L. Hohlfelder, and H. Wylde Swiny (Eds.), *Res Maritimae: Cyprus and the Eastern Mediterranean from Prehistory to Late Antiquity*, pp. 1–16. Atlanta: Cyprus American Archaeological Research Institute.

Aston, B. G. (1994). *Ancient Egyptian Stone Vessels: Material and Forms*. Heidelberg: Heidelberg Orientverlag.

Aston, B. G., J. Harrell, and I. Shaw (2000). Stones. In P. T. Nicholson and I. Shaw (Eds.), *Ancient Egyptian Materials and Technologies*, pp. 5–77. Cambridge: Cambridge University Press.

Astour, M. C. (1972). The Merchant Class of Ugarit. In O. E. Dietz (Ed.), *Gesellschaftsklassen im Alten Zweistromland und in den Angrenzenden Gebeiten*, pp. 11–26. Munich: Bayerischen Akademie der Wissenschaften.

Aström, L. (1967). *Studies on the Arts and Crafts of the Late Cypriot Bronze Age*. Lund: Berlingska Boktryckeriet.

Aström, P. (1972). *The Swedish Cyprus Expedition, Vol. 4 (Part 1B)*. Lund: Berlingska Boktryckeriet.

Aström, P. (1984). Aegyptiaca at Hala Sultan Tekke. *Opuscula Atheniensia 15.2*, 17–24.

Aswani, S., and P. Sheppard (2003). The Archaeology and Ethnohistory of Exchange in Precolonial and Colonial Roviana. *Current Anthropology 44 Supplement*, 51–78.

Attewell, P. B., and I. W. Farmer (1976). *Principles of Engineering Geology*. London: Chapman and Hall.

Aufrère, S. (1991). *L'Univers Minérale dans la Pensée Egyptienne*. Paris: Institut Français d'Archéologie Orientale du Caire.

Axelrod, R. (1990). *The Evolution of Cooperation*. New York: Basic Books.

Baer, K. (1960). *Rank and Title in the Old Kingdom: The Structure of the Egyptian Administration in the Fifth and Sixth Dynasties*. Chicago: Chicago University Press.

Baines, J. (1985). Color Terminology and Color Classification: Ancient Egyptian Color Terminology and Polychromy. *American Anthropologist 87*, 282–297.

Baines, J. (1995). Kingship, Definition of Culture, Legitimation. In D. O'Connor and D. P. Silverman (Eds.), *Ancient Egyptian Kingship*, pp. 3–47. Leiden: Brill.

Baines, J., and N. Yoffee (1998). Order, Legitimacy, and Wealth in Ancient Egypt and Mesopotamia. In G. Feinman and J. Marcus (Eds.), *The Archaic State: A Comparative Perspective*, pp. 199–260. Santa Fe: School of American Research.

Baines, J., and N. Yoffee (2000). Order, Legitimacy and Wealth: Setting the Terms. In J. Richards and M. van Buren (Eds.), *Order, Legitimacy and Wealth in Ancient States*, pp. 13–17. Cambridge: Cambridge University Press.

Banou, A. (2002). Ta Lithina Antkeimena apo to Minoiko Iero Koriphis ston Ag-Georgi sto Vouno Kithiron. *Pepragmena tou Dhiethnous Kritologikou Synedhriou H*, 383–394.

Banti, L. (1930–1931). La Granda Tomba Tholos di Haghia Triada. *Annuario 13-14*, 155–251.

Bar-Yosef Mayer, D. E., N. Porat, D. Shalem, and H. Smithline (2004). Steatite Beads at Pepi'in: Long Distance Trade and Pyro-Technology. *Journal of Archaeological Science 31*, 493–502.

Barber, E. J. B. (1991). *Prehistoric Textiles. The Development of Cloth in the Neolithic and Bronze Ages*. Princeton: Princeton University Press.

Barbieri, M., G. Testa, D. Merola, Y. Polychronakis, and V. Simitzis (2002). Comparative Strontium-Isotope Analysis and Petrography of Egyptian and Cretan Limestone and Calcite-Alabaster. In L. Lazzarini (Ed.), *Interdisciplinary Studies on Ancient Stone. ASMOSIA VI—Proceedings of the Sixth International Conference (Venice, June 15–18, 2000)*, pp. 415–426. Padua: Bottega D'Erasmo.

Bard, K. A. (1994). The Egyptian Predynastic: A Review of the Evidence. *Journal of Field Archaeology 21*, 265–288.

Bárta, M. (1995). Pottery Inventory and the Beginning of the IVth Dynasty. *Göttinger Mitszellen 149*, 15–25.

Basch, L. (1997). Une Représentation de Navire de Type égéen Dans l'Oasis de Dakhleh (Egypte) vers 1200 av. J-C. In S. Swiny, R. L. Hohlfelder, and H. Wylde Swiny (Eds.), *Res Maritimae: Cyprus and the Eastern Mediterranean from Prehistory to Late Antiquity*, pp. 17–29. Atlanta: Cyprus and American Archaeological Research Institute.

Bass, G. F. (1967). *Cape Gelidonya: A Bronze Age Shipwreck*. Philadelphia: Transactions of the American Philosophical Society.

Bass, G. F. (2006). Bronze Age Shipwrecks in the Eastern Mediterranean. In U. Yalçin (Ed.), *The Ship of Uluburun. A Comprehensive Compendium of the Exhibition Catalogue "The Ship of Ulu Burun—World Trade 3,000 Years Ago,"* pp. 1–5. Bochum: Deutsches Bergbau-Museum.

Baurain, C., and P. Darcque (1983). Un Triton en Pierre à Mallia. *Bulletin de Correspondance Hellénique 107*, 3–73.

Beale, T. W. (1973). Early Trade in Highland Iran: A View from a Source Area. *World Archaeology 5*, 133–148.

Bear, L. M. (1963). *The Mineral Resources and Mining Industry of Cyprus*. Nicosia: Ministry of Commerce and Industry.

Becker, M. J. (1976). Soft-Stone Sources on Crete. *Journal of Field Archaeology 3*, 361–374.

Bell, C. (2005). Wheels within Wheels? A View of Mycenaean Trade from the Levantine Emporia. In R. Laffineur and E. Greco (Eds.), *Emporia. Aegeans in Central and Eastern Mediterranean*. Liège: University of Liège.

Bell, C. (2006). *The Evolution of Long Distance Trading Relationships across the LBA/Iron Age Transition on the Northern Levantine Coast: Crisis, Continuity and Change. A Study Based on Imported Ceramics, Bronze and its Constitutent Metals*. Oxford: British Archaeological Reports.

Ben-Barak, Z. (1988). The Legal Status of the Daughter as Heir in Nuzi and Emar. In M. Heltzer and E. Lipinski (Eds.), *Society and Economy in the Eastern Mediterranean, 1500–1000 B.C.*, pp. 87–97. Leuven: Peeters.

Ben-Dor, I. (1945). Palestinian Alabaster Vases. *Quarterly of the Department of Antiquities of Palestine 11*, 93–113.

Bendall, L. M. (2003). A Reconsideration of the Northeastern Building at Pylos: Evidence for a Mycenean Redistributive Centre. *American Journal of Archaeology 107.2*, 181–231.

Bennet, J. (1988). Approaches to the Problem of Combining Linear B Textual Data and Archaeological Data in the Late Bronze Age Aegean. In E. B. French and K. A. Wardle (Eds.), *Problems in Greek Prehistory*, pp. 509–518. Bristol: Bristol Classical Press.

Bentley, R. A., M. W. Lake, and S. J. Shennan (2005). Specialisation and Wealth Inequality in a Model of a Clustered Economic Network. *Journal of Archaeological Science 32*, 1346–1356.

Benzi, M. (1984). Evidence for a Middle Minoan settlement on the acropolis at Ialysos (Mt. Philerimos). In R. Hägg and N. Marinatos (Eds.), *The Minoan Thalassocracy. Myth and Reality*, pp. 93–104. Stockholm: Paul Åströms.

Benzi, M. (1992). *Rodi e la Civiltà Micenea*. Rome: Gruppo Editoriale Internazionale.

Benzi, M. (1993). The Late Bronze Age Pottery from Vathy Cave, Kalymnos. In C. Zerner (Ed.), *Wace and Blegen. Pottery as Evidence for Trade in the Aegean Bronze Age*, pp. 275–288. Amsterdam: J. C. Gieben.

Bergoffen, C. J. (1991). Overland Trade in Northern Sinai. *Bulletin of the American Schools of Oriental Research 284*, 59–76.

Bernard, M. (1966–67). *Les Vases de Pierre de l'Ancien Empire (Ve et VIe)*. Ph.D. dissertation, Université de Louvain.

Bessac, J.-C. (1986). *L'Outillage Traditionnel du Tailleur de Pierre: de l'Antiquité à Nos Jours*. Paris: CNRS.

Betancourt, P. (1997). The Trade Route for Ghyali Obsidian. In R. Laffineur and P. P. Betancourt (Eds.), *Techne, Craftsmen, Craftswomen and Craftsmanship in the Aegean Bronze Age*, pp. 171–176. Liège: University of Liège.

Betancourt, P. (1998). Middle Minoan Objects in the Near East. In E. Cline and D. Harris-Cline (Eds.), *The Aegean and the Orient in the Second Millennium*, pp. 105–111. Liège: University of Liège.

Betancourt, P. P. (1985). *The History of Minoan Pottery*. Princeton: Princeton University Press.

Betancourt, P. P. (2004). Pseira and Knossos: The Transformation of an East Cretan Seaport. In L. P. Day, M. Mook, and J. D. Muhly (Eds.), *Crete Beyond the Palaces: Proceedings of the Crete 2000 Conference*, pp. 21–28. Philadelphia: INSTAP Academic Press.

Bevan, A. (2003). Reconstructing the Role of Egyptian Culture in the Value Regimes of the Bronze Age Aegean: Stone Vessels and Their Social Contexts. In R. Matthews and C. Roemer (Eds.), *Ancient Perspectives on Egypt*, pp. 57–73. London: University College London Press.

Bevan, A. (2004). Emerging Civilized Values? The Consumption and Imitation of Egyptian Stone Vessels in EMII-MMI Crete and Its Wider Eastern Mediterranean Context. In J. C. Barrett and P. Halstead (Eds.), *The Emergence of Civilisation Revisited*, pp. 107–126. Oxford: Oxbow.

Bevan, A. (2007). Wood-Worked and Metal-Shocked: Softstone Vessels in the Bronze and Early Iron Age Eastern Mediterranean. In C. Phillips and S. Simpson (Eds.), *Softstone in Arabia and Iran*. Oxford: Archaeopress.

Bevan, A., E. Kiriatzi, C. Knappett, E. Kappa, and S. Papachristou (2002). Excavation of Neopalatial Deposits at Tholos (Kastri), Kythera. *Annual of the British School at Athens 97*, 55–96.

Bietak, M. (1984). Zum Königsreich des Nehesi. *Studien zur Altägyptischen Kultur 11*, 59–75.

Bietak, M. (1989). Servant Burials in the Middle Bronze Age Culture of the Eastern Nile Delta. *Eretz Israel 20*, 30–43.

Bietak, M. (1991). Egypt and Canaan During the Middle Bronze Age. *Bulletin of the American Schools of Oriental Research 284*, 27–72.

Bietak, M. (1996). *Avaris: The Capital of the Hyksos. Recent Excavations at Tel el-Dab'a*. London: British Museum Press.

Bisset, N. G., J. G. Bruhn, S. Curto, B. Holmstedt, U. Nyman, and M. H. Zenk (1996). Was Opium Known in 18th Dynasty Egypt? An Examination of Materials from the Tomb of the Chief Royal Architect Kha. *Ägypten und Levante 6*, 199–201.

Black, J., and A. Green (1992). *Gods, Demons and Symbols of Ancient Mesopotamia*. London: British Museum Press.

Blackman, A. M. (1914). *The Rock Tombs of Meir (Part I)*. London: Kegan Paul.

Blackman, A. M., and M. R. Apted (1953). *The Rock Tombs of Meir (Part V)*. London: Kegan Paul.

Blackman, A. M., and T. E. Peet (1925). Papyrus Lansing: A Translation with Notes. *Journal of Egyptian Archaeology 11*, 284–298.

Blegen, C. W., C. G. Boulter, J. L. Caskey, and M. Rawson (1958). *Troy IV, Settlements VIIa, VIIb and VIII*. Princeton: Princeton University Press.

Bleiberg, E. (1996). *The Official Gift in Ancient Egypt*. Norman and London: University of Oklahoma Press.

Bloch, M., and J. Parry (1989). Introduction: Money and Morality in Exchange. In J. Parry and M. Bloch (Eds.), *Money and the Morality of Exchange*, pp. 1–32. Cambridge: Cambridge University Press.

Bloxam, E. (2003). *The Organisation, Transportation and Logistics of Hard Stone Quarrying in the Egyptian Old Kingdom*. Ph.D. thesis, University of London.

Boehmer, R. M. (1972). *Die Kleinfunde von Bogazköy-Hattusa*. Berlin: Gebr. Mann Verlag.

Boehmer, R. M. (1979). *Die Kleinefunde aus der Unterstadt von Bogazköy*. Berlin: Gebr. Mann Verlag.

Bonechi, M. (1992). Relations Amicales Syro-Palestiniennes: Mari et Hasor au XVIIIe siécle av. J-C. In J.-M. Durand (Ed.), *Florilegium Marianum: Recueil d'Etudes en l'Honneur de Michel Fleury*, pp. 9–22. Paris: Nouvelles Assyriologiques Brèves et Utilitaires.

Borchardt, L. (1910). *Das Grabdenkmal des Königs Sahu-Re (Vol. 1)*. Leipzig: Wissenschäftliche Veröffenliohung der Deutschen Orient-Gesellschaft.

Bosanquet, R. C. (1904). Some 'Late Minoan' Vases found in Greece. *Journal of Hellenic Studies XXIV*, 317–335.

Bosanquet, R. C., and R. M. Dawkins (1908). *The Unpublished Objects from the Palaikastro Excavations*. London: MacMillan.

Bosanquet, R. C., and F. B. Welch (1904). *Excavations at Phylakopi*. London: Society for the Promotion of Hellenic Studies.

Bouchard, J.-P., and M. Mézard (2000). Wealth Condensation in a Simple Model of the Economy. *Physica A 282*, 535–546.

Bourdieu, P. (1994). *Distinction: A Social Critique of the Judgement of Taste*. London: Routledge.

Bourke, S. J., and R. T. Sparks (1995). The DAJ excavations at Pella in Jordan 1963/64. In S. J. Bourke and J.-P. Descoeudres (Eds.), *Trade, Contact and the Movement of Peoples in the Eastern Mediterranean*, pp. 149–167. Sydney: Mediterranean Archaeology Supplement.

Bourriau, J. (1981). *Umm el-Ga'ab—Pottery from the Nile Valley Before the Arab Conquest*. Cambridge: Cambridge University Press.

Bourriau, J. (2004). The Beginnings of Amphora Production in Egypt. In J. Bourriau and J. Phillips (Eds.), *Invention and Innovation. The Social Context of Technological Change 2. Egypt, the Aegean and the Near East 1650–1150 BC*, pp. 78–95. Oxford: Oxbow.

Bourriau, J. D. (1996). The Dolphin Vase from Lisht. In *Studies in Honor of William Kelly Simpson*, pp. 101–116. Boston: Museum of Fine Arts.

Bowen, R. L. (1960). Egypt's Earliest Sailing Ships. *Antiquity 34*, 117–131.

Boyd, R. (1992). The Evolution of Reciprocity When Conditions Vary. In A. H. Harcourt and F. B. M. De Waal (Eds.), *Coalitions and Alliances in Humans and Other Animals*, pp. 473–489. Oxford: Oxford University Press.

Boyd, R., and P. J. Richerson (1985). *Culture and the Evolutionary Process*. Chicago: University of Chicago Press.

Boyd Hawes, H., B. E. Williams, R. B. Seager, and E. H. Hall (1908). *Gournia, Vasiliki and Other Prehistoric Sites on the Isthmus of Ierapetra*. Philadelphia: American Exploration Society.

Brady, J. E., A. Scott, H. Neff, and M. D. Glascock (1997). Speleothem Breakage, Movement, Removal, and Caching: An Aspect of Ancient Maya Cave Modification. *Geoarchaeology 12.6*, 725–750.

Branigan, K. (1968). *Copper and Bronze Working in Early Bronze Age Crete*. Lund: Paul Åströms.

Branigan, K. (1974). *Aegean Metalwork of the Early and Middle Bronze Age*. Oxford: Clarendon.

Branigan, K. (1982). Minoan Metallurgy and Cypriot Copper. In D. Muhly, R. Maddin, and V. Karageorghis (Eds.), *Early Metallurgy in Cyprus*, pp. 203–212. Nicosia: Pierides Foundation.

Branigan, K. (1993). *Dancing with Death: Life and Death in Southern Crete, c.3000–2000 BC*. Amsterdam: Adolf M. Hakkert.

Braudel, F. (1966). *La Méditerranée et le Monde Méditerranéen à l'époque de Philippe II*. Paris: Armand Colin.

Braun, E. (1990). Basalt Bowls of the EBI Horizon in the Southern Levant. *Paléorient 16.1*, 87–96.

Braun, E. (2004). *Early Beth Shan (Strata XIX-XIII): G.M. Fitzgerald's Deep Cut on the Tell*. Philadelphia: University of Pennsylvania Museum.

Breasted, J. H. (1907). *Ancient Records of Egypt*. Chicago: Chicago University Press.

Broodbank, C. (1999). Colonisation and Configuration in the Insular Neolithic of the Aegean. In P. Halstead (Ed.), *Neolithic Society in Greece*, pp. 15–41. Sheffield: Sheffield Academic Press.

Broodbank, C. (2000). *An Island Archaeology of the Early Cyclades*. Cambridge: Cambridge University Press.

Broodbank, C. (2004). Minoanisation: Beyond the Loss of Innocence. *Proceedings of the Cambridge Philological Society 50*, 46–91.

Broodbank, C., E. Kiriatzi, and J. B. Rutter (2005). From Pharaoh's Feet to the Slave-Women of Pylos? The History and Cultural Dynamics of Kythera in the Third Palace Period. In A. Dakouri-Hild and E. S. Sherratt (Eds.), *Ace High: Studies Presented to Oliver Dickinson on the Occasion of His Retirement*, pp. 70–96. Oxford: Archaeopress.

Broodbank, C., and T. F. Strasser (1991). Migrant Farmers and the Neolithic Colonisation of Crete. *Antiquity 65*, 233–245.

Brunner-Traut, E. (1970). Gravidenflasche: Das Salben der Mutterleibes. In A. Kuschke and E. Kutsch (Eds.), *Archäologie Und Altes Testament: Festschrift Für Kurt Galling Zum 8 Januar 1970*, pp. 35–48. Tubingen: J. C. B. Mohr.

Bruno, M. (2002). Alabastro Quarries Near Hierapolis (Turkey). In L. Lazzarini (Ed.), *Interdisciplinary Studies on Ancient Stone. ASMOSIA VI—Proceedings of the Sixth International Conference (Venice, June 15–18, 2000)*, pp. 19–24. Padua: Bottega D'Erasmo.

Brunton, G. (1927). *Qau and Badari I*. London: Bernard Quaritch.

Brunton, G. (1930). *Qau and Badari III*. London: Bernard Quaritch.

Brunton, G. (1937). *Mostagedda and the Tasian Culture*. London: Bernard Quaritch.

Brunton, G., and G. Caton-Thompson (1928). *The Badarian Civilisation and Predynastic Remains near Badari*. London: Bernard Quaritch.

Bryce, T. (2002). *Life and Society in the Hittite World*. Oxford: Oxford University Press.

Brysbaert, A. (2002). Common Craftsmansjip in the Aegean and Eastern Mediterranean Bronze Age: Preliminary Technological Evidence with Emphasis on Painted Plaster from Tell el-Dab'a. *Ägypten und Levant 12*, 95–107.

Buchholz, H.-G. (1963). Steineren Dreifussschalen des ägäischen Kulturkreises und ihre Beziehungen zum Osten. *Jarhbuch 78*, 9–11.

Buchholz, H.-G., and V. Karageorghis (1973). *Prehistoric Cyprus: An Archaeological Handbook*. London: Phaidon.

Buckingham, S. (1985). Archaic Decorative Stone Vessels: With Specific Reference to Fragments from the Petrie Collection. *Wepwawet 1*, 9–11.

Budd, P., and T. Taylor (1995). The Faerie Smith Meets the Bronze Industry: Magic Versus Science in the Interpretation of Prehistoric Metal-Making. *World Archaeology 27*, 133–143.

Burger, R. L. (1992). *Chavìn and the Origins of Andean Civilization*. New York: Thames and Hudson.

Buttler, S. (1991). Steatite in the Norse North Atlantic. *Acta Archaeologica 61*, 228–232.

Cahill, N. (1985). The Treasury of Persepolis: Gift-giving at the City of the Persians. *American Journal of Archaeology 33*, 55–64.

Callot, O. (1987). Les Huileries du Bronze Recent a Ougarit. In M. Yon (Ed.), *Le Centre de la Ville. Ras-Shamra-Ougarit III. 38e-44e campagnes (1978–1984)*, pp. 197–212. Paris: Etudes Recherche sur les Civilisations.

Callot, O., and Y. Calvet (2001). Le Bâtiment au Vase de Pierre. In M. Yon and D. Arnaud (Eds.), *Etudes Ougaritiques I. Travaux 1985–1995. Ras Shamra-Ougarit XIV*, pp. 65–82. Padua: Etudes Recherche sur les Civilisations.

Campbell, S. (2000). Domuztepe: The 2000 Study Season. *Anatolian Studies 6*, 2.

Carinci, F. (2000). Western Messara and Egypt During the Protopalatial Period. In A. Karetsou (Ed.), *Kriti-Aigyptos: Politismikoi desmoi trion chlieton*, pp. 33–34. Athens: Karon Editions.

Carruba, O. (1967). Rhyta in den Hithitischen Texten. *Kadmos I.1*, 88–97.

Carter, T. (1998). Reverberations of the International Spirit: Thoughts upon 'Cycladica' in the Mesara. In K. Branigan (Ed.), *Cemetery and Society in the Aegean Bronze Age*, pp. 59–77. Sheffield: Sheffield Academic Press.

Carter, T. (2004). The Stone Implements. In J. S. Soles and C. Davaras (Eds.), *Mochlos IC. Period III. Neopalatial Settlement on the Coast: The Artisans' Quarter and the Farmhouse at Chalinomouri. The Small Finds*, pp. 61–107. Philadelphia: INSTAP Academic Press.

Carter, T. (2006). Beyond the Mohs Scale: Raw Material Choice and the Production of Stone Vases in a Late Minoan Context. In Y. M. Rowan and J. R. Ebeling (Eds.), *New Approaches to Old Stones: Recent Studies of Ground Stone Artifacts*. London: Equinox.

Caskey, J. L. (1956). Excavations at Lerna, 1955. *Hesperia 25*, 147–173.

Casson, L. (1995). *Ships and Seamanship in the Ancient World*. Baltimore: Johns Hopkins University Press.

Castel, G., and L. Pantalacci (2005). *Les Cimetières Est et Ouest du Mastaba de Khentika*. Cairo: L'Institut Français d'Archéologie Orientale.

Caton-Thompson, G. (1929). Zimbabwe. *Antiquity 3*, 424–433.

Caton-Thompson, G., and E. W. Gardner (1934). *The Desert Fayum*. London: Royal Anthropological Institute of Great Britain and Ireland.

Caubet, A. (1991). Répertoire de la Vaisselle de Pierre. In A. Caubet, J. Connan, E. Coqueugniot, O. Deschesne, C. Eliot, and H. Frost (Eds.), *Arts et Industries de la Pierre: Ras-Shamra-Ougarit VI*, pp. 205–255. Paris: Etudes Recherche sur les Civilisations.

Caubet, A. (1998). The International Style: A Point of View from the Levant and Syria. In E. H. Cline and D. Harris-Cline (Eds.), *The Aegean and the Orient in the Second Millennium*, pp. 105–114. Liège: University of Liège.

Caubet, A., and V. Matoïan (1995). Ougarit et l'égée. In M. Yon, M. Sznycer, and P. Bordreuil (Eds.), *Ras-Shamra-Ougarit XI: Le pays d'Ougarit autour de 1200 av. J.-C.*, pp. 99–112. Paris: Edition Recherche sur les Civilisations.

Cauvin, M.-C. (1998). *L'Obsidienne au Proche et Moyen Orient: du Volcan à l'Outil*. Oxford: Archaeopress.

Cerny, J. (1935). *Catalogue Général des Antiquités Egyptiennes du Musée de Caire: Ostraca Hieratiques (Vol. I)*. Cairo: L'Institut Français d'Archéologie Orientale.

Chadwick, J. (1976). *The Mycenaean World*. Cambridge: Cambridge University Press.

Chanut, C. (2000). *Bois, Pierres et Métaux à Ugarit-Ras Shamra (Syrie)*. Paris: Atelier National de Réproduction de Thèses.

Chapouthier, F., and R. Joly (1936). *Fouilles exécutées à Mallia: Exploration du Palais, II (1925–26)*. Paris: Paul Geuthner.

Chapoutier, F., and P. Demargne (1942). *Mallia. Troisième Rapport. Exploration du Palais (1927–32) (Etudes Crétoises VI)*. Paris: Paul Geuthner.

Charpin, D., and J.-M. Durand (1991). La Suzeraineté de l'Empereur (Sukkalmah) d'Elam sur la Mésopotamie et le 'Nationalisme' Amorrite. In L. De Meyer and H. Gasche (Eds.), *Mésopotamie et Elam*, pp. 61–66. Ghent: University of Ghent.

Chase-Dunn, C., and T. D. Hall (Eds.) (1997). *Rise and Demise: Comparing World-Systems*. Boulder: Westview Press.

Chevallier, H. B., S. Détournay, R. Dupré, J.-P. Julien, M. Olivier, M. Séfériades, and R. Treuil (1975). *Fouilles Exécutées à Mallia: Sondages au Sud-Ouest du Palais (1968)*. Paris: Paul Geuthner.

Chippindale, C. (1989). Grammars of Archaeological Design: A Generative and Geometrical Approach to the Form of Artefacts. In J.-C. Gardin and C. Peebles (Eds.), *Representations in Archaeology*, pp. 251–276. Bloomington: Indiana University Press.

Chlouveraki, S. (2002). Exploitation of Gypsym in Minoan Crete. In L. Lazzarini (Ed.), *Interdisciplinary Studies on Ancient Stone. ASMOSIA VI—Proceedings of the Sixth International Conference (Venice, June 15–18, 2000)*, pp. 25–34. Padua: Bottega D'Erasmo.

Clamer, C. (1976). *Late Bronze Age Alabaster Vessels Found in Palestinian Contexts with an Emphasis on Calcite and Gypsum Tazze*. M.A. thesis, Hebrew University of Jerusalem.

Clamer, C. (1986). The Dayan Collection: The Stone Vessels. *Israel Museum Journal 5*, 19–36.

Clamer, C. (2002). The Stone Vessels. In A. Biran and R. Ben-Dov (Eds.), *Dan II: A Chronicle of the Excavations and the Late Bronze Age "Mycenaean" Tomb*, pp. 65–76. Jerusalem: Nelson Glueck School of Biblical Archaeology.

Clark, J. D. (1964). Stone Vessels from Northern Rhodesia. *Man 64*, 69–73.

Cline, E. H. (1994). *Sailing the Wine-Dark Sea: International Trade and the Late Bronze Age Aegean (BAR 591)*. Oxford: Tempus Reparatum.

Clunas, C. (2004). *Superfluous Things: Material Culture and Social Status in Early Modern China*. Honolulu: University of Hawaii Press.

Çolak, M., and L. Lazzarini (2002). Quarries and Characterisation of a Hitherto Unknown Alabaster and Marble from Thyatira (Akhisar, Turkey). In L. Lazzarini (Ed.), *Interdisciplinary Studies on Ancient Stone. ASMOSIA VI—Proceedings of the Sixth International Conference (Venice, June 15–18, 2000)*, pp. 35–40. Padua: Bottega D'Erasmo.

Coldstream, J. N., and G. L. Huxley (1972). *Kythera: Excavations and Studies*. London: Faber & Faber.

Coleman, J. E. (1977). *Keos I. Kephala: A Late Neolithic Settlement and Cemetery*. Princeton: Princeton University Press.

Coleman, J. E. (1999). An Early Cycladic Marble Beaker from Theologos in East Lokris. In P. P. Betancourt, V. Karageorghis, R. Laffineur, and W.-D. Neimeier (Eds.), *Meletemata: Studies in Aegean Archaeology Presented to Malcolm Wiener*, pp. 125–130. Liège: University of Liège.

Conchavi-Rainey, Z. (1999). *Royal Gifts in the Late Bronze Age: Fourteenth and Thirteenth BCE*. Beer-Sheva: Studies by the Department of Bible and Ancient Near East.

Cooper, E. N. (1992). Trade, Trouble and Taxation along the Caravan Roads of the Mari Period. In S. E. Orel (Ed.), *Death and Taxes in the Ancient Near East*, pp. 1–15. Lampeter: Edwin Mellen.

Corney, B. G. (1920). An Historic Stone Bowl. *Man 20*, 106–109.

Courtois, J.-C. (1984). *Alasia III: Les Objets des Niveaux Stratifiés d'Enkomi (Fouilles Claude F.-A. Schaeffer 1947–70)*. Paris: Klincksieck.

Courtois, J.-C. (1988). Enkomi (Fouilles Schaeffer 1934–66): Inventaire Complémentaire (Suite), les objets en terre cuite et en pierre. *Report of the Department of Antiquities, Cyprus*, 307–318.

Courtois, J.-C. (1990). Yabninu et le Palais Sud d'Ougarit. *Syria 67*, 103–141.

Courtois, J.-C., J. Lagarce, and E. Lagarce (1986). *Enkomi et le Bronze Récent à Chypre*. Nicosia: Zavallis.

Crawford, H. E. W. (1973). Mesopotamia's Invisible Exports in the Third Millennium B.C. *World Archaeology 5*, 232–241.

Croft, P., E. Peltenburg, and M. Tite (1998). Other Artefacts. In E. Peltenburg (Ed.), *Lemba Archaeological Project (Cyprus) II.1A. Excavations at Kissonerga-Mosphilia, 1979–1992*, pp. 188–201. Jonsered: Paul Åström.

Cummer, W. W., and E. Schofield (1984). *Keos III. Ayia Irini: House A*. Mainz: Philipp von Zabern.

Curle, A. T. (1937). The Ruined Towns of Somaliland. *Antiquity 29*, 315–327.

Curry, A., C. Anfield, and E. Tapp (1986). The Use of the Electron Microscope in the Study of Palaeopathology. In A. R. David (Ed.), *Science in Egyptology*, pp. 57–60. Manchester: Manchester University Press.

Curvers, H. H., and G. M. Schwartz (1990). Umm el-Marra: A Bronze Age Urban Centre in Western Syria. *American Journal of Archaeology 101*, 201–239.

Dalley, S. (1977). Old Babylonian Trade in Textiles at Tell al Rimah. *Iraq 39*, 155–159.

Dalley, S. (2002). *Mari and Karana: Two Old Babylonian Cities*. Piscataway: Gorgias Press.

Davaras, C., and P. P. Betancourt (2004). *The Hagia Photia Cemetery I. The Tomb Groups and Architecture*. Philadelphia: INSTAP Academic Press.

David, H. (1996). Styles and Evolution: Soft Stone Vessels During the Bronze Age in the Oman Peninsula. *Proceedings of the Seminar for Arabian Studies 26*, 31–46.

David, H. (2007). Three Examples of 3rd Millennium BC Softstone Vessel Imports from Syria. In C. Phillips and S. Simpson (Eds.), *Softstone in Arabia and Iran*. Oxford: Archaeopress.

Davies, N. D. G. (1902). *The Rock Tombs of Deîr el Gebrâwi (Vols. 1 and 2)*. Lonon: Kegan Paul.

Davies, N. D. G. (1922). *The Tomb of Puyemrê at Thebes*. New York: Metropolitan Museum.

Davies, N. D. G. (1925). *The Tomb of Two Sculptors at Thebes*. New York: Metropolitan Museum.

Davies, N. D. G. (1973). *The Tomb of Rekh-mi-re at Thebes*. New York: Arno Press.

Day, P. M., and H. Haskell (1993). Transport Stirrup Jars from Thebes as Evidence of Trade in Late Bronze Age Greece. In C. Gillis, C. Risberg, and B. Sjöberg (Eds.), *Trade and Production in Premonetary Greece: Aspects of Trade*, pp. 87–99. Jonsered: Paul Åströms.

Day, P. M., P. E. Wilson, and E. Kiriatzi (1998). Pots, Labels and People: Burying Ethnicity in the Cemetery at Aghia Photia, Siteias. In K. Branigan (Ed.), *Cemetery and Society in the Aegean Bronze Age*, pp. 133–149. Sheffield: Sheffield Academic Press.

De Cardi, B. (1970). *Excavations at Bampur, A Third Millennium Settlement in Persian Baluchistan*. New York: American Museum of Natural History.

De Conteson, H., J.-C. Courtois, E. Lagarce, S. Lagarce, and R. Sticky (1974). La XXXIVe Campagne de Fouilles à Ras Shamra en 1973. Rapport Préliminaire. *Syria 41*, 1–30.

De Jesus, P. (1980). *The Development of Prehistoric Mining and Metallurgy in Anatolia*. London: British Archaeological Reports.

de Miroschedji, P. (1973). Vases et Objets en Stéatite Susiens du Musée du Louvre. *Cahiers de la Délégation Archéologique Française en Iran 3*, 9–79.

De Morgan, J. (1894). *Fouilles à Dahchour*. Vienna: A. Holzhausen.

Debono, F., and B. B. Mortensen (1990). *El Omari (Vol. I)*. Mainz: Philipp von Zabern.

Degnan, P. J., and A. H. F. Robertson (1998). Mesozoic-early Tertiary passive margin evolution of the Pindos ocean (NW Peloponnese, Greece). *Sedimentary Geology 117*, 33–70.

Demakopoulou, K. (1988). *The Mycenean World: Five Centuries of Early Greek Culture 1600–1100 BC*. Athens: National Museum.

DeMorgan, J. (1897). *Recherches sur les Origines de l'Egypte*. Paris: Ernest Leroux.

Détournay, B. (1981). Vases de Pierre. In B. Détournay, J.-C. Poursat, and F. Vandhabiele (Eds.), *Le Quartier Mu*, pp. 19–69. Paris: Paul Geuthner.

Dever, W. (1995). Social Structure in the Early Bronze IV Period in Palestine. In T. Levy (Ed.), *The Archaeology of Society in the Holy Land*, pp. 282–295. London: Leicester University Press.

Dever, W. G. (1976). The Beginnings of the Middle Bronze in Syria-Palestine. In F. M. Cross, W. E. Lenke, and M. J. P. D. (Eds.), *Magnalia Dei: The Mighty Acts of God. Essays on the Bible and Archaeology*, pp. 3–38. Garden City: Doubleday.

Devetzi, A. (2000). The Imported Stone Vases at Akrotiri, Thera: A New Approach to the Material. *Annual of the British School at Athens 95*, 121–139.

Diamond, J. M. (1998). *Guns, Germs and Steel: A Short History of Everybody for the Last 13,000 Years*. London: Vintage.

Dickers, A. (1995). Spätbronzezeitliche Steingefässe des Griechischen Festlandes. *Studi miceni ed egeo-anatolici 92*, 125–223.

Dikaios, P. (1953). *Khirokitia*. London: Oxford University Press.

Dikaios, P. (1969). *Enkomi. Excavations 1948–1958 (Vol. I)*. Mainz: Philipp von Zabern.

Dikaios, P. (1971). *Enkomi. Excavations 1958–1959 (Vol. II) Chronology, Summary and Conclusions, Catalogue, Appendices*. Mainz: Philipp von Zabern.

Dilek, Y. (2003). Ophiolite Concept and Its Evolution. In Y. Dilek and S. Newcomb (Eds.), *Ophiolite Concept and the Evolution of Geological Thought*, pp. 1–16. Boulder: Geological Society of America.

Dominguez, V. R. (1990). Representing Value and the Value of Representation: A Different Look at Money. *Cultural Anthropology 5.1*, 16–44.

Douglas, M., and B. Isherwood (1979). *The World of Goods*. Harmondsworth: Penguin.

Doumas, C. (1977). *Early Bronze Age Burial Habits in the Cyclades*. Göteborg: Paul Åströms.

Doumas, C. (1992). *The Wall-Paintings of Thera*. London: Thera Foundation.

Drew, L., and D. Wilson (1980). *Argillite. Art of the Haida*. Vancouver: Hancock.

Dreyer, G. (1986). *Elephantine VIII. Der Tempel der Satet*. Mainz: Phillipp von Zabern.

Dreyer, G. (1992). Recent Discoveries at Abydos Cemetery U. In E. C. M. van den Brink (Ed.), *The Nile Delta in Transition: 4th–3rd Millennium BC*, pp. 293–299. Tel Aviv: Pinkhas.

Driessen, J., and I. Schoep (1999). The Stylus and the Sword: The Roles of Scribes and Warriors in the Conquest of Crete. In R. Laffineur (Ed.), *Polemos. Le contexte guerrier en Égée á l'âge du Bronze*, pp. 389–401. Liège: Université de Liège.

Duell, P. (1938). *The Mastaba of Mereruka*. Chicago: Oriental Institute Publications.

Duff, W. (1980). *Images Stone B.C.: Thirty Centuries of Northwest Coast Indian Sculpture*. Saanichton: Hancock.

Dumont, L. (1980). On Value. *Proceedings of the British Academy 66*, 207–241.

Dunand, M. (1939). *Fouilles de Byblos (Vol. I)*. Paris: Geuthner.

Dunand, M. (1958). *Fouilles de Byblos (Vol. II)*. Paris: Geuthner.

Dunham, D., and J. M. A. Janssen (1960). *Semna Kumma (Second Cataract Forts Vol. I)*. Boston: Museum of Fine Arts.

Durrani, F. A. (1964). Stone Vases as Evidence of Connection Between Mesopotamia and the Indus Valley. *Ancient Pakistan 1*, 51–96.

Edwards, I. E. S. (1979). *Tutankhamun: His Tomb and Treasures*. London: Victor Gollancz.

Effinger, M. (1996). *Minoischer Schmuck*. Oxford: Tempus Reparatum.

Eichmann, R. (1987). Uruk-Warka XXXVIII, Oberflächenfunde III: Steingefässbohrer. *Baghdader Mitteilungen 18*, 107–115.

Eiwanger, J. (1988). *Merimde-Benisalâme II*. Mainz: Philipp von Zabern.

El-Khouli, A. (1978). *Egyptian Stone Vessels: Predynastic to Dynasty III: Typology and Analysis*. Mainz: Philipp von Zabern.

El-Khouli, A. (1993). *Stone Vessels, Pottery and Sealings from the Tomb of Tut'ankhamun*. Oxford: Griffiths Institute.

Eliot, C. (1991). The Ground Stone Industry. In A. Caubet, J. Connan, E. Coqueugniot, O. Deschesne, C. Eliot, and H. Frost (Eds.), *Arts et Industries de la Pierre. Ras-Shamra-Ougarit VI*, pp. 9–99. Paris: Etudes Recherche sur les Civilisations.

Elliott, C. (1990). The Ground Stone Industry. In V. Karageorghis (Ed.), *Tombs at Palaepaphos*, pp. 129–143. Nicosia: A. G. Leventis Foundation.

Engel, A. E. J., and L. A. Wright (1960). Talc and Soapstone. In J. L. Gillson (Ed.), *Industrial Minerals and Rocks*, pp. 835–850. New York: The American Institute of Mining, Metallurgical and Petroleum Engineers.

Engelbach (1923). *Harageh*. London: Bernard Quaritch.

Espinel, A. D. (2002). The Role of the Temple of Baalat Gebal as Intermediary Between Egypt and Byblos During the Old Kingdom. *Studien zur Altgyptischen Kultur 30*, 103–119.

Esse, D. L. (1991). *Subsistence, Trade and Social Change in Early Bronze Age Palestine*. Chicago: The Oriental Institute of the University of Chicago.

Evans, A. J. (1906). *Prehistoric Tombs of Knossos, The Cemetery of Zafer Papoura and II: The Royal Tomb of Isopata*. London: Feinman.

Evans, A. J. (1928). *Palace of Minos at Knossos (Vol. II)*. London: MacMillan.

Evans, A. J. (1935). *Palace of Minos at Knossos (Vol. IV)*. London: MacMillan.

Evans-Pritchard, E. (1940). *The Nuer: A Description of the Modes of Livelihood and Political Institutions of a Nilotic People*. Oxford: Oxford University Press.

Evely, R. D. G. (1980). Some Manufacturing Processes in a Knossian Stone Vase Workshop. *Annual of the British School at Athens 75*, 127–137.

Evely, R. D. G. (1993). *Minoan Crafts: Tools and Techniques—An Introduction*. Götebörg: Paul Åströms.

Evely, R. D. G. (1999). *Fresco: A Passport into the Past*. Athens: British School at Athens and Goulandris.

Fabre, D. (2005). *Seafaring in Ancient Egypt*. London: Periplus.

Faure, P. (1966). Les Minerais de la Crète Antique. *Revue Archéologique 1*, 45–78.

Feenstra, A., E. Ockenga, D. Rhede, and M. Wiedenbeck (2002). Li-Rich Zincostaurolite and its Decompression-Related Breakdown Products in a Diaspore-Bearing Metabauxite from East Samos (Greece): An EMP and SIMS Study. *Geology 30.2*, 119–122.

Feenstra, A., and B. Wunder (2003). Dehydration of Diasporite to Corundite in Nature and Experiment. *American Mineralogist 88*, 789–805.

Feldman, M. H. (2002). Ambiquous Identities: The 'Marriage' Vase of Niqmaddu II and the Elusive Egyptian Princess. *Journal of Mediterranean Archaeology 15.1*, 75–99.

Feldman, M. H. (2006). *Diplomacy by Design: Luxury Arts and an 'International Style' in the Ancient Near East, 1400–1200 BCE*. Chicago: University of Chicago Press.

Finkelberg, M., A. Uchitel, and D. Ussishkin (1996). A Linear A Inscription from Tel Lachish (Lach ZA 1). *Tel Aviv 23*, 195–208.

Finley, M. I. (1973). *The Ancient Economy*. London: Chatto and Windus.

Firth, C. M., and B. Gunn (1926). *Teti Pyramid Cemeteries*. Cairo: L'Institut Français d'Archéologie Orientale.

Firth, C. M., and J. E. Quibell (1935). *Excavations at Saqqara: The Step Pyramid*. Cairo: L'Institut Français d'Archéologie Orientale.

Fischer, H. G. (1993). Another Pithemorphic Vessel of the Sixth Dynasty. *Journal of the American Research Centre in Egypt 30*, 1–9.

Fiske, A. P. (1991). *Structures of Social Life: The Four Elementary Forms of Human Relations*. New York: The Free Press.

Fiske, A. P. (2000). Complementarity Theory: Why Human Social Capacities Evolved to Require Cultural Complements. *Personality and Social Psychology Review 4.1*, 76–94.

Fiske, A. P. (2004a). Four Modes of Constituting Relationships: Consubstantial Assimilation; Space Magnitude, Time and Force; Concrete Procedures; Abstract Symbolism. In N. Haslam (Ed.), *Relational Models Theory: A Contemporary Overview*, pp. 61–146. Mahwah: Erlbaum.

Fiske, A. P. (2004b). Relational Models Theory 2.0. In N. Haslam (Ed.), *Relational Models Theory: A Contemporary Overview*, pp. 3–25. Mahwah: Erlbaum.

Fiske, A. P., and N. Haslam (2000). The Four Basic Social Bonds: Structures for Coordinating Interaction. In M. Baldwin (Ed.), *Interpersonal Cognition*, pp. 267–298. New York: Guilford.

Fitton, J. L., M. Hughes, and S. Quirke (1998). Northerners at Lahun. Neutron Activation Analysis of Minoan and related pottery in the British Museum. In S. Quirke (Ed.), *Lahun Studies*, pp. 112–140. London: SIA.

Floyd, C. R. (1998). *Pseira III. The Plateia Building*. Philadelphia: The University Museum.

Floyd, C. R. (2000). Chrysokamino. The Habitation Site. In J. D. Muhly and E. Sikla (Eds.), *Crete 2000: One Hundred Years of American Archaeological Work on Crete (1900–2000)*, pp. 65–68. Athens: American School of Classical Studies at Athens.

Foster, B. (1987). The Late Bronze Age Palace Economy: A View from the East. In R. Hägg and N. Marinatos (Eds.), *The Function of the Minoan Palaces*, pp. 11–16. Göteborg: Paul Åströms.

Foster, B. R. (1977). Commercial Activity in Sargonic Mesopotamia. *Iraq 39*, 31–43.

Francfort, H.-P. (2005). Observations sur la Toreutique de la Civilisation de l'Oxus. In C. Landes and O. Bopearachchi (Eds.), *Afghanistan: Ancien Carrefour Entre l'Est et l'Ouest.*, pp. 21–63. Turnhout: Brepols.

Frankfort, H., and J. D. S. Pendlebury (1933). *The City of Akhenaten II*. Oxford: Oxford University Press.

Freed, R. E. (1981). *Egypt's Golden Age: The Art of Living in the New Kingdom 1558–1085 B.C.* Boston: Museum of Fine Arts.

Friedel, D. A. (1993). The Jade Ahau. Toward a Theory of Commodity Value in Maya Civilisation. In F. W. Lange (Ed.), *Precolumbian Jade: New Geological and Cultural Interpretations*, pp. 149–165. Salt Lake City: University of Utah Press.

Frison, G. C. (1982). Sources of Steatite and Methods of Procurement and Use in Wyoming. *Plains Anthropologist 27*, 273–286.

Frodin, O., and A. Persson (1938). *Asine, Results of the Swedish Excavations 1922–1930*. Stockholm: General Straben Litografiska Förlag.

Furumark, A. (1941). *The Mycenean Pottery: Analysis and Classification*. Stockholm: Kungl Vitterhets Historie och Antikvitets Akademien.

Gachet, J. (1987). Objets en Os et en Ivoire. In M. Yon (Ed.), *Le Centre de la Ville. Ras-Shamra-Ougarit III. 38e-44e campagnes (1978–1984)*, pp. 249–272. Paris: Etudes Recherche sur les Civilisations.

Galili, E., M. Shmueli, and N. Artzy (1986). Bronze Age Ship's Cargo of Copper and Tin. *International Journal of Nautical Archaeology 15*, 25–37.

Garber, J. F., D. C. Grove, K. G. Hirth, and J. W. Hoopes (1993). Jade Use in Portions of Mexico and Central America: Olmec, Maya, Costa Rica and Honduras. In F. W. Lange (Ed.), *Precolumbian Jade: New Geological and Cultural Interpretations*, pp. 211–232. Salt Lake City: University of Utah Press.

Gardiner, A. (1935). A Lawsuit Arising from the Purchase of Two Slaves. *Journal of Egyptian Archaeology 21*, 120–146.

Gardiner, A. H. (1988). *Egytian Grammar: Being an Introduction to the Study of Hieroglyphs*. Oxford: Ashmolean Museum.

Gardiner, A. H., T. E. Peet, and J. Czerný (1955). *The Inscriptions of Sinai II: Translations and Commentaries*. London: Oxford University Press.

Garelli, P. (1977). Marchands et Tamkâr. Assyriens en Cappadoce. *Iraq 39*, 99–107.

Garstang, J. (1903). *Mahâsna and Bêt Khallâf*. London: Bernard Quaritch.

Gee, J. L. (1998). *The Requirements of Ritual Purity in Ancient Egypt*. Ph.D. thesis, Yale University.

Georgiou, H. (1991). Bronze Age Ships and Rigging. In R. Laffineur (Ed.), *Thalassa: L'égée préhistorique et la mer*, pp. 61–71. Liège: University of Liège.

Georgiou, H. (1995). The Role of Maritime Contacts in the Prehistoric Cyclades. In C. Gillis, C. Risberg, and B. Sjöberg (Eds.), *Trade and Production in Premonetary Greece: Aspects of Trade*, pp. 33–42. Stockholm: Paul Åströms.

Georgiou, H. (1997). Seafaring, Trade Routes and the Emergence of the Bronze Age. In S. S. Swiny, R. Hohlfelder, and H. Wylde Swiny (Eds.), *Res Maritimae: Cyprus and the Eastern Mediterranean from Prehistory to Late Antiquity*, pp. 117–124. Nicosia: Cyprus American Archaeological Research Institute.

Gerontakou, E. (2003). Dio Mesominoiki Apothetes sto Nekrotapheio tou Platanou. In A. Vlachopoulos and K. Birtacha (Eds.), *Argonautis: Timetikos tomos yia ton Kathegete Christo G. Douma apo tous mathetes tou sto Panepistimio Athenon (1980–2000)*, pp. 303–330. Athens: Kathemerini.

Getz-Gentle, P. (1996). *Stone Vessels of the Cyclades in the Early Bronze Age*. Pennsylvania: Pennsylvania State University.

Giddens, A. (1984). *The Constitution of Society*. Cambridge: Polity Press.

Gill, D. W. J., and C. Chippindale (1993). Material and Intellectual Consequences of Esteem for Cycladic Figurines. *American Journal of Archaeology 97*, 601–659.

Gillis, C. (1995). Trade in the Late Bronze Age. In C. Gillis, C. Risberg, and B. Sjöberg (Eds.), *Trade and Production in Premonetary Greece: Aspects of Trade*, pp. 61–86. Jonsered: Paul Åströms.

Gittlen, B. M. (1981). The Cultural and Chronological Implications of the Cypro-Palestinian Trade during the Late Bronze Age. *Bulletin of the American Schools of Oriental Research 241*, 49–59.

Gjerstad, E., J. Lindos, E. Sjoqvist, and A. Westholm (1934). *The Swedish Cyprus Expedition: Finds and Results of Excavations in Cyprus 1927–31.* Stockholm: Victor Pettersons.

Godelier, M. (1996). *L'Enigme du Don.* Paris: Fayard.

Goldman, H. (1956). *Tarsus II. Excavations at Gözlü Teke, Tarsus.* Princeton: Princeton University Press.

Gonen, R. (1992). *Burial Patterns and Cultural Diversity in Late Bronze Age Canaan.* Winona Lake: Eisenbrauns.

Gosselain, O. P. (2000). Materializing Identities: An African Perspective. *Journal of Archaeological Method and Theory 7*(3), 187–217.

Goyon, G. (1991). Les Instruments de Forage sous l'Ancien Empire Egyptien. *Ex Oriente Lux 21*, 154–163.

Grajetzki, W. (2003). *Burial Customs in Ancient Egypt: Life in Death for Rich and Poor.* London: Duckworth.

Grajetski, W. (2006). *The Middle Kingdom of Ancient Egypt.* London: Duckworth.

Grant, E. (1932). *Ain Shems Excavations II.* Haverford: Haverford College.

Grayson, D. K. (1988). Sample Size and Relative Abundance in Archaeological Analysis: Illustrations from Spiral Fractures and Seriation. In R. D. Leonard and G. T. Jones (Eds.), *Quantifying Diversity in Archaeology*, pp. 79–84. Cambridge: Cambridge University Press.

Graziadio, G. (1991). Social Stratification at Mycenae in the Shaft Grave Period. *American Journal of Archaeology 95*, 403–440.

Greenberg, R., and N. Porat (1996). A Third Millennium Levantine Production Center: Typology, Petrography and Provenance of the Metallic Ware of Northern Israel and Adjacent Regions. *Bulletin of the American Schools of Oriental Research 301*, 5–24.

Gregory, C. A. (1982). *Gifts and Commodities.* London: Academic Press.

Gwinnett, A. J., and L. Gorelick (1983). An Ancient Repair on a Cycladic Statuette Analyzed Using Scanning Electron Microscopy. *Journal of Field Archaeology 10*, 378–384.

Gwinnett, A. J., and L. Gorelick (1993). Beads, Scarabs and Amulets: Methods of Manufacture in Ancient Egypt. *Journal of the American Research Centre in Egypt 30*, 125–132.

Haldane, C. (1993). Direct Evidence for Organic Cargoes in the Late Bronze Age. *World Archaeology 24*, 348–360.

Hallager, B. P., and E. Hallager (1995). The Knossian Bull—Political Propaganda in Neo-Palatial Crete? In R. Laffineur and W.-D. Niemeier (Eds.), *Politeia: Society and State in the Aegean Bronze Age*, pp. 547–556. Liège: University of Liège.

Hallett, J. (1990). *The Early Islamic Soft-Stone Industry.* M.A. thesis, University of Oxford.

Hallo, W. W. (1992). Trade and Traders in the Ancient Near East. In D. Charpin and F. Joannès (Eds.), *La Circulations des Biens des Personnes et des Idées dans le Proche Orient*, pp. 351–356. Paris: Editions Recherche sur les Civilisations.

Hallo, W. W., and B. Buchanan (1965). A "Persian Gulf" Seal on an Old Babylonian Mercantile Agreement. In H. G. Güterbock and T. Jacobsen (Eds.), *Studies in Honor of Benno Landsberger on His Seventy-Fifth Birthday*, pp. 199–209. Chicago: The Oriental Institute of the University of Chicago.

Halstead, P. (2004). Life After Mediterranean Polyculture: The Subsistence Subsystem and the Emergence of Civilisation Revisited. In J. C. Barrett and P. Halstead (Eds.), *The Emergence of Civilisation Revisited*, pp. 189–206. Oxford: Oxbow.

Hamada, A., and S. Farid (1947a). Excavations at Kom el-Hisn. Season 1943. *Annales du Service des Antiquités de l'Égypte 46*, 101–111.

Hamada, A., and S. Farid (1947b). Excavations at Kom el-Hisn. Season 1945. *Annales du Service des Antiquités de l'Égypte 46*, 195–205.

Hamada, A., and S. Farid (1948). Excavations at Kom el-Hisn. Third Season 1946. *Annales du Service des Antiquités de l'Égypte 48*, 299–308.

Hamada, A., and S. Farid (1950). Excavations at Kom el-Hisn. Fourth Season 1947. *Annales du Service des Antiquités de l'Égypte 50*, 367–379.

Hamilakis, Y. (1998). Eating the Dead: Mortuary Feasting and the Politics of Memory in the Aegean Bronze Age Societies. In K. Branigan (Ed.), *Cemetery and Society in the Aegean Bronze Age*, pp. 115–132. Sheffield: Sheffield Academic Press.

Hankey, V. (1972). Stone Vessels at Myrtos Pyrgos. *Pepragmena tou Tritou Diethnous Kritologikou Synedriou 1*, 210–215.

Hankey, V. (1974). A Late Bronze Age Temple at Amman I. The Aegean Pottery; II. Vases and Objects Made of Stone. *Levant 6*, 131–178.

Hankey, V. (1995). Stirrup Jars at El-Amarna. In W. V. Davies and L. Schofield (Eds.), *Egypt, the Aegean and the Levant: Interconnections in the Second Millennium BC*, pp. 116–124. London: British Museum.

Harper, P. O., J. Aruz, and F. Tallon (1992). *The Royal City of Susa*. New York: Abrams.

Harper, P. O., E. Klengel-Brandt, J. Aruz, and K. Benzel (1995). *Assyrian Origins.Discoveries at Ashur on the Tigris*. New York: Metropolitan Museum of Art.

Harrell, J. A., and B. V. Max (2006). Discovery of a Medieval Islamic Industry for Steatite Cooking Vessels in Egypt's Eastern Desert. In Y. M. Rowan and J. R. Ebeling (Eds.), *New Approaches to Old Stones: Recent Studies of Ground Stone Artifacts*. London: Equinox.

Harris, J. R. (1961). *Lexicographical Studies in Ancient Egyptian Materials*. Berlin: Akademie-Verlag.

Hasel, M. G. (1998). *Domination and Resistance: Egyptian Military Activity in the Southern Levant 1300-1185 BC*. Leiden: Brill.

Haslam, N. (2004). Research on Relational Models: An Overview. In N. Haslam (Ed.), *Relational Models Theory: A Contemporary Overview*, pp. 61–146. Mahwah: Erlbaum.

Hassan, F. A. (1997). Nile Floods and Political Disorder in Early Egypt. In N. Dalfes, G. Kukla, and H. Weiss (Eds.), *Third Millennium BC Climate Change and Old World Collapse*, pp. 1–21. New York: Springer.

Hassan, F. A., G. J. Tassie, T. L. Tucker, J. M. Rowland, and J. van Wetering (2003). Social Dynamics at the Late Predynastic to Early Dynastic Site of Kafr Hassan Dawood. *Archéonil 13*, 37–46.

Hatzi-Spiliopoulou, G. (2000). A Mycenean Stone Vase from Messenia. In P. P. Betancourt, V. Karageorghis, R. Laffineur, and W.-D. Neimeier (Eds.), *Meletemata: Studies in Aegean Archaeology Presented to Malcolm Wiener*, pp. 343–349. Liège: University of Liège.

Hekman, J. J. (2003). *The Early Bronze Age Cemetery at Chalandriani on Syros (Cyclades, Greece)*. Groningen: University of Groningen.

Helck, W. (1987). The Dissolution of the Palace Economy in the Ramesside Period. In R. Hägg and N. Marinatos (Eds.), *The Function of the Minoan Palace*, pp. 17–18. Gothenburg: Paul Åströms.

Heldal, T., E. Bloxam, P. Storemyr, and A. Kelany (2003). The Geology and Archaeology of the Ancient Silicified Sandstone Quarries at Gebel Gulab and Gebal Tingar, Aswan (Egypt). *Marmora 1*, 11–35.

Helms, M. (1988). *Ulysses' Sail: An Ethnographic Odyssey of Power, Knowledge and Geographical Distance*. Princeton: Princeton University Press.

Helms, M. (1993). *Craft and the Kingly Ideal—Art, Trade and Power*. Austin: University of Texas.

Heltzer, M. (1977). The Metal Trade of Ugarit and the Problem of the Transportation of Commercial Goods. *Iraq 39*, 203–211.

Heltzer, M. (1978). *Goods, Prices and the Organization of Trade in Ugarit*. Wiesbaden: Reichert.

Heltzer, M. (1984). Private Property at Ugarit. In A. Archi (Ed.), *Circulation of Goods in Non-Palatial Context in the Ancient Near East*, pp. 161–194. Rome: Edizioni dell'Atene.

Heltzer, M. (1988). The Late Bronze Age Service System and Its Decline. In M. Heltzer and E. Lipinski (Eds.), *Society and Economy in the Eastern Mediterranean, c.1500–1000 B.C.*, pp. 7–18. Leuven: Peeters.

Heltzer, M. (1989). The Trade of Crete and Cyprus with Syria and Mesopotamia and Their Eastern Tin Sources in the XVIII and XVII Centuries BC. *Minos 24*, 7–28.

Hendrickx, S. (1996). The Relative Chronology of the Naqada Culture. Problems and Possibilities. In J. Spencer (Ed.), *Aspects of Early Egypt*, pp. 36–69. London: British Museum Press.

Hendrickx, S. (1999). La Chronologie de la Préhistoire Tardive et des Débuts de l'Histoire de l'Egypte. *Archéonil 9*, 13–81.

Hennessy, J. B. (1989). Amman Airport. In D. Homes-Fredericq and J. B. Hennessy (Eds.), *Archaeology of Jordan II: 1 Field Reports, Surveys and Sites A–K*, pp. 167–178. Leuven: Akkadika Supplementum.

Hennessy, J. B., K. O. Eriksson, and I. C. Kehrberg (1988). *Ayia Paraskevi and Vasilia*. Götebörg: Paul Åströms.

Hester, T. R., and R. F. Heizer (1981). *Making Stone Vases: Ethnographical Studies at an Alabaster Workshop in Upper Egypt*. Malibu: Undena.

Hiebert, F. T. (1994). Production Evidence for the Origins of the Oxus Civilization. *Antiquity 11*, 372–387.

Higgins, M. D., and R. Higgins (1996). *A Geological Companion to Greece and the Aegean*. Ithaca: Cornell University Press.

Hiller, S. (1993). Minoan and Minoanizing Pottery on Aegina. In C. Zerner (Ed.), *Wace and Blegen: Pottery as Evidence for Trade in the Aegean Bronze Age*, pp. 197–199. Amsterdam: J.C. Gieben.

Hirschfeld, N. (1993). Incised Marks (Post-Firing) on Aegean Wares. In C. Zerner (Ed.), *Wace and Blegen: Pottery as Evidence for Trade in the Aegean Bronze Age*, pp. 309–318. Amsterdam: J.C. Gieben.

Hoffman, M. A. (1982). *The Predynastic of Hierakonpolis: An Interim Report*. Giza: Cairo University.

Holladay, J. S. (1997). The Eastern Nile Delta During the Hyksos and Pre-Hyksos Periods: Toward a Systemic/Socio-economic Understanding. In E. Oren (Ed.), *The Hyksos: New Historical and Archaeological Perspectives*, pp. 183–226. Philadelphia: University Museum.

Holthoer, R. (1994). Vessels of K3fy from the Tomb of the Princesses Now in the Ägyptisches Museum in Berlin. In J. Phillips (Ed.), *Ancient Egypt, The Aegean and the Near East*, pp. 239–241. San Antonio: Van Siclen.

Hood, M. S. F. (1957). Knossos. *Archaeological Reports*, 21–25.

Hood, M. S. F. (1961–1962). Knossos. *Archaeological Reports*, 25–29.

Hood, M. S. F., and P. De Jong (1952). Late Minoan Warrior Graves from Ayios Ioannes and the New Hospital Site at Knossos. *Annual of the British School at Athens 47*, 243–277.

Horden, P., and N. Purcell (2000). *The Corrupting Sea*. London: Blackwell.

Hornung, E. (1992). *Idea into Image: Essays on Ancient Egyptian Thought*. Princeton: Timken.

Horowitz, W., and T. Oshima (2002). Two More Cuneiform Finds from Hazor. *Israel Exploration Journal 52*, 179–186.

Huot, J.-L. (1989). Scéne sur un Bol de Pierre de Larsa. In J.-L. Huot (Ed.), *Larsa: Travaux de 1985*, pp. 175–183. Paris: Editions Recherche sur les Civilisations.

Hurtado, V. (1997). The Dynamics of the Occupation of the Middle Basin of the River Guadiana Between the Fourth and Second Millennia BC: An Interpretational Hypothesis. In M. Díaz-Andreu and S. Keay (Eds.), *The Archaeology of Iberia*, pp. 98–127. London: Routledge.

Iakovidis, S., and E. B. French (2003). *Archaeological Atlas of Mycenae*. Athens: The Archaeological Society at Athens.

Ingholt, H. (1992). *Rapport Préliminaire sur Sept Campagnes de Fouilles à Hama en Syrie (1932–1938)*. Copenhagen: Wrapp.

Jackson, A. (2003). The Ground Stone Industry. In E. Peltenburg (Ed.), *The Colonisation and Settlement of Cyprus. Investigations at Kissonerga-Mylouthkia, 1976–1996. (Lemba Archaeological Project, Cyprus III.1)*, pp. 35–40. Sävedalen: Paul Åström.

Jacobsson, I. (1994). *Aegyptiaca from Late Bronze Age Cyprus*. Josered: Paul Åströms.

James, F. W. (1966). *The Iron Age at Beth Shan: A Study of Levels VI-IV*. Philadelphia: University Museum.

Janssen, J. J. (1975a). *Commodity Prices from the Ramesside Period: An Economic Study of the Village of the Necropolis Workers*. Leiden: Brill.

Janssen, J. J. (1975b). Prolegomena to the Study of Egypt's Economic History During the New Kingdom. *Studien zur Altägyptishen Kultur 3*, 127–185.

Janssen, J. J. (1982). Gift-giving in Ancient Egypt as an Economic Feature. *Journal of Egyptian Archaeology 68*, 253–258.

Janssen, M. A., T. A. Kohler, and M. Scheffer (2003). Sunk-Cost Effects and Vulnerability to Collapse in Ancient Societies. *Current Anthropology 44.5*, 722–728.

Jéquier, M. G. (1934). Vases de Pierre de la VIe dynastie. *Annales du Service des Antiquités de l'Egypte 34*, 97–113.

Jéquier, M. G. (1935). Vases de Pierre de la VIe Dynastie. Note Additionelle. *Annales du Service des Antiquités de l'Egypte 35*, 160.

Jidejian, N. (1971). *Byblos Through the Ages*. Beirut: Dar el-Machreq.

Joannes, F. (1991). Létain de l'Elam à Mari. In L. De Meyer and H. Gasche (Eds.), *M'esopotamie et Elam*, pp. 65–76. Ghent: University of Ghent.

Johnston, J. (1980). *Maroni de Chypre*. Göteborg: Paul Åströms.

Jones, A. H. M. (1964). *The Later Roman Empire*. Oxford: Oxford University Press.

Jones, R. E., and L. Vagnetti (1997). Traders and Craftsmen in the Central Mediterranean: Archaeological Evidence and Archaeometric Research. In N. Gale (Ed.), *Bronze Age Trade in the East Mediterranean*, pp. 127–147. Göteborg: Paul Åströms.

Joukowsky, M. S. (1986). *Prehistoric Aphrodisias*. Louvain: Université Catholique de Louvain.

Kaiser, B. (1980). Mykenische Steingefässe und Verwandtes im Magazin zu Nauplia. *Athenische Mitteilungen 95*, 1–19.

Karageorghis, V. (1960). Fouilles de Kition 1959. *Bulletin de Correspondance Héllenique 84*, 504–588.

Karageorghis, V. (1974). *Excavations at Kition*. Nicosia: Department of Antiquities.

Karageorghis, V. (1976). Chroniques des Fouilles et Découvertes Archéologiques à Chypre en 1975. *Bulletin de Correspondences Héllenique 100*, 839–906.

Karageorghis, V. (1990). *Tombs at Paleopaphos*. Nicosia: Leventis Foundation.

Karageorghis, V. (1996). Some Aspects of the Maritime Trade of Cyprus. In V. Karageorghis and D. Michaelides (Eds.), *The Development of the Cypriot Economy: From the Prehistoric Period to the Present Day*, pp. 61–70. Nicosia: Bank of Cyprus.

Karageorghis, V. (Ed.) (2000). *Ancient Art from Cyprus: The Cesnola Collection in the Metropolitan Museum of Art*. New York: Abrams.

Karetsou, A. (1974). Ieron Koriphis Ioukta. *Praktika tis en Athinais Etaireias 25*, 228–239.

Karetsou, A. (1975). To Iero Koriphis tou Ioukta. *Praktika tis en Athinais Etaireias 26*, 330–342.

Karetsou, A. (1978). To Iero Koriphis Ioukta. *Praktika tis en Athinais Etaireias 29*, 232–258.

Karetsou, A. (2000). *Kriti-Egyptos. Politismiki Desmi triun Chilietion. Katalogos*. Athens: Kapon.

Karo, G. (1930–1933). *Die Schachtgraber von Mykenai*. Munich: Bruckmann.

Kemp, B. J. (1989). *Ancient Egypt: Anatomy of a Civilisation*. London: Routledge.

Kemp, B. J. (1996). Old Kingdom, Middle Kingdom and Second Intermediate Period c.2686–1552 BC. In B. G. Trigger, B. J. Kemp, D. O'Connor, and A. B. Lloyd (Eds.), *Ancient Egypt: A Social History*, pp. 71–174. Cambridge: Cambridge University Press.

Kemp, B. J., and R. S. Merrillees (1982). *Minoan Pottery in Second Millennium Egypt*. Mainz: Phillipp von Zabern.

Kempinski, A. (1974). Tell el-'Ajjul - Beth-Aglayim or Sharuhen. *Israel Exploration Journal 24*, 145–152.

Kenyon, K. (1960). *Excavations at Jericho I*. London: Harrison Press.

Kenyon, K. (1965). *Excavations at Jericho II. The Tombs Excavated in 1955–1958*. London: Harrison Press.

Kestemont, G. (1977). Remarques sur les Aspects Juridiques du Commerce dans le Proche-Orient du XIV Siècle avant Notre ère. *Iraq 39*, 191–201.

Keswani, P. (2004). *Mortuary Ritual and Society in Bronze Age Cyprus*. London: Equinox.

Killebrew, A. E. (2004). New Kingdom Egyptian-Style Pottery in Canaan: Implications for Egyptian Rule in Canaan during the 19th and early 20th Dynasties. In G. N. Knoppers and A. Hirsch (Eds.), *Egypt, Israel and the Ancient Mediterranean World*, pp. 309–343. Leiden: Brill.

King, J. C. H. (1977). *Smoking Pipes of the North American Indian*. London: British Museum.

Kirman, A. (1993). Ants, Rationality and Recruitment. *Quarterly Journal of Economics 108*, 137–156.

Kitchen, K. A. (1987). The Basics of Egyptian Chronology in Relation to the Bronze Age. In P. Astrom (Ed.), *High, Middle or Low? Acts of an International Colloquium on Absolute Chronology Held at the University of Gothenburg 20th–22nd August 1987*, pp. 37–55. Gothenburg: Paul Åströms.

Kitchen, K. A. (1993). *Ramesside Inscriptions I*. Oxford: Blackwell.

Kitchen, K. A. (2000). The Historical Chronology of Ancient Egypt: A Current Assessment. In M. Bietak (Ed.), *The Synchronisation of Civilisations in the Eastern Mediterranean in the Second Millennium B.C.*, pp. 39–52. Vienna: Royal Austrian Academy.

Klemm, R., and D. D. Klemm (1993). *Steine und Steinbrüche im Alten ägypten*. Berlin: Springer-Verlag.

Knapp, A. B. (1983). An Alashiyan Merchant at Ugarit. *Tel Aviv 10*, 38–45.

Knapp, A. B. (1991). Spice, Drugs, Grain and Grog: Organic Goods in Bronze Age East Mediterranean Trade. In N. H. Gale (Ed.), *Bronze Age Trade in the Mediterranean*, pp. 21–68. Gothenburg: Paul Åströms.

Knapp, A. B. (1997). Mediterranean Maritime Landscapes: Transport, Trade, and Society on Late Bronze Age Cyprus. In S. Swiny, R. L. Hohlfelder, and H. Wylde Swiny (Eds.), *Res Maritimae: Cyprus and the Eastern*

*Mediterranean from Prehistory to Late Antiquity*, pp. 153–162. Atlanta: Cyprus and American Archaeological Research Institute.

Knapp, A. B. (1999). Thalassocracies in Bronze Age Eastern Mediterranean Trade: Making and Breaking a Myth. *World Archaeology 24(3)*, 332–347.

Knapp, A. B., and J. F. Cherry (1994). *Provenience Studies and Bronze Age Cyprus. Production, Exchange and Politico-Economic Change*. Madison: Prehistory Press.

Knappett, C. (1999a). Assessing a Polity: Protopalatial Crete. *American Journal of Archaeology 103*, 615–639.

Knappett, C. (1999b). Tradition and Innovation in Pottery-forming Technology: Wheel-throwing at Middle Minoan Knossos. *Annual of the British School at Athens 94*, 101–129.

Knappett, C. (2000). The Provenance of Red Lustrous Wheel-Made Ware: Cyprus, Syria, or Anatolia? *Internet Archaeology 9*. http://intarch.ac.uk/journal/issue9/knappett_index.html

Koepke, J., E. Seidel, and H. Kreuzer (2002). Ophiolites on the Southern Aegean islands of Crete, Karpathos and Rhodes: Composition, Geochronology and Position Within the Ophiolite Belts of the Eastern Mediterranean. *Lithos 65*, 183–203.

Kohl, P. L. (1977). A Note on Chlorite Artefacts from Shahr-I Sokhta. *East and West 27*, 111–127.

Kohlmeyer, K., E. Strommenger, and A. Abou-Assaf (1982). *Land des Baal. Syrien-Forum der Völker und Kulturen*. Mainz: Philipp von Zabern.

Komter, A. (2001). Heirlooms, Nikes and Bribes: Towards a Sociology of Things. *Sociology 35*, 59–75.

Kopytoff, I. (1986). The Cultural Biography of Things: Commoditisation as a Process. In A. Appadurai (Ed.), *The Social Life of Things: Commodities in Cultural Perspective*, pp. 64–91. Cambridge: Cambridge University Press.

Kroeper, K. (1985). Some Stone Vessels from Minshat Abu Omar—Eastern Delta. *Varia Antiquorum 1*, 51–57.

Kroeper, K. (1992). Tombs of the Elite in Minshat Abu Omar. In E. C. M. van den Brink (Ed.), *The Nile Delta in Transition: 4th–3rd Millennium BC*, pp. 127–150. Tel Aviv: Pinkhas.

Kroeper, K., and D. Wildung (1985). *Minshat Abu Omar*. Munich: Karl M. Lipp.

Krzyszkowska, O. H. (1988). Ivory in the Aegean Bronze Age: Elephant Tusk or Hippopotamus Ivory? *Annual of the British School at Athens 83*, 210–234.

Krzyszkowska, O. H. (2005). *Aegean Seals: An Introduction*. London: Institute of Classical Studies.

Krzyzaniak, L. (1989). Recent Archaeological Evidence on the Earliest Settlement in the Eastern Nile Delta. In L. Krzyzaniak and M. Kobusiewicz (Eds.), *Late Prehistory of the Nile Basin and the Sahara*, pp. 267–285. Poznan: Archaeological Museum.

Lackenbacher, S. (1995). Une Correspondence entre l'Administration du Pharaon Meneptah e le Roi d'Ougarit. In M. Yon, M. Sznycer, and P. Bordreuil (Eds.), *Le Pays d'Ougarit autour de 1200 av. J.-C. (Ras Shamra-Ougarit XI)*, pp. 77–84. Paris: Editions Recherche sur les Civilisations.

Lacovara, P. (1991). The Stone Vase Deposit at Kerma. In W. V. Davies (Ed.), *Egypt and Africa: Nubia from Prehistory to Islam*, pp. 118–128. London: British Museum.

Lamberg-Karlovsky, C. C. (1975). Third Millennium Modes of Exchange and Modes of Production. In J. A. Sabloff and C. C. Lamberg-Karlovsky (Eds.), *Ancient Civilization and Trade*, pp. 341–368. Albuquerque: University of New Mexico Press.

Lamberg-Karlovsky, C. C. (1988). The "Inter-Cultural Style" Carved Vessels. *Iranica Antiqua 23*, 45–95.

Lambert, M. (1976). Tablette de Suse avec Cachet du Golfe. *Revue d'Assyriologie et d'Archéologie Orientale 70*, 71–72.

Lambrou-Phillipson, C. (1991). Seafaring in the Bronze Age Mediterranean: The Parameters Involved in Maritime Travel. In R. Laffineur (Ed.), *THALASSA: L'égée préhistorique et la mer*, pp. 11–21. Liège: University of Liège.

Lambrou-Phillipson, C. (1993). Ugarit: A Late Bronze Age Thalassocracy? The Evidence of the Textual Sources. *Orientalia 62*, 163–170.

Lansing, A. (1917). *Excavations at Assasif, Thebes*. New York: Metropolitan Museum of Art.

Larsen, M. T. (1967). *Old Assyrian Caravan Procedures*. Instanbul: Nederlands Historische-Archaeologische Instituut.

Larsen, M. T. (1987). Commercial Networks in the Ancient Near East. In M. Rowlands, M. T. Larsen, and K. Kristiansen (Eds.), *Centre and Periphery in the Ancient World*, pp. 47–56. Cambridge: Cambridge University Press.

Lauer, P. (1939). *Fouilles à Saqqarah: le Pyramide à Degrees*. Cairo: L'Institut Français d'Archéologie Orientale.

Laufer, B. (1912). *Jade: A Study in Chinese Archaeology and Religion*. New York: Dover Reprint.

Lazzarini, L. (2004). Marmor Taenarium (Rosso Antico). Fortuna e Diffusione, Cavatura e Lavorazione, Caratterizzazione Scientifica e Provenienza di suoi Manufatti. In M. F. Santi (Ed.), *Studi di Archeologia in Onore di Gustavo Traversari*, pp. 583–599. Rome: Giorgio Bretschneider.

Leach, J. W., and E. Leach (Eds.) (1983). *The Kula: New Perspectives on Massim Exchange*. Cambridge: Cambridge University Press.

Leemans, W. F. (1977). The Importance of Trade: Some Introductory Remarks. *Iraq 39*, 1–10.

Leinwand, N. W. (1980). A Ladle from Shaft Grave III at Mycenae. *American Journal of Archaeology 84*, 519–521.

Lemonnier, P. (1993). Pigs as Ordinary Wealth: Technical Logic, Exchange and Leadership in New Guinea. In P. Lemonnier (Ed.), *Technological Choices: Transformation in Material Cultures Since the Neolithic*, pp. 126–156. London: Routledge.

Levi, D. (1961–1962). La Tomba a Tholos di Kamilari Presso a Festos. *Annuario 23-4*, 7–148.

Lichtheim, M. (1975). *Ancient Egyptian Literature I: The Old and Middle Kingdoms*. Berkley: University of California Press.

Lilyquist, C. (1988). The Gold Bowl Naming General Djehuty. *Metropolitan Museum Journal 23*, 5–68.

Lilyquist, C. (1993). Granulation and Glass: Chronological and Stylistic Investigations at Selected Sites, ca. 2500–1400 B.C.E. *Bulletin of the American School of Oriental Research 290-1*, 29–75.

Lilyquist, C. (1995). *Egyptian Stone Vessels: Khian through Thutmosis IV*. New York: Metropolitan Museum of Art.

Lilyquist, C. (1996). Stone Vessels at Kamid el-Loz: Egyptian, Egyptianizing, or non-Egyptian? A question at sites from the Sudan to Iraq to the Greek Mainland. In R. Hachmann (Ed.), *Kamid el-Loz 16: Schatzhaus Studien*, pp. 133–173. Bonn: Saarbrucker Beitrage Zur Altertumskunde.

Lilyquist, C. (2003). *The Tomb of Three Foreign Wives of Thutmosis III*. New York: Metropolitan Museum of Art.

Limet, H. (1985). Les Relations entre Mari et la Côte Méditerranéenne sous le Règne de Zimri-Lim. In E. Gubel and E. Lipinski (Eds.), *Phoenicia and Its Neighbours*, pp. 13–20. Leuven: Peeters.

Lipinski, E. (1988). The Socio-economic Condition of the Clergy in the Kingdom of Ugarit. In M. Heltzer and E. Lipinski (Eds.), *Society and Economy in the Eastern Mediterranean, c.1500–1000 B.C.*, pp. 125–150. Leuven: Peeters.

Liverani, M. (1990). *Prestige and Interest: International Relations in the Near East ca.1600–1100 B.C.* Padua: Sargon.

Liverani, M. (2000). The Great Powers Club. In R. Cohen and R. Westbrook (Eds.), *Amarna Diplomacy: The Beginnings of International Relations*, pp. 15–27. Baltimore: John Hopkins.

Liverani, M. (2003). The Influence of Political Institutions on Trade in the Ancient Near East (Late Bronze Age to Early Iron Age). In C. Zaccagnini (Ed.), *Mercanti e Politica nel Mondo Antico*, pp. 119–137. Rome: Bretschneider.

Logue, W. (2004). Set in Stone: The Role of Relief-Carved Stone Vessels in Neopalatial Minoan Elite Propaganda. *Annual of the British School at Athens 99*, 149–172.

Loud, G. (1948). *Megiddo II*. Chicago: University of Chicago Press.

Löwe, W. (1996). *Spätbronzezeitliche Bestattungen auf Kreta*. Oxford: Tempus Reparatum.

Lucas, A., and J. Harris (1962). *Ancient Egyptian Materials and Industries*. London: E. Arnold.

Luke, C. (2002). Mesoamerican White Stone Vase Traditions and the Use of Colour. In L. Lazzarini (Ed.), *Asmosia VI: Interdisciplinary Studies on Ancient Stone*, pp. 507–516. Padua: Bottega D'Erasmo.

Luke, C. (2006). Carving Luxury: Late Classic White Stone Vase Traditions in Mesoamerica. In Y. M. Rowan and J. R. Ebeling (Eds.), *New Approaches to Old Stones: Recent Studies of Ground Stone Artifacts*. London: Equinox.

Luke, C., R. H. Tykot, and R. W. Scott (2006). Petrographic And Stable Isotope Analyses of Late Classic Ulúa Marble Vases And Potential Sources. *Archaeometry 48.1*, 13–29.

Macalister, R. A. S. (1912). *Excavations at Gezer*. London: John Murray.

MacDonald, C. (1987). A Knossian Weapon Workshop in LMII and IIIA. In R. Hägg and N. Marinatos (Eds.), *The Function of the Minoan Palace*, pp. 293–295. Gothenburg: Paul Åströms.

MacDonald, C. F. (2002). The Neopalatial Palaces of Knossos. In J. Driessen, I. Schoep, and R. Laffineur (Eds.), *Monuments of Minos: Rethinking the Minoan Palaces*, pp. 37–64. Liège: University of Liège and University of Texas at Austin (Aegaeum 23).

MacGuire, J. D. (1894). *A Study of Primitive Methods of Drilling*. Washington: Smithsonian Annual Reports.

MacGuire, L. C. (1995). Tell el-Dab'a: The Cypriot Connection. In W. V. Davies and L. Schofield (Eds.), *Egypt, the Aegean and the Levant: Interconnections in the Second Millennium B.C.*, pp. 54–65. London: British Museum.

MacKay, E. J. H., and M. A. Murray (1952). *City of Shepherd Kings and Ancient Gaza V*. London: Bernard Quaritch.

Madjidzadeh, Y. (2003). *Jiroft: The Earliest Oriental Civilization*. Tehran: Ministry of Culture and Islamic Guidance.

Magee, P., D. Barber, M. Sobur, and S. Jasim (2005). Sourcing Iron Age Softstone Artefacts in Southeastern Arabia: Results from a Programme of Analysis Using Inductively Coupled Plasma-Mass Spectrometry/Optical Emission Spectrometry (ICP-MS/OES). *Arabian Archaeology and Epigraphy 16*, 129–143.

Magen, Y. (2002). *The Stone Vessel Industry in the Second Temple Period: Excavations at Hizma and the Jerusalem Temple Mount*. Jerusalem: Israel Antiquities Authority.

Maggidis, C. (1998). From Polis to Necropolis: Social Ranking from Architectural and Mortuary Evidence in the Minoan Cemetery at Phourni, Archanes. In K. Branigan (Ed.), *Cemetery and Society in the Aegean Bronze Age*, pp. 87–102. Sheffield: Sheffield Academic Press.

Malinowski, B. (1950). *Argonauts of the Western Pacific*. London: Routledge & Kegan Paul.

Mallet, J. (1987). Le Temple aux Rhytons. In M. Yon (Ed.), *Le Centre de la Ville. Ras-Shamra-Ougarit III. 38e-44e campagnes (1978–1984)*, pp. 213–248. Paris: Etudes Recherche sur les Civilisations.

Mallet, J., and V. Matoïan (2001). Une Maison au Sud du Temple Aux Rhytons (Fouilles 1979–1990). In M. Yon and D. Arnaud (Eds.), *Etudes Ougaritiques I. Travaux 1985–1995. Ras Shamra-Ougarit XIV*, pp. 83–190. Padua: Etudes Recherche sur les Civilisations.

Mallory-Greenough, L. M. (2002). The Geographical, Spatial and Temporal Distribution of Predynastic and First Dynasty Basalt Vessels. *Journal of Egyptian Archaeology 88*, 67–93.

Mallory-Greenough, L. M., J. D. Greenough, and J. V. Owen (1999). The Stone Sources of Predynastic Basalt Vessels: Mineralogical Evidence for Quarries in Northern Egypt. *Journal of Archaeological Science 26*, 1261–1272.

Malpas, J. (1992). Serpentine and the Geology of Serpentinized Rocks. In B. A. Roberts and J. Proctor (Eds.), *The Ecology Areas with Serpentinized Rocks*, pp. 7–30. London: Kluwer.

Manen, C. (2003). La Vaisselle de Pierre Pré-céramique de *Shillourokambos* (Parekklisha). Approche Technique et Typologique des Secteurs 1, 2 et 4. In J. Guilaine and A. LeBrun (Eds.), *Le Néolithique de Chypre*, pp. 187–201. Athens: école Fran caise d'Athénes.

Manniche, L. (1989). *An Ancient Egyptian Herbal*. London: British Museum.

Manning, S. W. (1995). *The Absolute Chronology of the Aegean Early Bronze Age*. Sheffield: Sheffield Academic Press.

Manning, S. W., W. Bronk Ramsey, C. Kutschera, T. Higham, B. Kromer, P. Steier, and E. M. Wild (2006). Chronology for the Aegean Late Bronze Age 1700–1400 B.C. Millennium B.C. *Science 312*, 565–569.

Mantzourani, E., and A. Theodorou (1989). An Attempt to Delineate the Sea-Routes Between Crete and Cyprus During the Bronze Age. In V. Karageorghis (Ed.), *The Civilisations of the Aegean and Their Diffusion in Cyprus and the Eastern Mediterranean 2000–600 B.C.*, pp. 38–55. Larnaca: Pierides Foundation.

Marangou, L. (1990). *Cycladic Culture. Naxos in the 3rd Millennium BC*. Athens: Goulandris Foundation.

Marcus, E. (2002a). Early Seafaring and Maritime Activity in the Southern Levant from Prehistory Through the Third Millennium BC. In E. C. M. van den Brink and T. E. Levy (Eds.), *Egypt and the Levant: Interrelations from the 4th through the early 3rd Millennium BC*, pp. 403–417. London: Leicester University Press.

Marcus, E. (2002b). The Southern Levant and Maritime Trade During the Middle Bronze IIA Period. In E. D. Oren and S. Ahituv (Eds.), *Aharon Kempinski Memorial Volume: Studies in Archaeology and Related Disciplines*, pp. 241–263. Beer-Sheva: Ben-Gurion University of the Negev Press.

Marfoe, L. (1987). Cedar Forest to Silver Mountain: Social Change and the Development of Long-Distance Trade in Early Near Eastern Societies. In M. Rowlands, M. Larsen, and K. Kristiansen (Eds.), *Centre and Periphery in the Ancient World*, pp. 25–35. Cambridge: Cambridge University Press.

Margueron, J. (1977). Ras Shamra 1975 et 1976. Rapport Préliminaire sur les Campagnes d'Automne. *Syria 54*, 151–188.

Marinatos, S. (1930–1931). Dio Proimoi Minoiki Taphoi ek Vorou Mesaras. *Archaiologikon Deltion 13*, 137–170.

Marinatos, S. (1974). *Excavations at Thera V*. Athens: Archaeological Society of Athens.

Martin, S., and N. Grube (2000). *Chronicle of the Maya Kings and Queens: Deciphering the Dynasties of the Ancient Maya*. London: Thames & Hudson.

Martlew, H. (2004). Minoan and Mycenaean Technology as Revealed Through Organic Residue Analysis. In J. Bourriau and J. Phillips (Eds.), *Invention and Innovation: The Social Context of Technological Change 2. Egypt, the Aegean and the Near East 1650–1150 BC*, pp. 121–148. Oxford: Oxbow.

Marx, K. (1969). *Das Kapital*. Moscow: Progress.

Mathiassen, T. (1935). Archaeology in Greenland. *Antiquity 9*, 195–203.

Matoïan, V., and A. Bouquillon (2003). Vitreous Materials in Ugarit: New Data. In T. Potts, M. Roaf, and D. Stein (Eds.), *Culture Through Objects: Ancient Near Eastern Studies in Honour of P.R.S. Moorey*, pp. 333–346. Oxford: Griffith Institute.

Matsas, D. (1995). Minoan Long-Distance Trade. In R. Laffineur and W.-D. Niemeier (Eds.), *Politeia. Society and State in the Aegean Bronze Age*, pp. 235–248. Liège: University of Liège.

Matthiae, P. (1979). Scavi a Tell Mardikh-Ebla 1978. Rapporto Sommario. *Studi Eblaiti 1*, 129–184.

Matthiae, P., F. Pinnock, and G. Scandone-Matthiae (1995). *Ebla: Alla Origini della Civiltà Urbana*. Milan: Electa.

Matz, F. (1969). *Corpus der Minoischen und Mykenischen Siegel: Die Siegel der Vorpalastzeit. II.1*. Berlin: Gebr Mann.

Mauss, M. (1990). *The Gift: The Form and Reason for Exchange in Archaic Societies*. London: Routledge.

Mauss, M., and E. Durkheim (1963). *Primitive Classification*. London: Cohen West.

Mazar, A. (1990). *Archaeology of the Land of the Bible*. New York: Doubleday.

Mazar, B. (1985). *Excavations at Tell Qasile, Part 2: The Philistine Sanctuary: Various Finds, The Pottery, Conclusions, Appendices*. Jerusalem: Hamakar.

McBrearty, S., and A. S. Brooks (2000). The Revolution That Wasn't: A New Interpretation of the Origin of Modern Human Behavior. *Journal of Human Evolution 39*, 453–563.

McCartney, A. P. (1970). "Pottery" in the Aleutian Islands. *American Antiquity 35.1*, 105–108.

McCawley, W. (1996). *The First Angelinos: The Gabrielino Indians of Los Angeles*. Banning and Novato, California: Malik Museum and Ballena Press.

McClennan, M. C. (1988). The Excavation of Mangia V/Tomb 5 and Tomb 6. *Report of the Department of Antiquities, Cyprus 1*, 206–222.

McGovern, P. E., J. Bourriau, G. Harbottle, and S. J. Allen (1994). The Archaeological Origins and Significance of the Dolphin Vase. *Bulletin of the American Schools of Oriental Research 296*, 31–44.

McGovern, P. E., and G. Harbottle (1997). "Hyksos" Trade Between Tell el-Dab'a and the Levant: A Neutron Activation Study of the Canaanite Jar. In E. Oren (Ed.), *The Hyksos: New Historical and Archaeological Perspectives*, pp. 141–157. Philadelphia: University Museum.

McGraw, A. P., P. E. Tetlock, and O. V. Kristel (2003). The Limits of Fungibility: Relational Schemata and the Value of Things. *Journal of Consumer Research 30*, 219–229.

Mellaart, J. (1959). The Royal Treasure of Dorak. *Illustrated London News 28.11*, 754–758.

Mellaart, J. (1964). Excavations at Catal Hüyük 1963. Third Preliminary Report. *Anatolian Studies 14*, 39–120.

Mellaart, J. (1970a). *Excavations at Hacilar I*. Edinburgh: Edinburgh University Press.

Mellaart, J. (1970b). *Excavations at Hacilar II*. Edinburgh: Edinburgh University Press.

Mellaart, J., and A. Murray (1995). *Beycesultan: Late Bronze Age and Phrygian Pottery and Middle and Late Bronze Age Small Objects (Vol. III.2)*. London: British Institute of Archaeology at Ankara.

Mercer, S. A. B. (1952). *The Pyramid Texts I*. New York: Longmans.

Merrick, H. V. (1973). Aspects of the Size and Shape Variation of the East African Stone Bowls. *Azania 8*, 115–130.

Merrick, H. V., and F. H. Brown (1984). Obsidian Sources and Patterns of Source Utilization in Kenya and Northern Tanzania: Some Initial Findings. *The African Archaeological Review 2*, 129–152.

Merrillees, R. S. (1962). Opium Trade in the Bronze Age Levant. *Antiquity 36*, 287–292.

Merrillees, R. S. (1974). Ancient Egypt's Silent Majority. In R. S. Merrillees (Ed.), *Trade and Transcendence in the Bronze Age Levant*, pp. 13–41. Gothenburg: Paul Åströms.

Merrillees, R. S., and J. N. Tubb (1979). A Syro/Cilician Jug from Middle Bronze Age Cyprus. *Report of the Department of Antiquities of Cyprus*, 223–228.

Méry, S. (2000). *Les Céramiques d'Oman et l'Asie Moyenne*. Paris: CNRS Editions.

Metaxa-Muhly, P. (1981). *Minoan Stone Libation Tables*. Ph.D. thesis, Bryn Mawr College.

Michailidou, A. (1990). The Lead Weights from Akrotiri: The Archaeological Record. In D. A. Hardy and A. C. Renfrew (Eds.), *Thera in the Aegean World III*, pp. 407–419. London: Thera Foundation.

Michel, C. (1992). Les "Diamants" du Roi de Mari. In J.-M. Durand (Ed.), *Florilegium Marianum 1. Recueil d'études en l'Honneur de Michel Fleury*, pp. 127–136. Paris: Nouvelles Assyriologiques Brèves et Utilitaires.

Midant-Reynes, B. (2003). *Aux Origines de l'égypte*. Paris: Fayard.

Milgram, S. (1967). The Small-World Problem. *Psychology Today 1*, 61–67.

Miller, D. (1985). *Artefacts as Categories: A Study of Ceramic Variability in Central India*. Cambridge: Cambridge University Press.

Miller, D. (1995). Consumption Studies in Anthropology. In D. Miller (Ed.), *Acknowledging Consumption*, pp. 264–295. London: Routledge.

Miller, M. A. (1993). On the Eve of Collapse: Maya Art of the Eighth Century. In J. A. Sabloff and J. S. Henderson (Eds.), *Lowland Maya Civilisation in the Eighth Century AD*, pp. 355–414. Washington: Dumbarton Oaks Research Library and Collection.

Millet, N. (1987). The First Appearance of the Loose-Footed Squaresail Rig in the Mediterranean. *Journal of the Society for the Study of Egyptian Antiquities 17(3)*, 90–91.

Minault-Gout, A. (1986). *Le Mastaba d'Ima-Pépi*. Cairo: L'Institut Français d'Archéologie Orientale.

Minault-Gout, A. (1993). Sur les Vases Jubilaires et leur Diffusion. In C. Berger and B. Mathieu (Eds.), *Etudes sur l'Ancien Empire et la nécropole de Saqqara dédiées à Jean-Philippe Lauer*, pp. 305–314. Montpellier: Université de Montpellier.

Miron, R. (1990). *Das 'Schatzhaus' in Palastbereich. Die Funde*. Bonn: Rudolph Habelt.

Moholy-Nagy, H. (1983). Jarmo Artifacts of Pecked and Ground Stone and of Shell. In L. S. Braidwood, R. J. Braidwood, B. Howe, C. A. Reed, and P. J. Watson (Eds.), *Prehistoric Archaeology Along the Zagros Flanks*, pp. 289–346. Chicago: Oriental Institute.

Molm, L. D., G. Peterson, and N. Takahashi (2001). The Value of Exchange. *Social Forces 80(1)*, 159–184.

Monaco, G. (1941). Scavi Nella Zona Micenea di Jaliso 1935–6. *Clara Rhodos 10*, 41–183.

Money-Coutts, M. (1936). A Stone Bowl and Lid from Byblos. *Berytus 3*, 129–136.

Montet, P. (1928). *Byblos et L'Egypte*. Paris: Paul Geuthner.

Moorey, P. R. S. (1987). On Tracking Cultural Transfers in Prehistory: The Case of Egypt and Lower Mesopotamia in the Fourth Millennium BC. In M. Rowlands, M. Larsen, and K. Kristiansen (Eds.), *Centre and Periphery in the Ancient World*, pp. 36–46. Cambridge: Cambridge University Press.

Moorey, P. R. S. (1994). *Ancient Mesopotamian Materials and Industries*. Oxford: Oxford University Press.

Moorey, P. R. S. (2001). The Mobility of Artisans and Opportunities for Technological Transfer Between Western Asia and Egypt in the Late Bronze Age. In A. J. Shortland (Ed.), *The Social Context of Technological Change. Egypt and the Near East 1650–1550 BC*, pp. 1–14. Oxford: Oxbow.

Moran, W. L. (1987). *The Amarna Letters*. Baltimore: John Hopkins.

Morgan, L. (1988). *The Miniature Wall Paintings of Thera*. Cambridge: Cambridge University Press.

Morricone, L. (1972). Coo - Scavi e Scoperte nel 'Serraglio' E in Localita Minori (1935–1943). *Annuario 35*, 139–396.

Morris, D. (1991). Stone Bowls in the Northern Cape: A New Find and Its Possible Context. *The South African Archaeological Bulletin 46*, 38–40.

Muhly, J. D. (1996). The Significance of Metals in the Late Bronze Age Economy of Cyprus. In V. Karageorghis and D. Michaelides (Eds.), *The Development of the Cypriot Economy: From the Prehistoric Period to the Present Day*, pp. 44–59. Nicosia: University of Cyprus.

Müller, S. (1999). Idiomorphies stin Tafiki Architectoniki tou Medeona Fokidos. In P. Dakoronia (Ed.), *H Periferia tou Mykenaikou Kosmou: A' Diepistemoniko Sympsio, Lamia 1994*, pp. 223–234. Lamia: TAPA.

Münch, H.-H. (2000). Categorizing Archaeological Finds: The Funerary Material of Queen Hetepheres I at Giza. *Antiquity 74*, 898–908.

Murnane, W. J. (1981). The Sed Festival: A Problem in Historical Method. *Mitteilungen des Deutschen Archäologischen Instituts Abteilung Kairo 37*, 369–376.

Murphy, J. (1998). Ideology, Rites and Rituals: A View of Prepalatial Minoan Tholoi. In K. Branigan (Ed.), *Cemetery and Society in the Aegean Bronze Age*, pp. 27–40. Sheffield: Sheffield Academic Press.

Murray, A. S., A. H. Smith, and H. B. Walters (1900). *Excavations in Cyprus*. London: British Museum.

Mussi, M., J. Cinq-Mars, and P. Bolduc (2000). Echoes From the Mammoth Steppe. In W. Roebroeks (Ed.), *Hunters of the Golden Age: The Mid Upper Palaeolithic of Eurasia, 30,000–20,000 BP*, pp. 105–124. Leiden: Leiden University Press.

Myers, J. W., E. E. Myers, and G. Cadogan (1914). *Handbook of the Cesnola Collection of Antiquities from Cyprus*. New York: Metropolitan Museum.

Mylonas, G. E. (1959). *Aghios Kosmas: An Early Bronze Age Settlement and Cemetery in Attica*. Princeton: Princeton University Press.

Mylonas, G. E. (1973). *O Taphikos Kyklos B ton Mikenon*. Athens: Athenais Archaiologiki Etaireia.

Nakou, G. (1997). The Role of Poliochni and the North Aegean in the Development of Aegean Metallurgy. In C. G. Doumas and V. La Rosa (Eds.), *Poliochni e l'Antica Età del Bronzo Nell'Egeo Settentrionale*, pp. 634–648. Athens: Scuola archeologica italiana di Atene.

Nash, J. F. (1950). The Bargaining Problem. *Econometrica 18*, 155–162.

Naville, E. (1914). *The Cemeteries of Abydos I*. London: Kegan Paul.

Negbi, M., and O. Negbi (2002). The Painted Plaster Floor of the Tel Kabri Palace: Reflections on Saffron Domestication in the Bronze Age. In E. D. Oren and S. Ahituv (Eds.), *Aharon Kempinski Memorial Volume. Studies in Archaeology and Related Disciplines*, pp. 325–340. Beer-Sheva: Ben-Gurion University of the Negev Press.

Newberry, P. E. (1893). *Beni Hasan I*. London: Egypt Exploration Fund.

Niemeier, B., and W.-D. Niemeier (1997). Milet 1994–1995. Projekt Minoisch-mykenisches bis Protogeometrisches Milet: Zielsetzung und Grabungen auf dem Stadionhügel und am Athenatempel. *Archaologischer Anzeiger*, 189–248.

Niemeier, B., and W.-D. Niemeier (2000). Aegean Frescoes in Syria-Palestine: Alalakh and Tel Kabri. In E. S. Sherratt (Ed.), *The Wall-Paintings of Thera: Proceedings of the First International Symposium*, pp. 763–800. Athens: Thera Foundation.

North, D. (1977). Markets and Other Allocation Systems in History: The Challenge of Karl Polanyi. *Journal of European Economic History 6(3)*, 703–716.

Novák, M., and P. Pfälzner (2003). Ausgrabungen im bronzezeitlichen Palast von Tall Misrife-Qatna 2002. *Mitteilungen Des Deutschen Orient-Gesellschaft zu Berlin 135*, 131–165.

Nylander, C. (1966). The Toothed Chisel in Pasargadae: Further Notes on Old Persian Stonecutting. *American Journal of Archaeology 70(4)*, 373–376.

Ogden, J. (2000). Metals. In P. T. Nicholson and I. Shaw (Eds.), *Ancient Egyptian Materials and Technologies*, pp. 148–176. Cambridge: Cambridge University Press.

Orel, S. E. (2000). A Reexamination of the 1943–1952 Excavations at Kom el-Hisn, Egypt. *Göttinger Miszellen 179*, 39–49.

Oren, E. (1973). The Overland Route Between Egypt and Canaan in the Early Bronze Age. *Israel Exploration Journal 23.4*, 198–205.

Oren, E. (1997). Early Bronze Age Settlement in Northern Sinai: A Model for Egypto-Canaanite Interconnections. In P. de Miroschedji (Ed.), *L'urbanisation de la Palestine à l'Age du Bronze Ancien: Bilan et Perspectives des Recherches Actuelles*, pp. 389–405. Oxford: British Archaeological Reports.

Ormerod, P. (1998). *Butterfly Economics*. London: Faber & Faber.

Ortman, S. (2000). Conceptual Metaphor in the Archaeological Record: Methods and an Example from the American Southwest. *American Antiquity 65*, 613–645.

Özgüç, T. (1959). *Kültepe-Kanis I*. Ankara: Turk Tarih Kurumu Basimevi.

Özgüç, T. (1966). Excavations at Acemhöyük. *Anadolu 10*, 29–52.

Özgüç, T. (1986). *Kültepe-Kanis II*. Ankara: Turk Tarih Kurumu Basimevi.

Özten, A. (1979). Two Stone Plates from the Sarikaya Palace at Acemhöyük. *Belleten 43*, 385–388.

Özten, A. (1988). Acemhöyük Tas Kaplari. *Belleten 52*, 393–406.

Panagiotaki, M. (1999). *The Central Palace Sanctuary at Knossos*. London: British School at Athens.

Panagiotakopoulou, E., P. C. Buckland, P. M. Day, A. Doumas, C. Sarpaki, and P. Skidmore (1997). A Lepidopterous Cocoon from Thera and Evidence for Silk in the Aegean Bronze Age. *Antiquity 71*, 420–429.

Pantalacci, L. (1997). De Memphis à Balat. In C. Berger and B. Mathieu (Eds.), *Etudes sur l'Ancien Empire et la Nécropole de Saqqara dédiées à Jean-Philippe Lauer*, pp. 341–349. Montpelier: Orientalia Monspeliensia.

Papadatos, Y. (2005). *Tholos Tomb Gamma: A Prepalatial Tholos Tomb at Phourni, Archanes*. Philadelphia: INSTAP Academic Press.

Pardee, D. (2000). Trois Comptes Ougaritiques RS 15.062, RS 18.024, RIH 78/02. *Syria 77*, 23–67.

Pareto, V. (1982). *Le Cours de l'économie Politique*. Geneva: Librairie Droz.

Parkin, D. (1999). Mementoes as Transitional Objects in Human Displacement. *Journal of Material Culture 4*, 303–320.

Parkinson, R., and L. Schofield (1995). Images of Myceneans: A Recently Acquired Papyrus Fragment from El-Amarna. In W. V. Davies and L. Schofield (Eds.), *Egypt, the Aegean and the Levant: Interconnections in the Second Millennium B.C.*, pp. 125–126. London: British Museum.

Parrot, A. (1956). *Mission Archéologique de Mari I. Le Temple d'Ishtar*. Paris: Paul Geuthner.

Pasztory, E. (1993). *Aztec Art*. New York: Abrams.

Paunier, D. (1983). La Pierre Ollaire en Valais. *Archéologie Suisse 6*, 161–170.

Payne, J. C. (1993). *Catalogue of the Predynastic Egyptian Collection in the Ashmolean Museum*. Oxford: Clarendon Press.

Pearson, M. (1998). Performance as Valuation: Early Bronze Age Burial as Theatrical Complexity. In D. Bailey (Ed.), *The Archaeology of Value*, pp. 32–41. Oxford: Tempus Reparatum.

Peltenburg, E. (1982). Early Copperwork in Cyprus and the Exploitation of Picrolite: Evidence from the Lemba Archaeological Project. In D. Muhly, R. Maddin, and V. Karageorghis (Eds.), *Early Metallurgy in Cyprus*, pp. 41–61. Nicosia: Pierides Foundation.

Peltenburg, E. (1991a). Greeting Gifts and Luxury Faience: A Context for Orientalising Trends in Late Mycenean Greece. In N. Gale (Ed.), *Bronze Age Trade in the Mediterranean*, pp. 162–179. Gothenburg: Paul Åströms.

Peltenburg, E. (1991b). Local Exchange in Prehistoric Cyprus: an Initial Assessment of Picrolite. *Bulletin of the American School of Oriental Studies 283*, 107–126.

Peltenburg, E. (2002). East Mediterranean Faience: Changing Patterns of Production and Exchange at the End of the 2nd Millennium BC. In E. A. Braun-Holzinger and H. Matthäus (Eds.), *Die Nahöstlichen Kulturen und Griechenland an der Wende vom 2. zum 1. Jahrtausend v. Chr. Kontinutat und Wandel von Strukturen und Mechanism Kultureller Interaktion*, pp. 289–346. Möhnsee: Bibliopolis.

Peregrine, P. N. (2001). Comment on Ratnagar 'The Bronze Age: Unique Instance of a Preindustrial World System?' *Current Anthropology 42.3*, 205–224.

Perles, C. (2001). *The Early Neolithic of Greece*. Cambridge World Archaeology. Cambridge: Cambridge University Press.

Persson, A. W. (1931). *The Royal Tombs at Dendra near Midea*. Lund: Berlingska Boktryckeriet.

Petrie, W. M. F. (1891). *Illahun, Kahun and Gurob*. London: David Nutt.

Petrie, W. M. F. (1900). *Royal Tombs of the First Dynasty I*. London: Egypt Exploration Society.

Petrie, W. M. F. (1901a). *Diospolis Parva: The Cemeteries of Abadiyeh and Ha*. London: Egypt Exploration Fund.

Petrie, W. M. F. (1901b). *Royal Tombs of the Earliest Dynasties II*. London: Egypt Exploration Society.

Petrie, W. M. F. (1902). *Abydos*. London: Bernard Quaritch.

Petrie, W. M. F. (1906). *Hyksos and Israelite Cities*. London: Bernard Quaritch.

Petrie, W. M. F. (1909). *Qurneh*. London: Bernard Quaritch.

Petrie, W. M. F. (1917). *Tools and Weapons, Illustrated by the Egyptian Collection in Univesity College, London*. London: Bernard Quaritch.

Petrie, W. M. F. (1931). *Ancient Gaza I*. London: Bernard Quaritch.

Petrie, W. M. F. (1932). *Ancient Gaza II*. London: Bernard Quaritch.

Petrie, W. M. F. (1933). *Ancient Gaza III*. London: Bernard Quaritch.

Petrie, W. M. F. (1934). *Ancient Gaza IV*. London: Bernard Quaritch.

Petrie, W. M. F. (1937). *Funeral Furniture and Stone and Metal Vases*. London: Bernard Quaritch.

Petrie, W. M. F., and G. Brunton (1924). *Sedment I-II*. London: Bernard Quaritch.

Petrie, W. M. F., G. Brunton, and M. A. Murray (1923). *Lahun II*. London: Bernard Quaritch.

Pettinato, G. (1986). *Ebla: A New Look at History*. Baltimore: John Hopkins University Press.

Philip, G., and T. Rehren (1996). Fourth Millennium BC Silver from Tell esh-Shuna, Jordan: Archaeometallurgical Investigation and Some Thoughts on Ceramic Skeuomorphs. *Oxford Journal of Archaeology 15*, 129–150.

Philip, G., and O. Williams-Thorpe (2000). The Production and Distribution of Ground Stone Artefacts in the Southern Levant During the 5th–4th millennia BC: Some Implications of Geochemical and Petrographic Analysis. In P. Matthiae, A. Enea, L. Peyronel, and F. Pinnock (Eds.), *Proceedings of the First International Congress on the Archaeology of the Ancient Near East*, pp. 1379–1396. Rome: University of Rome La Sapienza.

Phillip, G. (1995). Tell el-Dab'a Metalwork: Patterns and Purpose. In W. V. Davies and L. Schofield (Eds.), *Egypt, the Aegean and the Levant: Interconnections in the Second Millennium B.C.*, pp. 66–83. London: British Museum.

Phillips, C., and S.-J. Simpson (Eds.) (2007). *Softstone in Arabia and Iran*. Oxford: Archaeopress.

Phillips, J. (1992). Tomb-robbers and Their Booty in Ancient Egypt. In S. E. Orel (Ed.), *Death and Taxes in the Ancient Near East*, pp. 157–192. Lampeter: Edwin Mellen.

Phillips, J. (1996). Aegypto-Aegean Relations up to the 2nd millennium B.C. In L. Krzyzaniak, K. Kroeper, and M. Kobusiewic (Eds.), *Interregional Contacts in the Later Prehistory of Northeastern Africa*, pp. 459–470. Poznan: Studies in African Archaeology.

Phillips, J. (2001). Stone Vessel Production: New Beginnings and New Visions in New-Palace Crete. In A. J. Shortland (Ed.), *The Social Context of Technological Change. Egypt and the Near East 1650–1550 BC*, pp. 73–92. Oxford: Oxbow.

Phillips, J. (2005). The Last Pharaohs on Crete: Old Contexts and Old Readings Reconsidered. In R. Laffineur and E. Greco (Eds.), *Emporia. Aegeans in the Central and Eastern Mediterranean*, pp. 455–462. Liège: University of Liège.

Phillips, J. (2005b). A Question of Reception. In J. Clarke (Ed.), *Archaeological Perspectives on the Transmission and Transformation of Culture in the Eastern Mediterranean*. pp. 39–47. Oxford: Oxbow.

Phillips, J. (2006). Why?...and Why Not? Minoan Reception and Perceptions of Egyptian Influence. In E. Czerny, H. Irmgard, H. Hunger, D. Melman, and A. Schwab (Eds.), *Timelines: Studies in Honour of Manfred Bietak*, pp. 293–300. Leuven: Peeters.

Phillips, J. (in press). *Aegyptiaca on the Island of Crete in Their Chronological Context: A Critical Review*. Vienna: Österreichisches Akademie der Wissenschaften.

Pilø, L. (1989). Early Soapstone Vessels in Norway from the Late Bronze Age to the Early Roman Iron Age. *Acta Archaeologica 60*, 87–100.

Pini, I. (1990). Eine Frühkretische Siegelwerkstatt? *Pepragmena tou ST' Diethnous Kritologikou Synedriou A2*, 13–20.

Pini, I. (2000). Eleven Early Cretan Scarabs. In A. Karetsou (Ed.), *Kriti-Aigyptos: Politismikoi desmoi trion chlieton*, pp. 107–113. Athens: Karon Editions.

Pinnock, F. (1981). Coppe Protosiriane in Pietra dal Palazzo Reale G. *Studi Eblaiti 4*, 61–75.

Piperno, D. R., E. Weiss, I. Holst, and D. Nadel (2004). Processing of Wild Cereal Grains in the Upper Palaeolithic Revealed by Starch Grain Analysis. *Nature 430*, 672–673.

Pischikova, E. V. (1994). Representations of Ritual and Symbolic Objects in Late XXVth Dynasty and Saite Private Tombs. *Journal of the American Resource Centre in Egypt 31*, 63–77.

Platon, N. (1949). O Tafos tou Stafilou kai o Minoikos Apoikismos tis Peparithos. *Kretika Chronika 3*, 534–573.

Platon, N. (1971). *Zakros. The Discovery of a Lost Palace of Ancient Crete*. New York: Scribners.

Platon, N. (1978). Anaskaphi Zakrou. *Praktika tis en Athinais Etaireias*, 259–299.

Polanyi, K. (1977). *The Livelihood of Man*. London: Academic Press.

Polanyi, K., C. Arensberg, and H. Pearson (Eds.) (1957). *Trade and Markets in the Early Empires*. Glencoe: Free Press.

Pomerance, L. (1980). The Possible Role of Tomb Robbers and Viziers of the 18th Dynasty in Confusing Minoan Chronology. *Acts of the Fourth International Cretological Congress 1*, 447–453.

Popham, M. R. (1978). Notes from Knossos II. *Annual of the British School at Athens 73*, 179–188.

Porada, E. (1984). The Cylinder Seal from Tell el-Dab'a. *American Journal of Archaeology 88*, 485–488.

Portugali, J., and A. B. Knapp (1985). Cyprus and the Aegeans: A Spatial Analysis of Interaction. In A. B. Knapp and T. Stech (Eds.), *Prehistoric Production and Exchange: The Early Aegan and East Mediterranean*, pp. 44–78. Los Angeles: Institute of Archaeology, UCLA.

Postgate, J. N. (1991). *Early Mesopotamia: Society and Economy at the Dawn of History*. London: Routledge.

Postgate, J. N. (1997). Mesopotamian Petrology: Stages in the Classification of the Material World. *Cambridge Archaeological Journal 7(2)*, 205–224.

Postgate, J. N. (2001). System and Style in Three Near Eastern Bureaucracies. In S. Voutsaki and J. Killen (Eds.), *Economy and Politics in the Mycenaean Palace States*, pp. 181–194. Cambridge: Cambridge Philological Society.

Potts, D. T. (1999). *The Archaeology of Elam*. Cambridge: Cambridge University Press.

Potts, D. T. (2003). A Soft-Stone Genre from Southeastern Iran: 'Zig-zag' bowls from Magan to Margiana. In T. Potts, M. Roaf, and D. Stein (Eds.), *Culture Through Objects: Ancient Near Eastern Studies in Honour of P.R.S. Moorey*, pp. 77–91. Oxford: Griffith Institute.

Potts, T. F. (1989). Foreign Stone Vessels of the Late Third Millennium BC from South Mesopotamia: Their Origins and Mechanisms of Exchange. *Iraq 51*, 123–164.

Potts, T. F. (1993). Patterns of Trade in Third Millennium BC Mesopotamia and Iran. *World Archaeology 24(3)*, 379–402.

Poursat, J., and C. Knappett (Eds.) (2005). *Le Quartier Mu IV. La Poterie du Minoen Moyen II: Production et Utilisation*. Paris: école Française d'Athènes.

Poursat, J.-C. (1966). Un Sanctuaire du Minoen Moyen II à Mallia. *Bulletin de Correspondences Héllenique 90*, 514–551.

Poursat, J.-C. (1981). Conclusion. In B. Détournay, J.-C. Poursat, and F. Vandhabiele (Eds.), *Le Quartier Mu*, pp. 231–238. Paris: Paul Geuthner.

Poursat, J.-C. (1996). *Artisans Minoens: Les Maisons-Ateliers du Quartier Mu*. Paris: Ecole Française d'Athènes.

Powell, M. A. (1977). Sumerian Merchants and the Problem of Profit. *Iraq 39*, 23–29.

Powell, M. A. (1999). Monies, Motives and Methods in Babylonian Economics. In J. G. Dercksen (Ed.), *Trade and Finance in Ancient Mesopotamia*, pp. 5–23. Leiden: Nederlands Instituut voor het Nabije Oosten.

Prentice, J. E. (1990). *Geology of Construction Materials*. New York: Chapman and Hall.

Preston, L. (1999). Mortuary practices and the negotiation of social identities at LMII Knossos. *Annual of the British School at Athens 94*, 131–44.

Preston, L. (2001). *A Mortuary Approach to Cultural Interaction and Political Dynamics in Late Minoan II-IIIB Crete*. Ph.D. thesis, University College London.

Preston, L. (2004). A Mortuary Perspective on Political Changes in Late Minoan II-IIIB Crete. *American Journal of Archaeology 108(3)*, 321–348.

Pritchard, J. B. (1980). *The Cemetery at Tell es-Sa'idiyeh*. Philadelphia: University Museum.

Pryor, J. H. (1988). *Geography, Technology, and War: Studies in the Maritime History of the Mediterranean 649-1571*. Cambridge: Cambridge University Press.

Pulak, C. (2006). The Uluburun Shipwreck. In U. Yalçin (Ed.), *The Ship of Uluburun: A Comprehensive Compendium of the Exhibition Catalogue "The Ship of Ulu Burun—World Trade 3,000 Years Ago,"* pp. 6–40. Bochum: Deutsches Bergbau-Museum.

Quesada, F. (1998). From Quality to Quantity: Wealth, Status and Prestige in the Iberian Iron Age. In D. Bailey (Ed.), *The Archaeology of Value*, pp. 70–96. Oxford: Tempus Reparatum.

Quibell, J. E. (1934). Stone Vessels from the Step Pyramid. *Annales du Service des Anitquités de l'Egypte 34*, 70–75.

Quibell, J. E., and F. W. Green (1902). *Hierakonpolis I-II*. London: Bernard Quaritch.

Quinnell, H. (1993). A Sense of Identity: Distinctive Cornish Stone Artefacts in the Roman and Post-Roman Periods. *Cornish Archaeology 32*, 29–45.

Quintaes, K. D., J. Amaya-Farfan, M. A. Morgano, and D. M. B. Mantovani (2002). Soapstone (Steatite) Cookware as a Source of Minerals. *Food Additives and Contaminants 19(2)*, 134–143.

Raban, A. (1988). The Constructive Maritime Role of the Sea Peoples in the Levant. In M. Heltzer and E. Lipinski (Eds.), *Society and Economy in the Eastern Mediterranean (c.1500–1000 B.C.)*, pp. 261–294. Leuven: Peeters.

Radimilahy, C. (1998). *Mahilaka: An Archaeological Investigation of an Early Town in Northwestern Madagascar.* Uppsala: Uppsala University Press.

Rainey, A. F. (1964). Business Contracts at Ugarit. *Israel Exploration Journal 13*, 313–321.

Raisman, V. (1985). UC31922. *Wepwawet 1*, 1–3.

Randall-MacIver, D., and A. C. Mace (1902). *El-Amrah and Abydos 1899–1901.* London: Bernard Quaritch.

Ratnagar, S. (2001). The Bronze Age: Unique Instance of a Pre-Industrial World System? *Current Anthropology 42(3)*, 351–379.

Raven, H. C. (1933). Huge Stone Jars of Central Celebes Similar to Those of Northern Indo-China. *American Anthropologist 35*, 545.

Rawson, J. (1995). *Chinese Jade: From the Neolithic to the Qing.* London: British Museum Press.

Read, H. H. (Ed.) (1957). *Rutley's Elements of Mineralogy.* London: Thomas Murby.

Redford, D. B. (1992). *Egypt, Canaan and Israel in Ancient Times.* Princeton: Princeton University Press.

Redford, D. B. (1997). Textual Sources for the Hyksos Period. In E. Oren (Ed.), *The Hyksos: New Historical and Archaeological Perspectives*, pp. 1–44. Philadelphia: University Museum.

Rehak, P. (Ed.) (1995a). *The Role of the Ruler in the Prehistoric Aegean.* Liège: University of Liège.

Rehak, P. (1995b). The Use and Destruction of Minoan Stone Bull's Head Rhyta. In R. Laffineur and W.-D. Niemeier (Eds.), *Politeia. Society and State in the Aegean Bronze Age*, pp. 435–460. Liège: University of Liège.

Rehak, P. (2004). Crocus Costumes in Minoan Art. In A. P. Chapin (Ed.), *CHARIS: Essays in Honor of Sara A. Immerwahr*, pp. 85–100. Athens: American School of Classical Studies at Athens.

Rehren, T., E. Pusch, and A. Herold (2001). Problems and Possibilities in Workshop Reconstruction: Qantir and the Organisation of LBA Glass Working Sites. In A. J. Shortland (Ed.), *The Social Context of Technological Change: Egypt and the Near East 1650–1550 BC*, pp. 223–238. Oxford: Oxbow.

Reisner, G. A. (1931). *Mycerinus: The Temple of the Third Pyramid at Giza.* Cambridge: Harvard University Press.

Reisner, G. A., and W. S. Smith (1955). *A History of the Giza Necropolis.* Cambridge: Harvard University Press.

Renfrew, A. C. (1972). *The Emergence of Civilisation: The Cyclades and the Aegean in the Third Millenium B.C.* London: Methuen.

Renfrew, A. C. (1984). From Pelos to Syros in Kapros Grave D and the Kampos Group. In R. L. N. Barber (Ed.), *The Prehistoric Cyclades: Contributions to a Workshop on Cycladic Chronology*, pp. 41–54. Edinburgh: Department of Classical Archaeology.

Renfrew, A. C. (1986). Varna and the Emergence of Wealth in Later Prehistoric Europe. In A. Appadurai (Ed.), *The Social Life of Things*, pp. 141–168. Cambridge: Cambridge University Press.

Renfrew, A. C. (1993). Trade Beyond the Material. In C. Scarre and F. Healy (Eds.), *Trade and Exchange in Prehistoric Europe*, pp. 5–16. Oxford: Oxbow.

Renfrew, A. C., and J. F. Cherry (1985). The Other Finds. In A. C. Renfrew (Ed.), *The Archaeology of Cult: The Sanctuary at Phylakopi*, pp. 5–16. London: Thames and Hudson.

Renfrew, C. (1978). Trajectory Discontinuity and Morphogenesis: The Implications of Catastrophe Theory for Archaeology. *American Antiquity 43(2)*, 203–222.

Renfrew, C., and E. B. Zubrow (Eds.) (1994). *The Ancient Mind: Elements of Cognitive Archaeology.* Cambridge: Cambridge University Press.

Revere, R. B. (1957). "No Man's Coast": Ports of Trade in the Eastern Mediterranean. In K. Polanyi, C. Arensberg, and H. Pearson (Eds.), *Trade and Markets in the Early Empires*, pp. 38–63. Glencoe: Free Press.

Reyes, A. T. (2001). *The Stamp-seals of Ancient Cyprus.* Oxford: University of Oxford School of Archaeology.

Richerson, P. J., and R. Boyd (2005). *Not By Genes Alone: How Culture Transformed Human Evolution.* Chicago: University of Chicago Press.

Rizkana, I., and J. Seeher (1988). *Maadi II: The Lithic Industries of the Predynastic Settlement.* Mainz: Philipp von Zabern.

Roberts, B. A., and J. Proctor (Eds.) (1992). *The Ecology Areas with Serpentinized Rocks*. London: Kluwer.

Roberts, O. T. (1991). The Development of the Brail into a Viable Sail Control for Aegean Boats of the Bronze Age. In R. Laffineur (Ed.), *Thalassa. L'égée préhistorique et la mer*, pp. 55–60. Liège: University of Liège.

Roberts, O. T. (1995). An Explanation of Ancient Windward Sailing: Some Other Considerations. *The International Journal of Nautical Archaeology 24(4)*, 307–315.

Robertshaw, P. (1990). *Early Pastoralists of South-western Kenya*. Nairobi: British Institute in Eastern Africa.

Robertson, B. M. (1999). *The Chronology of the Middle Bronze Age Tombs at Tell el Ajjul*. Ph.D. thesis, University of Utah.

Robinson, P. (2003). "As for Them Who Know Them, They Shall Find Their Paths": Speculations on Ritual Landscapes in the 'Book of the Two Ways'. In D. O'Connor and S. Quirke (Eds.), *Mysterious Lands*, pp. 139–160. London: University College London Press.

Robson, E. (2001). Society and Technology in the Late Bronze Age: A Guided Tour of the Cuneiform Sources. In A. J. Shortland (Ed.), *The Social Context of Technological Change: Egypt and the Near East 1650–1550 BC*, pp. 39–58. Oxford: Oxbow.

Roccati, A. (2002). A Stone Fragment Inscribed with the Names of Sesostris I Discovered at Qatna. In M. Al-Maqdissi, M. Luciani, D. M. Bonacossi, M. Novák, and P. Pfälzner (Eds.), *Excavating Qatna I*, pp. 173–174. Damascus: Deutche Orient-Gesellschaft.

Roosevelt, C. H. (2006). Stone Alabastra In Western Anatolia. in Y. M. Rowan and J. R. Ebeling (Eds.), *New Approaches to Old Stones: Recent Studies of Ground Stone Artifacts*. London: Equinox.

Rosen, B. (1995). A Note on the Middle Bronze Age Cemetery at Jericho. *Tel Aviv 22*, 71–76.

Roth, A. M. (1991). *Egyptian Phyles in the Old Kingdom: The Evolution of a System of Social Organization*. Chicago: The Oriental Institute of Chicago.

Roth, A. M. (1992). The *Pss-kf* and the 'Opening of the Mouth' Ceremony. *Journal of Egyptian Archaeology 78*, 113–147.

Roth, A. M. (1993). Fingers, Stars and the 'Opening of the Mouth': The Nature and Function of the *Ntrwj* Blades. *Journal of Egyptian Archaeology 79*, 57–79.

Rottländer, R. C. A. (1990). Investigations into a Vessel of the Cyclades. *Fresenius' Journal of Analytical Chemistry 338*, 138–139.

Rouault, O. (1977). L'Approvisionnement et la Circulation de la Laine à Mari d'après une Nouvelle Lettre du Roi à Mukannilum. *Iraq 39*, 147–153.

Rouse, I. (1992). *The Tainos: Rise and Decline of the People Who Greeted Columbus*. New Haven: Yale University Press.

Rova, E. (1987). Usi del Cristallo di Rocca in Area Anatolica (Fine III – Inizi II Mill. A.C.). *Oriens Antiquus 26*, 109–43.

Rowan, Y. M. (1998). *Ancient Distribution and Deposition of Prestige Objects: Basalt Vessels During Late Prehistory in the Southern Levant*. Ph.D. thesis, University of Texas.

Rowe, A. (1940). *Four Canaanite Temples of Beth Shan*. Philadelphia: University of Pennsylvania Press.

Rowlands, M., M. Larsen, and K. Kristiansen (Eds.) (1987). *Centre and Periphery in the Ancient World*. Cambridge: Cambridge University Press.

Runnels, C. N. (1985). Trade and Demand for Mill-Stones in Southern Greece in the Neolithic and Early Bronze Age. In A. B. Knapp and T. Stech (Eds.), *Prehistoric Production and Exchange: The Early Aegean and East Mediterranean*, pp. 30–43. Los Angeles: Institute of Archaeology, UCLA.

Runnels, C. N., and J. Hansen (1986). The Olive in the Prehistoric Aegean: The Evidence for Domestication in the Early Bronze Age. *Oxford Journal of Archaeology 5(3)*, 299–308.

Runnels, C. N., and T. H. van Andel (1988). Trade and the Origins of Agriculture in the Eastern Mediterranean. *Journal of Mediterranean Archaeology 1(1)*, 83–109.

Rutherford, S. R. (1978). *The Attic Pyxis*. Chicago: Ares.

Rütimeyer, L. (1924). *Ur-Ethnographie der Schweiz*. Basel: Gesellschaft für Volkskunde.

Rutter, J. B. (1979). Stone Vases and Minyan Ware: A Facet of Minoan Influence on Middle Helladic Laconia. *American Journal of Archaeology 83*, 464–469.

Saghieh, M. (1983). *Byblos in the Third Millennium BC: A Reconstruction of the Stratigraphy and a Study of the Cultural Connections*. Warminster: Harwood.

Sahlins, M. (1972). *Stone Age Economics*. Chicago: Aldine-Atherton.

Sakellarakis, J. A. (1968). Excavation of a Tholos Tomb at Haghios Kyrillos, Messara. *Athens Annals of Archaeology 1*, 53.

Sakellarakis, J. A. (1980). Mycenean Stone Vases. *Studi miceni ed egeo-anatolici 17*, 173–187.

Sakellarakis, J. A. (1996). Minoan Religious Influence in the Aegean: The Case of Kythera. *Annual of the British School at Athens 91*, 81–99.

Sakellarakis, J. A., and J.-P. Olivier (1994). Un Vase en Pierre avec Inscription en Linéaire A du Sanctuaire du Sommet de Cythère. *Bulletin de Correspondences Héllennique 118*, 343–351.

Sakellarakis, J. A., and E. Sapouna-Sakellaraki (1997). *Archanes. Minoan Crete in a New Light*. Athens: Ammos Editions.

Sasson, J. M. (1966). Canaanite Maritime Involvement in the Second Millennium BC. *Journal of the American Oriental Society 86*, 126–138.

Saunders, N. J. (2005). The Cosmic Earth: Materiality and Mineralogy in the Americas. In N. Boivin and M. A. Owoc (Eds.), *Soils, Stones and Symbols: Cultural Perceptions of the Mineral World*, pp. 123–141. London: UCL Press.

Sbonias, K. (1995). *Frühkretische Siegel: Ansätze für eine Interpretation der Sozial-Politischen Entwicklung auf Kreta während der Frühbronzezeit*. Oxford: Tempus Reparatum.

Scandone-Matthiae, G. (1981). I Vasi Egiziani in Pietra dal Palazzo Reale G. *Studi Eblaiti 4*, 99–127.

Scandone-Matthiae, G. (1988). Les Relations entre Ebla et l'Egypte au IIIème et au IIème Millénaire av.J.Chr. In H. Weatzoldt and H. Hauptmann (Eds.), *Wirtschaft und Gesellschaft von Ebla*, pp. 67–73. Heidelberg: Heidelberger Orientverlag.

Schaeffer, C. F. A. (1936). *Missions en Chypre 1932–1935. Mission Archologique d'Alasia*. Paris: Paul Geuthner.

Schaeffer, C. F. A. (1938). *Ugaritica I (Missions de Ras Shamra III)*. Paris: C. Klincksieck.

Schaeffer, C. F. A. (1949). *Ugaritica II (Missions de Ras Shamra V)*. Paris: C. Klincksieck.

Schaeffer, C. F. A. (1952). *Enkomi-Alasia: Nouvelles Missions en Chypre 1946–50*. Paris: C. Klincksieck.

Schafer, E. H. (1963). Mineral Imagery in the Paradise Poems of Kuan Hsiu. *Asia Major 10*, 73–102.

Schaub, R. T. (2006). Basalt Bowls in Early Bronze IA Shaft Tombs at Bab edh-Dhra: Placement, Production and Symbol. In Y. M. Rowan and J. R. Ebeling (Eds.), *New Approaches to Old Stones: Recent Studies of Ground Stone Artifacts*. London: Equinox.

Scheel, B. (1989). *Egyptian Metalworking and Tools*. Risborough: Shire.

Schiaparelli, E. (1927). *La Tomba Intatta del Architetto Cha*. Turin: Loescher.

Schild, R., and F. Wendorf (2001). The Combined Prehistoric Expedition Results of the 2001 Season. *American Research Centre in Egypt Bulletin 180*, 16–17.

Schneider, J. (1977). Was there a Pre-capitalist World-System? *Journal of Peasant Studies 6(4)*, 20–29.

Schoep, I. (1994). Ritual, Politics and Scripts on Minoan Crete. *Aegean Archaeology 1*, 7–25.

Schörgendorfer, A. (1951). Ein Mittelminoisches Tholosgrab bei Apesokari (Mesara). In F. Matz (Ed.), *Forschungen auf Kreta 1942*, pp. 13–22. Berlin: W. de Gruyter.

Seager, R. B. (1905). Excavations at Vasilike, 1904. *Transactions Pennsylvania 1*, 207–221.

Seager, R. B. (1907). Reports of Excavations at Vasilike, 1906. *Transactions Pennsylvania 2*, 111–132.

Seager, R. B. (1909). Excavations at Mochlos. *American Journal of Archaeology 13*, 277–303.

Seeher, J. (2005). Bohren wie die Hethiter: Rekonstruktion von Bohrmaschinen der Spätbronzezeit und Beispiele ihrer Anwendung. *Istanbuler Mitteilungen 55*, 17–35.

Seidlmayer, S. J. (1990). *Gräberfelder aus dem Übergang vom Alten zum Mittleren Reich*. Heidelberg: Heidelberger Orientverlag.

Sentance, B. (2001). *Basketry: A World Guide to Traditional Techniques*. London: Thames and Hudson.

Serpico, M. (2004). Natural Product Technology in New Kingdom Egypt. In J. Bourriau and J. Phillips (Eds.), *Invention and Innovation. The Social Context of Technological Change 2. Egypt, the Aegean and the Near East 1650–1150 BC*, pp. 96–120. Oxford: Oxbow.

Shaw, I. (1999). Khafra's Quarries in the Sahara. *Egyptian Archaeology: Bulletin of the Egypt Exploration Society 16*, 28–30.

Shaw, I., and E. Bloxam (1999). Survey and Excavation at the Ancient Pharaonic Gneiss Quarrying Site of Gebel El-Asr, Lower Nubia. *Sudan and Nubia Bulletin 3*, 13–20.

Shaw, I., E. Bloxam, J. Bunbury, R. Lee, A. Graham, and D. Darnell (2001). Survey and Excavation at Gebel el-Asr gneiss and quartz quarries in Lower Nubia (1997-2000). *Antiquity 75*, 33–34.

Shear, I. M. (1987). *The Pangia Houses at Mycenae*. Philadelphia: University Museum.

Shear, T. L. (1940). The American Excavations in the Athenian Agora: Eighteenth Report. (Jul.–Sep., 1940). *Hesperia 9*, 261–308.

Shelmerdine, C. W. (1999). A Comparative Look at Mycenaean Administration(s). In S. Deger-Jalkotzy, S. Hiller, and O. Panagl (Eds.), *Floreant Studia Mycenaea, Akten des 10. Internationalen Mykenologischen Colloquiums in Salzburg 1.-5. Mai 1995*, pp. 555–576. Vienna: Veröffentlichungen der Mykenischen Kommission.

Shennan, S. (1999). Cost, Benefit and Value in the Organisation of Early European Copper Production. *Antiquity 73*, 352–362.

Shennan, S. J. (2002). *Genes, Memes and Human History*. London: Thames & Hudson.

Sherratt, A., and E. S. Sherratt (1998). Small Worlds: Interaction and Identity in the Ancient Mediterranean. In E. H. Cline and D. Harris-Cline (Eds.), *The Aegean and the Orient in the Second Millennium*, pp. 329–342. Liège: University of Liège.

Sherratt, A., and S. Sherratt (2001). Technological Change in the East Mediterranean Bronze Age: Capital, Resources and Marketing. In A. J. Shortland (Ed.), *The Social Context of Technological Change: Egypt and the Near East 1650–1550 BC*, pp. 15–38. Oxford: Oxbow.

Sherratt, A. G. (1981). Plough and Pastoralism: Aspects of the Secondary Products Revolution. In I. Hodder, G. Isaac, and N. Hammond (Eds.), *Pattern of the Past: Studies in Honour of David Clarke*, pp. 261–305. Cambridge: Cambridge University Press.

Sherratt, A. G. (1993). What Would a Bronze Age World-system Look Like? Relations Between Temperate Europe and the Mediterranean in Later Prehistory. *Journal of European Archaeology 1(2)*, 1–57.

Sherratt, A. G., and E. S. Sherratt (1991). From Luxuries to Commodities: The Nature of Bronze Age Trading Systems. In N. Gale (Ed.), *Bronze Age Trade in the Mediterranean*, pp. 351–381. Gothenburg: Paul Åströms.

Sherratt, E. S. (1982). Patterns of Contact: Manufacture and Distribution of Mycenean pottery 1400–1100 BC. In J. G. P. Best and N. M. W. de Vries (Eds.), *Interaction and Acculturation in the Mediterranean*, pp. 179–195. Amsterdam: BR Gruener.

Sherratt, E. S. (1998). "Sea Peoples" and the Economic Structure of the Late Second Millennium in the Eastern Mediterranean. In S. Gitin, A. Mazar, and E. Stern (Eds.), *Mediterranean Peoples in Transition: Thirteenth to Early Tenth Centuries BCE*, pp. 292–313. Jerusalem: Israel Exploration Society.

Sherratt, E. S. (1999). *E Pur Si Muove*: Pots, Markets and Values in the Second Millennium Mediterranean. In J. P. Crielaard, V. Stissi, and G. J. van Wijngaarden (Eds.), *The Complex Past of Pottery: Production, Circulation and Consumption of Mycenean and Greek Pottery (Sixteenth to Early Fifth Centuries BC)*, pp. 163–209. Amsterdam: Gieben.

Sherratt, E. S. (2000). Circulation of Metals and the End of the Bronze Age in the Eastern Mediterranean. In C. F. E. Pare (Ed.), *Metals Make the World Go Round: The Supply and Circulation of Metals in Bronze Age Europe*, pp. 82–98. Oxford: Oxbow.

Sherratt, S. (2001). Potemkin Palaces and Route-based Economies. In S. Voutsaki and J. Killen (Eds.), *Economy and Politics in the Mycenaean Palace States*, pp. 214–238. Cambridge: Cambridge Philological Society.

Sherratt, S. (2003). The Mediterranean Economy: "Globalisation" at the End of the Second Millennium B.C.E. In W. G. Dever and S. Gitin (Eds.), *Symbiosis, Symbolism, and the Power of the Past: Canaan, Ancient Israel and Their Neighbours*, pp. 37–62. Winona Lake: Eisenbrauns.

Sherwin, V. H., and A. C. Haddon (1933). A Stone Bowl from New Britain. *Man 33*, 160–162.

Shimy, M. A.-H. (1997). *Parfums et Parfumerie dans l'Ancienne Egypte (de l'Ancien Empire à la Fin du Novel Empire)*. Villeneuve d'Asq: Septentrion.

Shortland, A. J. (2001). Social Influences on the Development and Spread of Glass. In A. J. Shortland (Ed.), *The Social Context of Technological Change: Egypt and the Near East 1650–1550 BC*, pp. 211–222. Oxford: Oxbow.

Shortland, A. J., P. T. Nicholson, and C. M. Jackson (2001). Glass and Faience at Amarna: Different Methods of Both Supply for Production, and Subsequent Distribution. In A. J. Shortland (Ed.), *The Social Context of Technological Change. Egypt and the Near East 1650–1550 BC*, pp. 147–160. Oxford: Oxbow.

Sigmund, K. (1993). *Games of Life*. Harmondsworth: Penguin.

Silver, M. (1985). *Economic Structures of the Ancient Near East*. London and Sydney: Croom Helm.

Simmel, G. (1900). A Chapter in the Philosophy of Value. *American Journal of Sociology 5*, 179–186.

Sleeswyk, A. (1981). Hand-cranking in Egyptian Antiquity. *History of Technology 6*, 23–37.

Smith, J. S. (2003). International Style in Mediterranean Late Bronze Age Seals. In N. C. Stampolidis and V. Karageorghis (Eds.), *Sea Routes: Interconnections in the Mediterranean 16th–6th c. BC*, pp. 291–302. Athens: University of Crete and Leventis Foundation.

Smith, L. M. V., J. D. Bourriau, Y. Goren, M. J. Hughes, and M. Serpico (2004). The Provenance of Canaanite Amphorae found at Memphis and Amarna in the New Kingdom: Results 2000–2002. In J. Bourriau and J. Phillips (Eds.), *Invention and Innovation: The Social Context of Technological Change 2. Egypt, the Aegean and the Near East 1650–1150 BC*, pp. 55–77. Oxford: Oxbow.

Snodgrass, A. M. (1991). Bronze Age Exchange: A Minimalist Position. In N. H. Gale (Ed.), *Bronze Age Trade in the Mediterranean*, pp. 15–20. Gothenburg: Paul Åströms.

Sobhy, G. P. G. (1924). An Eighteenth Dynasty Measure of Capacity. *Journal of Egyptian Archaeology 10*, 283–284.

Solenhofen, A. (2003). Rock Properties: And Their Importance to Stoneworking, Carving, and Lapidary Working of Rocks and Minerals by the Ancient Egyptians. http://www.geocities.com/unforbidden_geology/rock_properties.htm

Soles, J. S. (1992). *The Prepalatial Cemeteries at Mochlos and Gournia*. Princeton: American School of Classical Studies at Athens.

Soles, J. S. (2005). The 2005 Greek-American Excavations at Mochlos. *Kentro. Newsletter of the INSTAP Study Centre in East Crete 8*, 10–13.

Soles, J. S., T. Nicgorski, A. M. Carter, M. E. Soles, and Carter (2004). Stone Objects. In J. S. Soles and C. Davaras (Eds.), *Mochlos IC. Period III. Neopalatial Settlement on the Coast: The Artisans' Quarter and the Farmhouse at Chalinomouri. The Small Finds*, pp. 35–43. Philadelphia: INSTAP Academic Press.

Sowada, K. N. (2002). *Egypt in the Eastern Mediterranean During the Old Kingdom: A Re-appraisal of the Archaeological Evidence*. Ph.D. thesis, University of Sydney.

Sparks, R. (1998). *Stone Vessels in the Levant During the Second Millennium B.C. A Study of the Interaction Between Imported Forms and Local Workshops*. Ph.D. thesis, University of Sydney.

Sparks, R. (2001). Stone Vessel Workshops in the Levant: Luxury Products of a Cosmopolitan Age. In A. J. Shortland (Ed.), *The Social Context of Technological Change: Egypt and the Near East 1650–1550 BC*, pp. 93–112. Oxford: Oxbow.

Sparks, R. (2003). Egyptian Stone Vessels and the Politics of Exchange (2617-1070 BC). In R. Matthews and C. Roemer (Eds.), *Ancient Perspectives on Egypt*, pp. 39–56. London: University College London Press.

Sparks, R. T. (2007). *Stone Vessels in the Levant During the Second Millennium BC*. London: Maneys.

Sperling, J. W. (1976). Kum Tepe in the Troad. Trial Excavation, 1934. *Hesperia 45(4)*, 305–364.

Stein, G. J. (1998). World Systems Theory and Alternative Modes of Interaction in the Archaeology of Culture Contact. In J. G. Cusick (Ed.), *Studies in Culture Contact: Interaction, Culture Change, and Archaeology*, pp. 220–255. Carbondale: Centre for Archaeological Investigations.

Steindorff, G. (1913). *Das Grab des Ti*. Leipzig: Hinrihs'sche Buchandlung.

Steinkeller, P. (1982). The Question of Marhaši: A Contribution to the Historical Geography of Iran in the Third Millennium BC. *Zeitschrift für Assyriologie und Vorderasiatische Archäologie 72*, 237–265.

Stewart, J. R. B. (1962). *The Early Bronze Age in Cyprus (Swedish Cyprus Expedition IV:1A)*. Lund: Berlingska Boktryckeriet.

Stocks, D. A. (1986a). Sticks and Stones of Egyptian Technology. *Popular Archaeology 7(3)*, 24–29.

Stocks, D. A. (1986b). Tools of the Ancient Craftsman. *Popular Archaeology 7(6)*, 25–29.

Stocks, D. A. (1993). Making Stone Vessels in Ancient Mesopotamia and Egypt. *Antiquity 67*, 596–603.

Stocks, D. A. (2001). Testing Ancient Egyptian Granite-Working Methods in Aswan, Upper Egypt. *Antiquity 75*, 89–94.

Stocks, D. A. (2003). *Experiments in Egyptian Archaeology: Stoneworking Technology in Ancient Egypt*. London: Routledge.

Storemyr, P., E. Bloxam, T. Heldal, and A. Salem (2002). Survey at Cephren's Quarry, Gebel el-Asr, Lower Nubia 2002. *Sudan and Nubia 6*, 25–29.

Takaoğlu, T. (2004). Early Cycladic presence in central-western Anatolia: Evidence for stone bowls. *Anadolu 26*, 65–72.

Takaoğlu, T. (2005). *A Calcolithic Marble Workshop at Kulaksizlar in Western Anatolia*. Oxford: Archeopress.

Takaoğlu, T. (2006). Neolithic stone vessels from Coşkuntepe in north-western Anatolia. *Archaeology, Anatolia and Eurasia 2*.

Thompson, M. (1979). *Rubbish Theory: The Creation and Destruction of Value*. Oxford: Oxford University Press.

Tilley, C. (1991). *Material Culture and Text*. London: Routledge.

Tiradritti, F. (1998). *The Cairo Museum Masterpieces of Egyptian Art*. London: Thames & Hudson.

Tournavitou, I. (1995). *The 'Ivory Houses' at Mycenae*. London: British School at Athens.

Trigger, B. (2003). *Understanding Early Civilisations: A Comparative Study*. Cambridge: Cambridge University Press.

Truncer, J. (2004). *Steatite Vessel Manufacture in Eastern North America*. Oxford: Archaeopress.

Tsountas, C. (1898). Kykladika. *Archaiologiki Ephimeris*, 137–212.

Tsountas, C. (1899). Kykladika II. *Archaiologiki Ephimeris*, 73–134.

Tsountas, C., and J. J. Manatt (1897). *The Mycenean Age*. London: MacMillan.

Tubb, J. N. (1995). An Aegean Presence in Egypto-Canaan. In W. V. Davies and L. Schofield (Eds.), *Egypt, the Aegean and the Levant: Interconnections in the Second Millennium BC*, pp. 136–145. London: British Museum.

Tubb, J. N., and P. G. Dorrell (1991). Tel es-Sa'idiyeh: Interim Report on the Fifth Season of Excavations. *Levant 23*, 65–86.

Tufnell, O. (1958). *Lachish IV*. London: Oxford University Press.

Tzedakis, Y., S. Chryssoulaki, Y. Venieri, and M. Avgouli (1990). Les Routes Minoennes: Le Poste de Cheiromandres et le Contrôle des Communications. *Bulletin de Correspondences Hélleniques 114*, 43–65.

Ussishkin, D. (1980). The Ghassulian Shrine at En-Gedi. *Tel Aviv 7*, 1–44.

Vagnetti, L. (1980). Figurines and Minor Objects from a Chalcolithic Cemetery at Souskiou-Vathyrkrakas. *Studi Micenei ed Egeo-Anatolici 21*, 17–72.

Vallat, F. (1991). La Géographie de l'Elam d'après Quelques Textes Mésopotamiens. In L. De Meyer and H. Gasche (Eds.), *M'esopotamie et Elam*, pp. 11–21. Ghent: University of Ghent.

Valloggia, M. (1986). *Le Mastaba de Medou-Nefer*. Cairo: L'Institut Français d'Archéologie Orientale.

Valloggia, M. (1998). *Le Monument Funéraire d'Ima-Pepy/Ima-Meryrê*. Cairo: L'Institut Fran cais d'Archéologie Orientale.

van den Brink, C. M., and E. Braun (2003). Egyptian Elements and Influence on the Early Bronze I of the Southern Levant. *Archéonil 13*, 77–91.

van den Brink, E. C. (1982). *Tombs and Burial Customs at Tel el-Daba'a*. Vienna: Beiträge zur ägyptologie.

van Dijk, J. (1983). *Lugal ud me-lám-bi Nir-gál: Le Récit épique et Didactique des Travaux de Ninurta, du Déluge et de la Nouvelle Création*. Leiden: E.J. Brill.

van Effenterre, H. (1948). *Nécropoles du Mirabello*. Paris: Paul Geuthner.

van Effenterre, H., and M. van Effenterre (1963). *Fouilles Exécutées à Mallia: étude du Site (1956–1957) et Exploration des Nécropoles (1915–1928)*. Paris: Paul Geuthner.

van Walsem, R. (2003). Une Tombe Royale de la Deuxième Dynastie à Saqqara sous la Tombe Nouvel Empire de Meryneith: Campagne de Fouille 2001–2002. *Archéonil 13*, 7–15.

Van Wijngaarden, G. J. (1999). An Archaeological Approach to the Concept of Value: Mycenean Pottery at Ugarit (Syria). *Archaeological Dialogues 1*, 2–23.

Van Wijngaarden, G. J. (2002). *Use and Appreciation of Mycenaean Pottery in the Levant, Cyprus and Italy (1600–1200 BC)*. Amsterdam: Amsterdam University Press.

Vandier d'Abbadie, J. (1972). *Les Objets de Toilettes Egyptiens au Musée du Louvre*. Paris: Louvre.

Vargyas, P. (1988). Stratification Sociale à Ugarit. In M. Heltzer and E. Lipinski (Eds.), *Society and Economy in the Eastern Mediterranean, c.1500–1000 B.C.*, pp. 111–123. Leuven: Peeters.

Veenhof, K. (1972). *Aspects of Old Assyrian Trade and Its Terminology.* Leiden: Brill.

Veenhof, K. (2003). Trade and Politics in Ancient Assur: Balancing of Public, Colonial and Entrepreneurial Interests. In C. Zaccagnini (Ed.), *Mercanti e Politica nel Mondo Antico,* pp. 69–118. Rome: Bretschneider.

Verbovsek, A. (2006). *Die sogenannten Hyksosmonumente: eine archäologische Standortbestimmung.* Wiesbaden: Harrassowitz.

Vickers, M. (1996). Rock Crystal: The Key to Cut Glass and Diatreta in Persia and Rome. *Journal of Roman Archaeology 9,* 48–65.

Vickers, M., and D. Gill (1994). *Artful Crafts: Ancient Greek Silverware and Pottery.* Oxford: Clarendon Press.

Vinson, S. (1993). The Earliest Representations of Brailed Sails. *Journal of the American Research Centre in Egypt 30,* 133–150.

von Arbin, H. (1984). The Alabastron-shaped Vases in the Throne Room. *Opuscula Atheniensia 15,* 7–16.

von Bissing, F. W. (1940). ägyptishe und ägytisierende Alabastergefässe aus den Deutschen Ausgrabungen in Assur. *Zeitschrift für Assyriologie und Vordasiatische Archäologie 46,* 149–182.

von Bissing, K. (1907). *Steingefässe (Catalogue of the Antiquities in the Cairo Museum).* Vienna: A. Holzhausen.

von der Osten, H. H. (1937). *The Alishar Hüyük. Seasons of 1930–32.* Chicago: University of Chicago Press.

Voutsaki, S. (1993). *Society and Culture in the Mycenean World: An Analysis of Mortuary Practices in the Argolid, Thessaly and the Dodecanese.* Ph.D. thesis, Cambridge University.

Voutsaki, S. (1997). The Creation of Value and Prestige in the Aegean Late Bronze Age. *Journal of European Archaeology 5(2),* 34–52.

Voutsaki, S. (2001). Economic Control, Power and Prestige in the Mycenaean World: The Archaeological Evidence. In S. Voutsaki and J. Killen (Eds.), *Economy and Politics in the Mycenaean Palace States,* pp. 195–213. Cambridge: Cambridge Philological Society.

Wace, A. J. B. (1955). Mycenae 1939–54. *Annual of the British School at Athens 50,* 175–250.

Wachsmann, S. (1987). *Aegeans in the Theban Tombs.* Leuven: Peeters.

Wachsmann, S. (1998). *Seagoing Ships and Seamanship in the Bronze Age Levant.* London: Chatham.

Wachsmann, S. (2000). Some Notes on Mediterranean Seafaring During the Second Millennium. In E. S. Sherratt (Ed.), *The Wall-Paintings of Thera: Proceedings of the First International Symposium,* pp. 803–820. Athens: Thera Foundation.

Wachsmann, S., and K. Raveh (1984). Concerning a Lead Ingot Fragment from Ha-Hotrim, Israel. *International Journal of Nautical Archaeology 13(2),* 169–176.

Wagner, G. A., G. Weisgerber, and W. Kroker (1985). *Silber, Blei und Gold auf Sifnos: prähistorische und antike Metallproduktion.* Bochum: Deutsches Bergbau-Museum.

Wagstaff, J. M., and J. F. Cherry (1982). Settlement and Population Change. In A. C. Renfrew and J. M. Wagstaff (Eds.), *An Island Polity: The Archaeology of Exploitation on Melos,* pp. 136–155. Cambridge: Cambridge University Press.

Walberg, G. (1997). The Date and Origin of the Kamares Cup from Tell el-Dab'a. *Ägypten und Levante 7,* 107–108.

Wallerstein, I. (1974). *The Modern World-System: Capitalist Agriculture and the Origins of the European World-Economy in the Sixteenth Century.* New York: Academic Press.

Wapnish, P. (1997). Middle Bronze Age Equid Burials at Tell Jemmeh and a Reexamination of a Purportedly "Hyksos" Practice. In E. Oren (Ed.), *The Hyksos: New Historical and Archaeological Perspectives,* pp. 335–367. Philadelphia: University Museum.

Ward, W. A. (1963). Egypt and the East Mediterranean from Predynastic Times to the End of the Old Kingdom. *Journal of the Economic and Social History of the Orient 6,* 1–57.

Ward, W. A. (1971). *Egypt and the East Mediterranean World 2200–1900 B.C.* Beirut: American University of Beirut.

Warren, P. (1965). The First Minoan Stone Vases and Early Minoan Chronology. *Kretika Chronika 19,* 7–43.

Warren, P. (1967). A Stone Vase-maker's Workshop in the Palace at Knossos. *Annual of the British School at Athens 62,* 195–201.

Warren, P. (1969). *Minoan Stone Vases.* Cambridge: Cambridge University Press.

Warren, P. (1972). *Myrtos: An Early Bronze Age Settlement in Crete.* London: Thames & Hudson.

Warren, P. (1978). The Unfinished Red Marble Jar at Akrotiri, Thera. In C. Doumas and H. C. Puchelt (Eds.), *Thera in the Aegean World I*, pp. 555–568. London: Thera Foundation.

Warren, P. (1979). The Stone Vessels from the Bronze Age Settlement at Akrotiri, Thera. *Archaiologiki Ephimeris*, 82–113.

Warren, P. (1981). Knossos and Its Foreign Relations in the Bronze Age. *Pepragmena ton Diethnous Kritologikon Sinedrion 4*, 628–637.

Warren, P. (1984). Knossos: New Excavations and Discoveries. *Archaeology 37*, 48–55.

Warren, P. (1989). Egyptian Stone Vessels from the City of Knossos: Contributions Towards Minoan Economic and Social Structure. *Ariadne 5*, 1–9.

Warren, P. (1992). Lapis Lacedaemonius. In J. M. Sanders (Ed.), *Philolakon. Lakonian Studies in Honour of Hector Catling*, pp. 285–296. Chicago: Oriental Institute.

Warren, P. (1995). Minoan Crete and Pharaonic Egypt. In W. V. Davies and L. Schofield (Eds.), *Egypt, the Aegean and the Levant: Interconnections in the Second Millennium BC*, pp. 1–18. London: British Museum.

Warren, P. (1996). The Lapidary Art: Minoan Adaptations of Egyptian Stone Vessels. In R. Laffineur and P. P. Betancourt (Eds.), *Techne. Craftsmen, Craftswomen and Craftmanship in the Aegean Bronze Age*, pp. 209–223. Liège: University of Liège.

Warren, P., and V. Hankey (1989). *Aegean Bronze Chronology*. Bristol: Bristol Classical Press.

Warren, P. W. (2005). A Model of Iconographic Transfer: The Case of Egypt and Crete. In I. Bradfer-Burdet, B. Détournay, and R. Laffineur (Eds.), *Kris Technitis. L'Artisan Crétois*, pp. 221–227. Liège: University of Liège.

Waterhouse, H., and R. Hope Simpson (1961). Prehistoric Laconia. Part II. *Annual of the British School at Athens 55*, 67–108.

Watrous, L. V. (1987). The Role of the Near East in the Rise of the Cretan Palace. In R. Hägg and N. Marinatos (Eds.), *The Function of the Minoan Palace*, pp. 65–70. Gothenburg: Paul Åströms.

Watrous, L. V. (2004). State Formation (Middle Minoan IA). In L. V. Watrous, D. Hadzi-Vallianou, and H. Blitzer (Eds.), *The Plains of Phaistos: Cycles of Social Complexity in the Mesara Region of Crete*, pp. 253–276. Los Angeles: Cotsen Institute.

Watrous, L. V., and D. Hadzi-Vallianou (2004). Emergence of a Ranked Society (Early Minoan II-III). In L. V. Watrous, D. Hadzi-Vallianou, and H. Blitzer (Eds.), *The Plains of Phaistos: Cycles of Social Complexity in the Mesara Region of Crete*, pp. 233–252. Los Angeles: Cotsen Institute.

Watts, D. J., and S. H. Strogatz (1998). Collective Dynamics of 'Small-World' Networks. *Nature 393*, 440–442.

Weeks, L. R. (2003). *Early Metallurgy of the Persian Gulf: Technology Trade, and the Bronze Age World*. Leiden: Brill.

Weiner, A. B. (1992). *Inalienable Possessions: The Paradox of Keeping-While-Giving*. Los Angeles: University of California Press.

Weir, S. (2007). The Contemporary Softstone Industry in Jabal Raazih, North-West Yemen. In C. Phillips and S. Simpson (Eds.), *Softstone in Arabia and Iran*. Oxford: Archaeopress.

Wengrow, D. (1996). Egyptian Taskmasters and Heavy Burdens: Highland Exploitation and the Collared-Rim Pithos of the Bronze/Iron Age Levant. *Oxford Journal of Archaeology 15(3)*, 307–326.

Wengrow, D. (2006). *The Archaeology of Early Egypt Social Transformations in North-East Africa, 10,000 to 2650 BC*. Cambridge: Cambridge University Press.

Wenk, H.-R., and A. Bulakh (2003). *Minerals: Their Constitution and Origin*. Cambridge: Cambridge University Press.

Whitehead, H. (1993). Morals, Models and Motives in a Different Light: A Rumination on Alan P. Fiske's Structures of Social Life. *Ethos 21(3)*, 319–356.

Whitelaw, T. (1983). The settlement at Fournou Korifi, Myrtos and aspects of early Minoan social organisation. In O. Kryszkowska and L. Nixon (Eds.), *Minoan Society*, pp. 323–345.

Whitelaw, T. (2001). Reading between the Tablets: Assessing Mycenaean Palatial Involvement in Ceramic Production and Consumption. In S. Voutsaki and J. Killen (Eds.), *Economy and Politics in the Mycenaean Palace States*, pp. 51–80. Cambridge: Cambridge Philological Society.

Whitelaw, T. (2004). Alternative Pathways to Complexity in the Southern Aegean. In J. C. Barrett and P. Halstead (Eds.), *The Emergence of Civilisation Revisited*, pp. 232–256. Oxford: Oxbow.

Whitelaw, T. (2006). The objectives and methods of the 1987 surface survey at Dhaskalio Kavos. In C. Doumas, L. Marangou, and C. Renfrew (Eds.), *Investigations at Dhaskaleio Kavos, Keros: Volume 1*. McDonald Institute of Archaeology.

Whitelaw, T. W. (2005). A Tale of Three Cities. Minoanisation and Chronology at Phylakopi in Melos. In A. Dakouri-Hild and S. Sherratt (Eds.), *Autochthon: Papers Presented to O. T.P.K. Dickinson on the Occasion of his Retirement*, pp. 37–69. Oxford: Archaeopress.

Whittemore, T. (1912). Stone Vases of the Bisharin. *Man 12*, 124–125.

Wiener, M. H. (2003). Time Out: The Current Impasse in Bronze Age Archaeological Dating. In K. P. Foster and R. Laffineur (Eds.), *Metron: Measuring the Aegean Bronze Age*, pp. 363–399. Liège: University of Liège.

Wiener, M. H. (2006). Chronology Going Forward (with a Query about 1525/4). In E. Czerny, I. Hein, H. Hunger, D. Melman, and A. Schwab (Eds.), *Timelines: Studies in Honour of Manfred Bietak*, pp. 317–328. Leuven: Peeters.

Wilkinson, R. H. (1994). *Reading Egyptian Art: A Hieroglyphic Guide to Ancient Egyptian Painting and Sculpture*. London: Thames and Hudson.

Wilkinson, T. (1999). *Early Dynastic Egypt*. London: Routledge.

Williams, B. B. (1986). *The A-Group Royal Cemetery at Qustul, Cemetery L*. Chicago: Oriental Institute of the University of Chicago.

Wilson, D. E., and P. M. Day (1994). Ceramic Regionalism in Prepalatial Crete: The Mesara imports at EM I to EM IIA Knossos. *Annual of the British School at Athens 89*, 1–88.

Winlock, H. E. (1948). *The Treasure of the Three Egyptian Princesses*. New York: Metropolitan Museum of Art.

Wlodarski, R. J. (1979). Catalina Island Soapstone Manufacture. *Journal of California and Great Basin Anthropology 1(2)*, 331–355.

Wlodarski, R. J., J. F. Romani, G. R. Romani, and D. A. Larson (1984). Preliminary Evidence of Metal Tool Use in Soapstone Quarry-Mining on Catalina Island: Jane Russel Quarry. *Pacific Coast Archaeological Society Quarterly 20(3)*, 35–66.

Wolpert, A. (2004). Getting Past Consumption and Competition: Legitimacy and Consensus in the Shaft Graves. In J. C. Barrett and P. Halstead (Eds.), *The Emergence of Civilisation Revisited*, pp. 127–144. Oxford: Oxbow.

Woolley, L. (1955a). *Alalakh: An Account of the Excavations at Tell Atchana*. Oxford: Oxford University Press.

Woolley, L. (1955b). *Ur Excavations II: The Royal Cemetery*. Oxford: Oxford University Press.

Wright, K. I. (1991). The Origins and Development of Ground Stone Assemblages in Late Pleistocene Southwest Asia. *Paléorient 17(1)*, 19–45.

Wright, K. I. (1993). Early Holocene Ground Stone Assemblages in the Levant. *Levant 25*, 93–111.

Wright, K. I. (1994). Ground-Stone Tools and Hunter-Gatherer Subsistence in Southwest Asia: Implications for the Transition to Farming. *American Antiquity 59(2)*, 238–263.

Wright, K. I. (2000). The Social Origins of Cooking and Dining in Early Villages of Western Asia. *Proceedings of the Prehistoric Society 66*, 89–121.

Xanthoudides, S. (1924). *The Vaulted Tombs of the Mesara*. London: Hodder & Stoughton.

Xenaki-Sakellariou, A. (1985). *Oi Thalamotoi Taphoi ton Mykenon: Anaskaphes Chr. Tsounta (1887–1898)*. Paris: Boccard.

Yadin, Y., and S. Geva (1986). *Investigations at Beth Shean—The Early Iron Age Strata*. Jerusalem: Hamakar Press.

Yasur-Landau, A. (1992). Socio-Political and Demographic Aspects of the Middle Bronze Age Cemetery at Jericho. *Tel Aviv 19*, 235–246.

Yon, M. (2003). The Foreign Relations of Ugarit. In N. C. Stampolidis and V. Karageorghis (Eds.), *Sea Routes. Interconnections in the Mediterranean 16th–6th c. BC*, pp. 41–51. Athens: University of Crete and Leventis Foundation.

Yon, M., A. Caubet, and J. Mallet (1982). Fouilles de Ras Shamra–Ougarit 1978–80 (38e, 39e et 40e campagnes). *Syria 59*, 169–192.

Yon, M., Karageorghis, and N. Hirschfeld (2000). *Céramique Mycéniennes (Ras Shamra-Ougarit XIII)*. Paris: éditions Recherche sur les Civilisations.

Zaccagnini, C. (1977). The Merchant at Nuzi. *Iraq 39*, 171–189.

Zaccagnini, C. (1983). Patterns of Mobility Among Ancient Near Eastern Craftsmen. *Journal of Near Eastern Studies 42(4)*, 245–264.

Zaccagnini, C. (1984). Transfers of Movable Property in Nuzi Private Transactions. In A. Archi (Ed.), *Circulation of Goods in Non-Palatial Context in the Ancient Near East*, pp. 139–160. Rome: Edizioni dell'Atene.

Zaccagnini, C. (1987). Aspects of Ceremonial Exchange in the Near East During the Late Second Millennium B.C. In M. Rowlands, M. M. Larsen, and K. Kristiansen (Eds.), *Centre and Periphery in the Ancient World*, pp. 57–65. Chicago: Oriental Institute.

Zachos, K. L. (1990). The Neolithic Period in Naxos. In L. Marangou (Ed.), *Cycladic Culture: Naxos in the 3rd Millennium BC*, pp. 29–32. Chicago: Oriental Institute.

Zapheiropoulou, P. (1968a). Cycladic Finds from Keros. *Athens Annals of Archaeology 1*, 97–100.

Zapheiropoulou, P. (1968b). Kyklades: Anaskaphikai Erevnai-Periodeiai: Keros. *Archaiologikon Deltion 25*, 428–430.

Zapheiropoulou, P. (1988). *Naxos: Monuments and Museum*. Athens: Goulandris Foundation.

Zarins, J. (1978). Steatite Vessels in the Riyadh Museum. *Atlal 2*, 65–94.

Zarins, J. (1989). Ancient Egypt and the Red Sea Trade: The Case for Obsidian in the Predynastic and Archaic Periods. In A. Leonard and B. B. Williams (Eds.), *Essays in Ancient Civilisation Presented to Helene J. Kantor*, pp. 339–368. Chicago: Oriental Institute.

Zonhoven, L. M. J. (1969). The Inspection of a Tomb at Deir el-Medina (O. Wien Aeg 1). *Journal of Egyptian Archaeology 65*, 89–98.

# Index